Urbi Et Orbi
And All That

FRONT COVER: Drawing in colour of the author Raymond Smith by Peter Nicholson based on an original caricature by Jim Cogan that appeared in the *Sunday Independent*.
BACK COVER: Clockwise from top left: Bobby Kennedy; Muhammad Ali with famous Kilkenny hurler, Eddie Keher, Raymond Smith, the author and Bob Ryan, then Public Relations Manager of A.I.B., the sponsors looking at a copy of *The Clash of The Ash* which was presented to Ali while he was in Dublin for his fight against Al 'Blue' Lewis in Croke Park in 1972; the Taoiseach, John Bruton presents former Taoiseach, Charles J. Haughey with the winning trophy after Flashing Steel, who carried his colours, had won the 1995 Jameson Irish Grand National in the hands of Jamie Osborne (right); Raymond Smith with legendary Kerry footballer, Mick O'Connell and a picture capturing the continued contribution of the Irish Army to the peace-keeping efforts of the United Nations.

Other Books by Raymond Smith include:

Under the Blue Flag (1980)
The Poker Kings of Las Vegas (1982)
Charles J. Haughey: The Survivor (1983)
Garret: the Enigma (1985)
Haughey and O'Malley: The Quest for Power (1986)
Vincent O'Brien: The Master of Ballydoyle (1990)
The High Rollers of the Turf (1992)
Tigers of the Turf (1994)

Urbi Et Orbi And All That

By
RAYMOND SMITH

Mount Cross Publishers
Dublin
1995

Urbi Et Orbi
And All That

First published 1995

Published by Mount Cross Publishers, Dublin

Contents

Author's Note

Close friends of mine – Val Dorgan, Andrew Sheppard and Mike Burns in particular – have been pressing me for a long time to put down on paper the stories that have evolved from a lifetime in journalism. Now I bend to their wishes.

This is not an autobiography in the normal sense. It concentrates on the moments that left an indelible imprint on my mind, especially the moments of laughter and the "crack."

I would like to think that readers of this book will take a journey with me – a journey sometimes into the realms of the absurdly funny where one meets those who live by the motto of the late Jack (Treetop) Straus, the great world poker champion: "Better one day as a lion than one hundred years as a lamb."

Sean O'Casey invariably saw comedy in the midst of tragedy as typified in his immortal works, *The Plough And The Stars* and *Juno And The Paycock*. In my travels from the Congo to Biafra, from China to the Lebanon, from Kenya to Rwanda and Burundi, I discovered high comedy in indescribably tragic situations although I was at the same time deeply moved by the overriding pathos stemming from the helplessness and hopelessness of refugees in a world not of their own making.

Covering the European scene and the domestic political scene in the Seventies and Eighties provided me with the opportunity to meet larger than life characters who made those times very special for me.

Many people co-operated with me in ensuring that this book met the publication deadline.

First of all, my special thanks and appreciation to Tony Lyster and Peter Nicholson for the professionalism they displayed in preparing the copy for the printers. I must pay tribute also to Peter for producing such a fine front cover from an original caricature by Jim Cogan in the *Sunday Independent*. And a word of thanks to Stephen Pepper for his input and advice on the cover design.

My thanks also to Michael Daly and the staff of Independent Newspapers Library and to Aengus Fanning, Editor of the *Sunday Independent* for permission to reproduce the caricature of myself which was originally used in the paper. My appreciation too, to the editors of other newspapers and magazine and book publishers for permission to quote data relevant to this book.

A special word of thanks to the staff of the Photographic Library in the United Nations Headquarters in New York for providing me with photos used in this book from U.N. operations in the Congo, the Lebanon and Sinai.

I started this book initially in Spain three years ago and worked on it intermittently in the following two years. The grind of the final intensive sessions of writing this past year was made easier by finding the right settings with the right atmosphere whether it was in Marbella or Rosslare, in Tara Glen near Courtown or Blackwater in County Wexford.

In this respect, I am deeply grateful to my friends, Dr. Michael and Sheila Mangan, Terence and Annette Sweeney, Gerry and Marie Fanning and Aidan and Mary Moriarty.

And I wish to put on record too my thanks and appreciation to all the members of the staff of Kelly's Hotel in Rosslare, who were so courteous and co-operative in every way, also to my friends in Rosslare Golf Club, where I have enjoyed so many happy and relaxed hours; to Phil Meagher of O'Ryans of Rosslare for the memory of great conversations on football and racing; and to the Courtown Hotel staff.

I express special thanks also to Patrick Ryan, Captain of the Aloha Golf Club in Marbella, where I had some very pleasant afternoons in his company and that of friends in the Spring of '95 after the grind of writing sessions. Not forgetting either relaxed interludes in the 19th in Puerto de Banus.

My wife Sheila and daughter, Bairbre committed themselves with commendable dedication to the task of checking the proofs and I would like to think that the finished work is all the better for their untiring efforts. My appreciation also to my son, Stephen for his helpful advice.

I dedicate this book to the memory of Rev. Con O'Mahony, who epitomised the spirit of deep commitment and courage of the Holy Ghost priests who served in Nigeria during the Biafran War and in other missionary fields. It is also dedicated to the Irish officers and men who have served the cause of peace under the Blue Flag of the United Nations and to those journalists, photographers and camera-men who have given their lives in the theatres of war and strife.

Dublin.   Raymond Smith
September, 1995

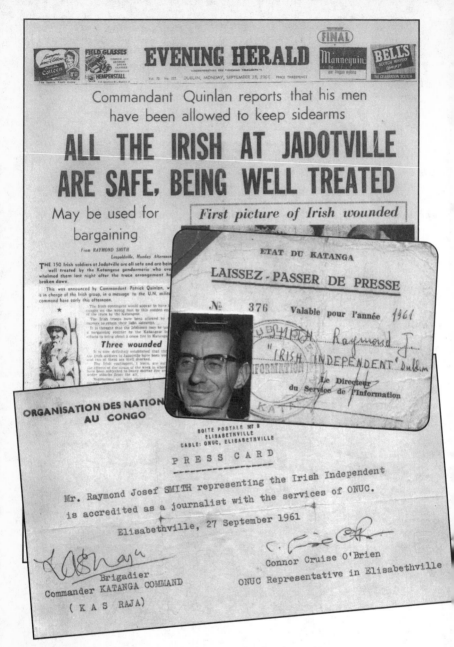

The front page of the *Evening Herald* carrying Raymond Smith's report from Leopoldville (now Kinshasa) telling readers that Comdt. Quinlan and his men had not been massacred after all in Jadotville in September '61. The Press Pass that Smith secured from the Katangese authorities to travel to Jadotville to meet the Irish company and (below) the Press Card that allowed freedom of movement in the area of U.N. operations in the Congo.

1

"A Little Pope Came Out And Said 'Urbi Et Orbi"

They were the best of times and the worst of times – the best in the sense that when you did at last hit the BIG assignment as a foreign correspondent no one counted the cost because it was the era before the accountants moved in.

They were the worst of times in the sense that mostly all that was going in the arena of foreign trips was the "plum" marking of covering the Dublin Diocesan Pilgrimage to Lourdes or being sent to Rome to cover the burial of a Pope or the elevation of a Cardinal to the seat of Peter.

The Lourdes trip meant being briefed before and after the great candlelight procession by the Archbishop of Dublin, Most Rev Dr John Charles McQuaid, the Stormin' Norman of the ultra-conservative brigade. It all acquired such a sameness and became so totally boring to the regulars on that beat that one intrepid veteran saw fit one year to report it from the bar of his hotel.

He filed an intro that had the sun shining on the basilica as the Dublin pilgrims chanted in prayer and sang their hymns of praise. And back from the News Desk came a wire to him enquiring cryptically and cynically: "Are you under the weather or off your rocker? Don't you realise it's an underground basilica now!."

Stories that have become legends in the Dublin newspaper world emerged from those trips, like the one about the group of reporters who brought a case of beer with them. They were having the proverbial "ball" in a carriage all to themselves when a dedicated young curate rushed down the train and this being the mystery of the Rosary to which these particular pilgrims should respond, shouted into the carriage: "Fifth sorrowful mystery!" and was left wondering for many a day subsequently why he was met with blank faces through the smoke-fog and veritable haze of popping beer bottle tops and a verse of *Molly Malone*.

Some of us, I must admit, were just not cast in the mould of "winning" that prestigious "marking." It was long before the time that the Dublin dailies decided to appoint Ecclesiastical Correspondents as such, though there were men who were considered in the higher echelons of the newspaper regimes to be "right" with Maynooth – whatever that meant!

It wasn't exactly that we, the "outsiders" from this privileged world of trips to Lourdes and Rome, bought the *Morning Star* (or was it the *Daily Worker?*) each day or had been invited on a familiarisation trip to Moscow by the Soviet Government – the ultimate black spot against you (one journalist who made such a trip was reputed to have lost his "spot" on the national radio network, though that could never be proved, of course).

No, it was that we were either too young to trust or else, because of our socialist leanings, there was perhaps a feeling that the Hierarchy would not be entirely comfortable in our presence and that our copy would lack the blandness that was certainly required in those days.

You wrote "nice" copy and nice copy meant that the sub-editors did not have to entertain qualms about letting it through. It was eminently suitable to the era when the Catholic Church exerted an influence in Irish life that was awesome and it extended into what went into the papers and what stayed out.

I mean when one esteemed colleague of my acquaintance, now happily gone to his eternal reward, the legendary Bill Shine, went to cover the funeral of a Pope, it took a team of reporters on the evening roster, acting as copy-takers, to take his report for the next day's *Irish Independent*. I recall one evening I was on my fifteen-minute shift and I could picture him high up in St. Peter's phoning his copy, dripping with colourful phrases that brought tears to the eyes of the good nuns in convents all around Ireland, who looked to the "Indo" to be the defender of faith and morals. A page fluttered down as he gasped "My God." No one counted the expense of the phone call as he made his way down the interminable steps to retrieve it and got back in due course to resume the filing of his story, his gasps for breath making the job all the harder and longer.

In time the phoning gave way to the telex and it created the legend of the mix-up in telex numbers that resulted in the manager of some creamery in the South of Ireland opening his office one Monday morning to be met by a tide of paper that almost overwhelmed him. And somewhere back in Dublin a distracted News Editor was tearing his hair wondering why the wrap-up story he was expecting from Rome never reached his desk.

Shock waves go through the system still at the memory from my days in the Newsroom of Independent House – Room 65 – in the early Sixties when I gathered with a few others of the "bachelor set" in their flat off O'Connell Street for a bit of a tea-time soiree (we were wont on some days a week to get an extra 7-11 shift, bringing us an additional £4 or so that we looked upon as money from America).

We got paid weekly then and there was such a shortage of food on that particular Thursday evening that I recall that the lads – Peter McNiff and Sean Duignan among them – were reduced to eating sandwiches with slices of orange in them when they ran out of bananas. One of the boys had earlier been handed the script of this most important statement by John Charles McQuaid, only that he did not think it was all that important.

Toilet paper was at such a premium that I squirm to think of it still – but I have this awful haunting feeling that the Archbishop's statement to the people of Dublin and the nation generally was flushed away.

My erstwhile colleague, never one lacking initiative, rang a friend in the *Irish Times* and duly scribbled down a short-hand abbreviated version of the Great Man's words – enough, as they say in the business, to "cover his flank." It appeared buried somewhere in the middle of the paper next morning.

The *Irish Press* and *Irish Times* had gone "big" on the story. Jack Flanagan, assistant to Brian Barrett on the News Desk, was appalled at the fact that the *Irish Independent* had been left trailing in the wake of both its Dublin rivals. The "Indo" was NEVER scooped on a religious story!

He was beginning to think that some sub-editor had missed the point of what the Archbishop was trying to convey when he got a call direct from the Archbishop's House – very discreet, mark you, but the message was loud and clear. John Charles didn't like the fact, didn't like it at all, that his statement should have been so hacked to pieces that the full weight of it was lost. The paper, it was suggested – rather hinted – would have to make due recompense.

The entire script, right down to "Yours in Jesus Christ" with the insignia of high office, appeared the next day, backed up by an editorial.

The lesson you learned in those days, if you wanted to make your way up the ladder in Independent House, was not to mess around with the Archbishop's House.

Those who made it to the top had an uncanny perception of what did not ruffle the feathers of the Hierarchy or bring blushes to the faces of the "good nuns", as we invariably seemed to describe them.

One executive in his anxiety that the nuns would not be offended, on finding on his desk for the next morning's paper, the photo of a prize bull that had swept the boards at a Southern show, gave instructions that the animal's magnificent specimen of bullhood – balls and all – be painted out. The climax to that episode was that an irate farmer arrived in the front office waving a blackthorn and demanded to know how his bull had suddenly been transformed overnight into a heifer!

*   *   *

I arrived in Independent House the very year – 1960 – that the Belgian Congo exploded with the revolt of the Force Publique and the raping of the women, with no mercy being shown even to the nuns. When I landed in the middle of it, I found myself sleeping under the stars with the refugees who had fled across the border into Rwanda-Burundi, originally inhabited (at the Rwanda end) by the Twa Pygmies but at that point by the Hutu tribespeople and the minority Tutsi. They eventually got involved in such butchering of each other that the country was split in two, into Rwanda and Burundi and the genocide would continue in the divided nations, with death on an unimaginable scale as an estimated 500,000 Tutsi ware slaughtered by the Hutu militiamen, the *Interhamwe* ('those who attack together') with machetes and nail-studded clubs and the bullet,

400 of them being massacred in a chapel in a wood fifteen miles south of the capital, Kigali where they had sought refuge. The legacy of the Killing Fields of Rwanda became piles of bodies, bloated and decomposing under the hot African sun, carrion birds circling above and scavenging dogs gorging themselves on the rotting human flesh, the stench of death hanging heavily in the air. Countless more corpses could be seen at the frontier with Tanzania drifting down-stream in the muddy flow of the Akagera River – innocent people cut down as they tried to escape.

Then over a million Hutu civilians, the *Interhamwe* mingling with them, fled in fear of reprisals before the advancing troops of the rebel Rwandan Patriotic Force (RPF), who inexorably and inevitably brought about the fall of the Hutu government. Thousands of Hutu died in the refugee camps near the Zaire town of Goma, home in 1960 of the 32nd Irish Battalion of the United Peacekeeping Force – the first Irish unit into the Congo. They died of starvation and cholera and dysentery before a massive relief effort, perhaps one of the greatest in world history, arrested what *Newsweek* described as "Hell On Earth" in a stark front page in August '94 and *Time* quoted a resident of Goma as saying: "This is the beginning of the final days. This is the Apocalypse" over a picture of trampled refugees at the Rwandan border and even more horrific pictures inside forming the background to the searing heading, "Cry The Forsaken Country."

The cycle of death came full circle in the Spring of '95 when the now Tutsi-dominated regime in Kigali, fearing that the Hutu militias in the refugee camps were fermenting trouble, set out to close down those inside its own borders. It all went terribly wrong at Kibeho camp and no one could say for certain whether it was hundreds or thousands who died from the bullets of the Rwandan army. But again the roads were filled with fleeing refugees who could see no end to the Hell On Earth that had scarred them for life. The dead at least did not have to live with what they had seen or experienced.

That was thirty-five years on from when I reported on the raping of the Belgian women and nuns and Ireland knew nothing about the Tutsi and the Hutu …

*   *   *

I found myself travelling one day from Goma, home of the 32nd Irish Battalion of the United Nations Peacekeeping Force – the first Irish unit into the Congo – to the capital, Leopoldville (now Kinshasa) on an over-used plane, sitting on a crate of fruit, to file a pooled report. And on arriving at the airport, I was so ravenously hungry that I would have eaten whole, legs and all, one of the frogs dancing in the tropical rain by the banks of the Zaire River, only to be told by Colonel Ferdie Lee that it was Lent and I couldn't eat a ham sandwich.

I settled for a cheese sandwich. The next morning he had me up at 6 a.m. with the crowing cocks acting as an altar-boy at Mass in a near-empty Church off the Avenue Boulevard. And I racking my brains trying to remember the Latin responses from my youthful days when I was a *real*

4

altar-boy.

Anyway, the Congo trip came up, or rather it was decided in Independent House that a reporter and a photographer had to be sent to cover the historic presence of an Irish contingent with the U.N. in the middle of "darkest Africa" (why had it always to be "darkest Africa"?). They didn't send any of the Lourdes boys on that one.

It was an age of powerful news editors and even more powerful editors – the kind of editors that young reporters never met in their daily rounds (and you addressed them by "Mr" when led into their august presence and NEVER by their christian or first names and the very thought of a copyboy in the corridor saying "How's she cuttin', Vinnie?" or "Will Kerry make it to Croke Park, Aengus?" would have been sacrilegious in the extreme – but times have changed, changed utterly!).

When these men decided to send a reporter abroad, it appeared to us that they just told the Board that their newspaper required a presence in a particular centre and we never heard the phrase so prevalent nowadays – "that will have to be a Board decision" or "the expense rules it out." The awesome "Fourth Floor" didn't exist. If it did, it didn't protrude into our thinking as the editorial executives in reality called the shots when the big stories broke.

No married reporter was risked on that first trip to the Congo. It had to be a single man. Come to think of it, I suppose single guys were dispensable – and the insurance cover was less.

I had just done the colour news coverage of the World Cup Golf Tournament out in Portmarnock and managed to snatch exclusive interviews with Arnold Palmer and Sam Snead and a few other big-name stars that kept my name "in lights" for a whole week in the *Evening Herald* and *Irish Independent*, with a few Page One specials for good measure. Perhaps somebody up there must have taken a mental note and concluded that the eager beaver who could land exclusives with Palmer and Snead might get close enough to Patrice Lumumba to file an exclusive.

There was a young journalist from the South, a real livewire who came up to Dublin for a week's briefing on Newsroom techniques before being located as a staffer in one of the offices in the Provinces. The first story he was handed to check out was the one about the bull with the cow's face. All right, you can laugh and say I am simply telling a tall one but it's the truth. To a paper like the *Irish Independent* that prided itself so much on its majority readership among the farming community, the story of a bull with a cow's face was certainly NEWS. I mean if you were a farmer in County Meath and you had purchased a bull that you believed was the last word in masculine virility and rearin' to go, only to discover that he was a fairy or rather had a cow's face, it would be no laughing matter.

Today, it would be worth a hefty sum in damages for a false sale but somehow or other men weren't as eager then to rush into the courts or maybe it was just that there weren't as many hungry, eagle-eyed legal luminaries about knowing where there were easy pickings to plunder and knowing that a paper was liable to settle right on the doorstep of the Four Courts before risking four days in the High Court and a kick-in-the-privates-type six-figure pay-out if you lost – with costs.

Anyway, the young livewire reporter didn't make a great deal of progress on that story of the bull with the cow's face. He admitted himself to me that he hardly covered himself in glory in getting to the heart of the matter. If he had, he might have been detained longer in Dublin and might well have beaten me to the Congo trip.

*   *   *

They did us proud in the generous way they treated us in making money available for all that was considered necessary for the jungle days ahead. No one had ever been sent on an assignment in Africa. It was still the era when you placed small change in the box with the black baby on top who nodded its head in gratitude at the sound of the click of the coins. We loved to make those little black babies nod their heads as we knew we were piling up the indulgences against the day we would arrive at the Pearly Gates.

So little was known, in fact, in Independent House about the Congo that, frankly, they thought that I would be hacking my way through the jungle and sleeping in a hammock.

I was handed £250 (a lot of "bread" in those days when you consider that the starting salary for a young reporter arriving in Dublin was £13-10s a week, old money) to go out and buy an assortment of powders and ointments to deal with snake bites and the like. And a hammock. And a machete.

No one realised they had modern hotels in Leopoldville like the Stanley, Regina and the Memling and broad avenues that would put O'Connell Street to shame, but of course there were the shanty-towns at the edge of the capital city that were not alone an eye-sore but an indictment of Belgian colonialism.

I was told that if I had to have a tooth pulled I could bleed to death in the Congo. So I went up by taxi to one of the top dentists in Fitzwilliam Square and had him look at every tooth in my head and deal with any that looked in the least suspect. The "Indo" paid for it all. He duly pulled two and filled three.

On to a specialist in tropical diseases to get all the necessary shots (against smallpox, cholera and yellow fever) recorded in your Yellow Card (International Certificate of Vaccination) which was every bit as important as your passport.

The late Hector Legge, then Editor of the *Sunday Independent*, had so much confidence in me that he detailed me to go to the Phoenix Park on the very day I had the two teeth pulled to cover a motor race in which his son, Simon was participating. I had never covered one in my life before. There I was in the Press tent still in a state of after-shock from the dentist's chair that morning trying to check how Simon Legge was faring and meanwhile sending back bulletins to his father, like a company commander in the forward lines, informing the Commander-in-Chief of the progress of the advance.

The space had been kept and I duly filled it, despite leaving some of my blood around that part of the Park where later Pope John Paul ll on his historic visit to Ireland in 1979 would concelebrate Mass for an estimated 1,250,000 people at a specially-erected altar and he was assisted by no less than 124 bishops and 31 priests at the Mass itself while 2,000 priests gave the Eucharist to 750,000 communicants. The choir numbered 6,000, the stewards totalled 15,000.

There were two births during the Mass – but, amazingly, not one person died (twelve years on from that day a Dublin free-sheet newspaper reported on its front page that a late-night parking ban was being considered by the Office of Public Works against courting couples who were littering the grounds with used condoms – and the spot where the Papal Cross still stood as a reminder of the glory of 1979, was "a particular black spot").

*   *   *

Incidentally, I had the privilege during the Pope's visit of being selected as one of the pool reporters – Julian de Kassel of the *Irish Press* was the other because he had fluent Italian – to be in the actual room with the Pontiff in Aras an Uachtarain as he met President Hillery. I thought I was getting on extremely well with His Holiness and was almost tempted to regale him with some of my experiences in the Congo when he suddenly turned away from me, leaving me for dead, and resumed talking to the President. I had had my fifteen minutes.

I reckoned he was a tough cookie. And he proved it when two years later he survived an assassination attempt in St. Peter's Square, supposedly master-minded by the Bulgarian Secret Service (though the Bulgarians have denied it since). Lucky for the Pope that it was a smoking gun that Mehmet Ali Agca held in his hand when he was overwhelmed by security guards and not a poisoned umbrella, like the one that was used to deposit the pellet the size of a pinhead in the thigh of Georgi Markov (a leading Bulgarian dissident and prominent writer before his defection to Britain in 1969) that killed him on London's Waterloo Bridge in September, 1978.

The Pope showed his mental toughness and political adroitness also at the height of the crisis in Poland involving Solidarity and Lech Wallensa when he ensured that the Catholic Church maintained its place and its profound influence in his native land – and the Russian tanks did not smash the surge to a new order as they had in Czechoslovakia. No, I reckoned you didn't make it to the Seat of Rome merely by the number of rosaries you said at night or how often you said novenas to Blessed Martin de Pores, the guy they got to know in Moore Street as "The Brown Bomber" (that is, if you bought the brown replica instead of the dearer black one!). You needed diplomacy – quite a bit of it.

Incidentally, during the Pope's visit to Aras an Uachtarain the delays that ensued, as the people pressed to meet him on the motorcade through the metropolis, caused an unexpected change in schedule. The Papal cavalcade never did get to stop outside Our Lady of Lourdes Parish

Church in Sean McDermott Street in the inner city area where the women-folk had their hubbies all spruced up and waiting, sashes in the Papal colours across their Sunday best and not even the hint of the smell of Guinness in the air (because they were kept out of the pubs through the long evening's wait as if they would catch the plague if they broke ranks). That was my "beat" because the "Indo" concluded that I might catch the subtle nuances. Now there was nothing for me to report only the disappointment, the incomprehensible inability to accept that they would not be greeting their Pontiff after all.

My piece told it factually this time – leaving out the colour – so factually that it got through the razor-sharp sub-editors who under no circumstances were going to ruffle the feathers of the Papal entourage. In a 32-page special supplement, wrapped in colour, it was carried down-page under the heading "Parish Dejected as Pope Passes Tomb".

"This was to have been their evening", I wrote, "the evening for which the Parish had prepared for weeks and, somehow, they came to be convinced that there would be a brief halt so that the Pope could pray at the tomb of the Venerable Matt Talbot.

" 'Pope John Paul – don't forget Matt', read one of the banners. The brilliant arc lamps for the TV cameras were set up and ready in the porch of the church. And outside, the stewards wearing yellow sashes, had a pathway clear for the Pope's walk to the church entrance.

"But the Pope's programme was already running two hours behind schedule – and if the motorcade stopped, there was little doubt that the Pontiff would have got involved in another long meet-the-people session. In addition, such was the press of people on the road outside the church, that the security men were known to be distinctly worried about getting him safely back to his vehicle if he had ventured in among the crowd.

"As the motorcade passed on and it finally dawned on the people of Sean McDermott Street that there would be no special moment for them, the stewards turned away in disbelief and, as they took off their sashes, utter disappointment was written on their faces.

"These were men for whom a word, a handshake from the Pope of the People would have meant more than it could ever have meant to the Cabinet members and heads of semi-State bodies who, in heavy concentration had greeted the Pontiff earlier in the day.

"If the Pope could have found the time to stop – or if the organisers of the motorcade could have made just a few brief moments – it would have conveyed a deeper message than any carefully worded address. In Sean McDermott Street you touch the heart of Dublin – and I would have liked to hear the reaction of those real Dubliners as the Pope moved among them.

"There may never be another opportunity. Somehow I fear that the opportunity of a lifetime was missed – an opportunity that can never be repeated."

It struck home like an Exocet missile in Archbishop's House and in the residence of the Papal Nuncio. And the following Sunday, a "representative", if not exactly a Papal legate, arrived in the same area and speaking from the pulpit at Mass said what had to be said but, stripped bare, it was a rank apology to the people of the inner city.

*   *   *

Before I took the Aer Lingus flight from Dublin to Brussels to link up with the Sabena flight to Leopoldville, I journeyed to Limerick to say farewell to my mother. She wept on the railway station platform as I boarded the train back to Dublin. She was convinced, I am sure, that she would never see me again and that the Balubas would make an appetising evening meal out of me.

But I survived – and left behind me enough anti-snake-bite powders and ointments to meet the requirements of a whole company plus one hammock and one machete.

Flying back from the Congo I stopped off in Rome and decided to buy Mother a suitable present. I mean I owed her so much. I recalled when I first left for Dublin how solicitous she was for my Christian welfare, reminding me to go to Mass and Holy Communion each morning and to say my Rosary in the evening – "and be careful, dear, of older women as they have tricks to catch you" (I didn't know then in my innocence what those particular tricks were!).

In the airport shop I found what I was looking for – a large model of St. Peter's. You plugged it in and it played holy music and the bells of St. Peter's pealed out as the window opened and a little Pope stepped out on to the balcony and said 'Urbi et Orbi' as he gave his blessing. It cost the equivalent of between £50 and £75, a lot of money in those days (but I knew I could put it down to a lunch on the Via Veneto with the Irish Ambassador to the Vatican, giving me a message to the Irish nation from Il Papa himself expressing the Vatican's gratitude for the role the Irish soldiers were playing in helping to bring peace to the strife-ridden Congo).

I got back to Dublin and after savouring the acclaim of my colleagues in Room 65, I took the first train to Limerick. And all the way I did not leave the model of St. Peter's out of my sight. I was greeted on the platform by members of the family. When I got to the house in Ballykeeffe, Mother burst into tears again – this time of joy at seeing me all in one piece.

"Look Mother what I have brought you", I said as proud as a peacock, as I unwrapped the parcel and presented her with the precious model of St. Peter's.

We plugged it in – the window opened and out stepped the little Pope but then there was an explosion as he bopped Mother on the nose and dangled forlornly at the end of his spring, as the words 'Urbi et Orbi' trailed away into the distance, broken and meaningless, like the sounds emerging from R2-D2 when he was damaged in *Star Wars*.

Unfortunately I had forgotten the difference in the voltage between Italy and Ireland …

9

$$\boxed{2}$$

"Make It a 32-Seater
For More Leg Room!"

Word for word the Congo was the most expensive story the world's media had had to cover since the Second World War. Telephone calls cost £1 a minute and the cable rate worked out at over 15p a word. It cost news agencies small fortunes each day.

In Leopoldville there were scores of international correspondents competing for three lines to the outside world. A tired and dwindling staff of European operators was gradually replaced by totally inexperienced Congolese – with the biggest story in the world to file.

We were pampered beyond belief. No expense was spared by rival papers – especially the British dailies – in trying to get the beat on being the first into a place where the real 'action' was taking place. Thus it could happen that I would find myself teaming up with the Associated Press man in hiring a plane and perhaps the *Daily Mail* man would row in with us, a three-way cut, and then the *Daily Express* correspondent would get wind of this and he would combine with the representative of Reuters, for example, and another paper to hire a bigger and faster plane.

It was crazy, you may say now, but "hang the expense" was the attitude then if you could put up a banner headline: "Our Man First Into Albertville." One evening I was hiring a 16-seater plane when our photographer, the late Gay O'Brien, a born character and wit, quipped: "Make it a 32-seater for more leg room!"

The only way to be certain in 1960 of getting pooled dispatches from Goma back to Dublin was to cross into Uganda as Cathal O'Shannon of the *Irish Times* did one day – making a 400-mile journey over winding dirt roads and through mountain and bamboo forests and past 12,000 feet high volcanoes, the home of mountain gorillas, to reach Kampala. Or else travel to Leopoldville – a distance of 750 miles – and trust in your luck that you could get a report away by telex (it was the era before the fax and the tandy made it all so different for the modern-day foreign correspondent working for a morning, evening or Sunday paper).

One day a single seat was offered on a plane leaving Goma for Leopoldville at short notice. I had just got over the vaccination effects which had kept me in bed for two days. But there was no time to think. I took a reckless ride back to my hotel in a jeep over the rutted road, bundled some overnight requirements into a bag, dashed out to the airport and on to the plane – to sit on a crate of tomatoes for the five hours journey to the capital.

That night I paced the floor of the telex room in Leopoldville for hours when every machine went dead – and they stayed dead to our agony and frustration. Next day they were back. You learned to be very generous in your tips to get the best man to punch your tape – and some of the Congolese employees in the telex room were earning more in gratuities in one day than their salaries would earn them in twelve months.

I received an urgent message from Gay O'Brien that £250 had been wired to the bank in Goma to see us through. When Gay went to collect it, he found that Jack Flanagan on the News Desk had designated it for both of us – and the bank would not pay until I returned.

But first I had a date in Kindu, to meet the men of "B" Company of the 32nd Battalion. Much of the spotlight in the papers at home had been on the men in Goma and the soldiers in Kindu must have been feeling by that stage that we had been ignoring them and that they were a forgotten Company. It was our custom to wear blue U.N. helmets and someone suggested to me during the drive over the red clay road into Kindu that I might talk to the soldiers and give them a morale-booster with some news from home, as I had garnered it from the papers I had seen in Leopoldville.

So you had the extraordinary sight of a reporter from Dublin in a blue helmet addressing a Company of Irish soldiers in the heart of Africa – and I often think that it was the nearest I ever came to emulating "Monty" or Rommel!

On to Goma to try and replenish our dwindling "tank" with that £250 wired out from Middle Abbey Street. Gay O'Brien met me crestfallen at the airport to inform me that the bank manager had been taken away into the bush and his fate and that of the £250 was unknown at that point.

I there and then took the first plane out of Goma back to Leopoldville to inform the *Irish Independent* of the "disaster" and to request that £250 be wired "immediate" to Ndola over the border in Northern Rhodesia (as Zambia was then).

The Congolese currency had collapsed. You could exchange your pounds sterling at an astronomical rate with Nick The Greek. I remember buying a French-made sports jacket that I could never have afforded at home for the proverbial buttons. You just had to get rid of the money on something concrete as it was no use bringing it home with you.

The £250 arrived quite swiftly in the Ndola bank I had named. Once Gay O'Brien and myself discovered this new route, everything went smoothly and it only entailed telling the Desk that expenses were running sky-high to have the figure topped up.

*   *   *

I digress here for a moment to recall the out-of-this-world experience I had when I returned to the Congo in the late Seventies on a nostalgic visit during the EEC-sponsored tour that carried me through five African countries in all. I was down to my last £500 in travellers cheques when I hit Kinshasa Airport, but I wasn't all that worried as I only intended spending a few days at most in Zaire and planned to fly home from there to London and then Dublin.

Anyway, I would be using one of my credit cards to pay my hotel bill.

I knew that corruption was endemic in Zaire but I certainly wasn't prepared for what I had to face on my arrival. I had been advised though that no matter what happened, I must keep smiling through it all – and not to forget either to make complimentary remarks about President Mobutu or to give him his full title, Marshal Mobutu Sese Seko Kuku Ngbendu wa za Banga ("The always victorious warrior who is to be feared"), President of Zaire, who nowadays with the roads so appallingly bad (the local cynics say that the potholes swallow cars the way the crocodiles swallow turtles – whole) uses his riverboat-cum-floating-palace, *Kamanyola* to steam up and down the Zaire River, eating like a king on board.

I was hardly off the plane when someone grabbed my bag and led the way into the terminal building and straight to customs. Now from long experience as a foreign correspondent, I believed that customs people were the last in the world to ask you for a bribe – but straight off cigarettes were demanded of me, as my bags were opened at the same time. I protested that I didn't smoke. My camera was taken and then my electric razor.

I could see myself growing a beard that would have done justice to Livingstone or Stanley (I presume they both had beards when they paved the way for the civilisation of this part of Africa). The hand signs and the chalk being waved over my bags made it clear to me the same as night follows day that unless I was prepared to fork out the necessary "dash" I could bid adieu to half my possessions – if not all. Imagine being in the fierce humidity of Zaire for a number of days without a change of clean underwear or socks.

I called over the bag carrier, who turned out to be also the taxi-driver who would bring me to the hotel, and got the message over to the bag rummagers that I would give him the money for them when I had changed some travellers cheques in the hotel. That did the needful. I got back my camera and razor and underwear and socks and nearly wept with joy as they duly put the necessary chalk marks on my bags.

But we had still to run the gauntlet of the Airport managerial staff and a few policemen. They threatened and harassed me for their bit of "dash" and again I had to promise that I would meet their demands when I got to the hotel. A belt of a truncheon across the backside speeded me on my way – and I was warned in no uncertain fashion that I would leave Kinshasa Airport in a coffin if I did not keep my promise – that is if they were kind enough to allow my remains to be returned to my nearest and dearest (more likely, I feared, that I would be dumped in the Zaire River with heavy weights around my ankles, never to be heard of again).

12

Luckily the soldiers at the roadblock outside the capital didn't stop the taxi and insist on cigarettes from me before letting us through. If it had been dusk, I know I wouldn't have been so lucky.

Arriving at the hotel, I nearly died of shock when the bag carrier-cum-taxi driver asked me as cool as a breeze to cough up the equivalent of £250 in Congolese money as he planked my bags beside the reception desk.

"Now hold on a minute, Moise or whatever they call you," I protested, "but I have never in my life heard of anyone asking that much for a taxi run from an airport to a hotel, even allowing for what I have to pay your pals at the airport itself."

I asked to see the hotel manager. The Belgian was very polite but firm. He conveyed to me that I had no option but to pay up and keep smiling. A German the previous day had been asked for £500. Later I would learn from a Dutch journalist friend of mine, Link van Brugen that he got so fed up with all the "dash" he had to pay that he went to the President himself and said he would do a documentary about it unless he got his money back. I believe they gave him a suitcase full of Zaires, but, having changed these back at the official rate, he found he was very much short-changed and would never contemplate now spending a holiday on safari in that region of Africa – even if given it free.

So there I was on the very first day of my return visit to Zaire down to £250 – and I hadn't as yet had a gin and tonic or a bite to eat.

A band was beating out cool African music in the garden restaurant of the Hotel of so many unhappy memories from the days of the revolution. I decided that I might as well be caught for a sheep as a lamb and lift my depression with a bottle of the best South African wine and whatever I could pick from the menu that suited a stomach still somewhat delicate after the long flight from Johannesburg (I had come the long way round from Kenya). I put it down to my hotel bill, knowing that I would be paying by credit card anyway.

Later I headed for the bar of the L'Orange Brasserie on the Boulevard du 30 Juin for a cool beer (it had been recommended in *Africa on a Shoestring* and I was certainly operating on shoestring now, cash-wise anyway!).

The official rate of exchange would make £250 seem like the proverbial drop in the sea and I was beginning to wonder if I would have to cut my visit short to just one day and get out of Zaire on the first jet to London the next morning.

Suddenly, I heard someone remark, "Sangonini?" (which in the Lingala language means, "What's new?").

Christopher Columbus was his name – or that is how I got to know him. He turned out to be a life saver to me.

When I told him I was a journalist from Ireland, his face beamed with pleasure and he confided that there was Irish blood in his veins. I suspected that way back some Irish missionary priest who had been inspired by the chronicles of Livingstone had, while pursuing his

13

converting zeal, strayed momentarily in his loneliness from the straight and narrow. I was now about to get the benefit of that indiscretion (or weakness of the flesh as the Redemptorists used describe it in my school-going days in Thurles as they gave one of those thundering hell-fire sermons in the Cathedral during the annual Mission and you jumped in your seat as you listened to the warning: "Beware the judgements of God, if thy right eye scandalise thee pluck it out – better to go to Heaven with one eye than to Hell's fire for all eternity with two").

Christopher Columbus, having heard my tale of woe as we drank cool beers together, laughed heartily at the thought of anyone even contemplating changing money at the official rate in a bank or Bureau de Change. In a word, if you found yourself in a country that was literally swimming in corruption, you might as well learn to swim with the tide.

"Come with me", beckoned Columbus and he led me to the Hotel Yaki on the Avenue du Stade, where I was introduced to a Mr Fix-It (every city in Zaire seems to have one to cater for travellers). I handed over my £250 in travellers cheques and was duly rewarded with more than treble the official rate.

My troubles were over in an instant. I invited Columbus to join me in a celebratory dinner of eels, caterpillars, grasshoppers, prawns and termites at the Chez Babylon and then we hit the town, taking in the rooftop night club at La Creche in Matongo, where the live band played the kind of music that would make a cripple want to dance.

*   *   *

Next morning he called early. He had managed to lay his hands on an old Mercedes-Benz that had long since seen its best days and had no doubt, been passed on to him by one of the elite ruling class for "services rendered" (Columbus, being into everything, knew how to grease the palms of those who dispensed favours). Soon I found myself down by the Zaire River looking at one of the most extraordinary sights I have seen in a lifetime travelling the globe.

The *Colonel Ebeya*, for all the world like a floating town with literally thousands of people packing every available inch of space, was about to begin its long, exotic journey of over 1,000 miles to Kisangani. You could not describe it simply as a single river-boat or ferry because linked to the basic structure were no less than half-a-dozen barges, each a double-decker, and in addition you had a plethora of pirogues, similar to the curachs the Aran Islands men use so expertly, only that these had been shaped out of hardwood trees cut down in the dense forest and outboard engines had been added to quite a number of them.

The words of the old newspaper poster – "All Human Life is Here" – summed it up. For life went on, even before the *Colonel Ebeya* left Kinshasa, as if the people on board were back in their home towns and villages … women could be seen washing clothes or dousing their kids with water taken with containers from the great flowing river; a barber was giving a man a haircut; a tailor was measuring someone for a suit; a group of men played cards languidly; a photographer was taking a snapshot of a

14

guy who had just disposed of his "bag" of tortoises, lizards and otters.

The smell of Congolese cooking in the morning air was not good, let me admit, for someone whose stomach was still rather queasy after I had gone too heavy the night before on the eels and the caterpillars, not to mention the termites. Michael Winner of the *Sunday Times*, I knew, would never sample the culinary delights of the *Colonel Ebeya* – he would never let his readers into the world of savouring white-nosed monkey stew or fresh palm grubs.

As it finally pulled away on the first leg of its journey I heard the sound of singing coming from the *Colonel Ebeya* and whenever I recall those voices rising above the River Zaire and the babble of noise made by the haggling merchants, I am reminded of the wonderful climax to that strange, haunting film I keep getting out on video, *Fitzceralgo* ... only that instead of a group of opera singers coming up the Amazon by river-boat to satisfy a crazy dream, and stirring us magically with wonderful singing from Bellini's *I Puritani*, here was a Congolese choir getting in some practice in a setting that was as incongruous as it was real.

Columbus could have got me a first-class cabin on the main boat. I still harbour a sense of regret that I turned down the offer as it could have formed the basis of a novel set among the thirty-five million people of a nation that thought freedom from the Belgians would bring a better way of life. But thirty-five years on they realised that the dreams Patrice Lumumba had harboured had turned to dust in the hands of President Mobutu, who abused power in such a way that he became immensely wealthy, so wealthy, in fact, that it was reckoned that he was a billionaire many times over while the ordinary people of a country that had been so rich in minerals subsisted on less than £100 a year, if any of them even had that much.

I feared perhaps that the journey along the seemingly endless, magnetic and majestic sweep of the Zaire River would seep into my bones and I would be hooked ... wanting to stay here and ending up living with a Bantu woman in a village at the edge of the rain forest ... waiting for the boat that would be my only lifeline to the outside world I had abandoned, familiar now with sounds that were so distant from the perennial city noises. And I would discover the true meaning of the silence that is special to this part of Africa, the silence that Conrad had discovered a hundred years ago and later Stanley and Livingstone.

That night I ran into a group of American pilots in the Memling Hotel and they offered me a seat on a plane to Goma. Again I regret very much that I did not accept the offer. You see it would have brought me back to the town standing at the foot of the Nyirangongo volcano, beside Lake Kivu in what we dubbed the "Killarney of the Congo" in 1960 on my first trip to the country.

*   *   *

When the rains came the dust, rising at times in blinding clouds as U.N. patrols went past along the road, was swept away and also the haze that dimmed the view of the magnificent mountains that formed the great Rift

15

Valley. Everything turned green during the rainy season, the mountains were etched sharp and clear and there was a profusion of flowers of every hue.

Due to the high altitude of close on 5,000 feet, the climate in Goma was temperate by African standards and the air was light, dry and invigorating. The Belgians in the days when they held sway over the Congo certainly knew where to besport themselves.

John Ross, covering that first Congo story for Radio Eireann, went with me one day to Goma golf course for a round and there on the walls of the clubhouse were the competition sheets showing the stage reached in each summer competition before the "Night of Terror" in July, 1960 when the Force Publique revolted. The mixed foursomes and the womens singles would never be finished now – would you want to return and go all out to win a cup after you had been raped?

John Ross was great when it came to the pooled reports (for those who do not understand this aspect of the foreign correspondent's work, it means that when there is only one line out the guys on the job will combine to write the one story, maybe in cablese and it goes to their respective media units, be it a newspaper, a television or radio station; it is then up to clever subs to add the meat, to expand and personalise and supplement with agency copy. I remember John pacing up and down one evening in Elizabethville (now Lumumbashi) and dictating to me as I sat at the type-writer, the sweat pouring from my brow in the fierce humidity. "Make sure this goes in, Raymond."

"The smell of Indian cooking drifting through the blue jacarandas …"

Could any line have caught more evocatively the presence of the Gurkha troops with the United Nations Peacekeeping Force?

The danger of one failing to survive that first trip came not from the possibility of contracting a fatal dose of malaria or some other tropical disease but that one of the planes you hopped on would go down somewhere in the jungle or crash on take-off or when coming in. The problem was that they had hardly got to one destination when they were pressed into service on another flight.

On one flight from Goma to Leopoldville, I seemed to be the only passenger on board. The radio officer came down to me from the cockpit and told me that they had received news that Congolese Army units were on the rampage at the airport. "If you are a Christian you might as well start praying now", he said. There was no guarantee that we would be able to land – and if the plane tried to make it to another airport, there wouldn't be enough fuel.

Fortunately, things had abated when the pilot began to circle over Leopoldville airport. He was able to land without incident, but as I walked through "Arrivals", I could see that passions and emotions were running high.

Patrice Lumumba was arriving back from a whirlwind tour of Africa, Europe and North America. He came down from the plane carrying his 6ft 2ins in that distinctive slight stoop, his spectacles of heavy horn and, of course, distinctive too with his goatee beard, trimmed as one correspondent wrote at the time "safely below the level of ostentation."

I shall never forget the wild look in his eyes – the look of a man who was under impossible strain, the strain that had mounted to heights he just could not cope with the pressures from Independence Day, June 30, 1960 when on becoming the first Prime Minister of the foundling Congo Republic, he made his famous remark in the presence of King Baudouin of the Belgians: "From today we are no longer your Makas (monkeys)."

Perhaps, as Colum Legum contended in the Foreword to *Congo My Country*, he was motivated at that point by his own restless energy – "fortified by drink and hemp-smoking."

The atmosphere was electric that night in Leopoldville under a Congo sky – the music of the bands and the cheers of the excited Congolese who had come out in their hundreds to greet him, all adding to the heightened sense of drama that he carried with him everywhere he went in just two months in power.

I recall how he could change the mood of the capital city with one ranting speech over the radio. If he said there were spies in the U.N. we walked the streets of Leopoldville in fear.

*   *   *

For myself and for those other newsmen who accompanied them to Goma there would remain always afterwards an aura of romanticism surrounding the 32nd Irish Infantry Battalion – wearing the old "bulls-wool" uniforms as they hit the dust after the first Lockheed troop-carrier had transported them from Baldonnel to Kivu Province.

When they made a stop at Kano on the way, they found they had to take off their tunics the heat was so great. Imagine their embarrassment as they met British Army personnel – revealing braces over heavy grey shirts and the Brits could not help but laugh at the "Paddy style" of things.

I pinpointed their humiliation in a blistering article in the *Sunday Independent*, calling for a proper tropical uniform and stressing at the same time that the armoured cars sent out with them had reached the stage where they were ready to be consigned to an Army museum as relics of the Emergency period – cars that would have offered protection maybe against Baluba poisoned arrows but which could not be expected to stand up to the shells and armour-piercing bullets of the Katangan armoured cars (not surprisingly, some of them were knocked out in subsequent fighting, the shells going through the armour like a knife through butter).

I had the satisfaction of seeing my article striking home like an arrow with the authorities. And the *Sunday Independent* won the eternal gratitude of the rank-and-file for helping to win a proper tropical uniform for them while never again did Irish contingents go abroad without armoured vehicles fit for modern battle conditions. When the 36th Irish Battalion left for the Congo in December, 1961, it proved in all respects the best-equipped and best-dressed of any of the Irish Battalions that had served up to that point with the United Nations.

*   *   *

However, irrespective of the incongruity of those old "bulls-wool" uniforms, the moment of their going away was the moment that those who experienced it with the 32nd Battalion could never forget. For they were the trail-blazers in the blue berets of the U.N.

It was the moment that opened a new era for the Irish Army, brought it into the arena of international involvement and ultimately greatly enhanced its image on the domestic front. It was to develop from a ponderous Army with outmoded equipment to a highly-motorised and extremely-efficient one and Irish officers showed their mettle by going right to the top in U.N. service (such as General Sean McEoin, General Bill Callaghan, General James Quinn and Major-General Michael Minahan).

July 27, 1960 was the day that the men of the 32nd Infantry Battalion paraded through the centre-city streets of Dublin behind their Commanding Officer, Kerry-born Lieut. Col. Murt Buckley. The salute was taken at the G.P.O. by the then Taoiseach, Sean Lemass.

One was reminded of Marilyn Monroe coming home after entertaining the American troops in Vietnam and telling husband Joe DiMaggio, the great Yankee baseball player, by now long retired and living in San Francisco: "Joe, I heard some cheering."

And Joe responded quietly: "I heard some cheering too."

The boys of the 32nd Battalion, on their arrival in Kivu Province, would talk long about how they were stirred as they marched down O'Connell Street – stirred by the great wave of cheering and the overflowing tide of emotion that saw them on their way. "There was many a stirring parade during the Emergency but this beat them all", said one officer.

The Pipe Band with the 32nd Infantry Battalion, wearing kilts and sporting black caps with feathers – would parade every evening in Goma and arouse wild enthusiasm among the local Congolese. One morning I saw a unique sight – a group of young Congolese had formed their own band with tin cans and, to cap it all, out front was one of them acting as Pipe Major with staff in hand, tossing it in the air and catching it better than any Irish Pipe Major. I didn't recognise the air but it seemed to have a touch of "*The Boys from the County Cork*" in it!

The band played at football matches in which the local villagers were involved.

And one day I saw them perform at the first hurling match ever played in the Congo, involving Army men of course who brought their camáns with them. The ball was actually thrown in from a hovering helicopter to start proceedings.

You can't beat the Irish for imagination!

Nobody talked of Aids in those days. But I recall the Army Chaplain addressing the assembled soldiers one day (and the journalist corps with them) and warning them that 90 per cent of the women of the night had "the pox." And we were informed that Congolese husbands, short of cash, thought nothing of sending out "the Missus" to earn the needful – and again the grave warning against getting involved with a married woman of easy virtue.

Anyway, avoidance of a dose of "the pox" could lead to the most bizzare happenings. Suffice it to say, that one chap of my acquaintance from those days told me that he had offered double the going rate for a "blow job."

"There she was lying stretched full length on the bed, a full moon silhouetting her ebony flanks and she turns to me and says that her religion didn't permit it. You could have knocked me over with a feather", he said.

Everywhere you saw large ant-hills rising like cones out of the ground. Ants crept all over the place. You fought through the night to keep your bed free of them – and it took you mind off sex!

I flew into Albertville after the serious disturbances there in which poisoned arrows were used by the natives. Still fresh in my mind was the story of how the natives tested the strength of the poison in the arrow-heads. They would scratch a chicken's leg and if it did not drop dead before it had walked five paces, then the natives knew that the poison was not potent enough.

* * *

The Irish troops were enjoying life in Kivu Province until the Niemba Ambush when a platoon, led by 30-years-old Lieut. Kevin Gleeson of Dublin, was ambushed by drug-crazed Baluba tribesmen. Nine soldiers died. There were only two survivors, Private Thomas Kenny and Private Joseph Fitzpatrick, both of Dublin.

The day was November 8, 1960.

The legends persist. Kenny being found by a search party on the side of a road and, on being asked his name, saluting and saying: "57 Kenny, Sir, and I'm glad to see you" to Comdt. P. D. Hogan (later Brig. General Hogan).

And the ultimate sacrifice made by 20-year-old Trooper Anthony Browne from Rialto Dublin, who played the guitar to his great friend Thomas Kenny's mouth-organ as they entertained their comrades. Kenny's daughter was two months old when he left for the Congo. And when the Balubas attacked the patrol and Browne and Kenny found themselves fighting side by side for their lives, Browne did not think of himself at that moment but of a mother and young child back home in Ireland. "Get away from here", he shouted at Kenny. "You are a married man with a kid. Get into the bush quick."

Kenny did not leave his friend. He fought on until he went down with one arrow in his back and one in his hip. Seeing Kenny fall, Trooper Browne decided to expose himself to try and save him. Stepping into the dirt track already red with the blood of the Irish who had fallen, he sprayed the Balubas with his light machine-gun and decoyed them away from Kenny's body.

When Kenny came to his senses the Balubas were gone – and there was no trace of Trooper Browne.

Trooper Browne was awarded posthumously the Military Medal for

19

exceptional gallantry.

There was to be no medal for Lieut. Kevin Gleeson, caught in a Catch 22 situation that day not of his making.

Civil War was raging in Katanga at the time of the Niemba Ambush between the Balubas and Conikat (the tribe of Moise Tshombe). Tshombe's decision to secede from the rest of the Congo was very much opposed by the Balubas.

Tshombe had been sending his gendarmes, led by white mercenaries, to suppress the Balubas. As their villages were razed to the ground, the Balubas grew daily more hostile and, unfortunately, it happened that the Katangese gendarmes used vehicles similar to those of the 33rd Battalion and their headgear too was quite like the U.N. beret.

One can conclude that the Balubas assumed in their simplicity that as the Irish soldiers – pursuing a policy of keeping roads open by removing road blocks and other obstacles – were opening the way for Tshombe's men.

The drums of the Balubas were beating for nights before the fateful ambush.

The normal approach of any Irish patrol when it came up with the Balubas was to greet them with the ubiquitous 'Jambo' (Hello). Lieut. Gleeson had being doing it every day. If there was a problem you parleyed. And generally it worked. This time it didn't. If Gleeson had turned the machine-guns on the Balubas and wiped them out, there would probably have been a U.N. inquiry and it would have been difficult for him to explain away the massacre. His career as a military officer would have been ruined – or at the very least there would have been a lasting cloud over it. As it was, the Irish Army authorities split hairs over why the classic military regime in such a situation was not observed, especially in relation to the siting of the vehicles with the weaponry that might have saved the patrol. For that reason Gleeson would never get a medal.

The rank injustice to him, to his wife and the other members of the family persists to this day and, to my mind, represents a serious blot on those in authority who indirectly made him the scapegoat for what happened.

His only daughter, Celine talked to me over lunch one day in Wynn's Hotel of the pain and deep disappointment she felt that her father had still been left unhonoured so long after the Niemba Ambush. (it's 35 years as I write this chapter).

She confessed that her mother never recovered from the tragedy and went to her grave with the feeling that a slur had been left on her husband's name, even though his Army comrades spoke of his qualities as a leader of men and the outstanding courage he had shown not alone at Niemba itself but earlier in the rescue of a Belgian missionary priest, Fr J. Peeters.

Celine was only five when her father died. She remembers going out with her mother to buy the present that would have been sent in November to reach Lieut. Gleeson in time for Christmas. She still has the Christmas card that would have gone with the gift. But it was never sent as over the radio that very day came the news that an Irish platoon had been ambushed at Niemba. She remembers the people crowding into the house to offer their condolences. There were so many people.

She was 8 or 9 before she started going to the annual Niemba Remembrance mass and ceremony. "I knew my father had been killed by the arrows of the Balubas. I always knew he was a hero, that he had died a hero's death.

"In school if I didn't do something as teacher wanted me to do it, I would be reminded that my father had been very brave and had died for the cause of world peace, that I must always be proud of him."

Before he went away to the Congo Lieut. Gleeson had gone on holidays to the Isle of Man with his wife. Celine had been with them. "We had a lot of photos from that last wonderful family holiday together. But Mother seemed to have a premonition of his death. She kept saying to him not to go – that she felt he was going to be killed. He responded that it was his duty to go.

"She was always a nervous and highly-strung person. He was calm, practical and down to earth and always cheerful. He was like an anchor to her. His death left her bereft and unable to cope. She couldn't accept that he was gone. She was in and out of hospital and, really, it was hopeless from then on."

Celine had to make sacrifices for her mother. She missed out on a university education at the time when she should have been going to college. Later she would get her chance but she accepted that her father's death had marked her for life, that the way the home was upset and the way it killed her mother's spirit, things could never be the same again.

The hurt would just not go away.

No detailed official reason has ever been given as to why Lieut. Gleeson was not honoured and successive Ministers for Defence have failed to respond properly when I put the question straight to them. I know from my own contacts, as I have indicated, the Army's attitude on the matter but, frankly, I don't accept it for one moment. Some day I would hope that there will be a Minister for Defence strong enough to say to the bureaucrats – "enough is enough; a stain must not be left on an Irish officer who died while doing his duty."

*　　　　*　　　　*

These niceties did not occupy the minds of the 300,000 people who turned out in Dublin as the victims were laid to rest in the Congo plot in Glasnevin cemetery on November 22, 1960. A nation would always remember how Lieut. Gleeson and eight of his men died with him. In the hearts of the people they had made the ultimate sacrifice for the cause of peace. Wearing the blue berets of the United Nations.

Where three months previously the nine men had left to echoing cheers, now there was only the plaintive music of the Dead March filling the air, catching the emotions of the silent thousands and intensifying that still silence as each coffin passed by. The beat of muffled drums, the tolling of

21

the church bells. They were buried in a mass grave beside that of General Michael Collins, first Commander-in-Chief of the National Army. Each coffin was draped in the Tricolour and the U.N. flag.

*   *   *

I was not home very long from my first trip to the Congo when the Niemba Ambush happened. I squirm still at the thought that if I had been with the Irish contingent, I would almost assuredly have gone down the road with Lieut. Gleeson and his platoon to the Tundala bridge and died in the hail of poisoned arrows. A day on patrol with an Irish unit was a story that would have attracted me very much and one I would have dearly loved to file.

On a lighter note, I cannot but record here that the Niemba Ambush and its aftermath gave rise to a phrase that has passed into Dublinese. If anyone says to you that you're "a bit of a Baluba", it means that you are the last word in uncouthness.

3

Dicing with Death on the Road to Jadotville

It was "Black Friday" in Dublin – September 15, 1961 to be exact – when the evening paper posters screamed out at us that 57 Irish soldiers had been surrounded at Jadotville and, amidst conflicting reports, it was even assumed initially that they had been wiped out.

So confused, in fact, were the reports reaching Dublin that Frank Aiken, then Minister for External Affairs, had decided to fly immediately to the Congo to study the situation and report back to the Government. Meanwhile, General Sean MacEoin, Supreme Commander of the United Nations Peacekeeping Force, radioed Dublin: "It now appears that the garrison at Jadotville has been overwhelmed by vastly superior numbers ..."

I was directed by the News Desk to prepare to leave for the Congo as quickly as possible. The fact that I had been there already and only needed a booster vaccination shot instead of the full treatment meant that no one else in the Newsroom was considered. And I was still single. I arrived in Leopoldville on the same plane as Frank Aiken.

The air service from Leopoldville to Elizabethville had been cancelled because of the fighting in the capital of Katanga. So I had to go the long way round via Johannesburg to Salisbury (now Harare) and Ndola and make the rest of the journey (168 miles) to Elizabethville by road and after that I would face another drive of 80 miles to Jadotville.

At last we reached Ndola and the Elephant and Castle Hotel which had become the headquarters of the corps of journalists. "I will see you in the lounge tonight", whispered the young man in the white shirt when he overheard me asking if it was possible to hire a car to Elizabethville.

He was willing to drive us – at a price. Of course, danger money entered into the bargain as there was a possibility of road-blocks and we had not yet acquired the special Laissez-Passer de Presse issued by the Katangese Director of Information. All we had were Irish passports which were considered anything but a safe possession, naturally enough, as the Irish were involved in the effort to end the secession of Katanga from the rest of the Congo.

As someone on the piano in the lounge played two of Louis Armstrong's greatest hits – *"When It's Sleepytime Down South"* and *"Ain't Misbehavin'"* – I concluded the deal on behalf of John Ross (*Radio Eireann*), Noel Conway (*Irish Times*), Des Fisher (*Irish Press*) and myself.

We were on the road the next morning at 4 a.m. and touched 75 m.p.h. on the way to the border. The fear was that we could be stopped by 'cowboy' units answering to no one. But personally I suspected there was more danger that the car would go off the road at the speed at which it was travelling and end up in one of the deep culverts specially cut by the roadside to take the monsoon rains.

No difficulty on the Rhodesian side. But I felt the rising tension as we neared the Katangan post. Everything depended on this and on the French that Nigel Ryan, the young Reuter's correspondent in those days, could muster for the occasion.

We were going into Katanga, we told the official, at the invitation of President Tshombe who wanted us to see for ourselves the way the Irish prisoners were being treated in Jadotville. It was plausible but it worked. One agonising moment. He nodded his head and we were through. Luckily enough we ran into no road-blocks on the rest of the journey and at last reached Elizabethville.

This city, which had delighted me with its easy atmosphere in the autumn of 1960, was now turned into a theatre of war with machine-gun nests everywhere and patrols of United Nations troops in jeeps and Katangan gendarmerie moving about. Twelve months previously the jacaranda trees were in full bloom and to get inside the borders of Katanga from the rest of the Congo was to attain some measure of security. Now Katanga had gone up like a bottle of champagne. Blossoms from the same jacaranda trees formed mauve shrouds over coffins of those who died in the fighting.

There were many strings to pull to get the necessary permission from President Tshombe to travel to Jadotville to see the Irish prisoners. We spent hours in Government buildings working our way from one official to the next until we presented our request to Tshombe's second-in-command. And finally President Tshombe himself granted our request.

At last we were on the road to Jadotville. We were carrying with us a bag of mail from home and, would you believe it, ballot papers as there was a General Election taking place back in Ireland and the Irish troops in the Congo had the right to vote. As if the men who had suffered the humiliation of being forced to surrender in face of overwhelming numbers would be that desperate to exercise the franchise.

The trip began in the gendarmerie headquarters in Avenue de la Reine where we picked up our escort, a young officer and a para-commando. For eighty miles we drove at 80 m.p.h. in a large American car. We had to pay a price to get it for it was not easy to find someone to hire out a car to Jadotville, because there was no great confidence in our returning.

We discovered almost to our grief that the car had no brakes.

It happened within sight of the bridge over the Lufira River, which figures so strongly in any debate in Irish Army circles on the effort to relieve the beleaguered Jadotville garrison. A commando carrying a sten-gun stepped out and waved us to a halt. Colleague Des Fisher of the *Irish Press*, who was at the wheel, jammed his foot down but the brakes didn't work and, as we were really going at speed at the time, we were gone half-a-mile before he could bring her to a halt.

"This is it", I said to myself as we went past the commando and I expected a burst of fire to end it all. But luckily he saw the escort Tshombe had provided, wearing the distinctive camouflage uniform with the epaulettes of an officer. He held his fire.

Still, it was a close call.

When we entered Jadotville, I felt like an explorer seeing one of the lost Inca cities. John Ross recorded his impressions for *Radio Eireann* as we approached the hotel prison camp. On the steps of the verandah were the Irish prisoners and across the road armed gendarmerie kept watch from the front of requisitioned cafes.

When the prisoners saw us coming towards them they could hardly believe we were Irish. Then we greeted them with "Céad Míle Fáilte", and they were all around us, smiling and laughing.

Before departing, we treated our escort to a drink in a bar in the native quarter. The tables were crowded with men and women drinking local beer. A record-player with a faulty needle blared out African dance music and couples went to the special dance platform in one corner to sway and swing with the rhythms as others clapped their hands to the beat.

*   *   *

The Congo was the most crazy mixed-up place imaginable in those days – so crazy at times that you had to scratch your head to convince yourself that you weren't living a nightmarish dream.

It's hard to imagine now how much was packed into eighteen frenetic months that elapsed from the time that Patrice Lumumba, a former beer salesman and postal clerk, became the first Prime Minister of the Congo Republic until he died at the age of 36 at the hands of his enemies in Katanga, having penned a last letter to his wife that proved that , despite his faults, his courage remained to the end: "Neither brutality, nor cruelty, nor torture will ever bring me to ask for mercy, for I prefer to die with my head unbowed, my faith unshaken and with profound trust in the destiny of my country, rather than live under subjection and disregarding sacred principles".

Lumumba never really had a chance to show what he was capable of achieving as a leader. Within a week of the Independence Day celebrations the Force Publique (Congolese Army) had mutinied. Then followed the days of turbulence – 68 to be exact – when on top of the mutiny he faced the secession of two provinces, an incursion by Belgian paratroopers, U.N. intervention, total disruption of his administration and eventually the loss of support of the Western powers, being labelled a communist because of calling directly for Russian support.

25

There was no rest or peace for him as crisis followed crisis – he had taken over a country that was totally unprepared to govern itself.

Lumumba's death was officially announced on February 13, 1961, a United Nations' Commission of Investigation finding that the weight of evidence showed that he was killed with two companions on the evening of January 17, 1961 "in the presence of high officials of the government of Katanga", having been brutally beaten by soldiers during the journey to Elizabethville. The word put out by the Katangese authorities was that Lumumba and his companions had been captured and killed by inhabitants of a small village near Kolwezi while trying to escape from Katanga.

Supporters of the late Premier had entrenched themselves in Stanleyville led by Antoine Gizenga. But on August 2, 1961 a new National Government was set up in Leopoldville with Cyril Adoula as Premier and Gizenga as Deputy-Premier.

It thus only remained for Katanga to be brought to heel. It would take almost two years, however, to achieve this aim. Finally, the secession of Katanga was ended on January 15, 1963 – but there was to be much bloodshed in the meantime and Irish soldiers died not from Baluba poisoned arrows this time but in full-scale fighting in what was then the capital of the break-away Province.

*   *   *

The generation not born then or those too young at the time to appreciate what was happening in the centre of Africa cannot comprehend the headlines commanded by developing events in the Congo at the time.

And what a spotlight turned on Dr Conor Cruise O'Brien, who had arrived as the United Nations special representative in Katanga and who was later to become a Cabinet Minister in the 1973-'77 Coalition Government.

The United Nations Security Council resolved on February 21, 1961 to use force if necessary to secure the withdrawal of the foreign political and military advisers from the Congo.

Six months went by and they were still there in strength.

The storm broke with the United Nations action of August 28, 1961 – a bloodless coup in which there was the element of complete surprise. "Operation Rum Punch" they styled it. In addition to taking the white officers and mercenaries into custody, the U.N. should also have taken full control of all key public buildings including the Post Office and Radio Katanga and strategic installations like "The Tunnel". And they should have been held as the bargaining ploy in ensuring that Tshombe acceded to the U.N.'s demands.

Events now began to deteriorate alarmingly, following the United Nations' failure to finish the job on August 28. Tshombe did everything to provoke the U.N., even to the point of one high-ranking official of the international organisation being "arrested". The Katangans brought their crack troops into Elizabethville in readiness for any bid by the U.N. to take over. These included the para-commandos, well-disciplined soldiers who wore camouflage uniforms. They occupied the Post Office. Heavily

26

armed patrols and guard posts were also maintained by the Gendarmeries at other public buildings and installations.

On September 13 the U.N. moved – the military action this time being styled "Operation Morthor" ("Smash and Grab").The U.N. appeared to have under-estimated the strength of the Katangese resistance. Once fighting broke out in Elizabethville it spread throughout the Province and the United Nations were to find themselves strongly criticised in many quarters for their action.

The "War in Katanga" was how the men of the Irish 35th and 36th Battalions would remember it.

It was an important event in Irish military history, because it meant that for the first time since the foundation of the Irish State in the early Twenties, Irish Army units were involved in full-scale battles.

For eight days young Irish soldiers, many of them no more than eighteen, experienced all the hardships of warfare and some knew fear when pitched into battle for the first time. By the time the cease-fire was arranged, they had experienced machine-gun fire and mortar shelling and they had even became accustomed to strafing attacks from the air. When later the fighting was renewed in Elizabethville and the U.N. made its final push that would ultimately end the secession of Katanga, the fighting was far more fierce and the Irish Army suffered casualties with the public at home having to accept that these were in the cause of world peace. Amazingly, the Irish people showed their maturity and their backing for the United Nations' efforts by not joining in any outcry for a pull-out of our contingents.

Irish troops were to distinguish themselves, even though they lacked much of the essential equipment of a modern fighting force. The truth is that they went out initially equipped for police action and not to fight a war. The Katangan armoured cars were of modern design and carried more powerful guns and every time the Irish armoured cars went out against them, they were at a distinct disadvantage. The Fouga jet dominated the skies over Katanga in the early September fighting because the United Nations had no air support for its troops. General Sean McEoin, Supreme Commander of the United Nations Force in the Congo had a plan to bomb Kolwezi airfield from which the jet was operating but it was vetoed by the political heads.

In the final analysis Jadotville and the forced surrender of the Irish garrison there, after they had put up heroic resistance, became the key to the September 13 action and represented a humiliation for the United Nations that should never have happened.

*   *   *

The company under 42-years-old comdt. Patrick Quinlan from Waterville, County Kerry was doomed from the moment it was sent to this mining town lying 80 miles north of Elizabethville. Their mission was to defend the white population from any molestation and to ensure that no outrages were committed there. The transfer of the 150 officers and men was completed by September 5.

It was soon evident to Comdt. Quinlan that there was no need for his Company to be in Jadotville. The town was peaceful and quiet. Nobody was being attacked and no request had been sent from there for U.N. troops.

Even though he reported this to the U.N. authorities in Elizabethville, the Company was kept in Jadotville. Why? That remained one of the great unanswered questions.

But, worse of all, no prior notice was given to Quinlan of the planned U.N. action in Elizabethville. As his unit came under attack, a wireless message was received to the effect that fighting had broken out in the capital of the Province. The message read: "Operation MORTHOR. Suspension of Katangan Government. Arrest of certain Cabinet Ministers and of white officers of Surete of Police. Seizure of Radio Station and all communications commenced 0400 hours today. Operation has been completed successfully".

But, of course it was not completed successfully. And soon it became clear the Jadotville garrison had been placed out on a limb – and Comdt. Quinlan had been left in a hopeless position.

Ultimately, when there was no break-through at the Bridge over The Lufira to relieve him, Comdt. Quinlan was faced with choosing between his garrison being wiped out or surrendering.

The Katangans launched their first major attack on the Irish defenses in Jadotville at eleven o'clock on Wednesday morning, 13 September 1961, and for four long, hot, torturing days there was to be no respite for the beleaguered garrison, ringed by the enemy and wondering how long they could hold out as more reinforcements were brought in against them and their rations got lower with each passing day.

The Fouga jet made its first appearance on Thursday. As it came in low, spraying the trenches with machine-gun fire, the Irish soldiers fired at it with small arms but they sadly missed anti-aircraft guns to give them proper cover.

Three times the jet came over the Irish positions that day, bombing and strafing them and the attacks were to continue on Friday and Saturday.

Now the U.N. log of the radio conversations proved beyond any doubt that with no relief column getting through, the Jadotville garrison was doomed.

JADOTVILLE: Ultimatum issued to us to capitulate by 1830 hours. We refused. Jet plane attacked our position twice. The enemy offensive fire still continues.

JADOTVILLE (later): Position desperate. Send reinforcements immediately.

ELIZABETHVILLE: Can you break out? Can you break out on foot, we will meet you at the bridge.

JADOTVILLE: Bridge about twenty miles. We do not know force between here and bridge. Unable to take all ammo and supplies. This would be suicide. Only hope remain here. You reach us.

The reveille for the Irish soldiers on Friday morning was another mortar barrage from the Katangan side. The fierce heat was now beginning to take its toll but the morale of the troops remained magnificently high. The news that a big relief force was being sent out on Saturday from Elizabethville sent their spirits soaring.

But the reinforcements never arrived and in the circumstances the surrender of the Jadotville garrison became inevitable.

In cold retrospect, the conclusion has got to be, firstly, that if there had been a break-through at the Bridge over The Lufira that same surrender would have been avoided.

Secondly, if the United Nations had the jets in service over Katanga then the Fouga jet, operating on the Katangan side, would have been quickly shot down. That same Fouga jet was not alone making matters impossible for the Jadotville garrison but also hampering the attempts by the relief columns to get through.

How ironic that the humiliation of the U.N. hostages in the former Yugoslavia in 1995 should have led to the decision to create a rapid reaction force. If there had been a proper rapid reaction force in 1961, equipped to throw extra bridges if necessary across the Lufira River, to outflank the Katangese, then Quinlan's company would not have been left to its fate in Jadotville. And the appalling genocide that was allowed to take place in Rwanda as the Hutus went on the rampage could also have been avoided. But insiders in the United Nations will admit to you that its greatest problem has always been to react quickly to a given set of events, even when the political will has been there to do so. The wheels of the organisation have always seemed to grind far, far too slowly – and death and misery had been the lot of thousands of helpless people as a result.

There were those who tried to make a scapegoat of Comdt. Quinlan because he took the fateful decision to surrender, for, as he put it himself, "if I continued my men would have been massacred by a vastly-superior force". Some of those who pointed the finger at him were hoping that it would divert attention away from the failure to break through at the Lufira Bridge.

Those gung-ho elements in the Irish Army who contended in the great debates on the issue that Quinlan should have been ready to die with his boots on, rather than suffer the ignominy of surrendering conveniently forgot the mandate under which he was operating. They failed to exclaim that the relief column should have been prepared likewise to die with their boots on to save a garrison that was thought initially to be in every danger of being completely wiped out, if not already wiped out.

I maintain that nothing – not even heavy casualties – should have prevented the relief columns going through.

Of course, there was the unexplained failure to inform Quinlan in the first place that "Operation Morthor" was planned for Elizabethville for September 13. He was actually in the act of shaving when he heard the news that the U.N. had moved against the Katangese in the Katangan capital.

The bottom line was that the Irish Company, who surrendered at

Jadotville were finally released with full ceremony in Elizabethville on October 25th, 1961 after being held prisoner in Jadotville from September 18. They received good food and good treatment and no harm had come to any of them.

*   *   *

Twenty-five Katangan gendarmerie died in the fighting at Radio Katanga and when the bayonets of the Indian Gurkha troops had finished, a strange silence fell over the building and its blood-stained floors and walls. They were buried in a common grave and questions were asked later whether the Indians need have gone so far. No prisoners were taken in that particular engagement.

The correspondent is left with an appalling dilemma – is the cause greater than one particular incident? You have Irish troops fighting in the cause of world peace and rules are breached on warfare that you know should not be breached – by others serving under the same flag. And yet if you reveal all at the moment of happening you sully those who have maintained their honour and not broken the rules – who have observed an ethic that they will never besmirch, like the born officers and men of the Irish Army who left such an imprint on my mind. And became close friends of mine.

That dilemma will remain for every correspondent in a theatre of war and, remember, the press liaison officers with an army can dictate the terms. An army in war does not operate to satisfy the day-to-day needs of the correspondents. It fights to win. And when the rules are broken, it can choose to hide this fact from the correspondents or paint a totally different picture – one that shifts the blame to the enemy – and the correspondent who tries to dig deeper can be blocked very effectively because ultimately an army at war can call the shots. And may have no qualms in doing so as it pursues its own agenda.

*   *   *

The failure to bring the September 13, 1961 operation in Elizabethville to a successful conclusion and the bloodshed that stemmed from it resulted in a hue and cry for the head of Dr Conor Cruise O'Brien. In the opinion of some sections of the British media he was personally responsible for everything that had gone wrong.

Indeed, so intensive became the campaign against him that, after being recalled to New York for discussions, he resigned his post and also gave up his job with the Irish Department of Foreign Affairs (he had been one of its most brilliant career diplomats). He announced at a press conference in New York that he was seeking a divorce from his wife Christine, whom he had married in a registry office twenty-two years earlier and by whom he had a son and two daughters. He made it known also that he planned to marry Miss Maire MacEntee, daughter of Sean MacEntee, then Tanaiste and Minister for Health.

His private life, he said, had been deliberately introduced by the British "gutter Press" in an attempt to deflect attention from what he had to say and to discredit him and his ideas.

30

I recall interviewing him as he stood under a tree, arms folded, in the grounds of his villa in Elizabethville. "The suggestion that I alone was responsible has been put out by parties who feel that it would be to their benefit to get rid of me", he said with emphasis.

"If a U.N. representative like myself were to take it upon himself to make decisions of such magnitude without consulting his superiors, he would not remain in his position twenty-four hours".

The whole matter had been discussed in Elizabethville, Leopoldville and New York before the final decision to go ahead with the operation was taken, he added.

Dr Conor Cruise O'Brien would probably have emerged as a world hero if the operation of September 13, 1961 had succeeded in ridding Katanga of the remaining mercenaries and reconciling the Tshombe regime with the Central Government. When it brought only bloodshed sections of the British Press picked on him and painted him as a headstrong Irishman who had plunged peaceful Katanga into warfare.

*   *   *

An uneasy peace reigned in Katanga between September 21, 1961 when the provisional ceasefire came into operation and December 5, 1961 when fighting was renewed in Elizabethville.

The atmosphere of growing tension gradually got worse in Elizabethville. Then in New York the U.N. Security Council voted 9-0 for a resolution demanding that all secessionist activities "cease forthwith" and authorising the Acting Secretary-General, U. Thant, to use force if necessary to remove the foreign mercenaries.

The die was cast. It was only a matter of time now before the U.N. began its final offensive to end the secession of Katanga on December 15.

The Battle of "The Tunnel" – the railway underpass near the centre of Elizabethville – resulted in one Irish Officer, 25-years-old Lieut. Patrick Riordan of Dublin and one Irish Soldier, Pte Andrew Wickham, also 25 and from Dublin, being killed in the assault. The storming of this strategic installation represented a singular triumph for the men of the 36th Battalion and for Comdt. Sean Fitzpatrick of "A" Company and Comdt. Bill O'Callaghan of "B" Company, who was later to become Supreme Commander of the U.N. Force in the Lebanon.

On Tuesday, September 26, 1961 22-years-old Trooper Edward Gaffney from Norrismount, Camolin, Co. Wexford had become the first official casualty in the Katangan fighting when the truck he was driving came under machine-gun fire. Trooper Patrick Mullins from Kilbeheny, Co. Limerick and Cpl Michael Nolan from Colbinstown, Co. Wicklow, both of the 35th Battalion, like Trooper Gaffney, were also killed in action in the September fighting.

Others who died in action in the December fighting were Sergt. Patrick Mulchay of Dublin, and Cpl Michael Fallon of Dublin.

Unlike the fighting in September, the U.N. now had control of the skies and its jets attacked where necessary with rockets and cannon-shells. The fighting in Katanga finally ended and Tshombe accepted the territorial integrity of the Congo and that foreign mercenaries must leave the breakaway Province.

Dr Ralph Bunche, the U.N. Under-Secretary for Foreign Affairs hailed the agreement as a "highly important step towards the unity, peace and stability of the Congo".

*   *   *

Correspondents came from many parts to cover the Congo story. At the height of the crisis there was hardly a leading paper in Western Europe or the United States that was not represented. Those who were my Irish colleagues on the first trip were John Ross *(Radio Eireann)*, Cathal O'Shannon *(Irish Times)* and Michael O'Halloran *(Irish Press)* while on the second trip Des Fisher was covering for the *Irish Press* and Noel Conway for the *Irish Times*. John Ross was still Radio Eireann's Man.

The team-work among the Irish correspondents was outstanding especially when finding ourselves with only one connection out by telex or cable. Then we combined together in the time-honoured institution of the "pooled" report.

Flying by air had become second nature to me by the end of my initial sojourn in the Congo. By the time I returned from my second trip I was a veteran.

You couldn't afford to be nervous about travelling by plane. In such a vast country, where distances between the major centres of population are so great, it was generally the only means of getting about. You learned fairly quickly that the roads could be diabolical and if you did decide to go by jeep, you arrived at your destination caked in mud and so bruised, battered and exhausted that you were good for nothing for a week at least.

The planes were so over-used that you lived with the fear deep-down that one day the ground engineers would not have the time to do a proper service on a plane you were taking and you would be lost in the jungle between Leopoldville and Elizabethville – to be buried by the pygmies.

One of the biggest risks of all during that second trip of mine in September, 1961 was the hazard of the spy-hunt. It was directed against presumed Belgian paratroopers in disguise. Reporters and photographers with blonde hair – which labelled them immediately to the Congolese as Flemish Belgians – were eternally at risk.

Fortunately, I had dark hair then, though it has long since turned grey!

Because we of the Irish contingent of correspondents had to go so much to the U.N. Headquarters in Elizabethville for briefings, we found one day that difficulties were being put in our path and we had a creepy feeling that we were suspected as spies.

We decided that it might be wise to spend a temporary "holiday" in Ndola while matters cooled down and we could return in a week or so.

Back in the Elephant and Castle hotel, the Irish community greeted us with a spontaneous party. The laughing nurses from the local hospital were only too happy to listen to the highly-coloured escapades of a team of Irish "war correspondents" (unfortunately, we hadn't any wounds to display!).

For my sins I missed a lot of the fun. There I was lying upstairs in my room in a state of fever. Endeavouring to do the best he could for me, John Ross began plying me with lucozade but it came up and went down the toilet bowl as fast as I drank it.

John then told a doctor from my own town of Thurles, who had come in for the party that I was looking distinctly jaundiced and that the lucozade had failed to solve the problem. Dr Hayes immediately came upstairs to give a look-over. He diagnosed that I was suffering a severe dose of gastroenteritis and that my temperature was such that unless I was moved to hospital right away, it could be curtains for me.

The ambulance arrived and I was whisked to the local hospital. I recall that I was back on the 'goodie' of my childhood days as I got well enough to eat something. Somewhere along the line I must have forgotten to peel an apple or else I had eaten a salad (salads, we were warned, were deadly).

When I felt well enough to resume, I wired Jack Flanagan on the "*Irish Independent*" Newsdesk: "Ready to proceed Elizabethvillewards. Wire £500 to Barclays Bank in Ndola".

Jack, who was a living monument to nervousness when the heat was really on in the kitchen, had been kept fully informed of my illness and I believe was appalled at the idea of having to make the arrangements to fly my remains back home from Ndola – if I didn't survive the bout of gastroenteritis. No man was more relieved to hear that I had survived and that I wouldn't after all become the first Irish media victim of the "War in Katanga". He wired back: "No need proceed Elizabethville. Come home on first available plane".

And not a word about the £500 …

*   *   *

Eighteen years on, I found myself in the Lebanon in the tightest of tight situations as I hit the road from Beirut airport to Tibnin and Shaqra, travelling with the resident Reuters man and a cameraman. The village of Shaqra was then (early May '79) the headquarters of "C" Company (Western Command) of the 44th Irish Battalion under Comdt. Brendan Maguire from Ballina, County Mayo.

The Israelis had come in at dawn, crossing their own border into the Lebanon at a point less than five miles from the Irish area of operations.

They moved into the enclave controlled by Major Saad Haddad's Israeli-backed right-wing militia and from there swept on into the outskirts of Shaqra itself. They numbered 400 and used twenty armoured personnel carriers.

Irish troops were put on full alert and their armoured units were mobilised. Comdt. Maguire ordered the road on the U.N. side of the village to be sealed off and called up reinforcements, which soon began to converge from other points. The Dutch and their armoured units were also called in.

Comdt. Maguire met the Colonel commanding the Israeli unit at the edge of the village and asked him why they had come into the Irish U.N. positions. The Colonel politely explained that Palestinian terrorists had

33

infiltrated the enclave and into Israel itself and had appeared to be ready to attack the Israeli village of Ramin when a number of them were captured. The others had escaped across the border into the Lebanon and it was to try and capture these that the Israelis had decided to cross right into the outskirts of Shaqra.

Lt.-Col. Vincent Savino, then O/C of the 44th Battalion, had gone to Beirut airport to greet the 45th Battalion on their arrival. It was while I was at the airport talking to him that word was received on the radio link with Battalion Headquarters in Shaqra of the Israeli incursion. Having filed a quick story to the *Evening Herald* with the information I had at that point, I headed for Tibnin and Shaqra.

Our urgings ensured that the taxi-man we had engaged kept his foot on the accelerator nearly all the way and there was little let-up even when we hit the winding mountain roads. Soon we were almost at our destination and Tibnin was within sight.

And then as we came around a sharp bend, a farmer and his cart confronted us on the wrong side and our driver only avoided them by mounting the ditch on two wheels and getting clear by inches.

Later that same afternoon when fourteen shells fell in the Irish area of operations from Major Haddad's guns, I was displaying no great alacrity to get in to one of the shelters. I was still too shell-shocked after that nerve-racking taxi ride and its so-near fatal climax.

Meanwhile, the Second-in-Command of the 44th Battalion, Comdt. Noel Bergin had arrived in Shaqra with Comdt. Mick Shannon, the Adjutant of the Battalion to join Comdt. Maguire. And a Colonel was airlifted from the U.N. Headquarters at Naquora as protracted negotiations began to try and resolve the tense situation that had developed.

The Israeli team included a general who had arrived on the scene. Later Major Haddad also made his appearance. The Israelis seemed determined that they and they alone would search the village for possible Palestinian terrorists.

"We will open fire if you press on," was the message delivered to them across the table.

And it was no idle boast. For the Dutch had that morning got delivery of powerful TOW missiles which, of course, had the capacity to easily knock out the Israeli armour.

I saw the Dutch and the Irish armoured units along the roadside overlooking the valley and their guns trained on the positions at the outskirts of Shaqra where the Israeli force was in position. It was an extraordinary sight and the nearest the U.N. came to becoming involved directly in a shooting war with the Israelis.

The Irish officers made it plain to the Israelis that only the U.N. troops would carry out the search for Palestinian terrorists in Shaqra.

Major Haddad threatened at one point during the negotiations that he would shell the villages in the area.

"If your artillery opens up and villagers are killed, you will be responsible," was the response.

In face of the firmness of the Irish officers, who did not waver once during the dawn duel of words – that went on for three hours – the Israelis eventually got in touch with headquarters back home and their force pulled out.

The one concession made to them was that the U.N. agreed to search two houses which the Israelis said they suspected as havens for the terrorists. But no terrorists were found.

*   *   *

I had been in China covering the visit of the first Irish trade delegation to the Peoples Republic, led by the Minister for Industry, Commerce and tourism, Mr. Des O'Malley. We had come out by rail from Canton to Hong Kong and from there I flew to Singapore and took the Singapore Airlines jet to Kuwait. Next morning I departed that perspiring hot-house and headed for Beirut.

It was like arriving in Belfast. As we passed through check-points on the road into town manned by Syrian troops of the Arab Deterrent Force, we thought again of the tragedy that emanates from communal strife wherever religion is confused with politics.

The scars one saw in Belfast at the time were nothing, however, to what was wrought in Beirut and in villages around it during the civil war that lasted from April 1975 to October 1976. It was undoubtedly one of the bloodiest ever recorded. The estimated toll was 40,000 killed, 100,000 wounded, 5,000 maimed and 500,000 rendered homeless or displaced out of a population of 3.2 million inhabitants. Some 300,000 Lebanese emigrated and the overall damage ran into billions and billions in Lebanese currency.

This was a civil war in which mortars and rockets were used in built-up areas with no thought to the destruction that would be done to property. It was brutal and it was terrible.

Tipperary-born Seán Whelan, Ireland's Charges d'Affaires in the Lebanon at the time (I would meet him again later in New York when covering the United Nations) brought me on a tour one morning of the devastated areas in the city where the fiercest fighting took place during the civil war. It was an experience that touched me very deeply. "Pret a repondre a ton appel, mon Liban," read the scrawled sign on a wall down by the port area. Yes, they had responded all right to the call – the Christians and Moslems but not to that of their country fighting against another power but in a civil war that reached a level of bestiality towards the end that saw bodies dragged through streets behind speeding cars and girl fighters posing for photographs standing over the victims they had shot.

Beirut – the capital that died and had come alive again, partially at any rate – left you at the time with memories of destruction that you knew would never be easily effaced. You felt the tragedy of the civil war even more in villages like Quarantina, Damour and Jiyeh. In the battle that raged in and around Quarantina no less than 600 people died.

Damour, Mon Amour ...

35

Always it will remain starkly in the mind – the rubble and the children playing on those rubble heaps that were once homes. The village was under siege for a week and after the intensive shelling had destroyed everything, 500 were dead. The remainder had fled in small boats.

The famous lines of W.W. Gibson's *Lament* went through my mind:

We who are left, how shall we look again
Happily on the sun or feel the rain
Without remembering how they who went
Ungrudgingly and spent
Their lives for us loved, too, the sun and the rain?

A bird among the rain-wet lilac sings –
But we, how shall we turn to little things
And listen to the birds and winds and streams
Made holy by their dreams,
Now feel the heartbreak in the heart of things?

And the equally-famous lines that Siegfried Sassoon wrote when he cried out in ironic fury as he saw the names of the war-dead written on a memorial stone also came to mind:

Who will remember, passing through this gate
The unheroic dead who fed the guns?

Yet in the middle of all this death and destruction before the U.N. arrived – including the Irish contingents and those from other nations – great courage was displayed by ordinary people. And among them Irish people who served in different fields in battle-scarred Beirut.

Fifteen years on again from that trip to the Lebanon the phrase "ethnic cleansing" had become an integral part of the everyday language used by the correspondents covering events in the former Yugoslavia. Much that had happened during the civil war in the Lebanon paled before the atrocities carried out by the Bosnian Serbs and Croats. The victims, as often as not, were innocent people. It was a tit-for-tat situation where the United Nations seemed helpless to act. And, yet ironically, you knew that if those in the blue berets were not there, the killing, the maiming, the torture and the rapings could be far, far worse.

Strangely enough, despite all its failures – and no one could deny them in '95 – my faith in the United Nations, as it celebrated the 50th anniversary of its foundation, remained unshaken for while the big powers could meet and talk in the Security Council, it reduced the appalling prospect of a nuclear war bringing the final Apocalypse.

One had only to reflect on Hiroshima and Nagasaki a half-a-century on to realise the need to have a forum for peace and if there was no Security council, no United Nations as the ultimate focal point – what then?

At least, we could hope, that talking in the Security Council could buy time … the time that might prevent the button being pressed.

*   *   *

The Commodore Hotel was the base for the corps of international correspondents covering the Lebanon scene – just as it had been the Ledra Palace in Nicosia or the Memling or Stanley Hotel in Leopoldville.

It was also the base for CIA men and others wearing all kinds of hats. You never knew for sure who you were rubbing shoulders with when you sat at the bar and ordered a gin and tonic or a scotch on the rocks.

But there was invariably a sense of excitement and intrigue from just being there. For those who passed through Beirut or who served there as correspondents at the height of the civil war or later, the Commodore will always occupy a special corner in their hearts. It was unique.

You paid a fee on arrival, for example, that ensured that you got the necessary papers that allowed you stay on in the Lebanon. It went on to your hotel bill like a round of drinks sent to your room. The management squared everything without any fuss. You left it to them to deal with officialdom. And if they took their "cut", what matter? It came out of expenses.

They seemed to be able to handle any crisis involving any correspondent patronising the hotel – right down to the personal level.

There was this Scandinavian journalist friend of mine who happened to have a fleeting affair with a beautiful Lebanese girl – or rather he concluded that it was fleeting until one morning her entire family arrived in the lobby for the wedding ceremony.

He rang reception and informed the manager that he was trapped in his room and inquired desperately if anything could be done to rescue him from his plight. "Not again", said the manager in a world-weary voice. He then indicated to my friend that the ladder that was kept for this very same eventuality would be available outside the window inside ten minutes and that he must act with speed and alacrity. He could settle his account in due course. It seemed that Jimmy Durante was singing "Woodman spare that ladder" as the reckless young Scandinavian broke all records in escaping his room and the hotel.

4

"Don't Eat Rat
– It May Be diseased"

I had flown into Uli airstrip in Biafra at the height of the Nigerian Civil War to be greeted on entering the terminal building – if you could call it such – with the sign scrawled in large letters: "DON'T EAT RAT IT MAY BE DISEASED".

As we made our way into town, I asked about the makeshift nets slung across the road. "They're to catch the bats – something of a delicacy these days, old man".

I took a mental note that I wouldn't be asking for filleted rat and I would only plump for steamed bat if I was on my last legs with hunger.

But beggars can't be choosers. When I saw the effects of hunger in Biafra, I was able to understand more fully why it was that if a plane went down in the jungle and you were one of the surviving passengers lost for weeks on end with nothing to eat, you could easily turn cannibalistic.

I recall one Kerry-born Holy Ghost priest telling me when I met him off the plane on his arrival back in Dublin that he would never eat tinned peas again. He had had his fill of them over a six-months period.

The sign warning all and sundry not to eat rat was one thing and the nets to catch the bats another – but hitting me like a sledge-hammer right in the solar plexus was the sight of a man being shot off the wing of a plane with one spray of machine-gun fire, the very same as I would use an insect repellent to kill a mosquito. And all he had done was creep out of the bush to steal one dried fish.

Planes bringing in dried fish. Others bringing in salt. Still others bringing in supplies of various kinds – and the suspicion always on the Federal side that guns and ammunition could be hidden in the holds of some of those planes.

I had been down on the Costa del Sol writing a sports book to a tight deadline over the Christmas holiday period, trying as far as I can recall to put enough money together for my wedding which was to take place the following August. I got a message to head for Madrid where I would link up with a Holy Ghost priest, Fr Tony Byrne, known as "The Green Pimpernel".

Fr Byrne would have a passport ready to hand over to me at Madrid Airport that would designate me as a "businessman" for the purpose of my trip into Biafra. It would make it easier than if I produced one showing I was a journalist.

I was being commissioned to write a book – for the love of God and the good of my soul – about the heroic efforts of the Irish missionary priests in helping to keep the starving Ibos fed while at the same time ministering to their spiritual needs. I could hardly refuse when my future brother-in-law, Fr Con O'Mahony was one of the Holy Ghost priests right in the front lines.

The Ibos had seceded from the Federation but ultimately their cause was hopeless as the big powers – Britain and the Soviet Union included – were backing the Federal Government.

On the road to the Mission Station I am given instructions on what I must do if the Federal jet comes over. You see someone who had failed to observe the code when getting out of his car a few days previously had his head blown off in a sudden air attack. I didn't want that fate to befall me and be buried under an African sky.

What I was told to do was immediately the car halted at the sound of the jet approaching, I must run as fast and as far as I could into the bush – on the other side of the road. It had to be the opposite side to where the car ground to a halt. Naturally the guns of the jet would be aimed at the vehicle – on its side of the highway.

We were passing by a gasoline station when I heard a loud bang. "This is it", I said to myself as my companion pressed the brakes to the floor-boards. Out I jumped and nearly set a new Irish 100-metres record as I plunged into the bush. Ants were crawling all over me but I wasn't thinking of them, only waiting for the first bullets to fly. They never did.

It transpired that it wasn't a jet attack after all, only the sound of a car back-firing.

Later when I was pulling out of Biafra on the second last plane, I was given further instructions on what I must do while waiting at Uli airstrip – if again the Feds attacked. They only lit up the runway at night when a plane came in to land or when one was ready to take off. And all the time they had to be prepared for a jet to come over and endeavour to put the airstrip out of action. The planes that had been destroyed and shifted to one side of the runway bore ample testimony to this ever-present danger.

They had dug these shelter-holes by the tarmac. "At the first sound of a jet coming in to attack, you must jump into one of these and remember to stay down", I was advised.

I decided on a practice run, so that my timing would be spot on. A little sprint and a leap that would have done justice to an Olympic hop-step-and-jump contestant and I was flying through the air and into what seemed to me then to be the black hole of Calcutta. There was a sudden scream mixed up in a babble of African voices, surprise and shock intermingled with pain as the toe of my right shoe struck someone in a very tender spot.

You see I had picked the wrong hole – and jumped right on top of a group of Ibos.

*   *   *

On that first evening at the Mission Station I could hear the sound of the big Russian-made guns in the distance, but obviously getting closer all the time. Their range, I was told, was a mile or more. I decided to check on the morrow how many miles we were from those guns and at the same time have a look at the Biafran defences.

As I headed for the "front", I saw this chap in a motley outfit pushing ahead of him a container of very weak-looking soup. I wondered if that was all that was left to feed the supposedly "elite corps" who would withstand the final Federal onslaught.

"Where is the second line of defence?", I enquired. "There isn't even a first", I was told.

And sure enough when I reached the Owerri River, I knew in my heart that it was over to all intents and purposes and that I wouldn't be sticking around too long.

There were disquieting reports reaching us that the Federal troops were shooting those they took prisoner into crocodile-infested rivers (all so much poppycock as it turned out and there was no genocide in the wake of the Federal victory). Still at the time it wasn't very pleasant to be faced with the prospect that you might end up as a juicy dinner for some croc.

All the time the dead and wounded were being brought in to the hospital not far from the Mission Station. There must have been a thousand there the day I visited it with one of the priests. Men who had lost both arms and both legs – and in addition you saw some even blinded. And amazingly enough still able to sing the Biafran National Anthem.

A veteran reporter who had seen it all in Vietnam emerged from the hospital feeling physically sick. I was no better.

But there was even worse to follow. I accompanied Fr. Con as he officiated at the burial of a number of Biafran soldiers. The coffins were of the most makeshift kind imaginable – just four plain planks of wood hammered together. Suddenly I hear a crack as one of the planks gives way and I see a leg protruding from the end of one of the coffins. There is a distinct smell of decaying flesh in the air, the stench of death.

They manage to get the coffin with the protruding leg to the graveside with the others. The priest never pretends he has noticed anything. He continues with the prayers for the dead and calmly does all that needs to be done – the same as if burying someone in a graveyard in Ireland.

But there are no relatives, no flowers – and no politicians with votes to win. Everything stripped completely bare as in a Beckett play. Four soldiers I would never know – unknown soldiers who had died in their minds for flag and country but in an unnecessary civil war, given a Christian burial because they had been brought up Catholics by Irish missionary priests.

Daily the face of starvation burned into the marrow of one's bones, left one marked indelibly for life with new philosophies, a new sense of priorities. Who was it, I reflect now, killed the beautiful white swans on

40

Lough Derg on the Shannon in my childhood days in Killaloe, County Clare?

Every time I see *Swan Lake* or play the tape of that ballet I can see those swans lying there in the street of Killaloe waiting to he shipped to England. Because it was during the Second World War and there were many hungry mouths to feed as the German U-Boats took a heavy toll and who was to know the difference between swan and duck?

But that was nothing, of course to Biafra. Nothing to seeing kids chasing after a lorry and picking up single items of food – even single peas – that might fall on the dusty road. Seeing the swollen stomachs of dead and dying babies. Going out into the bush with a Scottish missionary priest to try and save some of the children. We bring in quite a few. Remembering always now that man shot off the wing of the plane for the sake of one dried fish.

In a break during the writing of this chapter, I pick up the edition of *Newsweek* of May 20, 1991 spotlighting in the main Africa's famine areas, forgotten to a large extent because of the "disaster fatigue" that had set in on a world beset by a rush of calamity.

And in between all the evocative writing they put the spotlight on the very latest in veterinary care for animals and depict for us Rhonda lying trembling on the operating table as her cardiologist presses a small sensing device against her tiny chest ... an ultrasound image of Rhonda's wildly thumping heart flashes onto a video monitor, and a computer quickly outlines the direction of blood flow in bright reds and blues ... at the top of the video screen a turbulent splotch of colours spread toward the heart's aortic vale ... "it's a lesion" the doctor sighs, as the computer begins analysing the heart defect.

Rhonda, the six months-old Boston terrier may not be in the best of health but, as the writer in *Newsweek* noted, "she has one thing going for her – she was born into what is fast becoming the golden age of veterinary medicine. Barely a decade ago euthanasia was the standard prescription for pets with such serious ailments as heart disease and diabetes. Today there is an analog in the veterinary world for almost every procedure in human health care."

And he added: "Veterinary surgeons now implant pacemakers, donated organs and artificial joints in dogs and cats. Oncologists are diagnosing their cancers with CAT scans, then treating them with radiation and chemotherapy. Veterinary dentists perform root canals and fit crowns on animals, ophthalmologists strip away cataracts with ultrasound techniques and doggie dermatologists finally are addressing the heartbreak of Fido's psoriasis. All in all, many of America's 117 million dogs and cats receive better care than many of its citizens. As a result pets are living longer – and veterinary costs are spiralling into the stratosphere (Americans spent six billion dollars on veterinary care in one year, 1990, alone and experts estimate that this figure is rising by as much as ten per cent annually)".

Robert and Angela Maddix of Atlanta, according to the *Newsweek* man, had nursed Tanya, their toothless 19-year-old tabby through three years of severe diabetes. "She gets insulin daily, and once a week her skin is rehydrated with a water IV. After lapsing into a diabetic coma recently, she was rushed into intensive care. The bill: 400 dollars. "She's our only child", exclaimed 31-years-old Angela. I've had her since I was 12 and she's been a big part of my life. I have family members who are appalled by it all, but these don't seem to me extraordinary things to do for her".

And *Newsweek* concluded: "How much is too much? Fay McCoy (50) of Hardin, Mont. spent 3,200 dollars in 1990 on care for her two dogs. After an attack by a neighbouring stray, three-year-old Sadie underwent hours of surgery during which her external wounds were stitched and her chest cavity reconstructed. McCoy's 8-year-old cocker spaniel, Ebony died after being treated for bladder stones and cancer. "I had more invested in those two dogs and a horse than in all my three kids", says McCoy. "But you don't even think about it. You just want to keep them alive".

Across from me in the English Bar near the seafront in Marbella (at times when I see so much doggy excretion about I can be forgiven for thinking that this town on the Costa del Sol, haven of the retired, must be over-run by pets), there is a lady with a poodle. She's telling her friend over a G. & T. how happy she is really that Winnie the poodle got over her recent illness and happier still at the care the vet had given her. I am tempted to enquire about the cost. But what of it. My priorities and hers would be so different in this instance. So vastly different. Never could the twain meet.

Come to think of it, I didn't see one cat or dog in all my time in Biafra. Not even a stray. Starvation is a terrible thing.

*   *   *

Down the way the pilots who fly the relief planes in and out of Uli are having a party – and a ball. The sounds of clinking glasses and spontaneous laughter drift out to me from the verandah of the bungalow-style house they use as their base when over-nighting.

Before I join them for a night-cap, I must try and get a few more hours into the book I am writing about the starving Ibos and the great relief effort to reduce the toll of daily deaths and how the Holy Ghost missionaries are staying with the people in their hour of need. The provisional title I have hit upon is *Days of the Kwashiorkor* (Kwashiorkor being the disease of starvation).

I am down to the red part of my last dual ribbon. The sweat drops on to the page discolouring what I have written and making it run red if I forget now and then to wipe my brow. But I plough on. By now I must have 25,000 words typed and I feel satisfied that the back of the book is broken.

You learn to stop when the headaches begin to strike in the fierce humidity. Always they do and there are no headaches like these. Once I made the mistake in the Congo of typing non-stop through the midday hour forgetting Noel Coward's dictum ("only mad dogs …") – in order to get my despatches on a plane that was leaving Leopoldville Airport at around 3 o'clock and I paid a heavy penalty. I was more careful now in

42

Biafra. I came to know when to stop.

One of the pilots tells me over a stiff gin and tonic that flying the relief planes is just a job to him – his previous "marking" was flying diamonds in South America. He wasn't involved – didn't intend to be, couldn't really be worried about the way the Ibos were dying like flies. He was only interested in what was going into his numbered bank account in Switzerland in a solid foreign currency.

And in surviving.

I sensed a certain air of bravado as he dismissed the danger with a shrug but there was the ever-present possibility that he would be shot down by a Federal jet, assuming that one of the relief planes was carrying military equipment for the Ibos – and those Fed pilots knew how to heighten the drama as they warned on their radios: "We'll get you bastards if you try to take the mickey out of us".

If not shot down in flames, a guy could be caught like a sitting-duck on the tarmac at Uli airstrip, either before take-off or after landing, as a jet screamed in and sprayed the entire area with gunfire.

He wasn't being paid big money for nothing – and neither were the others. Having a ball at a party like this – the girls gravitating to them like bees to honey – was part of living life to the full, while you could enjoy it.

There's always tomorrow … but there might not be in this crazy theatre.

*   *   *

The effort on my book would come to nought in the end. Once Biafra fell, it wasn't considered wise or diplomatique that I should publish a work highlighting the role of the Holy Ghost missionary priests and – from the Federal Nigerian viewpoint at any rate – it was surrounded by controversy though they, for their part, saw it as their duty to stay with their people, come what may.

If it was the ultimate in service, then they served.

I had my own farewell with Fr Con before departing Biafra. He suggested some time in the early hours of the morning that I stay on a few more days.

Fr Tony Byrne was insistent that I get out as quickly as possible and tell the story of what I had seen of the starvation in Biafra's final days.

He himself was heading for Rome to see the Pope and impress upon him the need of appealing to the Federal Government not to allow genocide.

Fr Tony and myself had a deep discussion on the line the Pope might take. Here was I counselling and cajoling and pleading for carefulness in the line his Holiness should assume, in case he might go too far in offending the sensibilities of the Federal authorities.

I need not have worried. The Pope was going to have no rush of blood to the head. He had his own advisers, far more experienced than I was in how to frame a speech that would be heard by 600 million Catholics – and studied, into the bargain, by Heads of State and Government and diplomats in the corridors of power, including the U.N. Headquarters in

New York.

I heard part of what the Pope said on a transistor radio on San Tome Island as I sat at a cafe table having a drink, young Portuguese soldiers beside me writing letters and cards home to their sweethearts. He didn't put it as bluntly or directly as Fr Byrne might have liked to put it. He was extremely careful in his choice of words, as you would expect the Pontiff to be in such a situation but the message came across very clear – let reconciliation be the order of the day among "our brothers" in Nigeria (no sides were taken).

From San Tome I filed to the world the brief cabled story that told it all: "Federal troops have crossed the Owerri River. Biafra is no more".

And to Sheila, Fr Con's sister and my wife-to-be later that same year, I sent another short cable: "Don't worry. Fr Con is safe. I'm okay. See you soon. Love. Raymond".

*   *   *

Twelve years on I am back swimming in a sea of "dash". By now I have become immune to it, acquiring the necessary thick skin to accept it all as part of the African scene and realising that if you didn't learn how to work the system you were either a complete fool or a saint.

It's 1982 and I have returned to Nigeria. I had been to Abijan, capital of the Ivory Coast to cover the signing by Dr Garret FitzGerald, then Ireland's Foreign Minister of the Lome Convention on behalf of the EC (Ireland had the Presidency of the European Community at the time).

I had been warned what to expect once I hit Lagos but all the warnings in the world couldn't have prepared me for what was to evolve. I knew, for example, that a person applying for a driving licence had to be prepared to pay for the application form – and that was only the start of it. Everyone up the line from the humblest counter clerk got "dash" from what was forked out. You paid through the nose. If you didn't, you got used to the words "come back later" or being left sitting for hours in a waiting room or annex. So in the end you forgot your scruples and paid like all the rest.

Senator Charles McDonald – "Charlie" to his friends – was then a member of the European Parliament. He had been in Abijan and on the way home he planned to visit a priest relation of his in Ibo country. He wondered if I would accompany him. I felt it was a first-hand opportunity to see again that area of Nigeria which we had known as "Biafra" and assess too how it had recovered from the days of civil strife. It was a simple enough matter to re-route the air-flight ticket.

On arriving at Lagos airport we discovered that all flights in and out were grounded by a sudden storm. There would be nothing moving that day – and maybe the next also. It was essential then to get a room in the nearest hotel.

First I made the acquaintance of the "Jungle Bunnies" – or rather learned how the ladies of easy virtue who preyed on the business men with ample "readies" coming through the airport were christened. They were literally hanging out of the trees and if you shook one of the trees you were liable to get one of them dropping into your lap like a ripe melon!

Charlie McDonald was Chairman of a European Parliament Committee that gave him status and, as luck would have it, he happened to be carrying a document that had the word "President" written on it in gold lettering. They took it that he was President of Ireland. We didn't do anything to kill that assumption. A President was a very important person in their eyes. The Senator managed a suite – the Presidential suite.

I slipped the equivalent of a tenner in U.S. dollars into my passport as I handed it across the desk at reception. The man who took it never batted an eyelid. I was handed my room key. An exasperated German, who had been wrangling over the apparent non-receipt of a telex from his secretary back in Munich confirming his booking, never lodged the "dash" in his passport and was told quite blandly to move to one side. I then proceeded to get a room for another Irishman in our party. A raised eye-brow was enough to indicate to the man at reception that there was more money from America on the way to him.

We joined Charlie upstairs. There would now be the question of getting a table in the dining room, which we noted was over-crowded and with a long queue building up outside. I was instructed to tell my friend at reception that the "President" had not eaten as yet that day, that he was getting agitated and that the hotel had to appease that agitation forthwith.

Like any good Presidential aide I duly carried out my instructions and I was informed that the head waiter would be at our service.

I became Charlie's Press Officer for the purpose of that evening. The other man became his Economic Adviser. A President didn't move about without an entourage. I actually bowed Charlie into the dining room. I would have gone down on my knees and kissed his feet if necessary and as Charlie McCreevy would put it on another immortal occasion, sung a verse of *The Rose of Tralee* if that speeded our path to a good dinner.

I could see that the head waiter was eminently impressed. The queues parted before us like the waters of the Red Sea. They too were impressed by our princely entry. We passed them as if they didn't exist.

Back to the airport the next day when word reached us that one plane might get away after all but it is inferred that those who were first on the list when the planes were grounded would get priority treatment. Our chances didn't look very good.

We are in the VIP lounge naturally – again because a President doesn't wait in an over-crowded general area. Charlie, with that relaxed easy manner of his, gets into conversation with this man who turns out to be a Prince from the Port Harcourt region. In the most nonchalant manner imaginable the Irish MEP lets the Prince see his documentation. I can see that the man is impressed. Immediately standing to his feet, he leads the two of us to the departure desk.

He steps up on the baggage scales and in behind to the ticket office itself, as we follow. He demands to see the man in charge. Tells him to put the two of us on the plane that is about to leave. The man looks overwhelmed – but doesn't dispute matters with the Prince. He knows better. I can sense a thousand eyes staring in at me from the people waiting in the long queues outside.

Our baggage is handled for us. We are led by the Prince to the plane and he bids us a dignified farewell. I am hardly seated when I see an officer of the Nigerian Army suddenly enter the plane. He taps someone on the shoulder indicating that the seat must be vacated – and it is without a word.

The officer takes it without a word of apology.

* * *

The Holy Ghost missionaries dispersed after the ending of the Nigerian Civil War – that is those who had served in that part of the nation known as "Biafra". Some went to the States, some back to Ireland to other duties, a few left the priesthood altogether. The call of Africa was there for some that could never be dispelled. I met one of them in Sierra Leone and spent a memorable day in his company.

Fr Con found his way to Kenya, as did others. I renewed acquaintanceship with him among the runners of the Kangunda Hills. Youngsters who would run the 40 miles into Nairobi and back again, making it into the city on Friday and being back on time for school on Monday. Little wonder that they became great middle-distance and long-distance athletes, their names surfacing for their country at the Olympic Games. Back home on holidays Fr Con would be glued to the television following their progress and proud when he saw any of them mount the rostrum to receive a gold, silver or bronze medal – standing symbolically with them as the Kenyan national anthem flowed out over the sitting-room and we toasted them with our glasses of Scotch.

In Kenya I meet also two old missionaries, retired from their duties. Of course, they should have long since returned to the Mother House in Ireland, waiting for death. But they could not get Africa out of their bones, its sunrises and its sunsets, its way of life.

After dinner one evening in Nairobi, they bring me back to the time they officiated at the hanging of those who were caught causing havoc in the country-side in the unsettled period after Independence. Demonstrating for me how a convicted robber and killer with the rope around his neck would stand on the trap-door. The lever pulled and the spreadeagled legs would go with the opening of the trap-door as the neck snapped. On occasions if the guilty man was not killed outright when the trap-door opened, one of the missionaries would whisper another last prayer into the ear of the body dangling in mid-air, the legs giving a last kick like those of a dying hen or chicken.

It was gruesome, yes, and certainly far from pleasant. You could be forgiven for opening a bottle of whiskey when you got back from an evening of officiating at one or more hangings. Forgiven if you finished it off.

Sometimes instead of the hangings they would officiate at the shooting of a group of convicted criminals in the football stadium, packed to capacity as if it were a Cup final. Bussed in from all parts of the country-side around. A great roar would go up from the crowd when the officer gave the order "Fire" and the bodies of those, tied to their respective stakes, slumped forward.

It all became too much for one Irish priest. He cracked … cracked so badly that he ended up a gibbering wreck of a man, who would not leave his room. The price he had been asked to pay was too much for one human being.

*   *   *

I remember most of all from my trips to Kenya the length of the Masses and other religious ceremonies. One Sunday morning I went to Mass in Nairobi and after what seemed an hour the gospel had not yet been reached. I slipped out and bought an English newspaper and had a quick glance through it over a cup of coffee at a cafe convenient to the church. I returned to get an acknowledging nod of the head from the celebrant – a Holy Ghost priest who had talked hurling with me well beyond midnight the previous night. After the consecration had been reached, I slipped out again for a cure this time and came back to see the queue for Holy Communion. Another nod of the head from the altar. When it was finally over I felt like a man who had won an endurance test.

But that was nothing to the wedding ceremony Fr Con officiated at one day in the little church beside his Mission Station. They had a way of living together for a few years before they solemnised a union. You didn't question their morals but welcomed them into the fold of Mother Church, especially if they were getting baptised first. You learned that the ways of Africa were different to those of Catholic Ireland. The cook who served us breakfast, lunch and dinner had a number of wives.

I was making notes out of the heat of the noon-day sun for my biography of Dr Garret Fitzgerald – *Garret the Enigma* – as Fr Con led the procession into the church across the way from me. The hours passed. One after the other and still the singing went on. I had my siesta and it hadn't finished when I emerged again into the African sun. I reckoned it went on for almost four hours.

*   *   *

I made a trip to the Turkhana Desert to report on the European Community effort to get the nomadic people of that area to create a permanent base for themselves. It was their custom to follow their cattle. When the water in the water-holes became impure, the cattle died and the nomads frequently died with them.

The trip north gave me a chance to meet Bishop Lucey of Cork, who had opted for the mission fields on his retirement. He had a reputation for rigidity in his day that placed him second only to Most Rev Dr McQuaid.

We talk under a night sky. I proffer my philosophy – what I might term "the other side of the mountain" concept of belief in an after-life. Life is akin to a voyage and you merge eventually into the mountain at the level of beauty you have experienced in this life. Like the gannets drawn up in formation on the beach in Lahinch as the sun sets and the gulls swoop over the shoals of mackerel out in the bay. A golden sunset as you watch from a

47

sand dune beside the golf links. If you return in winter, you may see the flotsam from a wrecked ship being swept in on the same beach. The power of the Atlantic breakers can be awesome and so cruel, like life's tragedies but you know that, come summer, all will be dwarfed by the beauty you have known. I tell him there is no Hell's fire as such, just the awfulness of being cut off for eternity from the beatific vision. Only sins against Nature itself merit that.

I wondered whether the sojourn in the desert had broadened the thinking of this most-conservative of churchmen.

He puts it as Chancey Gardiner of Jerzy Kosinski's classic *Being There* might have put it: "There is Heaven. There is Hell. You go to Heaven if you avoid sin. You go to Hell if you are bad".

The European Community had promised to pay my flight to the Turkhana Desert from Nairobi and back to the Kenyan capital. Unfortunately, I had not written a letter to the Commission Headquarters in Brussels confirming what was agreed on the phone.

When I got back I duly made contact. It was agreed there had been a promise but, as there was no documentation, the bureaucratic machine could not pay the £400 in question. Sorry and all that. But that's the way the machine works, as you can appreciate. There has got to be something on paper.

So what must I do to get my £400 back, I ask?

"Make out another trip to Africa and incorporate the £400 in the cost of the ticket", was the solution offered. "But you must visit countries where the European Community is funding certain projects and we take it you will report on these".

I ask rather timidly but with the excitement already building in my blood if I can take in five countries in the course of the one trip. "Six if you want to", comes the reply. "Let us know when you have planned your itinerary and the cost of the ticket".

The return air ticket comes to a cool £2,300. I planned to take in Rwanda where Bord na Mona was involved in showing the natives how to save turf … neighbouring Burundi, where there was an Irish link with its tea industry … Zaire … Zimbabwe … and, of course, Kenya again to enjoy my sundowners with Fr Con and I might even fit in Botswana.

The *Irish Independent* wasn't paying full expenses this time but, to hell with it, I couldn't let that ticket go. Even though eventually it cost me an arm and a leg I entertain no regrets, for in many respects it was the trip of a life-time.

I had become very friendly with the EC delegate in Burundi, Richard le Sueur when he came on a visit to Ireland a few years previously and he promised to repay my hospitality if I ever happened to reach him in Africa. He met me at the airport. I have a memory of sitting with him on the veranda of his bungalow-style house drinking a gin and tonic as he played operatic tapes … Verdi's *Ernani*, *Don Carlos*, *Nabucco* and the timeless beauty of Maria Callas as Violetta in *La Traviata* flowing out over the African country-side.

I laughed as he told me of the Chinese workers who hadn't a clue about driving before they arrived in Burundi but, of course, that didn't deter them in the least and no chicken was safe crossing a road when they took their foot off the brake. No human either. They became maniacs once they sat behind the wheel of a car.

In Zimbabwe I had one hell of a day with the unofficial Mayor, the intrepid Tony O'Sullivan, the former Connacht and Irish rugby international, a great character.

The golf course up near the Victoria Falls, where I managed a round, had one of the most amazing holes in the world. You were allowed to place another ball – without penalty – if you went into the lake at one of the par threes. Why? Because you might lose your hand to one of the crocodiles if you tried to retrieve it.

The clubhouse was still damaged. I was told that one day one of Nkrumah's men fired a heat seeker missile across the A'Zambezi River. A guy who had just finished his round of golf had come in and ordered a toasted sandwich. It proved the fatal attraction for the missile and down the chimney it went … and zump up went the kitchen.

*   *   *

The epilogue to this chapter – to my African days – remains with Fr Con O'Mahony and in a way with all the outstanding Holy Ghost missionaries I came to know.

He came back from Kenya to work in the parish of New Barnet and "The Jester" became his local. And there on visits to meet him I would rub shoulders with Irish exiles who loved to talk hurling and football but who knew their soccer also and supported either Arsenal or the Spurs. On Ash Wednesday they would drink right up to closing time and then go off alcohol completely for Lent, allowing themselves a sabbatical on St. Patrick's Day. They had a great grá for Fr Con. Saw him as "one of our own" and actually honoured him at a special evening in "The Jester" that I know touched him deeply.

Fr Con suffered a heart attack during the Galway v Cork All-Ireland Hurling Final in 1990. He died two days later in the Mater Hospital. The last words I whispered to him as I touched his arm when he came briefly out of a coma were: "You served".

Tipperary-born Fr Denis Kennedy of Blackrock College, whom I remembered standing courageously in the ruin of his church in Biafra after the roof had been blown off by a rocket, said the Requiem Mass and spoke of service.

In 1982 on that return visit to Nigeria I had on my journey through Ibo land seen the crowded churches in the very areas where Fr Con and Fr Kennedy and others had worked. I heard the voices of the children coming to me everywhere I went. The legacy those missionaries had left would never die, I knew.

They played *Slievenamon* on the church organ during Requiem Mass. I was back in Nigeria as the big guns boomed in the distance and the Federal troops were preparing to break through across the Owerri River as

49

I sang *Slievenamon* with Fr Con during our impromptu farewell party.
And I remembered the lines that I composed later on San Tome:

The guns are silent now,
The jets no longer scream
Over the tarred incongruous road
Winding its way through bush
and jungle green,
In that country which we knew
briefly as Biafra.

5

When They Buried
Bobby Kennedy in Arlington

There we were in Arlington Cemetery in Washington waiting for the casket with the mortal remains of Bobby Kennedy to arrive. There was an early street edition of the *Sunday Independent* to catch and I had to be through by around six o'clock (GMT). So I duly filed a Page One lead story that saw the Senator buried by the light of the setting sun. But the train conveying the body was delayed and the original schedules went out the window.

The Kennedy clan had arranged things so meticulously that phones had been set up in the cemetery right on the grass margin beside the open grave where we were sitting. It was £1 a minute to phone Dublin. But hang the cost – this story was BIG, the biggest since Bobby's brother, President John F. Kennedy was assassinated in Dallas.

Anyway, I call Dublin collect and shout down the line – "Kill that lead", adding at the same time that I would be through with a new lead for the country edition. Now I had him buried in the gathering dusk. Eventually when we actually saw the cortege cross the Potamac River we got it exactly right.

The Newsdesk duly killed my first story – but it had hit the streets in Dublin.

This Dubliner, a Joxer-like character, was looking at the television in the pub as he drank his pint and there on the screen before him he could see the shots live of Bobby Kennedy's burial amid the candles. At the same time he was reading my initial story in the *Sunday Independent* about the burial taking place in the setting sun. Scratching his head, he turned to a companion beside him, who was half-way through his pint.

"How come I'm looking at Kennedy being buried in candle-light and Smith in the *Sunday Independent* has him being buried in the setting sun?"

"The time difference, Benny, the time difference", ventured his companion without batting an eye-lid.

The phone bill from Arlington was phenomenal but nothing was ever said to me because, as the calls were reversed, it got swallowed up in the Independent Group's annual bill. For many a journalist the lucky break has comes from being in the right place at the right time.

I had accompanied the Tipperary hurling team on a trip to New York for the 1968 National League final proper. I intended to use the material I gathered in a book I was planning.

Coming down the lift in the Manhattan Hotel I get the news from the lift operator that Bobby Kennedy had been shot.

I grab a copy of the *Daily News* and the banner headline screams out at me: KENNEDY SHOT.

I rush back up to my room, pack my bag and proceed to pay my account before taking a taxi to the airport and the first flight to Los Angeles. During a brief stop at Chicago I ring Bill Shine on the *Evening Herald* Newsdesk, tell him what I am doing and assume that the Independent Group will want me to take it from there.

First Bill Shine indicates that he wants me to work exclusively for the *Evening Herald* but I remind him that on a story like this you file for whichever paper of the Group hits the street first, be it evening, morning or Sunday. He comes back to say that I have read it correctly and to proceed on that basis. All expenses from the moment I took the taxi from my hotel in New York to when I get back to Ireland will be fully covered. Once I had booked into a hotel in Los Angeles I was to ring him and he would transfer "the necessary".

I was the first Irish journalist into Los Angeles and the Independent Group had the beat on all its rivals for almost twenty-four hours. Both the *Evening Herald* and *Irish Independent* sold massively.

I take a taxi to the Good Samaritan Hospital where Kennedy is battling for his life. The taxi-man is talking away … "dem Press guys is running around all morning like a chicken that has lost its head".

A special Press Centre has been set up. All seems confusion initially as they work at top speed to install more television cables and telephone lines. Pick up a phone and you are liable to hear a voice from Argentina or Brazil looking for someone or some information. You stop picking up phones, otherwise you will never get any information back to the paper at home.

After a while there comes a semblance of order. It's simply amazing how quickly and efficiently you get your own line. The Press gets every possible co-operation on a big story in the States. The coffee machines have been installed. Black coffee to stay awake. Plenty of it.

There is a photographer who has come in from a marking in Berlin. Thought he had a week off but was packed off to Los Angeles. Cannot remember when he last slept.

*   *   *

And now the long day's dying …

We know he is bad, that there is not a lot of hope. The faces of Frank Mankiewicz, Press Secretary to the dying Senator and of Pierre Salinger, who was Press Secretary to President Kennedy, are grave. Very grave.

But hope still lingers …

Two weeks earlier Senator Kennedy had told French writer Romain

Gary that "sooner or later" he would be the victim of an assassination attempt. "There is no way to protect a candidate during the electoral campaign", he had said. "You must give yourself to the crowd and from then on you must take your chance. In any case you must have luck to be elected President of the United States. You have it or you don't. I know that there will be an attempt on my life sooner or later. Not so much for political reasons, but through contagion, through emulation".

At 2 a.m. Los Angeles time Frank Mankiewicz announces that Senator Kennedy had died.

A strange silence falls over the Press Room. Hardened reporters who had campaigned with Kennedy through the California primary are visibly moved.

And then everyone seems to be talking into phones at the same time. The television cameras whirr. The representatives of the radio networks, who have been speaking incessantly it seems, capture the emotion of the moment brilliantly ... you marvel at their energy.

I phone the following to the *Evening Herald:*

"This is a day which I will never forget, the longest day I can remember. It has been a day of tension, of suspense, of false alarms, a day when the life of a great man hung in the balance – when not only the United States but the entire world followed his battle for survival.

"As I write this, it is 2.15 a.m. Los Angeles time and hundreds of people are coming from their homes and gathering outside the hospital, supplementing the faithful Kennedy supporters who had kept vigil throughout the day into the early hours of the morning. Death in a way may have been a release, as it was generally accepted that if he had pulled through he would have been paralysed for life. In conversations with friends a day or two before the shooting, he saw life as something to be lived fully, every minute of it – and he did not fear the game of politics".

His body came home to New York and we drove in the motorcade directly behind the hearse on the ten mile journey to the city. We had snatched just two hours of fitful sleep in the Hilton – lucky to get a bed from Cronin the Irishman behind the reception desk, who had never seen a Cronin on the cover of any book before until he saw John Cronin of Kerry on the cover of the 1968 edition of my book, *The Football Immortals* which someone had sent him from home.

All is a whirl of swiftly-developing events from the moment we hit New York to the last impressive act of the drama when the coffin is lowered into the earth in Arlington National Cemetery nearby to that of the late President Kennedy.

The big Air Force jet coming to a halt at La Guardia Field ... a composed Ethel Kennedy stepping into the glare of the lights alongside the coffin of her husband ... the ride into the city in the special Press bus, the police cars giving us a clear run ... thousands pressing against the barriers outside St. Patrick's Cathedral, floodlit by the spotlights of the T.V. camera teams ... Ted Kennedy spending the night by his brother's side, the last of the Kennedy boys keeping a sleepless vigil beside the coffin on the maroon-draped bier with one spray of white flowers.

There is no sleep for us this night either … to the Commodore Hotel to get our credentials for Arlington … next day thousands queue outside the Cathedral, stretching away down the avenue, around corners, away even further down other avenues, as far as the eye can see … the mourners include the rich from suburban homes and the poor from steamy tenements, white and coloured, young and old … the tribute of the people of his chosen State is solemn, silent and tremendously moving …

An invited congregation of 2,300 at the Requiem Mass. Millions in the United States, and throughout the world watch the ceremony on television (incidently, the television cameras catch me entering the Cathedral just behind U. Thant, the U.N. Secretary-General and when I return to Ireland a friend of mine asks me in Murphys of Baggot Street: "What did U. Thant say to you?").

The Archbishop of New York, Most Rev. Terence J. Cooke speaks the eulogy. Cardinal Cushing is present. There are moments I will remember always from that morning in St. Patrick's Cathedral … conductor Leonard Bernstein leading thirty members of the New York Philharmonic Orchestra in a movement from Mahler's Fifth Symphony during the Offertory of the Mass … Richard Tucker of the Metropolitan Opera singing *"Panis Angelicus"* … and Senator Ted Kennedy's tribute to his slain brother … "Love is not an easy feeling to put into words. Nor is loyalty, or trust or joy. But he was all of these. He loved life completely and lived it intensely" … with his voice failing with emotion, he concluded with the words of Bernard Shaw, which had been quoted by President Kennedy in his address to the historic joint meeting of the Houses of the Oireachtas on May 28, 1963 – "Other people see things and say: 'Why?' But I dream things that never were and I say: 'Why not?'."

They buried him near his brother, down a grassy slope from the columned portico of the Custis-Lee Mansion.

"We have come – in our lifetime at least – to an end of the Kennedy political period with its dynasty potential and its hero-worshipping followers", wrote Ted Lewis in the *Daily News*. "It will be a time to remember when we all grow old, for it was a hot-blooded, idealistic and high-spirited period, full of controversy but also full of the brilliant spark that makes life worth living …"

When finally I hit the sheets in the Mayflower Hotel I fell into the deepest sleep I ever experienced. It must have been fifteen hours later when I surfaced.

Two months after Dr Martin Luther King had been slain – two months to the day before his own assassination, Bobby Kennedy had said: "Violence is not the concern of any race. The victims of violence are black and white, rich and poor, young and old, famous and unknown. They are, mot important of all, human beings whom other human beings loved and needed".

Later I would listen to one of Kennedy's final campaign speeches in the JFK Library in Boston. I realised that his empathy with the oppressed and downtrodden and all the Willie Lomans put him outside the pale with the elements of the Right in a society where profit and the power of the dollar in the jungle of no-pity kept the wheels grinding relentlessly and no one cried "Stop – let's listen to the beaten dogs". And I wondered did the Right, who abhorred socialist principles in any form, really want him in the White House.

*   *   *

We had claimed the Kennedys as "our own" from the day in June, 1963 when President John F. Kennedy, only 46 then and two years and five months into his Presidency – the first Catholic, incidentally, to make it to the White House – stepped on to the tarmac at Dublin's Collinstown to begin his historic visit to Ireland. Sean Lemass was Taoiseach and Eamon de Valera was President. The entire Fianna Fáil Government of the day lined up to meet him, among them the "Golden Boys", Charles J. Haughey, Donogh O'Malley and Brian Lenihan, who was only 32 then and junior Minister for Fisheries.

"I remember him walking off the plane in the sunlight", Lenihan would recall thirty years later in the course of a *Sunday Press* interview with Orla Bourke. "He was tall, extremely tanned and he was wearing a light grey suit. It was all very dramatic. His hair was crumpled and brushed back in the fashion of the time.

"I was standing at the end of the line and I'll never forget the grin on his face when Lemass introduced me as the "baby" of the group. Kennedy's eyes twinkled in amusement. It was quite remarkable that here was a world hero, yet he seemed so completely Irish".

Those three days in June, taking in Dublin, Wexford, Limerick, Cork and Galway and most of all the Kennedy homestead in Dunganstown, a small cottage outside New Ross from where John F's great grandfather left as a poor labourer to take a coffin ship for America, created an indelible imprint from the moment of his arrival to his departure. And his departing words at Shannon would take on a new poignancy five months later ... "Last night somebody sang a song, the words of which I am sure you know, 'Come back to Erin, Mavourneen, Mavourneen, come back aroon' ... This is not the land of my birth but it is the land for which I hold the greatest affection and I certainly will come back in the springtime".

I joined the pool reporters in the car close behind the President as he was driven in an open-topped car through the centre of Dublin – on through O'Connell Street and around by Trinity College, to be welcomed by the greatest public turnout for any visiting dignitary (it was estimated that the cheering thousands totalled a quarter of a million) as he proceeded to the American Ambassador's residence in the Phoenix Park.

"America was at its peak in power and strength", was how Brian Lenihan put it to Orla Bourke. "It was the beginning of the Sixties, the Beatles and the power of youth ... Kennedy was setting in train something important between Ireland and America." And he added: "of course there was a certain amount of vote-catching involved. He was getting into his stride for the 1964 election and was going all out for the Irish-American

55

vote. But that didn't impinge on the fact that he was so obviously loving Ireland. Even the subsequent bits about his involvement with women didn't detract from him as far as I was concerned. It was quite obvious on meeting Kennedy that he wasn't going through an act, like so many do."

In fact, Ireland's love affair with the Kennedys became so intense that you hardly went into a home in rural Ireland – and right out to the Aran Islands – but you were greeted by a picture of the Pope above the mantlepiece side by side with one of John F. Kennedy. When the imposing Cathedral was built in Galway – for what seemed a fortune at the time – President Kennedy was featured in a mosaic beside Jesus and Padraig Pearse and, irrespective of the controversy it caused, there he remains to this day. Of course, the recording of Kennedy's brilliant address to the joint Houses of the Oireachtas became a prized possession in Irish homes and today when I play it I find myself admiring his easy references to Yeats and the way his speech was dotted with witty asides.

When President Kennedy was assassinated in Dallas the following November, the Irish nation was stunned and engulfed with a great sense of personal loss. For Kennedy in returning to lay claim to his roots had created very special bonds that could never be broken. And his brother Ted, who would remember him watching the home movies of that historic visit not just one night but three nights in a row on his return to the White House, was to work tirelessly in Ireland's cause, especially in the efforts to bring a lasting peace to Northern Ireland.

*   *   *

Other American Presidents came but none could arouse the same genuine feelings as President Kennedy. Nothing could ever surpass the famous picture of Kennedy cutting the cake, decorated with an iced portrait of himself, with Mary Anne Ryan beside him in the Dunganstown family home. Jackie Kennedy 34 then, was unable to come with John F. as she was pregnant with the couple's third child (Patrick who was born two months after the Irish trip but died just 48 hours old). Later, before she married Onassis, she brought John and Caroline on a private visit to Dunganstown, drank tea in the kitchen with Mary Anne senr, and sent the children down to the farm on their own with just one security man keeping surveillance.

The Camelot days touched Ireland deeply as they touched the world.

Kennedy had surrounded himself with the best and the brightest – the people captured for posterity in Dave Halberstam's book. They had the kind of grace that neither Nixon nor Reagan knew and so the visits of these two never captured the imagination of the Irish people as did the coming of John F. Kennedy.

"A grace of attitude, manner, form, social badinage, perhaps created out of generations of privilege, perhaps not; the underprivileged are also often born with grace", was how Roger Rosenblatt defined it in an incisive and often cruel profile of Nixon in *Time* magazine in April, 1988 – a Nixon trying to win rehabilitation after the ultimate disgrace of Watergate. Where Nixon, for example, had to claw and struggle to the top, you could

Celine Gleeson, who was brought up to be told in school that her father was a hero who gave his life for the cause of peace and (below) Lt. Kevin Gleeson with the Belgian priest, Fr. Peeters, whom he rescued from 300 Balubas by getting through 37 road-blocks to Nyunzu, after the Balubas at one point had threatened to kill him and the soldiers with him. He was congratulated by Col. Dick Bunworth for his bravery.

An Irish soldier doesn't forget to bring his guitar as he heads for the Congo for UN duty in 1960 And (below) the men of the 32rd Infantry Battalion, preceded by their colour party, parading past the saluting base at the GPO, as the Taoiseach, Sean Lemass and Frank Aiken, Minister for External Affairs look on and (inset) Capt. Jim Fives of the famous Waterford hurling family leads his detachment in the memorable parade.

NATION'S FAREWELL... thousands lined the streets of Dublin to cheer the first Irish contingent heading for the Congo in 1960. Here some of the soldiers are seen marching across O'Connell Bridge.

Gay O'Brien (top left), the *Irish Independent* photographer in the Congo (he was later a cameraman with RTE). John Ross of Radio Eireann and the author, who covered for the Independent Group, pictured (top right) outside the Memling Hotel in Leopoldville now Kinshasha (centre) and (below) the author with Army Chief of Staff, Lt. Gen. Carl O'Sullivan and Comdt. (now Lt. Col.) Dermot Earley at the launching of *Under the Blue Flag.*

Wounded and dazed, Pte Kenny staggers from the bush 41 hours after the Niemba Ambush and (top right) Pte Joe Fitzpatrick, the only other survivor, today makes painting one of his great hobbies and (below) the grief of a nation caught in this graphic *Irish Independent* picture as the remains of the men who died in the Blue Berets at Niemba are taken through O'Connell Street to Glasnevin Cemetery in November, 1960.

An Irish soldier stands guard over the square in Albertville (top) and (inset clockwise) General Sean McKeown, Supreme Commander of the U.N. Peacekeeping Force in the Congo, Dr Conor Cruise O'Brien, the U.N. Special Representative in Katanga and Major-General Bil Callaghan, Commander of the UN Force in the Lebanon. Two members of the Irish contingen with UNEF (below) observing activities in the Sinai Desert in November, 1973.

THE PITY OF WAR AND THE PITY THAT WAR DISTILS... the timeless face of a child in the arms of a young girl in a Lebanese Refugee camp in Beirut and (below right) Lebanese refugees returning to their homes in Abaseeyeh, which was destroyed during the Israeli invasion of southern Lebanon in 1978 and(left) the havoc and destruction wrought in downtown Beirut during the Civil War.

THE DAYS OF THE KWASHIORKOR... what starvation did to these Biafran children during the Nigerian Civil War and (below) the great relief effort brought the Churches together as these planes on San Tome proved; it was from here that the historic night flights to Uli originated.

say that prominence and power came as easily to the Kennedys as slipping on a coat.

Nixon and Reagan, both in advance of their arrival in Ireland, ensured that their links with the land of their ancestors were fully highlighted. But the cynics saw it as part of the agenda to catch the "Irish vote" back in the States. It seemed that you could not be a White House incumbent without making a trip to Ireland at some point in your Presidency.

By the time Nixon flew into Shannon Airport in early October, 1970 the Irish media were not as wide-eyed as had been the case when President Kennedy made his epoch-making visit.

Indeed, one reporter in the crime area was given strict instructions to report only on "incidents" and that meant clearly any attempts to disturb the composure of the visiting head of State.

This same reporter, when asked subsequently how he had fared with his expenses, responded: "I ran out of road".

I found myself also on the look-out for "incidents" rather than writing a colour piece about the overwhelming enthusiasm being shown by the crowds in Dublin and elsewhere. Indeed, the final drive through O'Connell Street to Dublin Airport for the flight out, was, as I reported next day, friendly – "but it did not seem to me to be over-enthusiastic and at no stage in Dublin was there the overflowing enthusiasm and excitement which I had experienced when I travelled in the motorcade with the late President Kennedy through the city seven years ago".

Now I was in the leading press bus, not far behind the Presidential car, as Nixon headed for a State luncheon in Dublin Castle. I had the Page One lead story in the *Irish Independent* next morning as I recounted how three times the President came under fire from egg-throwers. In Lord Edward Street, Nixon, who was standing up in the limousine, waving and smiling to the crowd, "suddenly dived for cover as eggs burst off the windscreen of his bullet-proof car".

I recounted how U.S. Secret Servicemen jumped out from their own bulletproof limousine and overpowered the man who had thrown the eggs from a satchel carried around his neck.

My report went on: "Four minutes earlier a young woman in a white rain-coat broke the Garda cordon at Cork Hill. I saw her with an egg poised to throw. The President seemed to see her and instead of waving, he put up his hand and shied away, and then ducked down into the car as she threw the egg, which spattered against the windshield. She had got to within 15 or 20 feet of the car.

"Two hundred yards further down the motorcade a young man in a sweater threw an egg which again broke on the windshield, and at this stage the driver of the Presidential car took diversionary tactics, pulling away from that side of the street."

"The egg-throwers were standing near a group of about 30 youths who shouted as the President passed: 'Vietnam, No, No' and 'Nixon, Fascist.'

"I saw the Gardaí push back other youths who kept up a chant of 'Victory to the Viet Cong' as the Presidential car accelerated and swung swiftly into the Castle yard."

*   *   *

I became the "pool" reporter for the entire Irish media when Mrs Pat Nixon sat down to high tea in the home of her nearest Irish relative, Miss Katie Naughton five miles outside Ballinrobe in County Mayo.

I nearly missed out on the assignment as just at the point when I was entering the cottage, I was told bluntly by a Secret Serviceman standing guard at the entrance to get lost. Never in my journalistic career in Ireland had the words "Raymond Smith of the *Irish Independent* (or *Sunday Independent*)" failed to get me past a Garda cordon or even members of the Special Branch and the showing of my N.U.J. card had even worked at awkward moments in the States.

I protested indignantly to the Secret Serviceman but he just ignored me. At that moment a burly American photographer, with whom I had been drinking the night before in a convivial gathering of Irish and American media folk, came along and seeing my predicament told the Secret Serviceman that he could vouch for my credentials.

In my pooled report, which was carried word-for -word in the *Irish Independent* next day, I bent over backwards to catch every weepy-weepy nuance of the occasion. I actually reported that "for me it will remain the most outstanding moment of the Nixon visit to Ireland".

It proceeded in this exotic vein:

"Katie herself had baked everything on the table and Mrs. Nixon wanted most of all to eat Katie's home-made bread.

"Visibly tense on Saturday evening at Shannon as security men battled on the tarmac with photographers to clear a passage for her and Mr. Nixon to the presidential car, the First Lady of the United States now sat happy and relaxed in Katie Naughton's sitting-room, drinking tea and eating a slice of home-baked bread.

"At the table , too, was Katie's brother, John Naughton, and his wife, Bridie; his sister-in-law, Nora Burke; and a shy, 10-year-old girl, Nora McWalter, who had had the honour of presenting a bouquet of flowers to Mrs. Nixon on her arrival in Ballinrobe.

"Katie pointed to the photograph of Mrs. Nixon's grand-uncle, Pat McHugh, who built the house, and was asked did she see any likeness to herself in it. 'I suppose you could say there is,' remarked Mrs. Nixon.

"Katie then took out a family album of faded photographs and went through it with Mrs. Nixon.

"I asked Mrs. Nixon what she thought of the welcome accorded her husband and herself on their arrival in Ireland.

"'Marvellous,' she said. She added that she had been particularly impressed with the turnout in the villages.

Tony Gallagher arrived from Dublin in a taxi just at the point when I had emerged from Katie Naughton's cottage. One of the most hard-bitten newsmen it was my pleasure to know, he was to succeed me as Press Officer of the IFA.

"What's the beat?", he asked. I told him I was doing the pool report and once I had it typed out I would give him a 'black' right away. 'Can't wait', he responded. "I have got to get back to Dublin as quickly as possible".

I began by painting a picture of Pat Nixon being greeted when she entered the cottage and of the spread on the table before her. "Cut the crap", said Tony. "All I want are the bare essentials. You don't have to tell me about every single cake and currant bun she ate".

He jumped back into the taxi with a "Cheerio, old boy" and left Katie Naughton's cottage and Ballinrobe behind him in a cloud of dust.

*   *   *

The members of the White House Press Corps accompanying Nixon, indeed all the American media representatives set the kind of pace that left us Irish media representatives drained when the visit was all over. Out of the Press Bus with the cry "move it", back into it and out again … it never seemed to end. We made a stop on the Curragh plains as Nixon was shown – or should I say introduced to – one of the leading colts of that season. All I can remember him saying blandly is "What a lovely animal". In a similar moment, President John F. Kennedy would have come up with something worth recording for posterity.

I concluded that Nixon had no style, no class – he who was described by Roger Rosenblatt in that cruel *Time* portrait as "of the contorted poses, the puckered face, the hunched-shoulder walk; he of the inability to lie and not get caught. Graceful people don't get caught. The graceless, awkward, stiff, stumbling character trips about in a world occupied by natural athletes and virtuoso statesmen, though once he commanded that world".

Were we really surprised when Watergate descended upon him or rather that he created it? I suppose the Irish people had to feel conned when they reflected on the way they had welcomed him and all the shenanigans about his ancestry. And I felt conned most of all when I reflected on what I wrote about Mrs Nixon loving Katie Naughton's homemade brown bread in County Mayo.

But at least you could say of Pat Nixon that she was a lady – far too good for "Tricky Dicky" who never displayed any affection for her in public and once forgot to mention her while profusely praising his late mother during his rambling final address of thanks to White House officials and staff on the day of his resignation from the Presidency (at least he did remember her with a phrase that served as her epitaph when he dedicated *Six Crises*, the first of his six books with the words: "To Pat – she also ran").

The Watergate tapes revealed more about the man and his mind than any biography.

One day the Chief of Staff offered the President a report from one of his economic advisers outlining the effect of Britain's floating of the pound on the world monetary system. Nixon brushed it aside saying: "It's too complicated for me to get into".

Haldeman said that Dr. Arthur Burns, Chairman of the Federal Reserve Board, expected the British move to result in a five per cent devaluation of sterling against the dollar.

The President: "Yeah, o.k. Fine."

Haldeman: "Burns is concerned about speculation about the lira."

The President: "Well, I don't give a (expletive deleted) about the lira." (Unintelligible).

*   *   *

And then President Ronald Reagan came in April, 1984 and the media circus was off again. Only that we were getting more cynical and blase – and downright weary – with each Presidential visit (as I write this chapter, President Clinton was due to hit our shores in September '95).

First, there was all the excitement engendered by the discovery of what was left of Reagan's Irish roots.

No tombstone with a fading inscription in a ruined graveyard; no thatched cottage where President Reagan could bow his head in tribute to long dead ancestors. Just one line in Latin told it all.

The yellowing pages of a church baptismal register contained conclusive proof of the President's Irish ancestry, Tom Shiels reported in the *Irish Independent.*

Among 40,000 names in the 1817-1872 Templetuohy Baptismal Register was an entry which showed that Reagan's great-grandfather, Michael was baptised there on September 3, 1829.

Michael married Catherine Mulcahy on October 31, 1852 in London and the couple later gave birth to Ronald Reagan's grandfather, John who died in Illinois in 1899.

According to Father Condon, the graveyard surrounding the ruined church at Templetenny, which pre-dated the modern-day Church of the Assumption in Ballyporeen, is presumed to be the burial ground of the Reagan family of Doolis.

President Reagan's great-grandfather, Michael would have been among the first to have been baptised in the new church at Ballyporeen when it was built in 1828, the year before Catholic Emancipation.

*   *   *

American security chiefs descended by helicopter on Ballyporeen. Indeed, one paper had it that the CIA were putting into motion an elaborate plan "to eliminate all risks to the President" when he arrived in the South Tipperary village of 350 souls, though, we have seen, 1,400 live in the parish itself (somehow CIA sounds better than "security chiefs" or "White House staff").

They travelled by limousine to the Reagan family burial ground in Templetenny, two miles outside Ballyporeen. No stone was left unturned as they assessed from what point on that lonely hilltop a would-be assassin might strike. They were reported to be appalled at the prospect that the Presidential Lincoln Continental, while being able to get up to the graveyard, might never get back down – because of the lack of turning space. And appalled too that Ballyporeen didn't have any skyscrapers from where marksmen could command a bird's eye view of everything that moved down below. But they had to accept that, having announced he was coming, the President could not snub the village, especially when you

60

reflected on all the trouble the villagers had gone to in order to spruce it up for the momentous visit (the smell of paint was everywhere and Gene Kerrigan caught it beautifully when he wrote in *Magill* that "the village looks as if a passing juggernaut crammed with assorted cans of Valspar hit a bump and disgorged its load").

The American security men with their eternal walkie-talkies had now come to be accepted as a necessary part of the "scenery" when an American President visited Ireland.

Such was the security cordon in the end around Ballyporeen – with parishioners having to get special passes – that a crowd of only 5,000 was present in the town itself when Reagan made his historic entry. A million sandwiches were reported to have been left over and they were distributed free to the six pubs in the town and then given out for nothing to every customer who bought a drink.

O'Farrell's public-house had stood on a corner of the long main street since 1922. John O'Farrell and his wife, Mary stuck a plastic sign above the door to the lounge that read "The Ronald Reagan" and one paper had a classic picture of a woman with a donkey and cart passing by right under the Guinness sign. But it would always be O'Farrell's. The plastic sign couldn't change that and neither could the fact that at the time of the Reagan visit, John O'Farrell was obliging the Yanks who got off the touring buses by selling them packets of authentic Ballyporeen clay at a quid a packet that could be placed proudly on the mantlepiece back home to proclaim to the world that you had been to the village from which the incumbent American President's ancestors had come.

And that inspired Gene Kerrigan to paint a picture in *Magill* of one Hiram J. Ignatowski landing at JFK and the customs officer looking at this dime bag and saying "would you mind stepping this way, sir," and Hiram would explain that it was, you see, clay from Ballyporeen, where Sherrif Reagan's folks had come from etc. etc.

White House aides brought in their own barrel of Smithwicks, with dispenser and glasses. They took them away with them when the visit was all over. The local wits reckoned this was carrying security to a ridiculous level. Who in Ballyporeen would want to slip a Mickey-Finn to the President of the United States – or was it possible that an agent from some country that had no love for America or Reagan himself would go to all the trouble of making it to this village to execute a Mafia-style scrubbing-out job.

Those White House security chiefs failed to counter the unexpected when it did happen – as it could only happen in Ireland. And it must have given some of them grey hairs.

Catherina Nancy O'Farrell, then only five weeks old, was one of the stars of the show when President Reagan finally made it to "The Ronald Reagan Lounge". The Secret Service men didn't mind Nancy Reagan holding the baby in her arms but they warned the O'Farrells that on no account must little Catherina Nancy be handed over to the President himself.

Mrs O'Farrell took up the story: " They were adamant that even if the President were asked to hold the baby for just one minute while a picture was being taken, he would refuse.

"The President had signed the visitor's book and he turned to Nancy and said: 'Honey, they want you to sign'. She looked up at him holding out the baby. There was a deafening silence and then she just walked across and put Catherina in his arms. I admit that he did look awkward holding the child, but he held on for dear life. I will treasure the picture of that moment always".

6

The Cheetah at Charlie's

A night-club in Luxembourg called Charlie's. A woman comes out wearing a Stetson, a G-string and carrying a pair of six-shooters. Her act is to have simulated sex with a cheetah.

The corps – or at least a hard core of that intrepid band of EEC correspondents – had gathered for some relaxation and late-night drinks after another intensive negotiating round had concluded in the tall building on the Kirchberg.

It always took some time to unwind after we had filed our stories to extremely tight deadlines for the final editions of the next day's papers.

I had managed to get a table right up front but my long-standing friend and colleague, Val Dorgan of the *Cork Examiner* had to make do with a perch behind a screen that missed out on the G-string and the cheetah. So I had to give a running commentary for Val and the other unlucky ones.

"What's happening?", Val calls out, with urgency in his voice.

"The cheetah has taken a classic horizontal position", I exclaim.

"Quick ... what's the story now?", is the eager inquiry from someone at Val's elbow.

"The lady has drawn her six-shooters from their holsters and is proceeding to seduce the cheetah".

"My God", groans Val, "why the hell didn't I get a proper seat".

At the climactic (simulated) moment the six-guns go off with a loud bang and the cheetah falls back limp with exhaustion – but with a very satisfied look.

We all applaud enthusiastically as the lady waves her Stetson. She comes back out with the cheetah for a second curtain call, as the applause breaks out with even greater enthusiasm.

We give her three curtain calls in all ... and an extra one to the cheetah!

I tell some good friends of mine in the British corps who missed out on that memorable night in Charlie's. And naturally they feel that they must see the steamiest show in town (even Ireland's Foreign Minister, Dr Hillery was tempted to make a visit but feared that it might reach one of the gossip columns back home).

Charlie's is crowded out the following night.

Six months later I pick up one of the British tabloids and learn of the untimely death of the cheetah.

Unfortunately, he died of the surfeit of sex.

*   *   *

The scene turns now to Copenhagen to the European Summit when French President Pompidou was so ill that the central heating was on round the clock at an inordinate level and you nearly fainted in the toilets.

We go out during a break in proceedings – Mick Mills of the *Irish Press*, Val Dorgan and myself – to see the film *Deep Throat*, the English version with Danish sub-titles. Naturally we are streets ahead of the Danish audience in our raucous laughter at the funny moments of this quirky film. One of the usherettes comes along with a flash-lamp and points it ominously at us, threatening at the same time to eject us if we don't stop laughing so uproariously.

Nothing funnier that when the lady goes along to the psychiatrist and tells him that she has had "it" something like forty eight times recently and still can't get any real satisfaction.

He looks down her throat and discovers that the nirvana point of real satisfaction is embedded there.

Where will she find the man who will give her THAT kind of satisfaction?

"I'm your man", comes the reply ... and, as he begins to pull down his trousers and she clears her throat, they both pop behind a screen.

We see a rocket take off from Cape Canaveral and again the flash-lamp shines on us as we explode into uncontrolled laughter.

The stoic Danes around us remain deadly serious through it all ... and we are quite happy to be told to leave, laughing all the way to the exit.

Sean Duignan, the incomparable "Diggy" of RTE, has missed the show because he has to catch a 9 o'clock News deadline that demands voice over film. I give a running commentary to Sean and the others back in the bar of our hotel. Sean quietly tapes it. All are agreed when they hear the replay that it's not necessary for those who had missed out to go to the film. The tape would suffice.

In one sex shop a small Chinese from Hong Kong is buying pornographic films. "Man and woman or man and man?", he is asked. "All man and man", he responds, his countenance as blank as the view from the Great Wall of China when it is shrouded in mist.

Val Dorgan and myself conclude after that it's time to get back to reality and we head for a Western ... this time with Danish voices dubbed on to it and sub-titled in English!

We don't mind in the least as we join the long queue (the Danes, it seems, are far more interested in Westerns, leaving the sex shops and shows to the innocents from the predominantly Catholic countries, Ireland and Italy especially).

The title is very promising ... *Exchange Your Gun For a Coffin.*

*   *   *

The previous occasion I had been to Copenhagen I was on an investigative story for the *Irish Independent* about a group of Irish girls who had answered an advertisement for chamber-maids and found themselves treated the same as migrant workers. Naturally, most of the Irish had been successful in the Leaving Certificate examination and their credentials were far too good for cleaning out bedrooms. Not to mention the accommodation in which they found themselves.

I was pictured over a splashed report pointing to the grim hostel, in which the Irish were housed, I quoted the female boss overseeing the girls (she wept in my presence as I grilled her in her office) that "it was all a mistake ... a dreadful mistake", as they assumed that the Irish they had engaged were simple, uneducated beings like those from another hemisphere and really they should never have come.

The *Irish Independent* claimed a famous victory and naturally I felt I had to celebrate the outcome of my investigative efforts.

I headed for the Penthouse Bar of the Sheraton Hotel (this was not the hotel, I hasten to add, that had employed the Irish girls).

As I sat at the bar drinking a Johnny Walker Black, I noticed that on my left was a lady sipping a dry martini and on my right was a thick-set guy consuming pink elephant cocktails.

Each time he ordered another one, he gave the bar attendant the nod to add it to his bill. The attendant was placing the chits in a cubicle behind him and I could not but help spotting that at this stage they had built up into quite a sizeable pile.

The lady presses her knee against mine ... and when I enquire blandly if she has a problem, she gives me the glad eye, like a cool Persian cat and lets it be known that she is working her way down to the Costa del Sol and is anxious to increase her bank-roll.

I decline and I'm given the quick brush-off as she moves to a spot further down the bar where she has spotted two Americans, obviously in high spirits.

Meanwhile, the attendant has just suggested to the guy drinking the pink elephants that he might want to settle his account.

"Look, you're not going back to the Gobi Desert tomorrow, young man ... let me have another and quick".

It turns out that he is an engineer supervising the drilling for water and he hits Copenhagen every few months ... and when he starts to drink, there's no one on this earth who's going to call 'time' on him.

"Have you ever seen the sun rise over the Gobi Desert?", he asks me.

I reply that I have seen the Niagara Falls and the Victoria Falls and I have been a number of times flying for hour after endless hour over the Sahara Desert and I have been to the Turkanah Desert, way up north in Kenya and I have crossed the Zaire River by helicopter and been to Burundi and Rwanda and places in Africa that are never mentioned in tourist literature but I had to admit I had missed out on the Gobi Desert.

He was going back in a private plane and he offered me a seat and he stressed that I would always regret it, if I missed the chance of seeing the sun rise over the Gobi Desert.

I looked at the ever-growing pile of dockets and another pink elephant being placed before him and I told him I still had to guard the fortunes of the group of Irish girls who had fallen on hard times in the Danish capital ... in a word that duty still called.

Somehow I regret now that I chickened out on that offer. There would have been an article in it, maybe even a chapter for a novel, that would far outstrip the pieces I had filed about the Irish scrubbing floors and cleaning toilets shoulder-to-shoulder with the Philippinos in a Copenhagen establishment.

Such is the life of a roving correspondent ...

*   *   *

Covering the Ireland v Britain "torture" case hearings before the Commission and later the Court of Human Rights resulted in many trips to Strasbourg over a period of two years – and even one to Stavanger in Norway (where evidence was taken from a "Mr X" – flown in by RAF jet for security reasons, – who gave his evidence from behind a screen). The irony of this case, won eventually by Ireland, was that it was of immense importance to the nationalist community in the North, especially those who had been victims of extreme torture methods (it was disturbing for us to see the coloured prints of mens' genitals after electrical appliances had been applied to them). But, of course, it was not the done thing at the time to mention the way the IRA had tortured those suspected of giving information to the Security forces or the way those in the building trade, who had done work for 'The Crown' on police barracks etc. had their bodies summarily dumped on the side of some road in the North after being executed without any proper chance to defend themselves.

The Strasbourg hearings were in camera and we had to garner what we could from our own "sources". It was a cat-and-mouse game between the rival Irish and British legal teams as to what could be fed without the accusation being levelled of "leaks" to the media and the British could be quite adept at letting out something if it suited their purpose – but in every instance, no matter which side it came from, you never even mentioned the word "source" or "spokesman". It was as if the information came out of thin air.

It called for constant burrowing and amazing initiative to piece together the happenings at each hearing. There were long days when you sat around waiting for a hearing to end and then you tried to get to "your man" or made a discreet call to a hotel room. A meaningful nod and a wink could convey a world of meaning.

The hearings overlapped at times with meetings of the Council of Europe and this gave us an opportunity to file stories that were ideal for early inside pages of the evening paper when they were not hot enough for the morning paper. And gave us an opportunity too of supplementing our expenses as we needed to be briefed over lunch or dinner.

I recall Val Dorgan and myself meeting this local councillor who was on a Committee examining a futuristic link between Athens and Cobh. It

66

was like manna from heaven for us on a day when there was nothing stirring in the news sense. We got the Council of Europe photographer to photograph our man standing by a map of the Continent of Europe and indicating how in time the new highway would meander its way through different countries and we even did a costing to give our stories greater strength.

The councillor in question never realised that he was simply fodder to the "guns" of Val and myself but he had his hour of glory when our features built around him and that large-scale map eventually appeared in the *Evening Herald* and *Cork Evening Echo*.

On another particularly dull day news-wise, the Irish corps travelled into Germany coming home by the border town of Keel, which had one of the finest sex shops that you could hope to find anywhere in the globe.

There was every contraption imaginable to stimulate sex and slow matters down, if needs be, and if you were so frustrated that you had to have someone with you in the bed in your lonely hotel room, they had thought up a life-size dolly, whose accoutrements were appealing beyond belief. All you had to do was blow the thing up as you would a balloon.

Anyway one wit in the company remarked to the staid German lady in the white coat who was giving a demonstration: "What happens if I have a row tonight in bed with Maria and prick her with a pin ... will I be arrested and charged with the murder of the Missus?".

The German lady wasn't at all amused ...

One member of our group was studying this book that had prints of the most extraordinary positions achieved by twosomes and threesomes together. He had never seen anything like it before in his life as this was his first *real* foreign assignment. As he turned a page, the German lady came over and standing at his elbow remarked: "We have even better books over in this section of the shop", as she sought to lead him to where she was pointing.

Like the good Catholic he was, he fled the shop ... and couldn't wait until he had seen the dust of Keel behind him.

Incidentally, this particular reporter was somewhat naive when it came to making out an expense account. I nearly suffered a heart attack when I saw what he had compiled. He was claiming lunch and dinner at the normal Dublin NUJ rate with a few suppers thrown in. His total bill for a week wouldn't have kept Val Dorgan or myself going for half a day. He could have wrecked everything for us in one moment of madness if I hadn't taken him in hand.

I told him that you NEVER eat lunch or dinner alone and enlightened him about the "briefing breakfast" which helped cover late-night drinking and other "diversions". And you never lowered your dignity or status by taking a bus. You always took taxis even though in reality you might avail of the bus service or metro.

His eyes nearly popped out of his head in amazement when I handed him the revised expense docket I suggested he should submit but then I learned later that he spoilt it all by looking for some days off for the overtime he had worked during the trip. He didn't realise that your expenses compensated for all the extra hours – even if it meant staying up through the night to cover an all-night sitting in Brussels, Luxembourg or elsewhere.

*　　　*　　　*

Stavanger was something else again. The price of everything was astronomical because it was here off the coast of Norway that they had struck oil and the town was a haven for those from the oil-rigs who were earning salaries at such a scale that the last thing they had to worry about was money.

The social fall-out was disastrous in many ways for the local community. Girls, even married women, who had known regular lives and were content with an evening out of two with the boyfriend or husband each week, were suddenly presented with a situation where those who were attracted by them or picked them up, could entertain them in a fashion beyond their wildest dreams. The sky was the limit.

Pregnancies, abortions, broken marriages – it all became par for the course. Some in their distress wished that oil had never been discovered off Stavanger, despite the fact that it brought wealth to those who were catering for the needs of the men on the rigs, whether it was in the restaurant business or the entertainment world or simply supplying the necessities of everyday life.

I met a stringer for one of the English dailies who had written a biography of Quisling – in defence (mark you) of the Norwegian collaborator with the Nazis.

He told me that it had wrecked his life as it resulted in his Norwegian-born wife divorcing him because of the pressure she had to withstand from friends.

All day long up to dinner hour he was in his room typing. Writing daily reports on the information I fed him from my contacts. He filed them faithfully and as far as I recollect he may have got just the one "situationer" par in during that entire week. Frankly, the charges against the security machine in the North of torturing didn't interest the paper in question. All that would stir them into action really would be a daring attack by the IRA that might 'take out' "Mr X".

I made the acquaintance of a young Norwegian journalist, Harald Offerdal, who impressed me so much with his sharpness that I told him I would have him signed up as our "stringer" in the Scandinavian Countries.

He did outstanding work for the Group papers, especially in the case of the major oil rig disaster when the legendary Red Adair was called in.

Harald decided at one point to visit Dublin to get an improved deal from the Independent Group. He travelled by land and ferry.

With that devil-may-care casualness that was an integral part of his make-up, he wore blue denim jeans and carried an overnight bag. His eyes were protruding from his head with sheer tiredness when he hit Rosslare. He was held on suspicion of being involved in drugs when, if he had been wearing a pin-striped suit and carrying the *Financial Times*, he would

68

have been nodded on his way.

When I got a call from Rosslare, I immediately rang the Department of Foreign Affairs and vouched for the identity and credentials of "Our Man" in Stavanger. The matter was resolved on the spot.

I told Harald that he didn't have the proverbial snowball's chance in hell of getting anywhere with the then Editor of the *Irish Independent*, Aidan Pender unless he got himself properly dressed out for the up-coming interview. He confessed to not having a lot of ready cash with him.

I knew he had ample money coming to him from the "Indo" for work already done, so I told him we would draw on this. I accompanied him to a shop – certainly by no means in the top range – where he got a new suit (made in North Korea), new shirt (made in Taiwan), new shoes (I am not certain where!) and a handkerchief for his top pocket – and all for around £19.50.

He came through the interview with Aidan Pender with flying colours and we had a ball of an evening together on the town.

* * *

Back to Brussels and our days covering the negotiations on Ireland's entry into the European Community ... sessions in Luxembourg also ... and to Strasbourg covering plenary sessions of the European Parliament. I must have made over 80 trips in all to Brussels and Luxembourg over a two-year period. Val Dorgan and myself travelled to Tromso, beyond the Arctic Circle in Norway on one occasion with Dr Hillery. I came to love every stone of Strasbourg ... its beautiful park opposite the Parliament building and La Petite France, down by the River Ile, where you dined at night in restaurants that had an atmosphere all their own. And you invariably ate lunch in the open when the weather permitted it.

"Bang The Bells" – as we knew it – became the haunt of the media corps, European parliamentarians and Parliament officials during plenary sessions and here too you heard rich Donegal accents mingling with Cork voices and voices from other parts of Ireland when MEPs brought out groups on "familiarisation" trips.

It was the late John Healy who christened it "Bang The Bells", I think. To gain entry you knocked on the door and the French proprietress looked out through the peephole to identify you and might even snatch a glance to see if the road was clear of the police and so we coined the phrase ... "Bang the Bells" in order to be admitted.

There were some great nights there as English Labour members of Parliament, maybe one or two from 'the valleys' joined in sing-songs with the Irish. And English Tories seemed to find no trouble either in mingling with the Celts. Those who are influenced by the hinge of history in Anglo-Irish relations, narrow-minded individuals of the ultra-Republican hue, talking in terms only of "700 years of colonial and imperialistic oppression" would have been appalled at how all barriers seemed to evaporate in "Bang The Bells".

"Bang The Bells" eventually died to the lasting regret of the Irish and

69

British journalists and MEPs something unique that can never be regained died with it.

My great friend Andy Sheppard of RTE who followed me later to the "Strasbourg beat" discovered an establishment called "The Coffin Bar". Yes, believe it or not, they had the replica of a coffin displayed in the bar. This was a haunt of ladies of the night who always seemed to be endeavouring to remain one step ahead of the law. They were generally left to their own devices by the journalists and MEPs and others who simply frequented it for a late-night aperitif.

Andy Sheppard's father was Jewish but got out of Germany before he could fall victim to the Holocaust. His mother spoke Russian fluently and that saved her from the fate of many other women when the Russian troops entered Berlin. Andy recalls the fall of the Third Reich in a way that is tragically amusing.

With food so scarce he knew what it was as a small child to pick flowers to eat among the ruins of once-proud buildings.

A man in their block of flats had reached his 100th birthday and, where in other times, a band might have come down that street as the cheque was presented, now a forlorn trumpeter in a uniform that had seen far better days stopped outside the building and played a few uneven notes. There was no cheque. Those notes still haunt Andy's memory ...

To this day Andy Sheppard speaks fluent German and we all felt immensely proud in the Irish Section of the Association of European Journalists when he was elected President of the organisation at overall European level and, did an outstanding job while he was at the helm.

*   *   *

One day Val Dorgan, myself and a few others went off for a long, lazy lunch down by the River Ile. We left Andy Sheppard behind forgetting to tell him that we expected him to file nothing for the lunch-hour news bulletin that might cause us to be disturbed with calls from our respective News Desks. Andy filed an innocuous story about European Community aid for housing projects in the North that would never have ruffled the *Evening Herald* had I sent it earlier but now when the News Desk heard it coming across on the airwaves it took on a new importance.

When I came back after two hours feeling very mellow after a bottle of the best Alsace wine, there was a message for me in the Salle de Presse to ring the *Herald* immediately. I was asked how I had missed out on the Northern Ireland story.

I immediately saw red. Val did also, as he too had a call from his Newsdesk. We decided there and then to banish Andy from the fold. His crime as such wasn't that he had scooped us as he would never, we knew, do that intentionally. It was simply that he had ruined the after-glow of mellowness we felt after lunch and that didn't wash with us at all.

We kept it up during a briefing by Michael O'Kennedy but, as the afternoon wore on and some real stories surfaced, we realised that our friendship with Andy was so deep that it couldn't last. Still we went off to the dinner thrown by MEP for Connacht, Sean Flanagan leaving Andy behind us, though we told someone to let him know in due course the restaurant where we were gathering.

No one can tell it better that Andy himself how in a downpour he arrived in the Rue des Juifs (the "Street of The Jews") feeling an outcast and wondering if he was ever again going to be welcomed back into the fold. Finally he found us and, of course, in the convivial atmosphere which only Sean Flanagan could create as our host for the evening, you would never have imagined that there had been a minor rift in relations around lunch-time that same day.

Incidentally, out of that same dinner we founded "The Januarians", a group of us discovering that our birthdays fell in January. Up to the time of his death Sean Flanagan would invite us to a reunion dinner in his home in Dublin where his wife, Pat and himself invariably made it an evening to remember. Mike Burns was there and Andy and Michael Roynane and Caroline Erskine. Then in 1995 we made Pat Flanagan the guest of honour for the evening when "The Januarians" met in Caroline Erskine's home and Barry and herself ensured that the tradition first created in Strasbourg was cemented in a fashion that did fitting justice to Sean Flanagan's memory among those of us who had such a high regard for his intellect.

*   *   *

The Metropole Hotel was the place we stayed in during our trips to Brussels. We had a special rate of £13.10s a night. If you thought that too much you could stay in the guesthouse which someone discovered that was run by a Cork woman married to a Turk working on the extension of the Metro. The nightly charge was a mere pittance for anyone on a liberal expense account. And with the bacon, egg, sausage, black pudding, tea and toast you might even be handed a copy of the *Cork Examiner* by the good lady herself as you feasted your eyes on those comely breasts of hers as she planted the tray on your lap with an enticing smile. The poor Turk was always dog-eared tired when he got back from working underground.

Our problem was that the negotiations had a way of extending on into the early hours of the morning and when you were finished filing for the final city edition of the daily paper, you had to be there on the spot to report on any important decisions for the first edition of the evening paper and then start on the follow-up stories for the daily paper of the following day. It became a never-ending cycle, fiercely energy-sapping and draining one's stamina to the limit but we were kept going by the adrenaline that stemmed from the fact that we knew these were epoch-making negotiations on which so much hinged for the country – and the people – back home.

Caruso's around the corner from the Berlaymont Building was our favourite Italian restaurant during breaks in negotiations or when we had met the deadlines for one edition and there was time to spare before squaring up to the next.

The Victoria and The Drum were the two pubs within walking distance of the EEC Commission Headquarters most popular with the Irish and British.

There was no government jet then. Dr Hillery, leading the negotiations at ministerial level, would sit in the front row of the Aer Lingus plane with his officials around him, frequently studying his brief during the flight. On one occasion a woman wearing a hat with a hat-pin on it walked up to him and asked if he could do anything about getting a job for her son, whom she suggested had the strength and physique to be an excellent bag-carrier!

We would generally get the opportunity to have a word with the Minister on the plane and file then on our arrival in Brussels as if the interview had taken place in the Belgian capital. On one occasion – at a late stage when the Coalition Government, headed by Dr Garret Fitzgerald was in power – Aengus Fanning, now Editor of the *Sunday Independent* but then Agricultural Correspondent of the *Irish Independent* travelled out on the same plane as Minister for Agriculture, Mark Clinton. He filed the interview Mark gave him during the flight, a perceptive insider piece about the significance of what was involved in the following day's talks. He left a "black" in the Metropole Hotel for Dick Cullinane of the *Cork Examiner*, who was flying in from Cork on a later plane. He stressed in a covering note that Dick should change the intro.

Dick went one better – he jazzed it up so well that he had Mark Clinton laying it on the line to the Brits and warning that Ireland would not stand idly by etc. etc.

Next morning Aengus Fanning received a call from Bill Shine inquiring how he had allowed himself to be scooped by the *Cork Examiner*. Aengus could only grin and bear it ...

Dick Cullinane became a legend in his own lifetime when he put through a call to home when his wife was expecting a baby. The girls on the switchboard in the Salle de Presse were accustomed to dialling numbers direct to all parts of the Continent and likewise to London and Dublin. They were completely stumped when Dick requested Ballinhassig 8. It took them two days to find it. Just at the point when the announcement was made that the German Minister was about to hold an important press conference and we all began rushing down the corridor to the room designated for the purpose, we heard over the public address system: "Ballinhassig 8 on the line".

Dick Cullinane could not help but be christened "Ballinhassig 8" after that.

Dick who was to die at a tragically young age, became legendary in another sense when he happened at an agricultural dinner in Cork one night to begin bidding to help a charitable cause on the assumption that someone would take over from him at the critical juncture. He woke up the next morning with a throbbing head to find himself looking at the replica of a prize bull and a bill for a few hundreds pounds staring him in the face. He had to make an urgent call to one of the Crosbies to get him off the hook.

In the era when the *Irish Independent* was sparing no expense to give its readers every detail of the "Brussels Story", especially in ensuring that it was ahead of all rivals on the farming deal, I found myself on one occasion doing a whole half-page on "What It Means For The Urban Dweller" while Aengus Fanning did another half-page outlining in detail "What It Means For The Farmer". Brought right down to the essentials, set out in simple and easy-to-read form but entailing a world of hard work as we got the officials to use their calculators overtime for us translating the gobblygook into the relevant facts and figures.

It was at the time when the paper was selling 170,000 copies a day under the editorship of Aidan Pender and cover prices had not zoomed very close to the ultimate reader-resistance point of £1 for a daily paper. And the slogan was "The Big One Gets Bigger", as the golden target was to hit the magic 200,000 mark. Aengus and I used to rib Dick Cullinane that he had no hope in trying to compete against the deadly duo from the "Big One" – but, of course, it was all in good fun as we would never dream of scooping him or the *Examiner*. When negotiating sessions were held in Luxembourg we would stay in the Holiday Inn, just across the road from the Kirchberg Building and the most popular restaurant was the Café du Commerce where you could select your dinner from the fish swimming in the tank. The guy on the piano in the Holiday Inn bar, a refugee from Eastern Europe, was outstanding and could play anything from classical to popular and was a brilliant accompanist to boot. We would ease the tedium of the all-night sessions by enjoying a sing-song around the piano – when we had a break between filing for different editions.

I still remember Aengus Fanning's rendering of *The Kerry Recruit* during one memorable sing-song and I remember too the top notes we hit as we sang *The Rose of Tralee*. Those were the days when journalism had a freedom for those born to the game that died when the accountants moved in.

Incidentally, Senator Daniel Moynihan, one of "The Four Horsemen" happened to arrive in the hotel one night when the bar was closed and let it be known that he would very much like a scotch on the rock. Aengus had built up an excellent relationship with the manager and a bottle of best Scotch was produced as if with the wave of a magician's wand for the good Senator, whose appreciation of Irish initiative in a mini-crisis was greatly enhanced.

You never could tell who would arrive at the Holiday Inn. Once the fly of my trousers went and, having no spare pair, I had to ask the girl at reception to get me a needle and thread in order that I could do a hurried job before catching a taxi for the airport. She was just about to oblige me when there was a sudden invasion by a group in for some contest. Richard Harris and Lulu were part of the group. All the passports were put up on the desk in front of my eyes in one big pile. My request for a needle and thread got buried in that awesome pile.

I introduced myself to Dickie Harris, who knew my brother, Gus very well (Gus was then writing the theatre column for the *Sunday Independent* and was later to produce a biography of the Limerick-born film star). Anyway, Harris in turn introduced me to Lulu and I can still see her face when I committed the appalling bloomer of inquiring "Lulu who?".

I wore my raincoat during the entire flight back to Ireland and each time any one of the hostesses politely suggested that I might take it off and place it in the rack overhead (it was the middle of July), I professed to be suffering from a troublesome summer flu. I didn't want to risk being accused of being a flasher on a flight to Dublin!

*   *   *

Joe Carroll *(Irish Press)*, Dennis Kennedy *(Irish Times)*, Val Dorgan *(Cork Examiner)*, John Feeney *(RTE)* and myself for the Independent Group formed the Irish corps during the negotiations on entry. John Feeney, who was later to become a Commission staffer after serving first in Dr. Hillery's Cabinet when the former Minister for Foreign Affairs became Commissioner for Social Affairs, died of a heart attack at a comparatively young age while out jogging one evening in Brussels.

Robin Fogarty, an outstanding career diplomat, who was to serve as Ireland's Ambassador in Tokyo, Bonn and Rome, was a key figure with Edwin Fitzgibbon in briefing the media on Ireland's stance in the negotiations. They would later both join the Cabinet of Dr Hillery, Robin as Chef. Unfortunately, it didn't work out and Robin returned to the Department of Foreign Affairs while Ed became the Chef de Cabinet.

Ed Fitzgibbon was masterly in his dealings with the press corps during the negotiations on Ireland's entry to the Community, building up excellent relations with the men from the "quality" English dailies like Reggie Dale of the *Financial Times* and Richard Norton-Taylor of *The Guardian*. What they reported was of immense importance to Ireland, as was the angle given by the man from *Le Monde*.

Ed was a man of diverse achievements and interests. He had made his mark with the Dublin Grand Opera Society and, in fact, cut a long-playing record (how often has he been compared in style to Count John McCormack) that became a collector's item among his friends and Eurocrats in Brussels. I prize my copy of *"Songs from The Green Isle of Eireann"*.

I remember when the fish deal was being completed, Ed would come down the stairs from the negotiating room and tell us that Dr Hillery had made a significant break-through and had won protection for Ireland's rights right around the coast. But then I would venture, with a feigned touch of cynicism in my voice: "What about the Dublin Bay Prawns Ed?"

Ed, fearing a headline that would indicate failure for his "Boss" rather than victory, would trudge back up the stairs and a few hours later we would see him descend waving a sheet of paper triumphantly. "We've got it, we've got it", he would exclaim and next day the banner headlines would scream that Hillery had scored another famous victory. Ed did not have to reflect: "I have signed my own death warrant on this night."

Then the negotiations on the sugar beet deal, ah yes, the sugar beet. That was perhaps the most highly-charged and emotional issue of all and in many ways the most memorable.

The beet growers marched at home in pressing their claim for the quota they were seeking. Bishops spoke out solemnly and one or two of them

74

were even prepared to march. Representatives of the beet growers' organisation arrived in Brussels and were in the lobbies at the height of the negotiations. There were dark hints of revolt if Dr Hillery failed to win what was being demanded. No one thought of asking could the beet growers grow all they were seeking. Later we thought of that.

It came down to an "A" quota and a "B" quota in the end. For the early editions, it looked as if Dr Hillery was heading for defeat. The French had dug in their heels. "We have beet growers too" was the now-historic comment by the French negotiator for The Six to Dr Hillery.

The hands of the clock had passed midnight when Dr Hillery rang the Taoiseach, Jack Lynch in Dublin to tell him the final offer. There were further hard negotiations – a final plea to the French negotiator and there it was; they had gone to the point beyond which they would not go further.

Even the threat of a blow from a bishop's mitre would not have improved the deal for Dr. Hillery at that moment ...

I remember going into the room to get a quick quote from him for the first edition of the Evening Herald. It had gone as late as that and dawn was already breaking over Brussels – over the Grand Place and the Metropole Hotel of happy memories. The ladies who sat knitting in the windows in the haunts where the unwary paid the proverbial moon for a bottle of champagne had long since ended the evening shifts. Dr. Hillery was looking utterly drained but happy that he had done his very best for his country – and the beet growers. "At least you rang back Dublin" I remarked, recalling the dilemma that faced Michael Collins and Arthur Griffith and the others when 50 years earlier they were threatened with "holy and terrible war"unless they signed on the dotted line.

"You're always good for a laugh", said Dr Hillery – and in shared moments like that the days and long nights of the negotiations forged a bond that nothing could break and created friendships that had a deep and lasting significance for us.

The bishops went back to Lenten pastorals and homilies on morals. And the beet growers grew their beet as before – and men were left to ponder why passions had run so high.

It had all started on a summer's day on the Kirchberg in Luxembourg in 1970 – 25 years ago as I type this chapter – the formal beginning of the negotiations on the entry of Ireland, Britain, Denmark and Norway (we hoped). The Irish flag flying proudly beside the others. We saw ourselves as a nation born anew – taking its place among the European family of nations at last. No longer would our farmers be at the mercy of Britain's cheap food policy, no longer would they have to march, as 30,000 of them marched through the streets of Dublin in October, 1966 when cattle prices collapsed.

We had high hopes for what the expansion of the European Community of Six would bring. They were heady days.

The lighter moments linger in the mind when many of the actual details of the negotiations have long since passed from the mind. Like the day I accosted Dr. Sicco Mansholt as he was going in for a key negotiating session and said to him: "I understand, Commissioner, that you will be walking out". His reply came quickly with an amused twinkle in his eye: "Observe that I am in the process of walking in".

Or when I asked the Norwegian Minister at a crowded news conference was there any truth in reports that his Government was about to fall. Naturally, he scoffed at the very suggestion. Next week he was gone.

It was to the same Minister that I suggested that "fish was now a dead duck".

*   *   *

Ed Fitzgibbon sang at my wedding in Rockwell College in August, 1970 – "In Happy Moments" from *Maritana* as Sheila and I came down the aisle. Charles Lynch, the noted concert pianist, who had been in "digs" with me at one stage in Yorkville, Cork, played the organ. With the cheque I gave him he spent a week in Hayes's Hotel in Thurles and each day he would drop into the Ursuline Convent to talk music and exchange adaptations with one of the nuns, whose knowledge was simply outstanding. Charles told me later that it was one of the happiest weeks of his life.

He was unique in that he lived totally for his calling in life. All else was secondary to him. He would recall for me that when he was young in Cork and already taking the first steps up the ladder, soldiers of the Free State Army, who were fighting the Civil War against the Anti-Treaty elements, actually came through the garden firing. "Who's causing all that noise?", was all Charles would ask his mother, as he practised a Chopin nocturne. Wars passed over his head. Sport was meaningless to him also. He dismissed the philistines out of hand, irrespective of what fortunes they had amassed.

One Sunday he got into a train in Cork on his way to Dublin for rehearsals for a programme he was recording for Radio Eireann. Little did he realise that it was Munster Hurling Final Day in Thurles. And, worse still, a clash between ancient rivals Tipperary and Cork.

A foxy-headed priest led a group of five headlong into the carriage. "Who do you think will win midfield?", Charles was asked by one of the quintet. He looked up at the foxy-headed priest and his companions from his copy of the *Sunday Times* and responded: "They say here that the concert in the Wigmore the other night was the best in London for years".

The foxy-headed priest sounded the retreat – and Charles was left alone. He begged me some times later to give him a calendar of big GAA fixtures so that he could avoid being swamped by the unwashed.

*   *   *

The Taoiseach, Jack Lynch and Dr Hillery, as Foreign Minister, signed the EEC Treaty of Accession on behalf of Ireland on a historic day in Brussels in January, 1972.

The mood at the reception afterwards was different from anything I can recall of any similar occasion in my journalistic career. We all knew we had seen a moment of history. Somehow there was a sense of pride in being Irish on this night – and our Irishness came through in the

76

spontaneity of the unrehearsed singing of *The Banks of My Own Lovely Lee* by Jack Lynch and I felt that I had to respond with a verse of *Slievenamon*. Colman Doyle the brilliant photographer of the *"Irish Press"* stepped out with Jack Lynch to dance a jig. It was that kind of evening.

Our friends Reginald Dale *(Financial Times)* and Richard Norton Taylor *(The Guardian)* shared the mood of that evening with us – and others of the corps too that we had come to know so well. Edwin Fitzgibbon was in fine voice.

It was impossible to go to bed. We ended up just sitting around in the lounge of the Metropole Hotel, talking over cups of coffee of days we knew in our hearts could never be recaptured. Some time in the early morning a group of pilgrims on their way to Mecca arrived and I heard them turning in prayer to Allah …

There is a memory of some Danes letting their hair down to such an extent that any unfortunate who had left his (or her) shoes outside a bedroom door to be polished discovered next morning that they had all been juggled and sent down the lift.

And it was reported that phones were pulled out of their sockets and left unusable when 'Room Service' (meaning whiskey and buckets of ice – no mixers) did not arrive on time. But then if you had been cooped up for example, in the Faroe Islands for a long, dull winter and suddenly found yourself celebrating a historic moment for your country in Brussels, you might go mad also ... in the Danish sense of the term!

It was that kind of night in the Belgian capital.

7

"Shut the Window or the Draught Will Kill The Pope"

The Pope was dying. The world's media waited, supplements prepared by some with End Of An Era-style headings that could be slipped into a paper at very short notice, others already pressing their Rome correspondents to try and ascertain who would emerge as the possible successor.

It was during the time that the late Julian de Kassel, later to become Foreign Editor of the *Irish Press,* was working as a stringer in the Italian capital for one of the Fleet Street dailies.

Julian had arranged with a comely, dark-haired Italian girl working inside the Vatican that at the moment the Pontiff expired she would shut the window overlooking the café seat where he sat each day drinking his favourite chilled white wine.

The missing link in this clever scheme was that Julian forgot to tell the nuns tending the Pope's needs with unselfish devotion of his little arrangement with Maria.

One of the nuns, passing down the corridor, noticed this window wide open and the breeze flapping the curtain. "I must shut that window or the draught will kill the Pope", she said to herself.

And duly banged it shut.

Julian immediately went into action and filed a story in time to catch the first edition that the Pontiff passed on around 6 o'clock Italian time.

Meanwhile, to add colour and body to the story he was planning for the next edition, he rang an "unimpeachable source" – as we say in the business – in the higher echelons of the Vatican to check on who might be in line from the College of Cardinals to succeed to the Seat of Peter.

"The Pope isn't dead ... he's sleeping quietly now, though he hasn't long to go", Julian was told.

Aghast, he rushed to the phone and literally screamed down the line to the News Desk to kill his first lead, replacing it with one that the Pope had lapsed into a coma, leading to the assumption that the end had come – but he had rallied remarkably and was now given a few more days to live.

Julian's arrangement with Maria had failed because of circumstances outside his control and like the other hacks and hackettes he decided next time to wait on the official announcement of the Pope expiring instead of trying to get a world scoop.

But the newshound in Julian could never prevent him endeavouring to beat the other resident correspondents and stringers to the draw.

Once, when Mario Lanza had gone into hospital, the official word was that he was suffering from exhaustion from too-strenuous a work-load. Julian learned from a nurse in the hospital that it was an alcohol-related problem and the phrase "drying out" was mentioned.

He duly produced a world exclusive built around this "inside" beat.

Some time later he was out walking his dog on a beautiful balmy Rome evening when an Alfa Romeo came round the bend heading straight for him. Spotting Mario de Lanza with murder emanating from his eyes, Julian dived over a wall into the nearest garden, ruining his Tom Wolfe-style white outfit in the process. As he picked himself up, bruised and shaken, he heard the shout: "I'll kill you, de Kassel".

It didn't end there.

Mario Lanza issued proceedings seeking the equivalent of one million pounds sterling in damages for defamation of character.

Julian was told that the paper would defend the action – if he could get his contact to sign a sworn affidavit backing up what she had already told him.

When Julian invited her for a drink and told her what he wanted from her, she looked blankly at him and remarked: "But I NEVER talked to you about Mario Lanza".

"I was lucky, very lucky", said Julian recalling that episode for me. "You see, Mario Lanza died of a massive heart attack just when I thought I was facing one hell of a time in the witness box and a verdict that would have finished my career".

*   *   *

Once he went to interview this famous film star whose bust was unquestionably part of her immense box-office appeal.

She told him to come up to her suite, as she had to keep an early appointment for dinner and time was limited.

He had hardly entered her suite when she asked him to help her to get her two outsize boobs into the 'cups' of her bra, designed to give the right lift behind a see-through dress.

"There she was lying languidly on the king-size bed", recalled Julian, "my right knee on her midriff and I pressing down on that right boob, pressing as hard as I could and it looking as ripe as an outsize melon, as I battled to get it into the cup. The sweat breaking out all over me and she exclaiming in those soft sexy tones that caused the hair to sit up straight on the back of my neck – 'you gotta press harder, man'.

"She didn't even say 'thanks' when I had finished the job but remarked 'Now let's get this thing over quick'.

"Impossible for me to concentrate on the interview after working on those boobs. I mean to say, you don't always as a working journalist find

79

yourself on a king-size bed astride someone who would have challenged Marlyn Monroe herself for curvature when you thought you were simply going along to a hotel suite for a politely-conducted interview".

On another occasion he was doing a feature on the set of a film when he learned how a famous male star amused himself before breakfast each morning.

This particular heartthrob invariably awoke with a massive erection. He would ring Room Service and ask for a boy to bring up a half-dozen oranges.

When the boy had duly entered the suite, Heartthrob would call to him: "Pitch me an orange".

And then with his cock he would hit a homer right out the open window that would have done justice to Babe Ruth or Mickey Mantle playing for the Yankees in the World Series.

"Now pitch me another one ..."

This time the boy might have to duck as a misdirected orange whizzed past his ear and smashed against the wall behind him.

All the oranges gone – either out the window or made into pulp – the boy would politely enquire, as the massive erection subsided: "Anything else I can do for your, Sir".

"That will be all" – and Heartthrob would duly slip a 1,000 lire note into his hand.

*   *   *

Julian was incorrigible, one of the funniest characters it has ever been my pleasure to know and Jeeves-like in some of the quaint touches he brought to the job.

It was Julian's custom when interviewing an important political personage or member of the Diplomatic Corps to wear a morning suit and I always thought that the striped trousers became a badge of his elitism on such occasions.

This particular morning he had an arrangement to interview the Taoiseach, Dr Garret FitzGerald. A Private Secretary rushes in and reminds the Taoiseach that a new Ambassador is presenting his credentials up "in the Park" (that is Aras an Uachtarain, the Presidential residence). As he was from a country with which Ireland was anxious to build new bridges, Garret had decided he should be there – but overlooked the fact that he had also agreed to meet Julian around the same time and had forgotten too about the required morning dress.

Julian, the perfect diplomat, intimated that the interview could wait in the cause of the pursuit of Irish foreign policy – and he was willing to lend his suit to the Head of Government if needs be.

In fact, he was just about to let down his trousers when another distracted Secretary rushed in with Garret's suit and all was well.

Then there was the time when Michael O'Kennedy was Minister for Foreign Affairs and Ireland had the Presidency of the European Community.

The news had broken earlier that a rugby team from South Africa was

80

about to visit Ireland – and Apartheid still very much in operation, those blinkered elements who salved their consciences by arguing that sport and politics should never mix must have known that they would be walking into a hurricane of opposition if they thought the South Africans would be welcome. Michael O'Kennedy, a son of the Tipperary heartlands, could read the mood. He revealed to us at a briefing to which we were summoned at short notice to Iveagh House that if the South Africans did arrive they would not be allowed into the country – whether they came by air or boat. Julian de Kassel and myself knew we had the Page One lead story for our respective papers next day.

As we came down the stairs in Iveagh House, Michael O'Kennedy suddenly appeared on the landing up above and shouted down to us that he had forgotten to mention that he was heading off for an ASEAN conference – in Singapore I think – the next day. He began to elaborate on some of the principal items on the agenda, which we knew hadn't a snowball's chance in hell of making it to the papers once the Newsdesk learned what kind of a reception was being planned for the South Africans.

Julian turned off his hearing aid.

We headed across Stephen's Green to the Shelbourne Hotel and phoned our stories and we didn't even need to exchange notes (a young reporter from RTE thought we were first going to type out our reports and asked us if we would oblige him with a "black").

In instances like this you learned to simply jot down your intro and ad lib after that, especially if it was coming close to a deadline. The copy girls in Independent House were brilliant – and patience personified – when they knew you were on the ad lib job.

We repaired to the Horseshoe Bar after the News Editors had agreed that what we had phoned was hot – very hot – and left us in no doubt whatsoever that our by-lines would be over the Page One lead next morning. We knew we could drink until closing time and even go for a late meal and a good bottle of wine around the corner in the Unicorn if we wished on what we would be claiming in expenses.

*　　　　　*　　　　　*

Fianna Fáil had teamed up with the Gaullists in the European Parliament to form the European Progressive Democrats Group. And Jacques Chirac, at a time when his dream of becoming President of France was still a long way over the horizon before its ultimate realisation, was invited to Cork in November, 1978 to address a big Convention that would effectively launch Fianna Fáil's campaign for the first directly-elected European Parliament elections the following year.

Julian de Kassel and myself travelled down together by train. First class. Julian was in tremendous high spirits because this story was so important to the *Irish Press* that he knew he need not scrimp and spare on anything as the expenses would be "liberal".

At dinner he ordered pâté de foie gras truffé to open, assuming it to be the real Strasbourg variety. When it arrived, it was obvious that it was a world removed from what Julian had intended. He beckoned the young waiter who had a rich Cork accent and, as he went back in through the swinging doors to the kitchen, he could be heard exclaiming: "There's a geezer out there who isn't happy with the fross grass".

Out comes the Head Chef and Julian explains to him in polite but very firm tones that there is only one kind of pâté de foie gras he would partake of and he wasn't going to be fobbed off with second best – not even by the Lee. The Head Chef, who happened to have had experience in France and realised that he was in the company of someone who really knew his goose liver – rendered a heartfelt apology and promised that he would personally get down to the task of ensuring that Julian would next evening be served with what he had demanded.

It was the famous occasion when Chirac decided that his English was sufficiently good that he did not have to resort to an interpreter to get his point of view across exactly to the representatives of the four Irish daily newspapers and RTE at the news conference he gave on his arrival in the Southern capital. He intended saying "If I had had my way there would be no European elections". This was said, of course, against the background of the stance he held and had expounded that national parliament, including the one in Paris, must not be weakened as greater sovereignty was given to the Strasbourg assembly (the cynics noted later that he had been on an intensive tour of France and might not have been quite aware that he had crossed over to Ireland and needed to amend his publicly-expressed views accordingly).

Anyway, Chirac missed out on the second "had" and all hell broke loose in consequence. There was consternation in the ranks of Fianna Fáil when the report appeared next morning in all the newspapers.

Here was their chief ally in Europe apparently insisting that the people should have no say in electing the Parliament and that the political parties should go on appointing their MEPs.

A bevy of Fianna Fáil Ministers and other "heavies" had assembled in Cork and other influential names from France, apart from Chirac. The Taoiseach, Jack Lynch was to address the Convention on the Saturday.

Jacques Chirac denied that he had used the words attributed to him and made it clear that the media had got it wrong. In fairness to the Gaullist leader, he probably knew in his mind what he had intended saying but his English didn't carry to two "hads" in voicing the past tense.

We took great umbrage at the fact that our integrity had been impugned. With Julian de Kassel, Val Dorgan and the other hacks, I framed a letter of protest to 'Jacques' and handed it to his aide-cum-Press spokesman. He looked into my eyes and saw fire in them and knew immediately that the letter spelt trouble,.

With cool Gallic aplomb, he handed it to the other Jack – Jack Lynch – just before lunch was about to commence.

That only added to the consternation.

Now instead of a grand Franco-Irish launch to the first direct elections of the European Parliament, the Fianna Fáil spin doctors knew that they were right into a damage limitation exercise and the priority was to get Chirac out of Cork before he could drop any more howlers.

Passing down a corridor, I heard one of the top Fianna Fáil lieutenants screaming into a telephone: "He has got to go and go right away, no matter what excuse we make …".

He obviously got the okay from Dublin to do the "needful" and soon the wheels were in motion to implement "Operation Damage Limitation" by the Lee.

Brian Lenihan meanwhile tried to calm the troubled waters. He made the kind of speech that only Brian was capable of making, talking about the marriage of two great Parties – Fianna Fáil and the Gaullists – on the European stage. He called up the French Revolution and the storming of the Bastille and he finished by saying there was "no problem" and they all applauded – but even Brian couldn't repair the damage that had been done.

They duly whisked Mr Jacques Chirac out of Cork. The bland excuse was given that "urgent business" in Paris necessitated his immediate departure but we weren't fooled and neither were all those attending the conference.

The wine at dinner that night was laid on by Fianna Fáil – one of the finest French wines available. Julian, having finished off the pâté de foie gras – perfection personified this time – was in his element as he proposed the toast "Jacques Chirac" and said that if he had his way, he would invite him over for every election and see to it that he NEVER addressed any gathering in French. Then we would be assured of stories that made headlines – and chateau wines of rare vintage.

*   *   *

At the time Chirac was Mayor of Paris, Clare-born Tom Earlie was Secretary-General of the European Progressive Democrat Grouping. Earlie was a product of the European Commission's student training scheme with attributes that commended him not alone to the Gaullists but to Chirac himself and the two were on very close and very friendly terms. Tom's fluency in French and his knowledge of the workings of the European Parliament, made him a superb technocrat and the roguish element in his character saw him revel in diplomatic intrigue (he was the bane, incidentally, of those dog-day bureaucratic types who seemed to delight in wading through mountains of paper-work and his rapier-like thrusts, couched in French that would have done justice to any Parisian, hit them right in the heart. Sometimes they found it hard to forgive him for opening to the cold light of day their total lack of any ingenuity or initiative).

Today he works with the European Commission in Vietnam. I am sure that when in the summer of 1995 Jacques Chirac triumphed in the second round of voting in the French Presidential election at the expense of the Socialist candidate, Lionel Jospin, Earlie was recalling with quiet amusement the 1978 Convention in Cork and also the press launch he organised for Paris later to reveal to the world the thoughts of Euro MEP, Noel Davern on an agricultural policy theme.

Only Tom Earlie, I know, would have the flair and panache to think of the French capital as the ideal venue for such an occasion but there was method in his madness.

Jacques Chirac was Mayor of Paris and Tom would see to it that the small corps of journalists that he had invited from Ireland would have stage-side tables at the Lido, a feat equal to block-booking the best seats at the Cup Final. We were going to be the guests of the Mayor of Paris on our night-out at the Lido.

Val Dorgan had a much better view of things this time than he had in Charlie's in Luxembourg. I didn't have to give him a running commentary as the line of dancing girls emerged.

We went on from Paris to Luxembourg in a high-powered car driven by a chauffeur who had a date with his girl-friend for 8 o'clock sharp and it saw him knock nearly an hour off the trip – and left me a total wreck in the front passenger seat.

In the Holiday Inn in Luxembourg we met a former American pilot who agreed to give us a lift to Brussels where we could catch the direct Aer Lingus plane to Dublin. During the journey he told us about the time he was serving in the Pacific at the height of the Second World War.

The fridge wasn't working. It was a priority to have cool beer. The only way to achieve that was to set up a red alert – in a word, sound an imaginary alarm that a Japanese plane was coming in to attack. "Up I would go with a crate of beer and, as I came down, I would exclaim 'here we go baby … cool it man, cool it' ". And the downward plunge of the plane from on high meant that there was cool beer all round to keep the boys happy … but the cost to the Pentagon ran into a frightening sum in dollars".

*   *   *

Julian de Kassel had an amazing knack of poring through the most involved EEC documents and coming up with clever and timely stories. Once he read a document that indicated that an effort was going to be made to break the airline cartels. He learned that the Dutch might set the ball rolling by giving a number of cheap flights out of Amsterdam. Julian decided to adapt this to the Irish situation and hinted that the day was at hand when we might see a number of nominal flights from Dublin to New York – at £1 a head!

It took the Aer Lingus Press Office two full days to try and convince people from Connemara and other parts of the Western seaboard – indeed, in all parts of the country – that they weren't going to be able to fly to the States to see relations there for a mere pittance.

Julian dismissed it as a little "temporary aberration".

There was the time when he got involved in a butcher's shop in Killiney which specialised in venison.

He decided, wearing his butcher's hat, that venison could be cheaper to the customers in his shop if certain action was taken by then Minister for Agriculture, Mark Clinton who, to put it mildly, had far more weighty problems on his mind than to be tossing and turning at night pondering the machinations of movements in the venison market. Julian wrote a second editorial (that is one below the main editorial for the day) that was critical of the Government's lack of action and, of course, this meant that he was taking a critical stance against Mark Clinton, who could never be accused of failing to act in any area of "vital interest" to Irish farmers.

Thurles-born Gerry Connaughton, the able Press Spokesman of the Department of Agriculture, who had a great grá for Julian and admired him very much, couldn't resist the opportunity of preparing a press release that was actually a riposte to Julian's editorial (Gerry had got to know on the grapevine about Julian's involvement in the butcher's shop). It wasn't sent out for general release but Gerry had it forwarded exclusively to Julian on Department-headed paper and Julian naturally got the message and the whole issue of non-Government intervention on the vexed problem of venison died a quick death. "How's the venison going?", Gerry would quip as he met Julian for a drink in one of the haunts that we were wont to frequent in those days.

*   *   *

There was the time too when T.J. Maher, former President of the Irish Farmers' Association and later an Independent Euro MEP for Munster decided to throw his hat in the ring and try and win a Dáil seat for Tipperary South in the 1981 General Election.

He was to make the announcement at a press conference in a hotel that was right in the shadow of the Rock of Cashel. It was anticipated that, because of the close and long-standing friendship I had with him, I would make it to Cashel to cover the news conference for the *Irish Independent*.

Coincidentally, at the same time Tom Earlie had arranged for a group of journalists to go to Morocco at the invitation of the Moroccan Government to report on the plebiscite that was being conducted on the Western Sahara issue. Paddy Lalor, former Minister for Industry and Commerce and at that point Leader of the Fianna Fáil Group in the European Parliament, had prepared a special report for the Parliament that promised to be the catalyst for the solution to the problem that King Hassan's regime was experiencing with the Polisario guerrillas, backed by Algeria, who were fighting to establish an independent Sahara homeland.

The Sahara War had been going on for years. Hassan's Government claimed the former colony of Spanish Sahara as part of the national territory. It was a claim, incidentally, that dated back centuries, before the establishment of Spanish rule. This in turn was hotly disputed by the Polisario, who proclaimed the Sahara Democratic Arab Republic (SDAR), with a government in exile in Algeria, and deeply angered the Moroccans by winning recognition from no less that 80 countries.

The continuing war was imposing enormous strains on the vulnerable economy of Morocco. A defensive wall, costing millions and millions of pounds, was built right around the disputed territory, stretching from the Algerian border for a distance of 1,500 miles. Frightening also was the cost of maintaining an army of 200,000 men, four times the normal requirement.

My great friends Val Dorgan, Andy Sheppard and Julian de Kassel were in the group scheduled to travel to Morocco. It seemed to me to be a trip that promised much in the way of "crack" and, frankly, was one that seemed too good to miss.

I duly rang Vinnie Doyle, Editor of the *Irish Independent* and indicated to him that I wanted his approval to cover the plebiscite on the Western Sahara.

"A plebiscite in the desert … am I hearing you right? What about the Election here in Ireland and what about your friend, T.J. running for the Dáil? I would prefer you here in Cashel rather than under a desert sky but go if you think fit to go, I'd be the last to stop you".

"An Editor's request to stay put?", came my response.

"Yes, if you would like to describe it that way".

Vinnie had always been very co-operative with time off for writing books in the valley periods and I knew I would be going back to him again. I took the hint and realised that my services were wanted in South Tipperary. I said goodbye there and then to nights of colour and excitement in bustling Casablanca and beating the Humphrey Bogart trail with Val, Andy and Julian to the toast, "Here's Looking At You Kid".

I sat down and framed a letter to King Hassan, opening it with the immortal words: "Dear King".

I conveyed my profuse apologies at not being able to make the trip and hinted as discreetly as I could that, because of a General Election in my own country, it was really a "second team" that was going and that Dennis Kennedy, Diplomatic Correspondent of the *Irish Times* and myself would be ready to go when next we got the call.

Julian de Kassel wisely opened it and concluded that the King would be deeply affronted at any suggestion of a second team heading for Rabat and, anyway, in Hassan's eyes the issue of who should rule the Sahrawis – natives of Western Sahara – and the nomads in that desert area far outstripped the question of whether one T.J. Maher made it to the Dáil or who would form the next government in the Republic of Ireland.

That trip to Morocco is remembered to this day by Val Dorgan with a vividness and clarity that put in the shade his memories of many other foreign trips for the *Cork Examiner*.

"Andy, Julian and myself hopping from city to city in a Hercules bomber with no seats only canvass webbing to sit on", recalled Val. "Young Moroccan lawyers acting as interpreters. Soldiers too being transported on the plane. There always seemed to be a mad scramble before it took off. Waiting for Julian, we always seemed to be the last on board.

"It struck us that quite a number of the Moroccan soldiers seemed to be holding hands together. I asked one of the lady interpreters what it signified. She told me that in a foxhole at night when there was danger from the guerrillas lovers looked after each other better.

"This same girl was at the centre of the strangest ceremony I ever witnessed. It was somewhere out in the desert and we were being entertained in a massive tent. We all sat bow-legged on the ground. Then they brought in a cooked goat on a silver salver.

"One of the young lieutenants, strikingly good-looking like the girl herself, took out a knife and cut off the vitals of the goat in one swift stroke. He handed them to the girl who nibbled on them as she would sweetmeats.

"We were so open-mouthed at it all that we hadn't the time – or the heart – to ask about its significance. We could only conclude that it had something to do with the transmission of vitality. Again, the girl never batted an eye-lid."

Julian de Kassel, reaching retirement age at that point, was by now at a stage of near-collapse. Val and Andy protested to the Moroccans that something would have to be done about ensuring that he got a seat rather than sitting on the floor of the plane. At last they put him up front and saw to it also that he was properly accommodated – as were Val and Andy – when they got to their hotel in Casablanca.

On his return home Val Dorgan filed a piece for the *Evening Echo* on the lines of a country and a society moving towards greater democracy – a feature painting a dawn of new hope.

It was carried in the inside page of an early edition of the paper when Val got word that coming through on the agency wires were reports of food riots in Casablanca.

"Pull it out, pull it out quick", he shouted down the house-phone line to one of the subs "on the stone" – and he didn't care at that moment if the ensuing blank half-page was filled with Curly Wee or the exploits of Donald Duck!

*   *   *

Julian de Kassel duly called it a day and lived in quiet retirement in Killiney with his wife Odette. His heart wasn't too good. The doctor told him to be careful of the "hard stuff". But, of course, Julian could take wine. He didn't stipulate exactly how much, whether it was a glass or two a day. I shared the odd bottle of Chablis with Julian when we sat through long, wonderful evenings remembering times past and laughing again at moments that could never fade.

When he passed on at a ripe age, we could not sink into an abyss of regret, when he was cremated at Glasnevin. He had been a stalwart of the Irish Section of the Association of European Journalists. Tom Earlie had flown in from Luxembourg and placed his own wreath.

We gathered afterwards – Val, Andy, Tom, Mike, myself and others – in the quiet lounge of a hostelry that luckily we had to ourselves through the long afternoon.

I laughed as I thought of Julian travelling back on the CIE express bus from an EEC seminar in Letterkenny in County Donegal, looking as immaculate as ever. He had to board it before he had put over everything to the *Irish Press*. The bus driver was obliging when first he told him that he was "Julian de Kassel, Foreign Editor of the *Irish Press*" and needed to ring the office. He was extremely obliging a second time in providing

87

Julian with the time he required to add to his report.

But the third time he said he didn't care if Julian was Foreign Editor of the *New York Times* or the *Washington Post* or *Pravda* – his bus had to get to Dublin and that was that.

Yes, Julian de Kassel, Foreign Editor of the *Irish Press* ... your spirit will never die.

"Class Distinction in the Graveyard in Templemore"

One particular evening, as a young cub reporter on The Tipperary Star, I was covering a meeting of Templemore Urban District Council.

The discussion turned to the issue of class distinction in the local graveyard. It was alleged that if you were from the working-class areas of the town you got buried in the shade; if you were wealthy you got buried in the sunlight.

The debate grew very heated. Someone had the temerity to blow a smoke ring from the cigarette held in a silver holder right into the face of the Council member who prided himself always on his defence of the interests of the people of his avenue.

"When we go to the Man up above, the sun will be shining the same on all", he shouted as one thing led to another and the meeting erupted. An inkwell hit the light and I found myself under the table with the Council clerk. The 'Revolution' had come to Templemore U.D.C.!

I wasn't yet born when what came to be known as the 'Templemore miracles' made headlines in the national media – long before the era of the moving statues.

Jimmy Walsh was his name and he was born in 1904 in the townland of Inch. He professed to have seen a vision of a bleeding statue – in a word when he looked at the statue of the Blessed Virgin during Mass, he saw her bleed for the sins of the world. And miracles, it was claimed, followed in his wake.

They poured into Templemore from all parts of the country – the sick, the indigent, the crippled, those dying of terminal diseases and the plain curious. The *Irish Independent* file for August, 1920 gives a vivid picture of the fever gripping the area.

It was that same month that he announced that the Blessed Virgin had appeared to him in a gravel pit in Curraheen. His word was accepted as he was an extremely devout youngster – the son of a devout mother while his father was said to have the gift of curing people.

The news spread like wildfire and people began to flock to the pit which became known as "The Grotto", where the Rosary and litany to the Blessed Virgin was recited daily. When questioned, Jimmy said he had seen tears of blood running down the Virgin's face. His fame spread and it was even reported that priests were leading groups of pilgrims from different corners of Ireland and joining in the prayers at "The Grotto".

Legend has it that every morning the money was being brought in bucket-fulls to the bank. A roaring trade was done in replicas of the bleeding statue.

A man of my acquaintance, a member of Thurles Golf Club, who served as an altar boy at some of the Masses, gave me a demonstration of how the blood would appear on the statue of the Virgin. Jimmy Walsh who was also serving at Mass was treated afterwards to breakfast in the parlour of the convent in the company of the celebrant and the Reverend Mother.

At the moment of the blessing of the Eucharist, when the congregation had their collective heads bowed, the bould Jimmy would split his lip and with perfect timing, work the miracle.

And, as heads were raised after the sounding of the bell, he would raise his hands to heaven and exclaim – "Praise be the Lord" – and a great audible gasp would arise from the congregation as they beheld the drops of blood around the Virgin's heart.

The sound of coins dropping into the buckets would echo through the church.

Soon the clergy, who had been slow to react initially, began to express caution and then outright doubt and by the end of October the *Irish Independent*, which always had the ear of Mother Church, had killed the story stone dead.

Jimmy Walsh entered the Cistercian monastery in Roscrea but did not remain long. Later he emigrated to Australia where he had a relative. The story goes that he entered another monastery there – but again only remained a short time. He died in Australia.

Breandan O hEithir, who wrote the highly-acclaimed autobiography, *Over The Bar* and the best-seller in Irish, *Lig Sin I gCathu* (later translated as Lead us into Temptation), travelled to Templemore to do a documentary on "the miracles" for RTE television but abandoned the project after admitting to friends that he had "never had so many threats in his life". Some time later Ennis writer, Meda Ryan started researching a book on the subject but met a stonewall in the area and "not so pleasant experiences", as she put it with classic understatement. Finally she decided "it wasn't worth it", concluding that the people who had been fooled by Jimmy Walsh were still very sensitive about it and preferred that it lie buried as far as they were concerned.

*   *   *

I supposed it was inevitable that I should go into journalism as there was writing in the family. My uncle, Walter worked on the *Catholic Standard* and some of his pieces were ahead of their time in finding the target on subjects that stirred him. My father wrote a film script that I recall was accepted but at that time there was no money for making films in Ireland.

Born in Loughrea, where the family had a hotel that has since gone out of existence, he joined the Garda Síochána at a time when it was deemed an honour to wear the uniform of the Security Forces, (whether Garda or Army) in the foundling State. But in reality my father was never happy as a Garda, hated the baton charges during the Blueshirt period in the Thirties when an order from the officer in command meant the clearing of a street and you had to use your baton on everyone in your path and that could even mean on innocent victims. Eventually he took early retirement, having made his mark as a regular contributor to *The Garda Review*.

We were all proud as a family of the Scott medal in our home with Garda Henry L. Smith inscribed on it. My father had won it for his courage in rescuing an entire family from drowning when their cottage at the foot of a hill was flooded in Ballina, across the bridge from Killaloe where he was stationed. It wasn't surprising that as a powerful swimmer himself he should insist that we all learned to swim from an early age.

He had married Ellen O'Mahony from Ballingarry, County Limerick and her brother, who got the name "Smiling Bill" when he ran a tavern in Chicago, was a great entertainer with the accordion at family gatherings. I have never heard anyone give a better rendering of *If You're Irish*.

The love of music and song – like that of writing – ran in the family and my father, out of a Garda salary, managed to get us a private piano teacher but I'm afraid I was so involved in sport that I didn't keep it up – to my eternal regret.

My father would travel with my mother on an old motor-bike to Galway Races and that is why this particular Festival meeting has always held a special appeal for me.

There were seven of us in the family – four boys and three girls and there is one outstanding shot in the family album of the seven of us in line behind our parents. Summer holidays were special. My father would hire a boat and bring us to Ballyvalley where he had permission to use a quiet cove in a private estate. We fished for pike from the boat itself along the reeds as we headed to the cove and back. We fished for perch from the shore of Lough Derg. The secret was to drop the pieces of a broken china cup or potato peels at a convenient point out in the lake waist-deep. You went out with your rod and dropped the hook with the appetising worm on it. The shoal of perch was invariably attracted by the shining pieces of broken delph or the potato peels. When a perch struck right at your feet, you learned to time the moment when you pulled, not too soon, not too late. And then you ran back to the shore with your catch, hauling him in the whole way and praying that you wouldn't lose him.

Mother fried them in bread crumbs for the evening meal. And no holiday in exotic places in the sun subsequently ever equalled the sheer joy and freedom of those summer days spent in Ballyvalley. At night we would go out fishing for bream, using dough this time instead of worms. The days were long, very long action-packed days.

Dapping for salmon with the Mayfly in May was one of the most wonderful and skillful forms of fishing. I always felt it was for the real experts. Once I saw a man fishing from the canal bank on a beautiful sunny day. He could cast the fly exactly on the spot where the salmon rose. Then eventually when it took the bait, he played with it for thirty minutes or more, letting out the right amount of line, then winding in, letting out more line until the exhausted fish finally conceded defeat. Landing it was another exercise in pure skill.

Lough Derg narrows into the River Shannon at Killaloe and a bridge links it with Ballina, which is actually in County Tipperary. We came to know every corner of Lough Derg – that is the stretch up from Killaloe where the pleasure boats, so popular with tourists, especially Continentals, begin their trips.

*   *   *

Killaloe lies in a valley steeped in legend and history, the megalithic tombs being a link with pre-historic man who first settled in the area 4,000 years ago. And then, as Sean Kierse has chronicled so well in his guide-book, Historic Killaloe, it was the home of scholars and saints, including Lua and Flannan. Killaloe is actually called after Lua or Molua. These two saints, in fact, belonged to the Golden Age of the early flowering of Christianity in Ireland and I recall my parents telling me about the shrine of St. Flannan and how it was venerated for centuries. Today whenever I return I invariably make a nostalgic visit to the oratory of St. Flannan and the Cathedral where the plaques on the walls recall the names of the powerful families who served the Empire in various wars.

But growing up in that so-picturesque of villages with its steep hill winding down from the church on The Green and the school run by the dedicated Edmonds brothers, where I started my secondary schooling, we had instilled into us the significance of how the course of Irish history was changed when King Brian Boru set off from here to the Battle of Clontarf in 1014, breaking the Viking supremacy. We knew the exact spot on Crag Hill overlooking Beal Boru, or Brian Boru's Fort on the Shannon's edge on the road to Scariff, where the Banshee sat and cried in warning the night before the battle but she went unheeded and Brian Boru died in his moment of greatest triumph.

You cannot, of course, visit Killaloe without seeing Brian Boru's fort and the spot beside it where Patrick Sarsfield, on his famous night-ride to intercept King William's siege train at Ballyneety, crossed the Shannon, led by the rapparee Galloping Hogan. And you must learn how Kincora, the royal palace of Brian Boru, stood on the summit of a hill on the very site now occupied by the Catholic church, though no trace of it remains today. Reading *Historic Killaloe* you will conjure up a picture of the twelve-year reign as High King of Brian Boru and the celebrations that followed his victory over Malachy and other great victories. It was an insult delivered by Murrough to Maolmordha, the King of Leinster during a game of chess that led inexorably to the Battle of Clontarf, for Maolmordha vowed vengeance and teamed up with the Vikings. Brian

Boru summoned all the chiefs of Thomond to Killaloe and from here went forth the summons to the fighting men of Munster and Connacht to rally to his flag.

There was no television in our childhood days and in many ways we were all the better for it. I have a memory of my father trying to adjust the outsize radio set endeavouring to catch the commentary by Michael O'Hehir on an All-Ireland senior football championship tie in which his native Galway were involved. I have a memory too of Lord Haw-Haw and the way he opened his broadcasts each evening "Germany calling, Germany calling". And the excitement of watching the men of the LDF out marching as they went on exercise, ready to die for flag and country, though the means at their disposal, if it came to stopping German panzers or even paratroopers, were pathetic.

I reckon many people were at heart secret sympathisers with Hitler's effort to defeat Britain, the "ancient enemy". In a strange, warped way they probably imagined that it would end the division of Ireland and the Border would be no more. Of course, if they had known about the concentration camps and what total victory for the Nazis would have meant, they would almost certainly have revised their opinion.

The irony of it was that De Valera had the support of the people in his policy of neutrality which later, it was revealed, leaned towards favouring – even helping – Britain as much as possible. German pilots who landed in Ireland after straying off-course found themselves imprisoned while British pilots were spirited out of the Republic via the North. And De Valera ensured that when Belfast was bombed Dublin did its bit in valiant fashion.

The Emergency, as we knew it, brought nothing like the hardship the British people experienced but we knew rationing and coupons for clothes that meant very little really, as there was no money anyhow for the buying of new outfits on a regular basis. In fact, when a hurling tournament was held with fifteen suitlengths as the prize for the winners, you could bet your last penny that they would battle for it with as much intensity and fervour as for a championship title itself – and sometimes more!

The scarcity of tea hit people hard because it was still the era when lunch in the middle of the day was still the main meal and it was a case of tea in the evening instead of dinner.

My father seemed to have the means of getting boxes of butter on a regular basis. And used great ingenuity in ensuring that we were never without tea. Those who got involved in the black market – charging people through the nose for tea – were abhorred by all decent-minded folk. It was claimed by my mother that the black-marketeers would never have any luck.

Women dutifully asked their husbands then how they should vote. "Go out and vote for Dev", my father would advise my mother and she did as she was told.

A tillage policy was carried out to the letter by De Valera's government. One of the tasks my father had to do each year was fill in what seemed to me to be an interminable pile of forms – listing the number of cows cattle and sheep a particular farmer had on his farm, the number of hens and ducks also. It was a wearisome task for any Garda to undertake and here was Dad trying to help us with our lessons and I think he became adept at taking short-cuts. If a farmer had ten hens and five ducks one year, no civil servant up in Dublin was going to worry too much if the form showed eleven and six respectively this time – especially if the civil servant in question received forms on a Monday morning when he had "a bit of a head" on him!

Every family knew how to grow vegetables for the luncheon table. My father got a plot on some farm and would bring me with him on the back of his bike when he went out to plant potatoes and cabbage, carrots and parsnips. We planted lettuce and onions in the back garden.

No one ate meat on Fridays. It was reckoned to be a mortal sin to do so. You had to get a dispensation if you wanted to get relief from fasting during Lent. You couldn't even take a cup of tea before you went to Holy Communion. No wonder it was a frequent sight to see delicate souls fainting in church and being carried out by strong men.

I remember the mountains of potatoes in the centre of the table on Fridays as Mother made colcannon for us (potatoes mashed and mixed into a lovely edible meal with butter and scallions).

The delicacy in those days was roast rabbit for the Sunday meal. Mother knew also how to stuff a sheep's heart to make it go around the whole family. And my father would kill a pig which would mean bacon and cabbage – the real McCoy – and home-made black pudding (I can still see in the mind's eye the making of those black puddings from the gush of the blood of the pig and all the rest that went into them).

We knew the finest white and brown bread made by Mother, the hot coals adding a flavour that could never be recaptured by bread bought in a supermart.

Father cut our hair with a scissors (non-electric, of course) that made you wince. So distant from the hair-cuts I get today that cost at least £11 when you add in the tip. He would sole our shoes with strips of leather cut from a large square. He could turn his hand to anything it seemed – apart from the writing.

He liked a bet on the Aintree Grand National. This lady in Ballina had a way of dreaming dreams that added up to predicting happenings in the future in a rather uncanny way. Now she told my father in the count-down to the Grand National that she had had this very clear dream of two horses ploughing in a field – the smaller of the two pulling all the time a head in front of the other. Up to the end of the furrow and back again.

My father studied the field and concluded that the small horse had to be Workman, who was to be ridden by Bruce Hobbs. The other was Royal Danieli. My father put 5/- (old money) on Workman who beat Royal Danieli – by a head. At odds of 40/1.

He brought us all into Limerick to collect his winnings. It seemed to me that all my birthdays had come together as I gorged myself on sweets and ice-cream and other goodies. I always had a soft spot for the National after that and in many ways it has been a lucky race for me.

My father was ahead of his time in that he was very ecumenically-minded when it came to religion. He had a great depth of belief that extended far beyond a simple Catholic faith to taking what was best from Hindu and Buddhist philosophers. He believed in doing rather than in the form.

Christmas times were special and the coming of Santa Claus a delight beyond reason itself. Once during the War I remember coming down to see all the toy soldiers drawn up in formation for a battle and we fought our battles in France and on the Eastern Front through a long, never-ending day. The turkey. The Christmas cake. The impromptu concert in the family circle to which we all had to contribute. My father writing the script. The sing-song around the piano. Following the wren on St. Stephen's Day.

And then we were invited to the Superintendent's house for a treat that included the showing of Charlie Chaplin films. And across the silent screen the line: "The birds shall sing sweetly tomorrow".

The sheer hilarity of Chaplin dropping an ice-cream cone from a balcony down on to the bare shoulders of a lady on the dance floor below and almost feeling the coldness as she squirmed.

*   *   *

Father was so independent-minded that it was inevitable, I suppose, that he would clash with his superiors.

I remember the shock that descended on our home when he got word that he was being transferred to Carrigaholt and Mother saying that we were going to "the last parish before America".

Father didn't allow the grass to grow under his feet but realised that we would be doomed if he did not act and act quickly. At least Killaloe had Benson's Box factory if the worse came to the worse and it was a question of working there rather than taking the emigrant boat to England. Carrigaholt had nothing.

So he pulled strings to get the transfer stopped. Not entirely though. He was told he would be moving instead to Thurles.

Destiny was certainly kind to us in that for it meant that my brothers and myself would finish our secondary school days in Thurles C.B.S. and my sisters would have the benefit of the Ursuline Convent, where you had the finest music teachers.

I travelled with my father to Thurles when he was renting a house. We stayed in Buggle's Hotel.

It was a night when snow fell heavily over the Cathedral town and all its environs. Liberty Square was a blanket of white.

We went together to see *Rose Marie* in the local cinema and I thrilled to the singing of Nelson Eddie and Jeanette McDonald.

Returning I asked Father to allow me to get involved in the great snow-battle that had developed in the Square. The world sang for me then with the lost innocence that could never be recaptured. And into that one White

95

Night merged the closeness I had with my father that blossomed in a strange way later. He inculcated me with his love of writing, with his belief in the meaning of the journey of life, with the significance of giving and serving. And if he was denied, by the times that were in it, from publishing the books I knew he had in him, he rejoiced at the publication of my first book by Hutchinson of London and the successes I knew in the journalistic field. And he was satisfied and fulfilled.

Thurles C.B.S. was unquestionably one of the best schools in the country, turning out a stream of boys who won scholarships to the universities and places in the Civil Service. Dick Burke, later to become an EEC Commissioner, cycled the fourteen miles into Thurles each day from Upperchurch and back home in the evening.

I was weak at Irish and no great shakes at Maths. So I went with others, my brother Gus included, into the "B" Class and it meant that all you needed was a bare pass in Irish and a pass in drawing and you were through. The irony of it was that in those pre-points days I was seeking honours in English, History and Geography and three honours meant honours in the Leaving Certificate itself.

It was a mixed school in the sense that you had lay teachers working side-by-side with the Christian Brothers. Some of the brothers were tough to say the least. I developed a speech impediment which only struck me inside the gates of the school. One day when the roll was being called, I couldn't give my name and the brother in question pummelled me around the room, until I ended up cowering in a corner. When later I informed him why I wasn't able to give my name, he was very apologetic and we became very good friends. I have a picture of him at the launching of one of my books on hurling.

Others were not as fortunate as I was. One Brother used the stick indiscriminately, slapping boys in a way that went well beyond the bounds of correction. Some unenlightened parents blamed their sons for provoking the Brother in question. But eventually a few parents, who were ahead of their time in their awareness of what was actually happening in the class-room, went direct to the Head. The Brother was summarily removed and the word on the grapevine was that he had gone to a mental home as a result of a break-down.

I was warned by my parents not to take sweets from a character, who looked quite amenable to me who stood at the door of his house with a bag of liquorice all-sorts in his hand, ready to offer them to young passers-by. Let's just call him Pete for the sake of this book, though that was not his real name.

Now and then a friend, greying at the temples and immaculately dressed in the kind of pin-striped suit so popular with members of the legal profession, would arrive on an evening train and make his way to Pete's house. The Gardaí, who kept a watching brief for the protection of the young and unwary, would nab the visitor and bring him to the station. When he was about to be charged under some ancient law before the phrase "consenting males" had ever entered the vernacular in Thurles,

Canon Fogarty would arrive post-haste in his old Dodge car and see to it that matters did not proceed further so that there would be no scandal created in the town.

And our visitor in the pin-striped suit would find himself being put on the mail train – to endure an excruciating journey back to Dublin, getting into the metropolis in the early hours of the following morning. And, as he headed home, he was left to ponder why the Church adopted such a stern stance towards his friendship with Pete.

Canon Fogarty would lean over the pulpit and, clapping his hands, warn: "I can't be looking after your daughters down the watery Mall" (that was the walk by the banks of the River Suir so popular with courting couples).

*   *   *

The retreats and the missions given by the Redemptorist Fathers were legendary. Fierce sermons for the first three days before God was produced as a God of mercy. Anyone involved in sex outside of wedlock was heading for Hell's fire for all eternity and if married couples indulged in any kind of contraception outside of the "rhythm system" or sleeping in separate rooms, they too faced the terrible fate of being banished by Peter when they arrived at Heaven's gate.

You tried to wait and see could you pick the softest of the visiting Fathers before venturing to confession. Certainly you kept well away from the confessional box from which the words "What, when, where?" could be heard emerging loud and clear and then the door opened to allow every head to turn and peer straight at a young man whose face was scarlet with embarrassment.

One summer the great two-week Mission came right in the middle of a heat-wave. The young bloods chose a popular spot for swimming on the banks of the River Suir and Dudley Farrell, who used to play the organ at Mass in the Cathedral, and was if anything 6ft 6ins tall, was brought into service with the words; "Depth it Dud" and he duly dived in and if the water came up only to his waist, we knew there was no danger.

There was this Redemptorist back from the mission fields whose voice was going or nearly gone (poor man he would eventually end up with a voice-box after cancer had been diagnosed). A half-empty Cathedral for that first sun-drenched week and, as he looked at the empty pews and exclaimed in that sad voice "there is no response to our appeal", you knew deep down that Canon Fogarty would never allow it to continue.

A discreet word and a quick change was made. Out from Limerick came a real fire-brand with a shock of grey hair. His arrival coincided with a change in the weather and the young bloods and the lassies with them who hadn't been too concerned for their souls as they courted by grassy river-banks, began to drift back first in dribs and drabs and then in something of a flood-tide for the grand climax of the Mission.

He struck the fear of God into us as he hopped off the pulpit. This guy wasn't appealing. He was delivering it to us right on the button, stripped of any sense of mercy. Those who felt the adrenalin flowing in their veins, the hotter a sermon, loved every minute of it. There was the sound of angels singing in the air. Showers of indulgences now where there had been but swimming and sex the previous week.

It was voted by general consent to have been the greatest climax to the most successful second week of a Mission ever seen in Thurles. It went into the annals of the Redemptorist Fathers. Your man with the shock of grey hair was a hero in the eyes of Canon Fogarty.

They don't make them like that anymore!

The teacher we had for Irish around Fourth Year wasn't very good and we arrived in the Leaving Certificate year paying the price for his sins of omission. A dedicated Brother took us in hand and started right at the bottom. He even got a dunce's cap to ensure that there would be no messing.

He would hold up a pen and ask: "Cad é sin"

And, if after a lot of tutoring, you could not answer: "Is peann é sin", then you were told to go into the corner and put the dunce's cap on you.

I know it may have seemed the most incongruous sight imaginable to see a strapping country lad of seventeen, going on eighteen, wearing a dunce's cap in the corner of a class-room with six weeks to go to the Leaving Certificate examination. But that was the way it happened in that immortal year.

Amazingly, I don't think there was one failure at Irish in the whole class. Some got the bare pass but they got through.

Frankly, I won't have a word said against the Christian Brothers. Too many of us owe too much to them. In the days before free secondary education they were really magnificent. I remember my mother going up with the money (was it £10 a quarter, I just can't recall exactly now) to pay the fees for Gus, Brendan, Noel and myself. If your parents hadn't the wherewithal to pay, no questions were asked. No boy was ever turned away.

*   *   *

Emigration was now a cancer affecting Irish society. There was an advertisement in *The Tipperary Star* for jobs in the mines in Wales. Pals of mine who had done far better in Maths ended up working in those mines.

I entered a competition, run by an English newspaper, to finish a cartoon detective story. I won £10. With the tenner I went to Dublin – partly on a holiday but at the same time taking in the Lower Civil Service exam. I came something like 266th out of 300.

I was 17 and living out a year of unemployment, being not in the least enamoured by the prospect of life in the Welsh mines, now beckoning more strongly than ever. The writing bug was beginning to catch me and to pass the time I wrote a story about a rebellion in an animal kingdom and the Phoenix rising from his ashes.

One day Bill Myles, Editor of *The Tipperary Star* sent word over to the Christian Brothers that he needed a boy to be trained as a junior reporter.

I had come first in English, getting one of the highest marks ever recorded in the school, and was duly recommended.

I was on my way.

On the eve of the 1984 All-Ireland Hurling Final – the memorable Centenary week-end in Thurles – I was walking across Liberty Square to Hayes's Hotel. A middle-aged man hailed me. "You won't remember me, Scoop", he remarked (they all knew me as "Scoop" in Thurles before I went to the Congo and then quite a number of them began to call me "Congo"!).

"Don't remember you", I said. "You were the best header of a ball in those matches we had when we started off playing soccer".

He was one of the guys who had been forced to emigrate to England which I always felt was a terrible cruelty. We spent that evening drinking together and reminiscing about boyhood days.

I started off at £2 a week and gave £1 a week to my mother as I was living at home still. I could manage very well on £1 a week, which shows how the value of money has declined.

The paper was owned by Kitty Long, a small rather hunched creature, who used to arrive in the car driven by Jerry and he would drive me in the same car to hurling and football matches on Sunday afternoons and to council meetings and out-of-town courts that had to be covered.

We knew her simply as "Miss Long". She left the running of the paper to Bill Myles, the Editor, who gave me a great grounding in the essentials of journalism and it was from him I first leaned the dictum – "when in doubt, leave it out". As the years progressed I was able to split the reports of council meetings into readable "takes" and could even plan and edit the entire GAA page.

I learned shorthand and typing on my arrival at the paper and also how to proof read and the various markings. There were no schools of journalism as such then and, frankly, I thought in one way it was better than the present system as you were not selected because you hit a very high points mark in the Leaving Certificate examination but you got into journalism because you impressed an Editor who knew what he wanted and could make a judgement on the essential qualities he knew the profession demanded.

Miss Long never married. Neither did Billy Myles, who was a fine cut of a man. She had a crush on him from the moment he assumed the editorial chair and she conveyed to him that he had a choice – either he could play along with the fallacy that he was tied to her or else lose the post of Editor. If he fell in love and married someone else it was curtains for him.

So he would go for drives with Miss Long and for Sunday lunch but they were never, as far as we knew, involved sexually. It was a charade. We all felt rather sorry for Bill Myles and wondered why de hadn't the gumption to tell her to get lost and go his own way, even if it meant sacrificing the editorial chair.

There was one attractive lady across the street who used drop in now and then to say "Hello" and across the table I might notice her hand running through Bill Myles's hair as they laughed and joked together. Somehow or other Miss Long would "get wind" of the fact that there was a rival on the prowl and Myles would be put into cold storage or the "blue room" for a few days.

A man in the printing room was big into the greyhounds and actually named one of his pups Mileslong. It ran fourteen times and never reached the first three.

When Myles was away on holidays we worked far, far harder that when he was around us, apart from writing copy, we had to edit the pages. After putting the paper to bed and hearing the presses roll, we would sit back and relax as we glanced through the first copies checking for any serious errors that might allow us to make changes to the run.

One day Miss Long dropped in suddenly and happened to come down the corridor and look into the room while I was telling a funny yarn to my fellow-staff members.

She said something to the effect that we were wasting time while the Editor was away. I immediately saw red and responded in a way I should not have responded to the owner of the paper. But I had broken my back, so to speak, all that week to ensure that deadlines were met and I wasn't going to be told that I was a waster – not even by Miss Long herself.

She there and then gave me the sack. I had joined the National Union of Journalists on becoming a junior reporter and the Limerick Branch, of which we were all members, was duly informed of what had happened.

The wheels were immediately set in motion and a delegation, led by Bill Shine (later to be my superior in Independent House in Dublin), came to see Miss Long, after ascertaining all the facts from me and my colleagues. The outcome was that I had to make a profuse apology – just to satisfy Miss Long's hurt pride – but I was reinstated in the job and Bill Myles on his return and, learning what had happened, ensured that she never bothered us again when he was away.

Her end was a sad one. She hired maids for a pittance – country girls from large families whose parents were grateful to get another mouth that had to be fed off their hands.

There came a time when you could no longer get a maid for 5/- to 10/- a week and "the keep". Miss Long couldn't understand it. And she was so mean that she actually went without a maid while the money piled up in the bank. She couldn't cook for herself and, as she became more helpless, she could hardly get out of bed to make a cup of tea or coffee. The rats were running about the place and, word had it, that when she died, things were in an appalling and very sad state in her house – palatial by Thurles standards and standing in its own grounds.

*   *   *

I was writing the Thurles Notes every week – not a gossip column like the Terry Keane column, the Trevor Danker column, or the Angela Phelan column. Straight news items and there was one headed "Social Changes" which told of the new girl bank clerks who had come to town (if they were good-looking, we ensured that we were in quick to take them out to be interviewed!)

I also wrote the Golf Notes and obituaries and great care had to be taken in a county like Tipperary with the obituaries of those who had played a role in the War of Independence (remember, this was the country of Dan Breen and Sean Treacy and Bill Myles had served in the Army of the Free State before entering journalism and laughed as he told us of going up the hills after Dan Breen and his column and he had no heart or inclination to wound or kill or even capture Dan Breen and Breen himself had no heart for a Civil War that saw him on the opposite side to Michael Collins; so really Myles and Breen were playing games with each other in the hills).

I was instructed by Bill Myles how to see to it that no "freedom fighter" got credit beyond what he had actually done. If his courage and actions were beyond question he got the full "works" in an obituary notice. If there was clearly a major question mark, you simply wrote "identified with the Cause" and in the case of a woman who was "out" in "The Troubles" and again didn't satisfy Myles that she was a true-blue "freedom fighter", he would dismiss her with the words "carried messages for Cumann na mBan".

All the names of the clergy officiating at the Requiem Mass of some important personage had to go in and the list might run to a column or half-a-column. You had to give them their full titles and if you made a mistake, you would have to go back and retype the whole thing and, God help you, if you failed to spot some parish priest who felt he should have been mentioned.

I had played hurling in Thurles C.B.S. and at a time when there seemed to be a never-ending stream of outstanding talent, I felt honoured to be selected at left corner forward in the final trial for the Croke Cup team. In earlier matches I had been scoring regularly but now I came up against one named Tony Wall and , as we said then in Thurles, I "never got a look in" for fully thirty minutes. I was replaced at the interval and that was the end of my career as a budding exponent of the national game. Come to think of it, the school never contemplated forming the discards from those trial matches into a "B" team and even a "C" team, so that their education into the skills and crafts of the game could be continued. We were simply discarded in an era of riches beyond belief and allowed to go our own way and it meant that we turned to soccer as an alternative, which was a pity in one way.

But the grounding you got in Thurles when it came to a knowledge of hurling was really outstanding. The town produced Jimmy Doyle, one of the finest artists of the caman the game has known, and Tommy Ryan, who was like Manolete in the ascetic quality of the way he wielded the stick on sun-drenched days and Tommy Doyle, who had the distinction of holding Christy Ring through the drawn game and marathon replay in Limerick in 1949 and that born character Mickey (The Rattler) Byrne who was in the company of Jim Devitt of Cashel – a brilliant sticksman in defence – at the funeral of Mick Mackey and I recall Devitt telling a story against himself of the day he was referee at a junior football match and someone shouted from the sideline: "Go home Devitt, you wouldn't see a foul in a hen house.

Thurles Sarsfields dominated the scene as one of the greatest club sides in the country in the fifties. Bobby Mockler, the Keane brothers, Tony Wall and Jimmy Doyle all wore the Blue jersey backed by an immense tradition. Later Paddy Kenny, a deadly forward, would join the club from Borrisoleigh making them more unbeatable.

On a paper like *The Tipperary Star* you turned your hand to everything, to both news and sport. But progressively I became more and more involved in covering the GAA scene and my reports were signed simply "By Our Reporter".

Michael O'Halloran was the senior GAA writer and Tom Higgins the senior reporter on news. The 1951 All-Ireland senior hurling final between Wexford and Tipperary was the first I actually wrote about for the paper. It was agreed with Bill Myles that, while I wouldn't qualify as yet for a ticket for the Press Box (that went to Michael O'Halloran), I could give my impressions in a column for the following week's paper. I watched the game from Hill 16 and the Rackard brothers, Bobby, Willie and Nicky, the captain for the first time and Nick O'Donnell and Tim Flood and saw a side that would reach greatness in 1955 and '56 fail for want of experience and a terrible weakness in goal before a Tipperary side that attained its peak that day as the third-in-a-row was clinched.

My expenses for the day in Dublin came to less that 30/- (old money), comprising 14/- for the train fare, 4/6d for lunch and 6/6d if you had meat tea and 4/6 for the plain tea. A bunch of reporters could mix the meat and plain teas and share the ham and claim for a meat tea. You could fiddle your expenses by putting down two shillings for "incidentals", which was a banana split or an ice sundae in Caffola's.

I reported on two matches every Sunday during the summer and evening matches as well. There was no such thing as a week-end off. You worked a five-and-a-half day week in the office, which meant coming in on Saturday mornings. And you were back in on Monday morning bright and early after doing your stint of matches on Sunday.

In 1952 I was thrown right in at the deep end when Michael O'Halloran suddenly left to join the *Irish Press*. It meant that overnight I became the chief GAA writer and had to cover the dramatic Munster Final in Limerick between Tipperary and Cork when the men in the Blue and Gold were seeking a fourth successive All-Ireland crown.

Fierce controversy surrounded the game as the referee, having first blown the whistle for a free, allowed a goal to Cork after being spoken to by Christy Ring. Tipperary protested vehemently but it was to no avail. Cork went on to record a three-timer and Christy Ring won his eighth All-Ireland medal – a feat to be equalled by Tipperary's sterling defender, John Doyle. Ring was denied a ninth by Wexford and Art Foley and John Doyle missed out on his when Tipperary were beaten by Kilkenny in 1967. But it has to be said of both Doyle and Ring that neither of them would ever agree to be "carried" as a sub just to go one ahead of the other. Both won their eight medals on the field of play and in that respect their record is unsurpassed.

*   *   *

I wrote my first book, *A Lifetime In Hurling* in 1955 or rather it was published that same year. It was in actual fact the "ghosted" autobiography of Tommy Doyle. I sent the manuscript to Hutchinsons, the big London-based publisher, pointing out in a covering note that up to 80,000 fans could attend an All-Ireland Hurling Final, so they were on to a winner. It was the era when the ghosted autobiographies of famous soccer stars were appearing with monotonous regularity. Anyway, Hutchinson accepted and the book came out in hardback at 10/6 a copy. I got £100 as an advance.

They printed 5,000 copies. It wasn't the runaway bestseller I had hinted to them it would be but, amazingly enough, it became a collector's item in time and I recall when I ran out of copies for my personal use, I advertised in *The Tipperary Star* and had to pay £10 to get one.

Around the same time I was an avid fan of the Sunday paper crosswords, which carried a first prize of £500 and there were also prizes if you submitted an entry that had just one clue incorrect. My father had been my mentor and he was brilliant at these competitions. Together we won something like twenty prizes in the one year and I recall missing £500 and a car and the clue I had incorrect in the first coupon I submitted I had right in the next. Of course, we used special systems to permutate a number of clues after making our bankers and we learned to keep past results, as the adjudicators had a way of doing repeats.

My great moment came when I won the *Sunday Chronicle* crossword outright and first prize of £650 and a hamper and a fireside set. I was actually down to my last 2/6d in the form of a postal order on Tuesday evening and, as I had lost that evening at the dogs, I pondered whether I should change the 2/6d postal order the next day or go ahead and use it to cover my entry. Fortunately, I took the right decision.

The *Sunday Chronicle* was actually an English Sunday paper and they got quite a shock when they learned that a local journalist in Thurles had won the top prize. But they went ahead with the presentation of the cheque to me in the local cinema and carried a report in their Irish edition the following Sunday of my being cheered to the echo by an over-flow attendance. Totally exaggerated, of course.

Shortly afterwards the paper closed down and the local wits said I was the cause of its demise.

I didn't have a bank account then, only a Post Office savings book. I knew nothing about overdrafts or deposit accounts. I went into my friend Patsy O'Connell in one of the banks and asked him to change the cheque for "readies" – and I told him I wanted £400 in singles. Patsy tried to advise me to open a current account and said they would have to go around to other banks in town to get some of the £400 in singles and, really, I was causing a lot of trouble.

But I had a bag with me and filled it with all the notes and, bringing it

103

home, turned the whole lot out on the kitchen table. There and then I counted out £100 in singles to my father and £100 in singles to my mother and gave a present to each of my brothers and sisters. I put the rest in the Post Office savings account and didn't know a rainy day for a long time after that.

Of course, when I joined Independent Newspapers I had to give up doing the crosswords and it wouldn't have been diplomatic of me to win the *Sunday Press* crossword either. So I duly retired. But all the other syndicates around the country who were expert at winning the crosswords knew our address – 9, Thomond Road, Thurles. A very lucky address I might add.

*   *   *

After spending ten years on *The Tipperary Star* I felt it was time to broaden my horizons. I had an offer of £13-10s a week from the *Irish Press* and was about to accept it when out of the blue, I was asked if I would accept the editorship of *The Munster Tribune*, which was at that stage in a terminal illness.

I signed a six-months contract and moved to Clonmel. I was earning £17-10s a week as Editor and had a further £8 for writing on the greyhound scene for *The Sporting Press* (I had started in Thurles covering the dogs at the local track and also Kilkenny) and I was giving tips to the *Sunday Review*. On a total income of £25 a week I thought it beneath me to stay in "digs". For something like £7.10s a week I lived in the lap of luxury in Hearne's Hotel across the road from my office and enjoyed a fillet steak every evening.

My contract wasn't renewed, as the paper by this time could hardly afford an Editor. It dragged on for another while with Mick Strappe and the late Mick Hogan doing trojan work but ultimately it could not win the auctioneers' and other lucrative advertisements from *The Nationalist* (Clonmel) and went out of existence. Sad really when you reflect on the outstanding reporters who worked for it in the brief High Noon when it was a weekly paper that broke moulds and set new standards in reporting and presentation.

Four papers in County Tipperary was perhaps too much. You had *The Nenagh Guardian* in the North Riding, *The Tipperary Star* in the Mid and *The Nationalist* in the South. To set up *The Munster Tribune* in direct opposition to *The Nationalist* in Clonmel was a very brave move by Tommy O'Brien or 'The Coalminer' as he was known (he came back from England to get the Ballingarry mines going and he was an awesome gambler in his day and would have netted £100,000 had his horse Moss Bank won the Champion Hurdle in 1961).

It was a lucky break for me that my contract with *The Munster Tribune* was not renewed as it saw me moving to Dublin in 1960 and joining the Independent Group.

Incidentally, Sean Duignan used come down from Galway to Limerick for Branch meetings of the NUJ. He had learned about my first book being published by Hutchinson and then when he walked into Cruise's Hotel, he was introduced to Mick Strappe who had produced The Mick Delahunty Story (Mick Del, of course, was a legend in his own lifetime in the Ballrooms of Romance).

"On the one afternoon I was meeting the authors of two tomes. I felt then I had really arrived among the greats", is how "Diggy" recalls it.

9

"What Would You be Doin' in Danang"

The two pals had gone from the West of Ireland to the United States and, rather than wait to be drafted, they volunteered to fight in Vietnam.

That way, they knew, a better future would be opened for them in America when they returned – that is if they were to be among the soldiers from the War returning.

Let's call one of them Billy and the other Joey for the sake of this story.

Joey reached Saigon (now Ho Chi Minh City) ahead of Billy. When they discovered that he had been a butcher back home in Ireland, they wouldn't even let him leave Tan Sun Nhut airfield, through which so many American GIs passed over the years, either heading for the war zone or going back home.

There was enough dead meat in the form of bodybags coming back from the front lines, that is if there was such a thing as a front line in this strangest of wars where an invisible Viet Cong killed young GIs from the tree line, maimed and killed with Claymore mines and even children carrying concealed grenades could contribute to the dirty work. And the frustrated Americans, many of them hooked on drugs and prepared to leave behind them dog tags that were liable to read 'Don't Fuck With Me I'm Already Dead', replied with napalm and gunship strikes, leading to appalling massacres like Mai Lai that could never be effaced from the mind.

Anyway, Billy arrives at Saigon Airport and Joey, as he takes a break from his duties as a butcher, spots him coming across the tarmac, weighed down with the wares of war: "Billy, Billy … where are you headin?"

"Danang", comes the instant reply.

"Danang?"

"Yes, Danang".

"What would you be doin' in Danang?"

He didn't tell Billy about the dope pushers and the pimps and the prostitution that made this city into a veritable giant brothel. He simply said: "Sure there's nothin' but bodybags comin' back from Danang. What in the name of the Blessed Virgin would you be doin' goin' there?"

Then he added: "They've plenty of guys for the fightin' and the dyin' up around Danang. But they still ain't got enough butchers".

So Billy, on the recommendation of his friend, became a butcher in Vietnam serving the American and South Vietnamese cause.

Billy and Joey were long gone back to the States when the North Vietnamese swept south, columns of refugees struggling towards Saigon ahead of the collapsing ARVN (South Vietnamese) army. The city fell in April, 1975 and by then the war had claimed 58,000 American dead, left 300,000 wounded and overall had cost 150 billion dollars.

The boys did well in the States – very well – and Joey came home to open his own butcher's shop in the West of Ireland. And sold the finest lamb that you could get anywhere in your travels – so good, in fact, that his business expanded beyond the confines of his own county, its tentacles reaching into the metropolis itself.

His name could have been on the memorial stone in Arlington if he had never learned the butchering business. Another martyr for old America, another martyr for the cause.

*   *   *

I was reminded of that story as I sat on a coffin in the ferry bringing Andy Sheppard and myself from the island of Kos to the port of Pothia in Kalymnos. On the coffin they had written an instruction on the lines: "Transmit body from the Bronx to Kalymnos". A son of the soil of the Island of the Sponge Fishers who believed that his soul would never rest unless interred in the Greek island where he was born and reared and, no doubt, experienced something in childhood and youthful days that, alas, could never be recaptured again in the pressure-cooker daily round of New York.

We had accompanied Foreign Minister, Michael O'Kennedy on a trip to Athens. A jaunt, to put it frankly, because when the offices would not cover the full cost, the Greek Government was happy enough to lay on the return flights and the hotel accommodation. You don't turn your back on a gift horse like that. They were angling at the time to push their claims for membership of the European Community and wanted all the backing they could command – including that of the Irish Government and Opposition.

We were put up in the Grand Bretagne Hotel right in the centre. The old guy behind the bar had waited on them all. He remembered serving Goering and Goebbels and, am I right in saying, that he had even served Hitler on one occasion. "What were they like?", I hastened to ask. With a countenance that gave away nothing of his emotions – nothing whatsoever – he enumerated what each one of them liked to drink – one preferring his Scotch neat, the other on the rocks and the third with soda. But each, it seemed, was an excellent customer in his own way. I thought it better not to enquire if they had the Scotch neat or on the rocks as they were sending the victims of the Holocaust to the gas-chambers.

Michael O'Kennedy was all excitement as he told Andy and myself that he had slept in the same bed that Karamanlis had occupied after his triumphant return to Greece. "Goebbels slept in the same bed too", said Andy laconically.

Later at the Foreign Office for a full-scale morning briefing by the Greek Foreign Minister. I knew that what we would be told about Greek foreign policy wouldn't command a headline in the *Evening Herald*. Initiative was called for in this instance.

The Rhodesian conflict was at its height at the time and it was being watched closely by the media back home because of the sizeable Irish community. I asked the Foreign Minister what plans his Government had to get Greek nationals out of Rhodesia should it come to a "Doomsday Situation". He revealed that the Greeks, together with the Irish and others from countries that hadn't embassies there, would gather in the grounds of the British Embassy and would be whisked out to safety, if necessary in RAF jets.

A lead story had fallen into my lap without really working for it. The *Evening Herald,* as I anticipated, went BIG on Page One on the "Doomsday Plan" and Andy Sheppard, who didn't consider it was just right for the one o'clock News, was asked by his Newsdesk why the Greeks were suddenly getting so hot around the collar about the deteriorating situation in Rhodesia.

The Foreign Minister never did quite understand why I didn't ply him with questions about the build-up to Greece's bid for EEC membership.

That would have to wait for an *Irish Independent* or *Sunday Independent* feature page article – a studied feature!

M. (my nom-de-plume) of the Foreign Office brought us to a late-night drinking spot off the Plaka. Suddenly, I felt M's hand on my left leg as he suggested that, after the round of briefings and all the filing, we might need a rest for a few days on one of the islands. "What about Rhodes?", he asked. "I'd be squashed like a sardine on the crowded main beach", I responded. His hand moved up my leg, as he ventured: "Kos is a nice island?". "Yes, quite nice – but too many Germans", came my reply. "Kalymnos – now that is my favourite of all the islands", he said then. "That will do fine", I splurted out, grabbing his hand before it reached the zone marked "Private".

The air tickets were sent around to the hotel. There was an apology over the fact that they would not be able to provide us with tickets for the ferry. That was all we would have to pay. A chauffeur-driven limousine would convey us to Athens Airport and meet us on our return. We would be met also at Kos Airport and conveyed to the ferry. They even gave us books of tickets that could be used for any meals we bought in tavernas or snacks at ouzerias.

A Greek Orthodox priest was waiting on the pier to meet the coffin. The smell of ouzo lingered in the air from the circle of relatives. There was also the scent of incense under a clear night sky as the priest sprinkled the coffin. The owner of our hotel was down to greet "the important journalist from Irish television" (it appeared that I was not in the same category as Andy as a VIP!)

Ravenous by now, we asked if there was any restaurant or taverna open. None, the hotelier indicated, in keeping with the tastes and status of two representatives of the Irish media.

But was there anything – ever so humble – within striking distance of the hotel where we might satisfy the pangs of hunger?

He pointed to a taverna about five hundred yards down the way but shrugged his shoulders at the same time as if to say that he wouldn't be responsible should it fail dismally to come up to standard.

The proprietor was beginning to put up the shutters. There was one last chicken roasting on a spit. His young daughter was playing around outside.

With that true hospitality that one always experiences from island people, he informed us that he would serve us. He set up a table outside under the stars. He split the chicken in half – one portion to Andy , the other to myself. Salad to go with it and a bottle of red wine.

I gave some coins to his daughter who was now dancing around our table. A second bottle of wine was brought – on the house.

The memory of that simple chicken dinner on Kalymnos somehow outstrips so many other dinners in so many prestigious restaurants and hotels around the globe. You won't find the name of the taverna in any guide-book. But it doesn't matter, anyway.

The taxi-man with the moustache a-la-Charlie Chaplin called for us next morning and brought us to a secluded beach that we had all to ourselves. We lazed the hours away between swimming in the blue-green water acquiring a tan without risking the noon-day sun. A succulent fish lunch followed on the veranda of some taverna to which Charlie conveyed us at noon. Paid for with piles of coupons. Wine. Ouzo. All were included.

Charlie was gone for his siesta by now, but he would be back, of course.

Beep-beep, beep-beep. Hard to imagine it is five o'clock already. There he was winding his way down the narrow road, maybe killing a chicken along the way that had the temerity to cross his path at the inopportune moment.

We learned of local men afflicted with the Bends. They were of the tradition of those who would have departed for five or six months to dive for sponges in the southern waters of the Libyan Sea off the coast of Africa – the only way they knew of earning a living outside of eking an existence from the barren rocks of much of the island itself. They would have left after a big farewell party when they danced until the dawn came up and they were happy for a time.

Away from the island then for what seemed an eternity to wives and sweethearts and other dear ones. The black flags flying on the boats on the returning indicate that there have been burials at sea. Now the weeping where there had been laughter and gaiety. Now the island wakes, like the Aran Island wakes, bringing matters full circle from the going-away parties.

Those who suffered the Bends rather than being buried at sea – the result of going down too deep after the prize – could count themselves lucky in a way. Or were they so lucky after all? A terrible price to pay, you concluded, as the bloom of youth was blown away in an instance.

Today disease and other factors have hit the deep-water beds that were the target of the sponge divers from Kalymnos and, tragically, many of the fleet of 30 and more boats are no longer being used for the purpose for which they were built originally. They have been converted for use in the tourist trade.

In the taverna where Andy and myself ate our chicken dinner under a star-lit sky, you might well be served by a young man who might have been a brave sponge diver.

More tourists, yes, but changing very fast from the Kalymnos that left an indelible imprint on me close on twenty years ago.

*   *   *

I find myself in Madrid with Andy Sheppard, Val Dorgan and Donal Byrne of the *Morning Ireland* RTE Radio programme. We are attending a Congress of the Association of European Journalists.

At a reception we meet a high-ranking member of the Spanish navy (one Gallagher by name, as far as I recall), who is proud to talk about the Irish blood in his veins. As he tries to explain that his blood lines go back to the Wild Geese, his English fails him in grappling with the word "geese". He gets over the problem by flapping his arms after the fashion of a gaggle of geese in flight.

I am so taken by his story and his enthusiasm in elaborating so vividly on the "Irish Connection" that I cannot refrain from promising to write about it in the *Sunday Independent*. But I put it far more colourfully when I inform him: "You'll be big in Backchat". (I was making quite an input at the time into the widely-read column, the anchor-man and main writer of which was Kevin O'Connor who had excellent contacts in the Leinster House arena and who, incidentally, with his stage experience from his days in Limerick has always been a great comic performer and singer at social gatherings of journalists, in particular of the Dublin Journalists Golfing Society).

Donal Byrne does a brilliant take-off of that moment – flapping wings for emphasis! I cannot but regret the fact that he did not follow his brother, Gabriel into the acting profession, for Donal is a natural, spontaneous in the way he sees the humour in a given situation. However, he only reveals his unique gifts to friends and acquaintances when a certain mood has been created. I regard myself as very fortunate to have shared the laughter that has sprung from the tide of his talent in full flow whether in Dublin or the quiet backwater of a pub in some Continental city when the day's work was ended.

That Spanish trip coincided with much controversy about an "alternative Pope" who had reared his head, or was it his Red Hat, down Seville way. Val and myself realised that there was an angle there that could capture that attention of the News Desks back home – if we could somehow or other get to Seville for on-the-spot despatches. As guests of the Spanish Government, of course!

Another of those interminable briefings. This had nothing whatsoever got to do with the "alternative Pope" but was into the serious business of fishing, Spain's fishing rights within the European Community and naturally the Foreign Ministry wanted to get across their position as clearly as possible to us, while ensuring that they did not raise the blood pressure of Irish fishermen in the process.

Somewhere along the line the official giving the briefing looked distinctly puzzled when Val suddenly raised the issue of the "alternative Pope" and wondered if it might be possible for certain "arrangements" to be made to fly us to Seville.

But what had the "alternative Pope" and Seville and the orange trees in the little squares there or any memorable feria in the bull ring for that matter which you might wish to recall got to do with Spain's rights – that is the rights of the fishermen. He brushed aside the "alternative Pope" as he would a fly from his nose. And Val and myself concluded that it was best to stick to fish. Out the window went any prospect of exclusive stories over our by-lines from Seville telling the Irish nation and the world what the "alternative Pope" thought about contraception, abortion and divorce and the English Mass as against the Latin version and maybe a viewpoint on the issue of celibacy and the clergy.

Donal Byrne was as funny about the "alternative Pope" as he was on the Navy man and the Wild Geese.

No wonder Madrid has a special place in my heart.

*   *   *

There were quite a number of trips to New York, mainly to cover sessions of the United Nations. These provided the opportunity of seeing outstanding performances of favourite plays of mine by Eugene O'Neill in off-Broadway theatres, like the *The Iceman Cometh, A Moon for the Misbegotten* and *Desire Under the Elms*. And I saw the late Jackie MacGowran, so brilliant an interpreter of Beckett, in a play about Gandhi, written by a lady from out of town. One of the New York critics who wielded a hatchet that could kill off a new work overnight, wrote that she should never have come to town, or rather that she should have seen to it that her play didn't hit Broadway. We gathered in Sardi's waiting for the reviews. The initial ones were not too bad but then after midnight came the key notices and we knew that the play was doomed. They closed it the next night. Nothing sadder than to be in Sardi's at a moment like that.

I had the good fortune to hear Joan Sutherland in *La Traviata* and I must say that a great night at the Metropolitan is a night to remember.

Val Dorgan and myself went along another evening to see the Yankees play. The baseball fans in New York, whether they follow the Mets or the Yankees are a law – and a breed – unto themselves, especially when they give "the bird" to some super-star in the million-dollar bracket as an earner who has got under their skin. "Go home ya bum", can be mild compared with some of the taunts and insults shouted from the stands. You wouldn't survive in that climate long if you hadn't a reasonably thick

111

skin.

Now China is the other side of the coin – in totality – from the skyscrapers of New York, the never-ending swish of its traffic and the hot-house pressure of day-to-day living in the ultimate in a winner-loser culture. Or rather the China I experienced in 1979 when I was one of the small band of media representatives who accompanied the first trade mission from Ireland to the People's Republic – and this vast country of 900 million people (by 1993 the population was being put at 1.2 billion) was still struggling to come out from under the yoke left by Chairman Mao of the *Little Red Book* and the horrors of the Cultural Revolution (which, incidentally, produced two classics, *Wild Swans* and *Life and Death in Shanghai*). And it was a country only then becoming aware of the consumer society of America and the West.

Fifteen years on from my eye-opening trip all would be changed, changed utterly. China was experiencing an economic boom that was breath-taking. Powerful ministries were being stripped of their monopolies in strategic industries and forced to compete in the market-place. Foreign investors were tripping over one another to get a piece of the action and were either buying out existing factories or getting directly involved. The Tiananmen Square massacre of '89 and the crushing of the pro-democracy movement looked as if it might bring a pause to China's sweep to becoming a 21st century powerhouse but nothing could halt the onward surge, the implications of which were awesome for a country that still had stark contrasts between traditional methods in the rural areas and modern technology.

Under the heading "Deng's Dollar Revolution" and pictures of a burger parlour and a chic Chinese girl getting out of a luxury car carrying a pekinese that could have cost over 10,000 dollars, Jon Swain was writing in the *Sunday Times* of how Deng Xiaoping, the ruthless pragmatist, had at 88 turned the world's largest nation upside down in a "socialist market" revolution. The new slogan was "money, money, money" with people prepared to go to any lengths to get rich. The egalitarian dream had died and with it the gulf between rich and poor was widening. One elderly Chinese, who grew up under Mao and remembered the idealism of the Revolution, complained to Swain: "In the past people were friendly, honest and pure. But now people are lazy, tricky and subtle, especially the young people. We were ready to die for the Revolution. But how can you die for a television set?".

But all that lay ahead in '79 when in one of my first reports from the Orient I described how the majority of Chinese lived on £20 a month and a bicycle, a radio and a record-player in that order were luxuries and there were no privately-owned cars. And when I walked the Bund, Shanghai's famed waterfront promenade and students heard me talking to colleagues in English, they swarmed around us as though we were creatures from another planet, staring at us and touching us and then asking how many cars and coloured television sets democracy had brought us (I'm afraid that some of them had concluded that democracy meant the freedom to buy all the consumer goods you wanted and I knew it was not the time or place to explain to them about complete freedom of speech and expression of thought).

*   *   *

It took weeks, indeed months, of negotiations before agreement was reached on six – and six only – from the Irish national media travelling with the trade mission to China. Apart from myself (representing the Independent Group), the others were: Maeve Kennedy *(Irish Times)*, John Wallace *(Irish Press)*, Donal Musgrave *(Cork Examiner)* and Dermot Mullane (the News Representative) and Jack Merriman (cameraman) from RTE. No soundman was permitted from the national television network.

Because no photographers were allowed either from the print media, the Editors of the dailies won permission from the RTE executives for Jack Merriman, who had started his journalistic career as a newspaper photographer (like his brother, the legendary Bill Merriman), to take shots that could be used with our stories and features.

The trade mission, led by Des O'Malley, then Minister for Industry, Commerce and Energy and comprising also Jim Godfrey, Deputy Secretary of the Department, Sean Condon, Chief Executive of Coras Trachtala (the Export Board) and Paddy McKernan, Counsellor of the Department of Foreign Affairs left Dublin Airport by Aer Lingus jet on the first leg of the journey on April 18, '79. From there we would fly by Chinese National Airlines to Peking (now Beijing).

I very nearly didn't make it. I went down with shingles. And when my doctor saw the red sports around the region of my waist, he said it was to hospital I should be going rather than heading for China. I explained to him that if I backed out, it was odds-on that the Independent Group would end up with no one covering the trip as the Chinese, with the tortoise-like slowness of their bureaucratic system, would never give agreement in time for a replacement to catch the flight out of Dublin. In a word, if I was out, the "Indo" was out.

He acknowledged my problem, stressing that there was only one thing for me to do and that was to stay in bed to the very last minute – until I was able to get around without suffering excruciating pain. The pain initially was the worst I have ever experienced in my life and Sheila had to help me in and out of bed.

Miraculously, I was fit enough to go out of doors the day before departure. But I still had a wrapping around my waist and I was applying the talc liberally at night to my spots. They had not vanished – though the danger that they might link up in the closed circle that tradition had it spelt instant death for the victim had vanished. My doctor advised me what I must do each evening before I went to bed. I knew then that I would be tending my spots rather than savouring the night life (if there was any!) of Peking and Shanghai.

The memory of the 25-hour flight is one of agony endured for the sake of recording for the readers of the *Irish Independent, Sunday Independent* and *Evening Herald* the forging of historic new links between Ireland and

113

China on the level of trade that would lead on to the opening of full diplomatic relations before the year was out.

In Peking when the others were going out for a drink, I had to pretend that the bears paws and soup made from ducks tongues or that Chinese delicacy, a nice little dish of dog meat hadn't exactly agreed with my stomach and I was happier to stay in. That meant changing my wrapping and applying my ointments. Embarrassing yes. A total embarrassment for a veteran of foreign arenas!

Then we hit Canton, where incidentally, cats and monkeys were made into dishes that were as palatable to the Chinese as snails and frogs are to the French in their cuisine. The city was enjoying a tropical-like climate at the time, with temperatures soaring into the 80s and higher. I suddenly became a new man. Off went my wrapping and I felt like Lazarus rising from his tomb. I was game for anything. The boys who couldn't get me out on the town in Peking and Shanghai now found themselves crawling into bed in the early hours of the morning and wondering what the hell had come over me. Let someone turn on a juke-box playing music that would have been deemed decadent and anti-revolutionary in the days of Mao and I was first on the dance floor. There I was swinging fat American ladies on interminable packages – taking in the Great Wall, the Ming Tombs, the Museum of the Revolution, the Garden of Ease of Mind and the Forbidden City and culminating in a dollar-spending spree in the Friendship Store in Canton – around the floor until they were gasping for breath. They were left to wonder who allowed this "crazy Irishman" loose in China and word was passed around discreetly that he must be avoided like the plague (or the shingles!).

Again all that lay ahead as I stoically endured with my journalistic colleagues and the members of the trade mission the food on the Chinese airliner now bringing us on the long haul from Zurich to Peking via Belgrade and Tehran. The food did nothing to ease my intense feelings of discomfort when the slightest turn in my seat made me wince with pain.

We had a very mundane chicken and rice dinner. When I woke from a fitful sleep, after dreaming for some strange reason of partaking of a magnificent Irish breakfast of bacon, egg and sausage with tea and toast, I found in front of me another dish of chicken and rice. You see, we had picked up in Belgrade a group of Communist workers, who were heading for an indoctrinisation "holiday" in the People's Republic and it happened to be dinner time (or was it lunch-time?) for them.

When we stopped at Tehran, I was struck by the notice at the Airport Bank proclaiming that it was closed because they were out of all the "forein money" (sic). Photos of the Shah had been replaced everywhere by those of the Ayatollah Khoemini.

Before we got off the plane, someone mentioned to me that if you were caught with a bottle of spirits, you could have your hand chopped off at the wrist by the Holy Man. I went to the toilet and flushed away with a heavy heart the bottle of whiskey I had purchased at the Duty Free Shop in Dublin Airport – just in case the Holy Man came on board on a quick inspection tour.

Sure enough, I saw the Holy Man with the chopper resting between his knees, before I got back on to the plane and again I was reminded that he had far, far more power than any Customs official ("You might get past Customs but you're a goner if you offend the Holy Man"). His scowl was enough to send a shiver down my spine.

*   *   *

Tony Ryan (later to become Dr Tony Ryan) was my travelling companion for the leg of the journey from Zurich to Peking. He had been a pupil of my old Alma Mater, Thurles C.B.S. and we found that we had a lot in common. Still only in his early forties at the time, he was playing for high stakes on this trip, hoping to lease Jumbo jets to the Chinese, thus helping to build the capacity of its national airline to meet the new tourist boom. He was also aiming to discuss the possibility of his Shannon-based company using its expertise to establish for the Chinese a light aircraft assembly plant for crop-spraying.

It didn't surprise me later when Tony Ryan with his dynamism became the pioneering force in establishing Ryanair which revolutionised the service that the public got between Ireland and Britain, in particular. The fares structure that had obtained when Aer Lingus dominated the scene on these routes changed overnight for the better. Today reality has become the norm where once one paid a ludicrously-high fare to fly to London and back.

One of the industrialists in the trade mission was prepared to make beet harvesters available to the Chinese at very competitive rates but they said "sorry"; they knew they should have them – and needed them badly – but it would mean putting hundreds out of work. Keeping people employed seemed to be a priority at that point in time.

Little wonder then that I saw ten men across the lawn of a hotel picking weeds at a snail-slow pace when one man with a machine could have completed the task in double-quick time.

Again all that was before Deng launched his "socialist market" and the catchphrase on every official's lips was "speed up the pace of reform".

As I type this chapter within a stone's throw of the seashore in Rosslare Strand in the glorious sun-drenched summer of '95, memories of the arrival in Peking and the overwhelming impact of first impressions of China come flooding back and so vividly is everything etched in the mind that it's really very difficult to believe that sixteen years have elapsed in the meantime.

I remember the endless cups of green tea at every negotiation session between Des O'Malley and the members of the Irish mission and their Chinese counterparts and the sucking sound the Chinese made that had your nerves tingling in a crowded room.

I remember the first big formal nine-course dinner in Peking's Great Hall of the People – crossing the vast expanse of the lobby where Mao had lain in state and then mounting the red-carpeted stairs to the banqueting chamber, with room for 1,000 guests seated, and the Chinese dignitaries

115

lined up bowing in greeting. I remember the endless toasts, the Chinese raising their glasses in "Gan Bei" (Cheers). The powerful local mao tai, very like schnapps and every bit as lethal, had one's legs feeling rubbery and one just prayed that the speeches that made the longest Lenten Pastoral seem short, would come to a sudden and abrupt halt.

I remember the staccato, totally monotonous way, in which the Vice-Chairman of the Revolutionary Committee of the Peoples Commune of Machao proudly reeled off the production figures – 27,000 head of pigs a year to the cities, 240,000 chickens and ducks and 100 milk cows and then he told us: "The commune members are paid on the principle of each according to his ability – each according to his labour. There is more for the people who work more".

I remember the castle-like dwellings dotting the country-side that once housed the rich landowners who treated the peasants like slaves and whose word could mean death or the chopping off of a limb for even minor misdemeanours. Because of lack of irrigation, they failed to cope with floods and there were frequent disasters. And due to lack of any proper medical service for the peasants, disease and death (with a frightening infant mortality rate) were taken for granted – as was the scourge of famine.

I remember that all the senior politicians we met, men who commanded positions of real power and influence in the party and the governmental structure, were old men, sons of the Revolution and heroes of the Long March (Bertie Ahern would be waiting a long time in this climate to make it to the top of the ladder!). The Minister for Foreign Trade, Li Chian who greeted Des O'Malley and the Irish trade mission on arrival, at Peking Airport, was 73, having joined the revolutionary movement back in 1920. He served in Russia and returned to a revolutionary base in China in 1939. The very fact that later he was made Head of the Chinese Broadcasting Authority showed that the Party wanted one they could completely trust in charge of the most influential arm of the media.

And also 73 was Vice-Premier Li Xiannien, the second most powerful figure in the Chinese Government. I was allowed with the rest of the Irish journalists to interview him. Initially our brief was that we would be permitted just two questions. But as it turned out, when the two questions had been put he took a few more. And then this elderly statesman stood up and chatted informally for some minutes with us and even posed for photographs. I could not but help wondering how many he had stepped on in making his way to the top and how many more he had consigned to the wilderness in the Party maze as he fought to retain his position. These senior statesmen didn't let go the reins of power very easily.

I remember most of all the bicycles. Everywhere we went in Peking we couldn't get away from them. But at the same time we were left rubbing our eyes in wonderment at the absence of the kind of traffic congestion that can make the centre of Dublin a living hell at rush hour.

In the great wide expanse of the Square of Heavenly Peace where 800,000 could gather for a rally, what traffic there was in 1979 – and it comprised mostly official cars – was lost in its vastness. You simply weren't aware of it.

As we came in from the Airport in our line of official cars, we saw the men and women cycling home from work or going to the evening eight-hour shifts. The women on bicycles which we would call mens' bicycles at home (women workers wore trousers, so there was total equality in the type of bicycle used). At the intersections you were struck immediately by the hundreds of cyclists waiting to go when the lights turned with them – or for the signal from the policeman on traffic duty. You realised that the plain bike was the king here rather than the car.

At midnight on our first night in Peking, as I came back with a few colleagues from the Post Office after we had filed our first dispatches home, it was all so quiet in the centre of the capital city. Only a few cyclists about. At that hour too, you saw the horse-drawn cars going to the market – none of the night life swish of cars that one took for granted in Dublin, especially around the Leeson Street disco belt.

At one formal dinner in the Great Hall of the People, I was sitting beside a Government official who would have had hundreds of civil servants under him. When it was all over and we had gone out into the night to take our chauffeur-driven limousines back to the residential compound where we were staying, I saw my friend of the dinner party get on his bicycle and head home, as if it was the most natural thing in the world for him to do. He hadn't exactly said before he left the table – "bring around my bicycle". But in the world that was China in those days, it was the bicycle to work and home again and the bus or train when you had to make a longer journey (then, of course, buses and trains are subsidised to the extent that they are relatively cheap).

* * *

Shanghai was another city of bicycles. It had no less than four million of them. This total had to be set against the background of a population of eleven million souls, five million of them living in the heart of the city with another six million in the greater city area (it had risen to 13 million by 1995).

If you think that dear old Dublin is so over-crowded nowadays that it's no longer heaven to have coffee at eleven and take a stroll down Stephen's Green, then I suggest that you get to Shanghai before you die and walk among the seething tide of pedestrians in Nanjing Road. This is congestion with a capital "C".

What hits you above all else is that the footpaths cannot contain all the people. I saw them crowd the streets in an ever-flowing, ever-moving solid mass and in between this tide the cyclists wended their way, fighting a constant battle with the pedestrians and taxis.

One morning I took a taxi down town and the experience, I knew, would remain with me for the rest of my life. Suddenly a cyclist would loom right in front of our path and I would put my hand involuntarily to my eyes and say silently to myself: "It's curtains for Mr Wong". But then the blare of the horn and a last-second swerve and before I could say a

117

prayer of thanks, another cyclist was cutting across an intersection. Eventually you gave up worrying, just held tight and wondered why there wasn't constant carnage.

But cars inevitably knock cyclists off their bicycles and cyclists in turn run into pedestrians and pedestrians, getting in the way of cyclists, cause them to fall in a city where space is at a premium. They think in inches in Shanghai where we think in yards. The cold statistics show that some 350 cyclists die in accidents every year.

When the rains come the poncho-clad cyclists, commuting to and from work, present a kaleidoscope of colour. By the early Nineties city planners were experimenting with bicycle-only streets but with the sheer volume of two-wheeled traffic, just walking the streets in the rain or in the sunshine could be a perilous adventure at the best of times and not one for the meek of heart.

In colonial times Shanghai was the glamour city of the Orient, famous for its sing-song girls and its 30,000 prostitutes. Szechuan Road, as it then was, used to be full of brothels, opium dens and gambling halls and visiting sailors were easy targets – and victims – of the vice kings. But when I arrived in the city in '79, these same brothels, opium dens and gambling halls had given way to bookstores with long queues of people – mainly young people – clamouring for new books, especially works that opened up for them new light and greater insights into the great world beyond China's borders.

The majestic historic buildings along the waterfront, a legacy of colonial days, have a timeless quality about them when viewed from the Huangpu River. But, sadly, as China moved into the mid-Nineties and experienced to the full the effects of the great Leap Forward, high-rise construction had become the norm with new apartment blocks sprouting like mushrooms above the Pundong Area, a 200-square-mile complex of industrial parks, foreign factories and housing developments. Here you touched the very heart of what *National Geographic* magazine writer, William S. Ellis described as "China's economic renaissance". Yes, Shanghai had come a long way from the city of the Twenties and Thirties when it was known as the "Paris of the Orient" or "The Whore of the Orient" and inspired the film in which Marlene Dietrich said ever so softly, "It took more than one man to change my name to Shanghai Lily".

I kept asking myself in '79 the question: Are they happy? Yes, I concluded, in the sense that their expectations were low as the expectations of the people of Ireland were in the Twenties, Thirties and Forties.

An a-la-carte menu and a wine list meant nothing to the average Mr Lu. He was unaware of a prawn cocktail or smoked salmon or lobster dishes or duck-à-l'orange. He ate his rice-based dishes at home and was quite content in "the small seas of his dreams" within the family circle.

He had a job, he had a bicycle and he had social security. For ordinary workers, pay in 1979 was the same for men and women – roughly £5 a week. And a person in one of the professions or highly-skilled crafts or art work got about £16 to maybe £20 a week.

How could anyone live on £5 a week or even £16 to £20? The Chinese had no tax to pay on their meagre incomes, health services were completely free in the cities and towns, electricity and heating bills were nominal, transport costs very low and with all property owned by the State, rents were not an intolerable burden.

In China a wife worked just the same as the husband – getting the same opportunities to reach the top in her job or profession. If the children were not yet going to school and the mother was working by day, there was no shortage of kindergartens and of nurseries where the children could be placed. The extended family system, where the parents and grandparents lived with or near couples, also eased the problems of looking after young children while the mother was at work in the city or out in the fields of the commune.

There were no set annual fortnightly holidays then, only a few days around New Year's Day and four days for the Spring Festival – the big holiday of the year.

A bus outing on Sunday to the Great Wall and a picnic with the wife and kids in the shadow of this timeless wonder could give as much joy as a holiday for any of us in Ireland on the Costa del Sol or the Canary Islands or the Caribbean.

Mr Lu takes his camera with him on the outing to the Great Wall – that was a luxury too in '79 – and takes family shots that he will cherish and he will return home in a crowded bus asking no questions as to why he can't afford a car.

It's all relative, you conclude, in the end. It revolves around the happiness and the joy that can be found with children or the happiness that young couples can discover in the first flowering of love, walking hand in hand in the Square of Heavenly Peace, in the Forbidden City or at the Great Wall.

A girl interpreter recalled for me in Shanghai her grandmother going to the Buddhist Temple to pray that somehow she would have rice for the next meal. Her grandmother did not go to the Temple any more when the rice was no longer scarce. That in itself showed the extent of the hunger.

The old people's eyes clouded over when you asked them through an interpreter to recall the "bad times". Because you were probing them to tell again of the acts that they preferred to forget – acts forced on them by the terrible gnawing hunger. Like having to give away a new baby because there was not enough rice to feed another mouth or, worse still, having to dispose of it in the river (many baby girls suffered this fate as the boys were kept) ...

In the China of today there is no hunger. Rigid birth control, with couples encouraged to have only one and not more than two children, keeps the population in check. The solution that Chairman Mao brought was eminently suitable for China and had provided a basic standard of living where there had been none. The old people who remembered the old days never wanted to go back to them. It was wrong for the outsider to

119

pass judgement on a system that was unique to that country. The great sores that repelled the society of the old China were gone – and the masses had a life.

The masses in China were brought up from childhood to conform – to work to targets in the factories and in the communes, to be content with the necessities and small luxuries and certainly not to think in terms of amassing a fortune. There was great pride of country, a tremendous sense of patriotism expressed in working for the country and society.

One of the finest officials I met was a young man who during the Cultural Revolution was banished from his college and found himself working behind a plough in a commune. The girl he was later to marry also was forced from her college and she too worked in a commune. It brought them closer to the soil, closer to the heart of the rural people.

He came back to finish his studies and got his degree.

He was worth far, far more with his qualifications than the very meagre salary he was getting. In Continental terms he was a £40,000-a-year professional – if not worth more in today's terms.

But he was proud to be working to build the new China, even though he was sharp enough to realise how far his country was behind the rest of the world.

*   *   *

The saddest aspect of the Communist system, as it operated in the China I visited, was that once you started life as a commune worker, it was almost ninety per cent certain that you would remain one for the rest of your working days.

And that meant in '79 working for an average wage of roughly £3 a week. Unless your son was a really brilliant child, he too would follow you into the commune. There was no freedom of choice for the parents and none for the children.

The sons and daughters of the peasants went to school until they were sixteen and then the really top ones got the opportunity of going away to college, leading on to a degree and the professional life. But the number who got the chance would be small compared with the total families comprising a commune or collective farm unit.

For example, Machao commune – one of the best in the area outside Shanghai – comprised 37,000 people or 9,300 families.

It was the absence of the freedom of choice you had in a democracy that made it all so different. In a way you were like a human robot, complying with targets and part of a production team. Ambition took the form of making you want to be the leader of a team, which would possibly give you more privileges than the ordinary member of the team. But, of course, corruption was also rife among the top officials in the Communist system. They had their perks – and guarded them – and they didn't worry that much about the lot of the commune workers, who had no hope of ever breaking out of the system.

It was an unforgettable sight to journey through the country-side and see the industry in the fields – men and women working together to the

120

THE FACE OF A GAMBLER... the late Jack (Treetop) Straus from San Antonio, Texas, who lived by the motto "Better one day as a lion than one hundred years as a lamb", is rated by the author one of the most fearless High Rollers and greatest characters he met covering the Las Vegas scene.

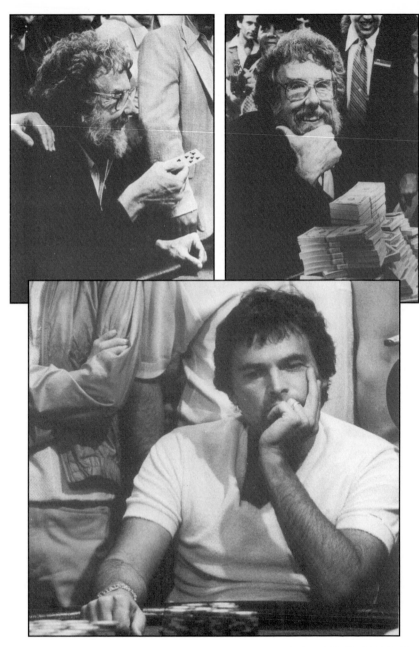

Straus savours the unforgettable moments after he had won the 1982 World Hold 'Em Poker Championship, first displaying the winning card and then posing behind the piles of greenbacks while Dewey Tomko is philosophical in defeat.

The colourful "Amarillo Slim" Preston, world champion in 1972, who went on record once to state "I will slit my throat if a lady ever takes the crown".

Jack Binion (left), who has maintained the high traditions set by his founding-father, Benny Binion (right) at Binion's Horseshoe Casino (centre), now completely modernised and refurbished and (bottom) Raymond Smith with Colette Doherty and Stu Ungar (winner) at the end of the 1980 World Championship.

Tom McEvoy, the 1983 world champion (top left) and Donnacha O'Dea (top right), son of Denis O'Dea and Siobhan McKenna, who has proved that he can compete with the best on the world stage and (below) three characters who add colour to the circuit in the States, Doddy Roach (left) with his distinctive suspenders, Buster Jackson, with equally-distinctive eye-shade and one of the most consistent of the old-timers, Gene Fisher, who would be lost without his Stetson.

GALLERY OF CHAMPIONS... (clockwise from top): Doyle "Texas Dolly" Brunson (1976-'77 world champion), Johnny Moss (1970-'71 & '74), Puggy Pearson (1973), Berry Johnston (1986), Bobby "The Owl" Baldwin (1978) and David "Chip" Reese, voted the best all-round player in the world by his peers.

Dubliner Noel Furlong (top left), who stood to win a cool £4 million in double bets had The Illiad taken the 1991 Champion Hurdle at Cheltenham, kept Ireland's flag flying when reaching the final table in the 1989 World Poker Championship losing out in a tremendous duel with Johnny Chan (right) the reigning title-holder, and (below) Texan Bill Smith shows his delight at winning the title in 1985.

The author taking part in the special Media Poker Tournament, which each year precedes the World Hold 'Em Poker Championship in Las Vegas. On this occasion he reached the final table.

background music from transistors beside them and with even jobs to do for the old (I saw one old man driving hundreds of ducks along a roadside).

You still had the sight of ploughs pulled by water-oxen contrasting with modern hydro-electric plants. And this was what made China then so fascinating for the visitor.

The Army was a people's army in every sense of the word. It totalled three million. They alternated between normal army duties and working in the fields beside the peasants. But then the majority of them were of peasant stock anyway.

I went into the homes of some of the commune workers and talked to them through an interpreter. The little houses were spotlessly clean. The women were very well dressed and seemed to me to be very happy. They took pride in the fact that they had such "luxuries" as radios and record-players and they did not seem to want for anything more.

The cynical may claim that we were only introduced to hand-picked commune workers and that they were hardly going to be critical of the system.

But again I must stress that you had to judge their lot against that of their parents and grandparents. There was no hunger. And the old fatalism about death by disease or flooding had been banished.

If the commune worker had to undergo an operation, the commune saw to it that he was sent to a city hospital for the best surgical treatment. When he died (if the family did not express a wish to have him buried in the normal manner), his remains were sent to the urban crematorium at the commune's expense to be cremated (cremation is encouraged because it cuts out the problem of opening new graves).

Yes, it was all highly organised – from the cradle to the grave.

Incidentally, I asked about the white objects on the hillsides – like handkerchiefs. I was told that these marked the places where people had been buried, especially believers who did not favour being cremated. Belief had lived on among many of the older people, even though under Chairman Mao there was no religious freedom.

It was very easy to contend that life in China was so terribly dull, especially for those in the communes and factories. The same around-the-clock routine – from work to bed and to work again, the sameness too in the smocks the men and women wore. We could not suffer this world because we had come to know another. Frankly, a person accustomed to life in Ireland or in Europe or the States could not move to China to live there on a permanent basis as you would miss too much.

And yet when I returned from that trip to China, Ireland was experiencing a major shortfall in petrol supplies. On the day that the Cabinet was expected to discuss rationing, I wrote a piece for the *Irish Independent* under the heading "Why Mr Wong Doesn't Rate The Oil Crisis".

I described how nobody queued for petrol in Peking and it wouldn't worry the ordinary Chinese if the petrol stations never opened. Because the ordinary Chinese didn't have a car.

Mr Wong and others like him were not yet in '79 the victims of the consumer society that we in Ireland had allowed ourselves to become.

Then I wrote (against the background of a long queue outside my front window in Mount Merrion winding its way a long way around to a petrol-filling station on the Stillorgan Road): "People protest about the lack of petrol in Ireland and stoically sit for hours now at filling stations hoping for a few gallons and one even hears of incidents at filling stations as tempers become frayed.

"I asked myself over the week-end, conscious of my Chinese experience, for what? If I had got the petrol, I would have headed with the family for the Wicklow hills or for the seaside. As it was, I was content to sit in the sun in the back garden and pity those tearing their hair in the queues.

"We have come to regard as essential what is not essential at all. Supposing the petrol ran out, could some of us buy a season bus ticket or take out the old bicycle and accept again the kind of life that is normal every-day living to the Chinese. Somehow I doubt it".

Gay Byrne took it up in his morning Radio programme. The thrust of his argument was: Had we allowed ourselves to become victims of the consumer society?

I wrote a series for the *Irish Independent* on my Chinese Experience and concluded thus: "What the future holds for China is anybody's guess. As the country modernises and television and foreign films give the people an insight into a world beyond their own frontiers, when they realise that there are consumer goods they cannot enjoy now, expectations will begin to rise. The tragedy would be if they mistook the consumer society for happiness. Are we happier now with our two cars and our holidays in the sun than our parents were with simple fare and a day out by the seaside?"

That was written before the boom days arrived under Mr Deng and the face of China was changed beyond comprehension.

*   *   *

Today Buddhists, Moslems and Christians are allowed to worship freely again, even if all religion remains under strict Communist control.

The epilogue to my China trip was the moment I put in a request in Shanghai to be brought on a visit to a Catholic church and be allowed talk to a practising priest (my reason for doing so was that some bishops and priests were still in prison because they had not "conformed", that is they still wanted to maintain the link with Rome when the Chinese authorities wanted only a Catholic Church under their heel).

All kinds of obstacles were placed in my path. Why did I want to meet a representative of a decadent form of worship that went out with the Revolution? Why was I pressing so hard to be allowed talk to a priest and visit a church?

The first official who got my request had to hand it on to a higher official. He in turn had to send it on to someone above him. There was a lot of shuffling, a lot of vagueness. "We may know tomorrow". Tomorrow came and then I was told: "It could be tomorrow". It seemed that all my tomorrows were going to lead me up a cul-de-sac.

Fortunately, I had an interpreter who was the very essence of intelligence and political savvy. I emphasised to him that unless my request was met, I was going to write a hard-hitting article when I got back home about the denial of religious freedom in the "new China". I told him that this would not be a good curtain-raiser to Mr Li Chian's visit to Ireland later that year (it appeared that it was being planned that he should reciprocate Des O'Malley's trip to the People's Republic by leading a return Chinese mission).

That did the trick. The interpreter conveyed my feelings to someone in the higher echelons who had the power to act – and act quickly.

I was picked up at my hotel next morning after breakfast and brought to a church which was opened each Sunday for Mass for members of the Diplomatic Corps. They opened it specially for me that day. The Chinese priest told me how one day in a road to Damascus-like experience he had suddenly got the vocation to join the Priesthood, leaving the job he had been working in. He was a man of unquestioned belief in an after-Life, whose philosophy was one of service.

I knew he was part of the "Chinese Church" and I knew it wasn't for me to ask if he had any hankering to ever visit Rome or meet the Pope. I knew also that it would spell the end of his vocation if he did not conform. But talking to him I didn't think of conformity. He was what he was – a priest, simple but saintly and totally dedicated.

He would probably go back to working in the garden when I was gone, after he had posed for photographs taken by Jack Merriman of the two of us together, both shaking hands. It was the first time he had ever been photographed by a professional photographer from abroad. I could not imagine any of the fat American ladies I had danced with to Elvis and those Blue Suede Shoes on the juke-box wanting to pose with him. They would not want to know. They would not understand because it was not part of the package.

He stood there in the Spring sunshine at the door of the gateway leading to the garden, waving to me as our chauffeur-driven car pulled away. A smile across his countenance.

Whatever happened to him, I wonder, when the tanks moved in on Tiananmen Square ten years later and the blossom of democracy was crushed.

Was he there to give succour to the dying – or did he just continue to conform?

10

"The Cock of the North Atlantic is no More"

O ver and back across the Atlantic she had gone with her pet cock, this millionaire Texan lady. They wouldn't let her bring the cock ashore when the luxury liner on which she was travelling first-class called at Cobh. Neither would they allow her to bring it ashore at Le Havre or Southampton. She wouldn't leave the liner without her cock. She was happy to eat her meals aboard. The cock, of course, got first-class treatment too.

Every morning he would crow at cock-crow. It happened with such monotonous regularity on the run between New York and Cobh, Le Havre and Southampton and back again to New York that this Italian cook found that it was getting to him in such a way that he would have to do something about it or go stark raving mad.

The final solution was that the cock had his head chopped off somewhere out of Cobh on a balmy morning at sea when it was cruel for a cock full of virility to be so summarily dispatched from this world. He was never seen or heard of again. The millionairess was inconsolable.

Larry Lyons, one of the most famous journalists to pass through the portals of the *Cork Examiner* and one of the truly great characters of the newspaper business that I came to know, picked up the story when he met the liner on its customary call. He filed the immortal intro to one of the English dailies: "The cock of the North Atlantic is no more ... but his spirit goes marching on".

His staff job with the *Examiner* provided the bread-and-butter for Larry. The cream came from working as a "stringer" for a number of the Fleet Street dailies, evenings and Sundays (they hadn't as yet moved out of the Street of Adventure). Larry wasn't the only member of the Newsroom staff who supplemented the weekly pay-packet in this way. Indeed, they had one phone that was set aside solely for the use of the "stringers".

In the era when the liner traffic was at its peak, in the fifties and sixties, and before jet travel really changed attitudes and modes irrevocably, Larry Lyons got to meet and interview many famous names including Rita

Hayworth, Prince Aly Khan, Jack Doyle, Brendan Behan and Eleanor Roosevelt.

Hitting Cobh from Cork after one of the liners had arrived at around 6 a.m., it was his practice to have a sumptuous breakfast in the dining-room on board – before he went scouting for stories. He was acknowledged as the doyen of the team covering this particular beat and young greenhorns who might be marked for it now and then, sat in awe at his feet.

"A legend in his own lifetime" is one of the most over-used and abused phrases used by journalists, especially when caught with a deadline to meet. But if it was ever true of any one person, it was true of Larry Lyons.

Incorrigible. Another over-used word and I'm afraid I have been guilty of abusing it myself from time to time. Again, however, Larry Lyons was not only incorrigible but impossible.

It never surprised his colleagues to see Larry writing notes on his shirt sleeve, the back of cigarette packs, even on the palm of his hand with a minute stub of pencil. But the end story, of course, was always entertaining and readable.

He was wont to drive up to a filling station and exclaim imperiously: "Fill her up". But, searching in his pockets, He would find only 5/- (old money) and then indicate that, on second thoughts, he would leave the topping up of the tank until he got to his own garage where he had an account. "Just the 5/- worth will suffice" he would inform the somewhat bewildered pump attendant.

On occasions he would run out of petrol altogether. A *Cork Examiner* colleague heading into the office for an early-morning shift – one maybe from the "stringer" stable – recognising Larry's car parked in some-out-of-the-way place would immediately conclude that he had happened on a major scoop. The lines would hum then as other "stringers" went in search of Larry.

The reality was, of course, that Larry would surface some hours later when the heat had abated after all the leads had ended up dead alleyways and he would be spotted discreetly pouring a can of petrol into the tank to enable him to get to the nearest garage.

Embarrassment wasn't in Larry's vocabulary when it came to those who were closest to him. Once he was in Dublin judging some contest and that meant a night in the Shelbourne with everything laid on by the organisers. I didn't hear from him that day. Or the next when, wearing his Larry Lamb hat (as television critic of the *Examiner*) he was wining and dining in the Montrose Hotel and staying there overnight. The third day he surfaced to call me.

"A bed is it you need, Larry?"

"Don't be so vulgar, my good man … the God of Friendship has asked me to visit my subjects and naturally you are No. 1 on the list", came his disarming response.

"We're low on the bed clothes", I told him.

"Don't worry about such inconsequential matters … friendship is all".

At that I was totally disarmed.

From the delights of the Shelbourne and the warmth of the Montrose, he descended to my bachelor flat in Raglan Road, immortalised by Paddy Kavanagh.

I still remember his two feet sticking out at the end of the bed (I think his toe-nails needed to be cut!) and over him I had put one sheet, one blanket (very thin), a raincoat, an overcoat and a pile of old *Sunday Independents*.

Joe Buck did better when he was put up by Ratso in *Midnight Cowboy!*

*   *   *

Mention Larry Lyons' name in the haunts in Dublin and Cork where media folk gather and the stories flow – and the laughter with them. Larry had an unique ability that enabled him to enter fully into the spirit of the occasion when we were recounting the legends he helped to create, even though he might pretend to be dismissive with the words: "Tut, tut, old man".

Like the time when a major shipping story was breaking and it was necessary that one of the *Cork Examiner* reporters work out the longitude and latitude for the following morning's paper (this was always considered essential on the paper as the Crosbie family were big into yachting and the Chairman, the late Tom Crosbie was a stickler for exactness in such instances).

Larry went into print with the necessary back-up data. The next day the booming voice of Tom Crosbie was heard demanding to know who was responsible for the "vital statistics". Proud of his work and already visualising a bonus, if not a pay-rise, Larry jumped up and announced to Tom Crosbie and the world that it was he who provided the longitude and latitude figures.

His deflation was sudden and complete when he was informed that he had planted the *Innisfallen* in the heart of County Tipperary!

The Cork show was an important marking in the purely domestic, insular sense for it meant columns of names of winners and runners-up and other prize-winners. And that meant more papers sold. For some reason that will never be known, Larry on being switched to this slog of a marking when one of those who had covered it year in, year out went down with the flu at the eleventh hour, got his hand on the wrong catalogue. It was the catalogue not for that particular year but for a previous year.

Next morning he was in the Newsroom when he was called by the girl at reception downstairs to tell him that there was an angry farmer wielding a blackthorn stick wanting to know how a Mister Lyons had him being best in one of the flower classes when he presented the prize bull at the show. "My dear girl, tell him that Lyons will be dismissed right away for his bloomer", was Larry's escape mechanism on that particular occasion. And with that he slipped out a back door in case the farmer should storm the barricades and make it to the Newsroom.

It was Larry who first informed *Examiner* readers that Pope John Paul II was coming to Ireland. "We all laughed at him but he was proved right",

126

said colleague Maureen Fox after his death.

Later when the Papal visit became a reality, Larry travelled to Rome with other journalists in order to accompany the Pope on his historic trip to this country.

At best Larry was disorganised, so it didn't surprise any of the party of media representatives that when he asked the Pope to bless a medal for him, he couldn't find it – so he produced a handful of coins instead!

One of his most famous sayings was "Who cares about the facts – give me the story".

I must have been following that dictum when I accompanied Paddy McCarthy and himself to Cobh on a story centring around a ship that had been wrecked at sea in a storm and a battle for the prize among those that went to the rescue. Larry loved the "split-the-village" angle, or a straight head-on conflict between warring parties. He knew that is what the English papers would go for rather than a dull, factual account, which they would have got already from the agencies.

I followed Larry, of course, while Paddy McCarthy was researching the facts for his *Irish Press* story. I ended up with a graphic intro that commenced: "With a forty-eight hours growth of beard …".

It petered off into nothing and I had to tell the copy-girl on the *Irish Independent* to hold on while I ran to Paddy McCarthy and asked him to fill me in quickly on what had exactly happened. As he duly obliged, I swore that in future I would be more circumspect following Larry like a lap-dog when he was on the scent of "an angle" and the *Irish Independent* wanted basically a straight story from me.

Larry loved colour. Loved nothing better than to sit at a typewriter and produce one of his very distinctive pieces, masterpieces of their genre, born of an interview with someone maybe in the film or theatrical world. He had the born newsman's gift of getting behind the people he interviewed, looking into their souls and making them reveal facets of their lives they had no intention of revealing when first he got talking to them. He often did his interviews with the minimum of notes and relied heavily on getting his subjects to relax.

He was never intimidated by the famous and he never forgot to drop their names casually into conversations. Maureen Fox recalled one famous aside as he was talking to some students: "After a champagne breakfast on the terrace of David Niven's mansion …".

The outsize cigars – did it matter whether they were Havana cigars or not? – became his badge as he went about his interviews and his work. There seemed to be ash everywhere all over his suit.

There was a period when he worked as Editor of the *Waterford News* which had been acquired by the *Examiner*. I called to see him one day when I was down that way.

He deliberately kept me waiting downstairs out of the pure fun of it. He got one of the girls in the front office to go out and get one of the largest cigars she could find but not to let me see it as she came back.

Eventually I was ushered up to his office – feeling in anything but a good mood – and found myself staring straight at his back. Suddenly he swivelled around in his chair, flipped some ash off his cigar and said: "And what can I do you for you, young man".

Then he broke into spontaneous laughter and, of course, realising that it was all a game, I could not but sit back and savour the moment.

He noted that when he left Cork to come to Waterford he had two suits and some money in the bank. Now he had one suit and an overdraft and those who didn't understand or appreciate that Editors in Ireland, whether on Provincial, daily, evening or Sunday papers commanded nothing like the salaries paid to Editors in Britain thought he was smiling all the way to the bank.

"If they only knew", said Larry, indicating that his shoes could do with new soles or rather he could do with a new pair of shoes.

Later over a drink I said to him: "Relatively speaking, I suppose we were better off when I started on *The Tipperary Star* in 1950 on £2 a week, giving £1 to my mother and you arrived in Cork from Mooncoin, County Kilkenny in 1945 to start your career".

He nodded. "But we didn't know life – and living – as we know it now".

*   *   *

I first really got to know him early in 1961. After returning from my first trip to the Congo, I was assigned to the Cork Office of the Independent Group as the district staff man (in fact, when I initially arrived in Dublin in May of that year it was to undergo training in the ways of a daily paper before moving to the Southern capital).

One night Larry Lyons told me that he was on his way to Passage West to gather material for a special article for *The Guardian* on Father Seamus O'Flynn. He suggested that I come along with him. I agreed as I was anxious to be introduced to the priest who had suddenly gained renown far beyond the confines of his parish after being featured by the BBC in the edition of "It happened to Me" televised in January, '61.

The 30-minute film showed Father O'Flynn taking a Shakespearean production class in The Loft – the school of drama and philosophy above the old sweet factory which he had founded more than thirty years earlier and which occupied a special place in the affections of Cork people, situated, as it was, at the base of Shandon steeple and resounding night and day to the chimes of its famous bells.

In the television documentary, Father O'Flynn demonstrated the techniques he used in curing one of his pupils of a stammer and this boy was later seen interpreting beautifully a Shakespearean role.

The programme created a sensation. A new spring had arrived for Father O'Flynn in the autumn years of his life. But death, the reaper, claimed him just one year later. In the brief twelve months until his death on January 18, 1992 – almost the first anniversary of his famous television appearance – he tirelessly devoted himself to helping the people who wrote to him in their hundreds asking him to cure them of stammers. The medium of television, with its mass appeal, had in one short half-hour spotlighted the work of a life-time – made him not merely a local personality but an international one.

When Larry and myself called to his house, we found him sitting in his famous old armchair in front of a blazing fire in the sittingroom replying to a letter from a Scottish housewife whose brother had a speech defect.

My eye was immediately caught by the big bundle of letters, divided into two piles – those already answered and those yet to be answered.

"It's so easy to show how stammers can be cured but so hard to put it in writing", he said with a sigh.

"But surely you cannot possibly answer all those letters", I said, almost aghast at the magnitude of the task facing a man of his years.

"People are in need of help and we must give it to them", was his simple reply.

And it was freely given. Any money enclosed was immediately sent back; also money sent for special prayers by people, even non-Catholics, who had been deeply moved by the television programme. They unburdened themselves to a priest whom they had never met but who had suddenly exerted a compelling influence on their lives.

There was one pound note which Father O'Flynn could not return, for all that was enclosed with it was a covering note that read simply: "From a black Ulster Protestant".

He confessed to me afterwards more than once that he cherished that note most of all and he carried it with him to his death-bed. Unconsciously, he had broken down the barriers that divide for "his business was with universal humanity and not with a fragment of it".

He gave renewed hope not only to those afflicted with speech impediments but to many who despaired of their lot. A young polio victim interviewed on BBC television said that life began anew for her the night she saw Father O'Flynn on the screen.

I do not know what inspired me to suggest to Father O'Flynn a series of articles for the *Sunday Independent* outlining his methods. Going down to Passage, I had no intention of taking on such a heavy task for, looking back on it now, more sweat and toil went into that series than into any I ever did in my Journalistic career. And yet in the end it was a labour of love.

The rain-swept road to Passage West that night provided something of a Road to Damascus experience. Father O'Flynn made such a deep and lasting impression upon me during that first meeting that I came away a disciple, intent on lifting from his shoulders, if I could, some of the burden of answering all those letters. For then he could refer those seeking advice to the newspaper series rather than try to reply to each letter individually.

The idea appealed to him greatly, as did the suggestion I made during a later meeting that the ideas in these articles be expanded in a book.

On the way back to Cork we talked, Larry and I, of the priest and his work and the inner force that drives men on unselfishly to give all in the service of others

*   *   *

Larry's *Guardian* article, written a few days after his return from Passage, added still further to Father O'Flynn's stature and was, incidentally, reprinted subsequently in two magazines while I included excerpts from it in my book *Father O'Flynn – The Well of Love.*

Even now at a distance of nearly thirty-five years it stands for me as one of the best pieces Larry Lyons ever wrote:

"Father O'Flynn was framed in the doorway: a barrel-chest man with a mane of white hair and the commanding presence instinctive in the actor.

"He began to talk. 'There is so little time left and so much to be done", he said. And the words began to flow. Slowly at first, then into a turbulent stream which whirled and eddied but flowed on and on. Words in full spate, sprawling all over the place, full of troubling truths, snaps and flashes of satire, with the actor's gift of interfusion of caricature and characterisation, flaying the fatuities of the the age. There was laughter and paradox – 'An actor never acts'.

"A priest who walks against the wind. And he was 80 last birthday. A rock of his Church with the exuberant rhythmic drive, his message was the doctrine of beauty which comes from the infinite love of the Supreme Being 'in transcendental rays of truth and beauty'. Amid all the angry lashing of decadence, the whipping of pseudo-art, the songs and the laughter, that was the recurring theme. Through the medium of Shakespeare could be found a deeper understanding of the Christian approach to life. Father O'Flynn wants everybody to know Shakespeare".

Then Larry went on to write about Father O'Flynn and his work, about his charity, of his weight-lifting feats in his younger days – he could lift two half-hundredweights over his head in each hand – and of his interpretation of King Lear, so haunting – because he had been Chaplain to the Cork Mental Hospital for a number of years and knew what madness really was – that the Church authorities asked him to stop playing the role.

I returned from Cork to Dublin and made my second trip to the Congo in '61 and the plan for the book had to be temporarily shelved. But always at the back of my mind was the memory of that first meeting with the kindly, white-haired priest in Passage West and the promise I had made him.

Then I was summoned to his bed-side as he lay dying in the North infirmary in Cork. It had been an urgent message that had reached me in Dublin. The end was near.

My thoughts were a whirl as I tip-toed down the corridor to his room. The table beside the bed was stacked with "get-well-soon" cards from the children of Passage and from pupils of the Loft. Messages of hope and love.

His face was much thinner now, his hands more wrinkled. But his eyes lit up as he recognised me and there was the old familiar firmness in his grasp.

The great mind was as clear as ever, though, the words came slowly where once they had flowed like a river in full spate.

"I wish I were up", he murmured as he thought of the pupils of The Loft getting ready for their production of *Macbeth*. At his request the Sunday morning rehearsals went on as usual during his illness.

He could still speak of his love of Shakespeare. Hamlet's soliloquy was his favourite passage. He had no need to ponder about the undiscovered country ... here, if ever, I was in the presence of a man at peace with himself and his God.

"Speak in similes", he often said, and he spoke in similes to the end. "If there is no Light there is no Life and no Love that moves the sun and stars ...".

His thoughts during that last meeting were mainly with those suffering from speech impediments. He was impelled with a deep intensity of spirit to use the last ounce of his ebbing strength to give a final message to sufferers. When I had recorded all he said and read it over slowly to him, a smile spread across his countenance and a look of complete resignation came into his eyes, as if he had now completed his task and there was nothing left to do.

It was a message of hope that he gave me that day, telling sufferers never to despair, for he was convinced that there was no speech impediment that could not be cured.

I promised him that the book would come out, though I had no agent, no publisher and no idea whatsoever at that moment when or how it would appear.

In his case I always felt later I was in some strange way but an instrument of the Divine. I went to Lourdes with a rugby team, including a number of Irish internationals. I remember dancing in "The Winger" on the Saturday night with a comely French maiden and, frankly, the thought that it was a pilgrimage I was making was the furthest thing in my mind.

I met a man on the plane into whom I would run on O'Connell Street by a chance-in-a-million two years later. He told me he had bought a printing works in Langrishe Place in Summerhill, Dublin, had established a publishing company called Little & McClean and was looking around for a book to publish. His name was James F. Walsh, a chemist from Roscrea, County Tipperary.

I told him about the book I had in mind on Father O'Flynn. He agreed there and then to publish. It came out in June, 1964 and was reprinted in September '64.

We formed the Father O'Flynn Society in Dublin, dedicated to the task of helping those with speech impediments. The primary aim was to have a College established in the capital for the training of speech therapists (those pursuing the profession were being forced to go to Britain to get their qualifications). We also acted as a lobby to ensure that on RTE television and radio programmes the practice was stopped of making people with speech impediments the butt of jokes. I remember I was part of a delegation that saw the Head of Programmes at the time and we were given a promise that everything would be done that could possibly be done to ensure that the sensitivities of stammerers would not be upset.

We got in touch with the Minister for Education, Donogh O'Malley and presented the case for a College of Speech Therapy. Swift action followed. I concluded that whatever his faults, Donogh could be relied upon to move when he realised that the cause demanded it and he certainly moved quickly in this instance.

So the torch that Father O'Flynn had lit was taken up and the work carried on by therapists trained in this country. Nora Dawson, an outstanding speech therapist, had been deeply involved in the Father O'Flynn society with us. Her advice on the course we should take proved invaluable.

She went to Greece and married there, dying at a tragically young age from cancer.

But I like to think that the finest monument to her unselfish contribution is what evolved in a better deal all round for sufferers from speech impediments and the fact that those in a position to give them professional treatment could be trained in their own country.

*   *   *

You covered everything as a district staff man for a Group of papers like the Independent Group, embracing, as we have seen, the *Irish Independent, Evening Herald* and *Sunday Independent*. The Independent Group had this special arrangement with the *Cork Examiner* whereby a member or members of its night journalistic staff ensured that there was the necessary coverage on any important news stories that broke late. This meant, of course, that I didn't have to go to bed worrying that my flank would not be covered during the night and into the early hours of the morning.

But there was a tacit reciprocal "understanding" stemming from that – an unwritten one.

You scooped the *Examiner* at your peril. If you were foolish enough to do so, a quiet word could be dropped in someone's ear and the night cover could be withdrawn temporarily and then you could find yourself deep in the mire. And if you tried to explain to Dublin that all you had done was produce a scoop for which they might already have lauded you, they would suddenly go very cold and tell you that it was for you to know the score by the Lee – and take it from there.

So the outcome was that while you didn't actually go on your knees and apologise in abject fashion, you conveyed it quite clearly to the powers-that-be in the *Examiner* that you had learned the error of your ways, that you would be a good boy in future and never again breach the "understanding". You were then accepted into the fold. You tipped off the *Examiner* whenever you got first beat on a hot story and, if it was a Sunday paper special, you quietly dropped a few pars to the *Evening Echo* that ensured that they could say "we had it" and, as no one on the Dublin Newsdesks saw the *Echo* on a Saturday evening, you had no cause for worry.

The pay-off was that if you wanted a quiet day out with the wife and kids by the seaside, you had no trouble in getting a "black" or the

132

necessary cover. Life went along merrily and you drifted along with it, not caring that much anymore. Meanwhile, "up in Dublin" the livewire young bloods, overflowing with enthusiasm and nose for a story, were wondering aloud why Smith seemed all washed up, why his time was past, why he never appeared to scoop the *Examiner*, why he had simply lost the edge and was ready to be consigned to the place where old elephants are left to wander in peace.

But the young bloods didn't understand that Cork is a Republic all its own and you operate there on its terms – that is if you wish to survive as the staff representative of one of the Dublin dailies, doing the district round.

Paddy McCarthy, the *Irish Press* district staffer and myself had long since learned to operate the reciprocal "understanding" with the *Examiner* (in fact, after replacing me as the Independent's Man in Cork when I moved back to Dublin, Paddy would in time become a member of the *Examiner* staff). He had this message displayed on the wall of his office: "WE MUST GET ORGANISED – TOMORROW". But that was typical of Paddy's sharp wit and gift of repartee. As a newsman he was red-hot and became completely turned-on when a big story broke. And with his American experience, he operated best on the plane when there were *real* stories to cover. He could quickly get bored otherwise.

We would go for coffee in the morning at eleven to Joe Kealys – Paddy, Larry, Steve Coughlan and myself and others of "the gang". Long sessions. Memorable sessions.

In the afternoon, as we waited for *The Echo* to hit the streets, Paddy and I would join Larry and Steve upstairs in Joe Dignam's pub on the corner within a stone's throw of Russells Bookshop. Tea and hot apple tart and cream and conversation ranging over a wide range of topics.

There was a lady's hairstylists beside Joe's place. The girls would come in during their break for tea or coffee. Very shapely girls. Not afraid to show plenty of leg.

Larry was never averse to a bit of leg – in a harmless way – though Eileen and himself had a marriage "made in heaven", as they say and, really, her spirit died the day he passed on.

"Down Fido", Paddy McCarthy would exclaim, as he spotted Larry's attention straying from the apple tart in front of him. "Tut, tut, old man", Larry would respond.

Then Paddy McCarthy would spin the yarn about this black guy in the States bidding a fond farewell to his mother before heading off for the Korean War. And she saying sadly: "Rastus, I've this awful burnin' sensation in my breast that you won't be back, that I won't be seein' you again."

"Ah, shucks, Ma don't be talkin' that way".

"Rastus the sensation is gettin' worse. I can't stick the burnin' in my breast".

"That's no burnin' sensation, Ma … that's your tits in the coffee".

When Paddy McCarthy hit a mood like that he was unstoppable. Now he is back in his *Irish Press* days in Dublin and recalling the legendary Limerick-born reporter, Maurice Liston, a larger than life character whom I once accompanied along with Dan Duffy of the *Irish Times* to an annual conference of the NUJ (Maurice was a founder-member of the Union in Ireland) in Blackpool and on the boat back I recall that Maurice was drinking whiskey out of a cup and telling me I had a future both as a journalist and a Union man. We of the younger school idolised him.

Maurice was a nervous passenger at the best of times and Paddy McCarthy recalled how one day he was heading with intrepid photographer, Duggie Duggan to a marking down the country. Duggie was pressing the accelerator somewhat to make time on the country road when Maurice shouted: "Mind the cow".

"I see no cow", said Duggie as he brought his foot down hard on the brake.

"One might jump out", came Maurice's classic response.

Then, of course, there was the one that has gained in the telling and retelling about Maurice making inquiries about a reported fire in a convent and managing to get the Reverend Mother on the other end of the line and being assured that everything was under control. Someone on the Newsdesk is still not too happy and presses Maurice if he has checked it out fully. "The Reverend Mother herself told me it wasn't worth a fuck", said an exasperated Maurice as he brought the curtain down firmly on any more annoying queries.

When Paddy McCarthy first arrived in the *Irish Press* Newsroom from the States, he happened – as luck or misfortune would have it – to find himself taking copy from an agricultural show from Maurice Liston. "Troubadour III" says Maurice in his rich Limerick accent as he gives the name of a prize bull. Paddy hasn't a clue as to what he is saying. "Come again", is all he can shout down the line. Maurice repeats the name of the bull as if the whole world and his mother should be acquainted with the name by now.

It's hopeless. Paddy can't understand Maurice and Maurice, in turn, cannot for the life of him accept that his dulcet tones are undistinguisable to a reporter accustomed for so long to cryptic American accents.

Maurice hangs up. The Newsdesk rescue the situation by quickly ringing him back and informing him that one of the girl copy-takers who knows every nuance of his voice, as she would a Russian from Siberia, has returned from her tea-break and is now ready to begin the task of recording the names of prize bulls and other winners of rosettes at a show that represented Maurice's kingdom for the day. And, believe me, his name was a by-word to the organisers of these events.

One day Maurice's wife rang up the office looking for him. Paddy McCarthy took the call. He puts his hand over the mouthpiece as he signals to Maurice that "herself" is on the line. "Tell her I'm down the country".

"You hardly expect me to believe that ... I can hear his voice ... it carries," was the frosty response Paddy got when he conveyed the message from his erstwhile colleague.

Old Ned Cannon (*Irish Independent*) and Tom Knightley (*Irish Press*) were the district men who had manned the fort before Paddy McCarthy and myself hit Cork. We would see them sometimes, after they had long retired, having a quiet afternoon drink in a corner and Larry Lyons would look at them and then at us and remark: "That's the way you'll both end up … two relics of ould decency … living with your memories".

He knew it was the fate that neither of us wanted.

Paddy McCarthy recalled accompanying Ned Cannon to West Cork when a press day had been arranged that entailed the spraying of crops from the air with a commodity that was supposed to be the answer to the farmers' prayers.

Cannon was a wonderful note-taker of the old school and took a perfect short-hand note of every blessed speech that was made by every single dignitary down to the last comma and full-stop. But the actual spraying of the crops was taking a long time to happen. Finally, Ned called over the guy who was in charge of press relations and made his point abundantly clear in very quick time: "When are they going to spray this shit from the air".

"My, my Mr Cannon … how can you be so rude".

"My, my okay … but I have to get back to Cork".

And with that he turned on his heel and headed back to Cork where in Paddy McCarthy's presence he went through his notes, swiftly turning the pages of his reporter's note-book one after the other.

"So much shit", he exclaimed as he put it aside and headed home.

The press relations man must have been wondering for a many a day afterwards where he went wrong to deserve that kind of fate.

*   *   *

Back from the tea and apple tart and the leggy girls who would have been "occasions of sin" to tell in confession had we still been going to confession, Paddy McCarthy and I, would rifle *The Echo*, for any stories we considered worth filing and, where necessary, make a few calls to get a new lead. But, stories that were "news" by the Lee were not always the same in the metropolis. You had to pick and choose. And sometimes we just filed "to show the flag" – to indicate to the Newsdesks that we were still alive and well and totally dedicated. There was too, I think, a certain sense of guilt that we were being paid to enjoy a camaraderie and comradeship that we knew somehow deep down could never be recaptured, as Scott Fitzgerald wrote of the South singing for him in carefree days of romance as it never sang again.

But stories did break that represented a call to arms and made us forget about our lazy tea-and-apple tart afternoons in Dignams. Like the day this girl was found brutally murdered in a lonely spot at the outskirts of the city. The *Irish Independent* had a great penchant then for highlighting the qualities in any female victim of rape or murder that indicated solid ties to Mother Church and all she held dear. I found myself writing that the girl in this instance was a daily communicant, that she wore the Brown

135

Scapular, that she did the Monthly Novena. I omitted nothing that was relevant to her saintly nature.

I'm afraid that by the time it came to the follow-up stories, further research revealed that I had gone over the top. But I had to let it ride. Anyway, I couldn't disabuse the "good nuns" in convents around the country who would have taken every word of my original story as the gospel. It was a strange old time, for, come to think of it, when I was in the Congo I would hardly write about a soldier or officer without saying that he had a brother or sister "serving on the African Mission". We always had to give the "holy angle" or felt that it was expected of us.

The *Sunday Independent* has come a long way from those days!

I was paid extra for all the specials I filed to the *Sunday Independent*.

I had formed a very good relationship with the Editor, Hector Legge and he expected me to deliver for him every week without fail. I'm afraid that my enthusiasm to keep a conveyor-belt like flow of specials to the *Sunday Independent* meant that at times the *Irish Independent* was left somewhat in the lurch.

Larry Lyons, Paddy McCarthy and myself went chasing a poltergeist in some out-of-the-way village. Slipping into the local pub like three sleuths. Trying to look nonchalant as every head turned our way, appraising us as if we were three Department inspectors out to catch those who were getting the farmers' dole without meeting in any way the necessary qualifications.

We were acting on reports that one poor farmer was experiencing a hell of a time with the delph flying off the dresser in the kitchen, the stool being knocked from under him as he milked the cows and the free-range eggs being spirited from under his wife's nose as she was in the process of collecting them.

"Strange things going on around here?", I venture to a man beside me who is half-way through his pint.

Looking straight ahead and not even giving me a sideways glance, he responded: "There might now and there might not".

We went in search of the local sergeant but he was away "on business" and the parish priest also but he was "on a call". We came away no more enlightened as to the reasons why a poltergeist should have surfaced like the Loch Ness monster in the locality.

We had gone up a cul-de-sac. The lesson was that when a village puts up the "Close Ranks" sign to the media, you are wasting your time looking for angles – unless it's a major story that merits real investigative reporting.

This was a long way from being in that category.

*   *   *

We travelled on the last train to Bantry – what an evening – when they closed the West Cork line.

And that had its own sequel. I went to Sherkin Island to do a *Sunday Independent* special on how the closure of the line had killed the rabbit trade. When they had the train, they knew, by linking up with the main-line train from Cork to Dublin, what time rabbits would get to the city. Now it was all different and they couldn't be certain if they would arrive fresh and still edible. The photographer who accompanied me took a shot of an islander walking into the setting sun with a pole over his shoulders and on it two dead rabbits, one on either side.

The *Sunday Independent* duly splashed it in the South edition. Next morning Paddy McCarthy was sitting in his office, his feet up on the desk as he read the papers when he was disturbed by the arrival of a Sherkin islander in the front office who made it clear that my report had seemed to insinuate that his family were surviving on rabbit-catching. But, no, his family were not rabbit-catchers but had links, going back a long way, with the Royal Navy and the head of everyone of them would be taken by this story in places that mattered to them.

Paddy didn't tell him that he was in the wrong office in the first place. He made an excuse that Smith was a junior, a cub reporter who wouldn't know a rabbit from a hare or a tortoise for that matter and really he should never have been let loose on Sherkin. Paddy promised personally to see to it that he was dismissed that very day. Your man left still huffing and puffing – "we were never rabbit catchers" – but satisfied that there would be retribution for the shame brought to his kith and kin.

Paddy, Larry and myself go on a story that also attracts one of the *Examiner* stringers who is working on this night for a foreign radio network. He comes up with the immortal opening sentence: "Tonight I saw the strangest ship on the ocean ...".

When the stringer arrives back at the *Examiner* and is heading up the stairs to the Newsroom to get his report across, he is met by one of the editorial executives who suggests that he might put first things first – "and remember the old *Examiner*".

"The old *Examiner* is entitled to f-all", is the dismissive missile fired on target with deadly effectiveness.

Our man goes into a phone booth and the stringers, who have not gone out on the story and have tight deadlines to meet for various papers, gather outside, note-books and biros at the ready.

Because of a problem at the other end, the sentence "Tonight I saw the strangest ship on the ocean" is repeated not just once but twice.

One of the boys sticks his head into the phone booth and says in all haste: "Christ, we have that already".

Like Terminator Mark One, the stringer delivers the withering riposte: "Depart from me ye parasites".

Meanwhile, Larry Lyons who is hammering away at the typewriter on a colour story for one of his Fleet Street outlets – a morning after piece which he will get over for the early editions of one of the evenings – is approached diffidently by the editorial executive who earlier had been left for dead on the stairs and asked would he ever remember "the old *Examiner*" in its hour of need.

Like a true professional, Larry leaves aside the colour piece momentarily and rallies to the flag of De Paper while in the phone booth over beyond, the stringer has at last got beyond "Tonight I saw ..." and has the boys outside taking shorthand notes at a furious pace.

The *Examiner* was quite unique before the market forces of arresting falling circulations and going tabloid with the *Echo* brought a new sense of reality. But it was still a "family paper" that placed a great store on loyalty and no one could ever accuse the Crosbie family of being "absentee landlords" so to speak (what nights we had with Donal Crosbie and later, Billy at the piano and I have always been happy at the thought that I was accepted into the family circle though working for a rival Group). There was a time when it was not unknown for mortgage payments to be met when a long-serving staff man fell ill or for other gestures of great generosity to be shown that made it an unique institution.

Larry Lyons was "Institute", meaning he was a member of the Institute of Journalists along with Steve Coughlan when Paddy McCarthy and myself were – to use Larry's phraseology – "NUJ types". That meant that Larry wore an Institute tie that put you above the plane of mere hacks and Union rabble-rousers in that era (later Larry and all the "Institute types" were more than happy that the NUJ fought and won for them wages and conditions that they could have looked in vain to the Institute to garner for them).

Larry Lyons brought Paddy McCarthy along one night as his guest to an Institute dinner in Cork. The devil in Paddy allowed his cynical wit to flow like the tide. Larry introduced Paddy to a Scottish delegate wearing a kilt. "And who might you represent?", Paddy inquired, somehow deducing that your man was not a professional journalist.

Larry nearly collapsed in embarrassment when the kilted one conveyed that he happened to be the local greengrocer in his particular area and an occasional stringer for a chain of small papers.

They sat down to dinner and the opening course was consommé. Along comes the waitress and asks: "Thick or thin, Mr Lyons?".

"Institute types, did you say, Larry?", remarked Paddy McCarthy ... and Larry could not refrain from bursting out laughing.

*   *   *

It's back to where we came in – to the liners.

Sean O'Brien, who was for twenty years Manager for Ireland of the United States Lines and who experienced at first hand the glory days, now lives in retirement in Cork but recalls vividly the impact made by Larry Lyons as the doyen of the "Cobh beat".

"I knew him simply as ''Scoop' Lyons", Sean told me. "The reason for that was that as I headed with Steve Coughlan and himself to meet one of the liners calling at Cobh, he would invariably ask: 'And what's going to be the scoop today, Sean?'.

"If there wasn't one handed to him on a plate, he had this amazing knack of conjuring one out of the air like a magician. Sometimes he would interview famous or newsworthy personalities on board. At other times he would talk to them on the tender as they were being brought ashore. He was razor-sharp in spotting an angle. And he could differentiate perfectly between what suited the *Cork Examiner* and what was ideal for export.

"As far as I was concerned, my job was to ensure that everything went off without a hitch but at the same time I loved the comradeship of Larry and Steve and the others who met the liners. It was a special time ... a time like no other. Only those of us who were close to it and part of it know how special it really was".

Yes, the liners of the United States line and the Cunard line.

Do the names ring a bell for you? the America (the first luxury liner after the War) ... the United States ... the Mauritania ... The New Amsterdam ... the Olympic.

One day I was in Cobh – when Brendan Behan came back from a barnstorming trip to the States. Cathal O'Shannon had arrived down from Dublin and we had a soiree that meant we didn't get to bed until the early hours of the morning. It seemed to me that I was up again before I had settled down properly between the sheets.

One of the stringers had demanded of Paddy McCarthy and myself that we ensure that he made it to the liner. When we called to his flat, he was out for the count. We pleaded with him to get up, shook his shoulders violently, twigged his nose and his ears, tickled his toes – but it was all to no avail. Finally, we dumped him on the floor, encircled in the bed clothes. He slept on.

He was looked after in the time-honoured fashion but when one of us told him later "you don't have to worry", he had the audacity to upbraid the carrier of the good tidings for cutting in on his ground.

It seemed that every media representative in Cork, supplemented by others from further afield, had hit Cobh for Behan's homecoming. For some reason or other, Tom Barker of the *Examiner* staff, a man we always associated with the courts, was there and someone thought up the idea of telling Behan that Tom was a martyr for the whiskey, when nothing could be further from the truth. When we had all assembled in the dining room, Behan entered waving a bottle of Paddy and exclaiming: "Where's Barker ... I want him to share this with me".

Poor Tom was utterly mortified.

After the main news conference was over, I had a quiet word with Brendan Behan and whatever he told me, I gave him a promise that he could check through my report later in Cork. He actually came into the *Irish Independent* office in Patrick Street (sadly, it's long gone in the interests of centralisation) and read what I had just telexed and, as far as I can recall, advised that I shouldn't bury myself too long in Cork but move on to broader pastures. We both adjourned to Kealys to join the others for what was a memorable afternoon.

*   *   *

Larry Lyons had drafted a sizeable portion of a planned book on the liner run before his death in September, 1989. A pity in a way that it wasn't completed and published.

But he had the pleasure of enjoying marked success with his book, *The Gay Future Affair*, launched by the Mercier Press in 1983. It told how

Larry's great friend, the Cork builder and racehorse owner, the late Tony Murphy was one of the central figures in the Cartmel coup on August Bank Holiday '74 that would have made a "killing" of more than £100,000 if every bet laid in Britain had been honoured. I chronicled the details also in my own book, *The High Rollers of The Turf.* I recounted how it has gone into the folklore of racing as a coup that can never again be repeated in all its machinations – down to the London police touring the Soho betting shops helping Tony Murphy as he tried to collect the winnings!

They opened 'The Gay Future Cocktail Bar' in the New Victoria Hotel in Cork in December '81 and Larry Lyons was there in the company of Tony Murphy. Other members of the Syndicate were there also with Niall Tobin, who starred in the brilliant documentary film, *Murphy's Stroke.* What a night!

The Gay Future colours worn by Timmy Jones as he powered to victory at Cartmel were on display in the bar and the boys were laughing uproariously as they recalled one Mr. T.A. Jones, as he prepared to mount Gay Future, trying to get into the saddle on one side and falling off the other. Some amateur! And all to fool the unsuspecting onlookers at the parade ring. And these same onlookers would have noticed that Gay Future was sweating up rather badly. The Lux soap flakes, liberally applied in the gathering ring prior to Gay Future being saddled, had done the job well!

Best of all Tim Finn had been given instructions that there must be no show of emotion as Gay Future left his field for dead. As it was, as Gay Future skipped over the last, Finn could not contain himself. He threw his cap in the air and rather upset the dear old lady beside him as he exclaimed: "You little beaut!".

Sheila and myself joined Larry Lyons for a long lunch in the Lord Edward in Dublin – a celebratory lunch just after *The Gay Future Affair* appeared.

Larry promised a repeat – an even bigger one – when next I arrived in Cork. As it happened, he was stripped for ready cash that particular day and I enjoyed instead the tea and apple-tart served up by Eileen – with Larry apologising that he would have to get something done about the arm-rest of the easy chair that kept falling off!

The man was incorrigible …

*   *   *

He had more than nine lives, it seemed to all of us, when it came to surviving heart attacks. I think that it was at a race meeting in England that he got his first. He was the staffer for the *Examiner* at the Olympic Games in Munich in 1972. No easy assignment as the emotions and the tension ran high following the horrific attack on the Israeli athletes. Larry became unwell but filed his copy before he went to hospital. He lived on the story for months afterwards.

There's an apocryphal story told that when he was hospitalised after another setback, his bed gave a view of the dogs being put into traps and Larry would signal his bet to a contact at the track. The sign on the door to

140

his room warned that Larry must not be disturbed under any circumstance. When they discovered what was happening, they quickly moved him to another room.

On another occasion when he was lucky to survive, Eileen told me that no visitors were being allowed – outside of herself and other family members. "I know that if he sees you, it will do him the world of good. Go and talk to him about old times".

There was no need for Eileen to press me. The doctor and the nurses understood. There was never any sense of time when I was in Larry's company. It was simply a case of picking up where we had left off. A friendship that transcended the barriers of time itself.

He loved the challenge of a bet whether it was on the horses or the dogs. After he had retired, they made available a special seat for him in the Ladbrokes office where he held court each day with a coterie of erstwhile punters like himself. All his life Larry had indulged in doubles and trebles and Yankees and these bets for a minimal outlay became his lifeline now in retirement. Sometimes he would bring a good one off and he would be on top of the world. You would see him going through the dockets, pulling them out of every pocket, ticking off the winners and scoring out the losers. It was an exercise in hope and despair but Larry got his kicks out of the masochism it provided. "You'll never need a whip". I cracked one day. "Tut, tut, old man", he laughed.

I got the call in Dublin when he passed on – not just one call but numerous calls from the Leeside from friends who knew I would take the first train south. I remembered how he had discussed with me whether he should go for a by-pass but both Eileen and himself knew that, with his history, the risks were too great. "Enjoy it while you can" – and he did.

Eileen's sense of humour had always matched Larry's. She understood him with his foibles and idiosyncrasies to a tee. She was his anchor in the impossibility of the disorganised world he lived in.

I remember a moment shared in the aftermath of the burial with Eileen and Eddie and Paula and the other five children. Eddie had followed Larry into journalism being attached to the *Echo,* and Larry was so proud that the link with the *Examiner* group was maintained.

Steve Coughlan, Paddy McCarthy and myself had our own private get-together. As it had been on the day we bade farewell to Julian de Kassel, the memories of the good times flowed in such a way that we laughed hour after hour away in a hostelry where Larry's spirit seemed to hover overhead. And we knew that Larry would want it that way. Steve has since joined Larry way up yonder.

Steve Coughlan had said to Maureen Fox for her tribute in the *Examiner* that Larry's passing meant the loss of "a journalist in the true sense".

It's all summed up in those six words.

Maureen Fox herself concluded her tribute thus: "No one will ever take the place of Larry Lyons".

141

11

When Old Nelson Took a Powder

Old Nelson took a powder in the early hours of the morning of Tuesday, March 8, 1966. When I listen to Ronnie Drew and The Dubliners on tape singing the evocative number, I think of the morning when I was sent out by the *Evening Herald* into O'Connell Street to garner the reaction of onlookers to the effect of the "necklace" of high explosives that demolished Dublin's most famous landmark.

All that remained of The Pillar was a ragged stump. I joined true-blue Dubliners straining at the Garda rope barriers and noted their spontaneous wit at the unseating of the hero of Trafalgar.

One enterprising reporter climbed what remained of The Pillar – for no charge this time. He discovered that there were only 93 steps now where previously there had been 168. "The Pillar vanished into nothingness a short distance beyond the 93rd step", he told readers of the *Herald*. But soon there would be no steps at all, nothing left of the great granite monument that had stood there since 1808 as City Hall revealed its plans to clear away the remnants of the column.

Millions had filed through the turnstiles to climb to the top in the days when Nelson looked down proudly from his high perch.

I recalled the occasion when a guy decided to commit suicide by jumping from the top, landing right in the middle of the lush table of fruit displayed by one of the vendors at the entrance to the 168 steps."You ould ee-jit, could you pick no spot but me luv'ly oranges to land on", said the Biddy Mulligan type who forgot momentarily to even whisper a prayer in the victim's ear.

So they enclosed it at the top to ensure that others wouldn't follow his example and cause the fruit vendors to bring claims against "the Corpo" for loss of earnings!

Dickie Rock's homecoming from Luxembourg after representing Ireland in the Eurovision Song Contest coincided with the blowing up of Nelson's Pillar. "Fans Rock Airport To Greet Dickie", read the heading in the *Evening Herald* – and such was the reception he received, though beaten out of first place by Austria's Udo Jurgens singing the romantically-haunting *Merci Cherie* that you would have been forgiven for thinking that he carried off the main prize.

"COME BACK TO STAY" read the placards carried by the excited fans who greeted him, echoing the title of the number he sang. The fans were shouting "We Want Dickie" as he walked across the tarmac and then he was hoisted up and carried shoulder-high the rest of the way, the Ballyfermot Boys' Band giving a rousing rendering of, yes, "Come Back To Stay".

"I must admit I had turned the blind eye on the old Admiral when he was 'alive', never honouring him with a visit", said Dickie afterwards. "He certainly got his own back on me on his deathbed by taking over the front pages and relegating me to the inside".

"But I can assure him that the Dickie Rock flagship is not that easily sunk", added the popular Dublin singer and entertainer.

The Hon. George Nelson, brother of the seventh holder of the title awarded to his ancestor, the Admiral, saw "nothing personal" in the destruction of The Pillar but the Hon. Mrs Charles Nelson (widow of Charles Lord Nelson who died two years previously), speaking from her home in Dun Laoghaire, thought it a "horrible thing" to destroy such a landmark. "This fine column was part of Dublin and if the cranks did not want Nelson atop of it, then they could have taken him down and put someone else there. But to destroy it for all time – I was shocked when I heard the news".

Had a poll been held among Dubliners that same evening, it would have come as no great surprise if they had voted that Dickie Rock replace Admiral Nelson. And I'm sure that Butch Moore, who had represented Ireland in the 1965 Eurovision Contest in Naples, finishing in sixth place, would also have polled extremely well. Brendan Bowyer might have come into the reckoning too.

America nurtured Elvis Presley, England The Beatles and Ireland was swept at the time by the phenomenon of the Showband Craze.

An English observer likened this thriving business to the leprechaun – "a purely native product".

A cult had grown up around the strumming guitars, beating drums and the distinctive sounds that made the fans go wild.

The "kings" of the business, the pop idols whose faces peered out at us from the pages of magazines and newspaper dance columns, were mobbed at functions or when they performed opening ceremonies. They earned big money and drove sleek cars that were the status-symbol of success in the business.

The showband scene just grew and grew. One of the most significant developments of all was the evolution of chains of big ballrooms – the Ballrooms of Romance – with a capacity of 2,500 and shrewdly located to draw the crowds from the big centres of population and from the surrounding rural areas.

The sweeping tide did not falter until the Government in 1966 slapped a ten per cent tax on gross takings at ballrooms. For the first time the ballroom managers experienced a sharp slump in attendances.

The Clipper Carlton Showband from Strabane started the rage. Impossible to forget the excitement that swept through the ballrooms wherever they played, especially when they beat out a Dixieland number. The sight of the dancers surging around the stage and wildly applauding Fergus O'Hanlon as he hugged the microphone and poured out the big numbers. "The Clippers Are Coming" was the cry of the day in every city and town. Led by ace trumpeter, Hugo Quinn they were 'tops".

The arrival of the Royal Showband in the late Fifties was a moment of historic significance. The unstoppable 'Royal' blazed a glory trail – a trail that others eagerly followed. The memory lingers to this day of the ecstatic fans screaming for Brendan Bowyer as he broke into *The Hucklebuck*, which, incidentally, sold 250,000 records or Tom Dunphy in *If I Didn't Have A Dime* or Charlie Matthews' No. 1. number *Somewhere My Love*. The Royal Showband (let's not forget bandleader, Michael Coppinger ... Jim Conlon, guitar ... Eddie Sullivan, trumpeter ... and Gerry Cullen, piano) had eight No. Ones in the Top Ten and they gave new meaning too, when they went on tours abroad, to old favourites like *The Croppy Boy, Galway Bay, Boolavogue* and *The Rose of Tralee*. How the exiles thrilled to them.

My own special memory is of an evening in Salthill, Galway in the Seapoint Ballroom during the Festival race meeting and the impact made by the number that I can only remember as *For She's Got Personality*. I walked out into the night and down the Prom under the stars with a Protestant girl from County Tyrone. All the world was young and sang to us in a way that there was no need to contemplate the building of bridges between divided communities. The eruption of violence in the North was still a long time away.

So they mushroomed and even spawned a book in 1966 titled *The Showband Stars* by my brother Gus with a Foreword by Eamonn Andrews, detailing the achievements of Joe McCarthy and the Dixies, big in the South initially but national in the image they forged for themselves ... the Miami and Dickie Rock ... the Drifters and Joe Dolan ... the Capitol and Butch Moore and Paddy Cole (whose virtuoso playing on the sax was still delighting the fans in '95) ... the Mighty Avons and Larry Cunningham (*Lovely Leitrim* and *Among The Wicklow Hills*) ... the Royal Blues and Doc Carroll ... Sean Dunphy and the Earl Gill Showband (later the Hoedowners) ... Donie Collins and his band.

There was a night in 1965 when Larry Cunningham and his Mighty Avons played with Mick Delahunty and his orchestra at the great charity ball, the 31st Le Bal des Petite Lits Blanc in the magnificent setting of Powerscourt. It was as if two worlds in Irish dancing history had been bridged.

Princess Grace and Prince Rainer of Monaco headed the distinguished and wealthy guest-list. They came from the Continent, from Britain and the United States to make this one of the biggest society balls in years. Yes, certainly it was a night to remember.

The Sixties was the decade of vitality, the decade of change and advancement not just on the economic front but in almost every field. Ireland caught the world-wide tide of growth. The unemployment and nightmare emigration of the Fifties suddenly became a bad memory as people reaped the benefits of industrial expansion. The building trade knew a new and sudden prosperity.

It seemed that the whole nation could go "walkin' tall" with Butch Moore down those streets in the rain. Only that somehow we didn't notice the rain when it fell. The sun seemed to be shining eternally in the Sixties.

It was the decade of the final rumbustious years of Brendan Behan, the decade of the Camelot days of the Kennedy Presidency in the States, of the excitement of John F. Kennedy's visit to Ireland and later the numbing shock of his assassination in Dallas; the decade of the advent of Telefís Éireann and of the arrival of Gay Byrne and the *Late, Late Show*; the decade of the internationalism of the Dublin Theatre Festival and of great nights at the opera in the Gaiety Theatre as there was still a substantial Italian Government subsidy to help bring some of the finest Italian voices for the Spring season. How I remember Ugo Benelli and the young Guiseppe de Stefano. And wonderful moments from *La Sonnambula, Norma, Nabucco* and *Lucia de Lammermour*. Hilton and Michael were still there serving art with total dedication beyond any thought of personal gain in The Gate.

It was the decade too of the boom in ballads, of Ronnie Drew and The Dubliners and the Clancy Brothers and Tommy Makem.

Even the poets knew a new dawn. And I remember Patrick Kavanagh strolling down Grafton Street, maybe coughing and spitting, and on into Bewley's. We had not discovered yet the true depth of the sweeping, epic grandeur of *The Great Hunger*. Later, of course, we would purchase in the Eblana bookshop at the top of Grafton Street a copy of the so-prized record of Kavanagh reading his own poems, glorying in *Come Dance With Kitty Stobling* and one of his finest of all, *Intimate Parnassus:*

> *It is not cold on the mountain, human women*
> *Fall like ripe fruit while mere men*
> *Are climbing out on the dangerous branches*
> *Of banking, insurance and shops; going*
> *To the theatre; becoming*
> *Acquainted with actors; unhappily*
> *Pretending to a knowledge of art.*
>
> *Poet, you have reason to be sympathetic –*
> *Count them the beautiful unbroken*
> *And then forget them*
> *As things aside from the main purpose*
> *Which is to be*
> *Passive, observing with a steady eye.*

The "in" eating places were the Russell Hotel, the Red Bank, Jammet's and the Royal Hibernian, so popular with Ulick O'Connor and Mary Lavin, who could be seen in the afternoon sitting in the lounge area chatting with friends.

The Leeson Street "Strip" was all in the future. The politicians had yet to discover their own favourite haunts like Frank Conway's Joys in Baggot Street and George's Bistro not far from the PDs Headquarters in South Frederick Street. A girl was happy after a film show if you brought her to the Kilimanjaro or The Paradiso (upstairs in The Paradiso with its grand piano provided that extra touch which invariably impressed!).

*   *   *

The Sixties was the decade of the "Young Tigers" – Charles J. Haughey, Donogh O'Malley and Brian Lenihan. It was the time when all was high promise and achievement for Haughey – before his personal Armageddon in the shape of the Arms Trial. It was the time when Lenihan and O'Malley, both made Parliamentary Secretaries after the General Election of 1961, formed a very close friendship with C.J. They had the panache and the flair that made him gravitate to them and they to him and the three became inseparable pals politically and socially. As Haughey himself would recall later – "we were know as 'The Three Musketeers' ".

Donogh O'Malley carried with him an air of swashbuckling bravura and he became a legend in his own lifetime. The stories that grew around his name could fill a book, like the night a Garda stopped his car going down a one-way street in Dublin and inquired if he had noticed the arrows and Donogh replied: "I haven't seen any Indians about!"

Or the famous moment when de Valera carpeted the head-strong young Minister whom "The Chief" personally had a great grá for and Donogh, with a mischievous gleam in his eye, said something to the effect: "I have been hearing a few stories about yourself also!"

Or again when the Russell Hotel was the regular haunt of the "Young Tigers" and the mohair-suited brigade, Donogh walked into the foyer leading a greyhound – yes, a greyhound. He called the Head Waiter and told him that this particular greyhound "must be fed today as well as I am, for we are planning to land a coup with him at Shelbourne Park on Saturday night".

They put up a screen around a corner of the dining room. A journalist from a prestigious American paper couldn't believe what his eyes were telling him and included it in the feature about Ireland, its people and its ways, which he wrote on his return to the States. Far from losing in image through having to serve lunch on the grand scale to a greyhound, the Russell gained customers from across the Atlantic who were compelled to visit the establishment that could be so accommodating to patrons of the four-legged kind!

When Donogh got the bill, he queried nothing but the £60 for what was taken from the sweet-trolley. "I never take sweet", he told the member of the Hotel staff in the politest tones he could muster. "But the greyhound nearly cleaned the trolley", came the response.

Donogh once confided to a friend that his long-term ambition – when he tired of the heat of the political "kitchen" – was to run for the Presidency and if he succeeded to "have a few greyhounds up in the Park". Imagine Mary Robinson out walking a string of greyhounds of a summer's morning!

Donogh had great friends in the media. They liked his style, his frankness, the sense of devilment in him, as later they identified with the easy, relaxed personalities of men like Brian Lenihan and Albert Reynolds who could always be trusted to engage in banter and "crack" and spin a "good one", in or out of power (like Albert, for example, recalling the shock he got when a taxi-man in Tangier asked him how the pubs were in Longford, rattling off the names, and he only regained his composure when the Arab told him that he had been an acrobat in Fosset's Circus and had become familiar with nearly every town in Ireland; or Brian Lenihan standing one New Year's day beside me as the Vietnam "boat people" were being entertained in his constituency and, after they had been presented with a cake they sang *Cockles and Mussels* for "The Minister", responding perfectly to their leader's commands and Brian could not refrain from remarking in an aside to me – "what a good Cumann secretary that chap would make!").

It was Donogh O'Malleys' practice when he returned to his constituency at week-ends to meet a group of journalists in the bar of the Brazen Head in Limerick every Saturday morning, including the Limerick-based representatives of the national papers. Donogh held court during these sessions and he seldom failed to "deliver" a story. And, like any born politician, he was able to use these sessions also as a sounding-board to get the journalists' response to national and local issues.

His impetuosity and his penchant for "bouncing" the Fianna Fáil Government into what seemed initially to be impossible and highly-embarrassing situations led, amazingly enough, to the most enlightened measure of all in the Sixties.

He was Minister for Education when during the week-end of September 10, 1966 he broke the story in Limerick that he would be introducing in the Dáil before the end of the year his plan for a free post-primary education scheme to be launched in 1967. And he did it without consulting the Minister for Finance, Jack Lynch, who wasn't at all happy when he got back from an engagement abroad to find that Donogh's announcement had got "splash" treatment under Noel Smith's by-line in the *Sunday Independent.* Anyone reading the report would naturally have concluded that O'Malley's Plan had the full blessing of the Taoiseach, Seán Lemass, and the entire Cabinet (it has never been fully established whether, in actual fact, O'Malley confided to Lemass beforehand that he intended "floating" the new plan in Limerick, though some of his Cabinet colleagues at the time were convinced he did).

It was a classic instance of cherishing all the children of the State equally and the introduction of a free school bus service in rural areas made Donogh O'Malley the white-haired member overnight of the Fianna Fáil Cabinet. He could do no wrong after that in the public eye – just as Dr. Noel Browne was forgiven much in his later career as a politician after the manner in which he had tackled the scourge of T.B. when Minister for Health in the Inter-Party Government. Of course, if Donogh O'Malley had many friends, he also made enemies – even bitter enemies in Limerick itself. Charles Haughey put this down to the fact that "a lot of people were jealous and resented his popularity, his way of doing things and the way he was inclined to sweep all before him".

In a way an era died when O'Malley fell victim to a heart attack while addressing a meeting in 1968. "For me to a large extent, the fun went out of politics the day Donogh died", said Charles Haughey. "When he was there, things were lively. He had a great sense of humour, larger than life and full of enthusiasm. Donogh was irresistible and impetuous and he had a great way of bouncing you into situations".

*   *   *

Sean Lemass had become leader of Fianna Fáil and Taoiseach in 1959 when de Valera retired at 77. It makes me almost weep when I think of Dev staying at the helm well beyond the point when he could be an effective and dynamic Taoiseach. His time was long past.

He had his hour during the Second World War when he ruled his Cabinet and the nation with an iron fist and showed no pity for 'subversives' who, he feared, might upset his policy of neutrality.

The Cabinet papers of the period from 1939-'43 reveal in startling light how Dev could operate on the high plains of preparing, on the one hand, for possible invasion and, at the next, not overlook some small matter of importance in his own Clare constituency on which votes could hinge for him in a General Election.

In November '39 we find the Cabinet discussing air raid precautions, including the provision of air-raid shelters and in December of the same year fixing the establishment of the Defence Forces – all ranks – at 29,000.

In April of 1940 we find a decision taken that the collection of dog licences will be strictly enforced with March 31st fixed as the latest date for payment in each year. Inside a month a substantial number of units of the Army were placed on a war footing and it was decided to procure right away 492 bren guns, 60 Bofors AA guns and 100,000 rounds of ammunition, 20,000 steel helmets and 100 field cookers. Civil servants were liable to be called up for Army service but the members of the Dáil and Seanad were exempted.

By September compulsory tillage was introduced with a guaranteed price for wheat and a special priority was placed on turf production.

Ten words in the Cabinet papers for July 2, 1940 showed that Dev would not be swayed where he believed that IRA men should pay the full penalty for their actions. "It was decided that the law must take its course" spelt out the fate of Tomas McCurtain, who had been sentenced to death by the Special Criminal Court on June 13, 1940.

The Cabinet declined to commute the death sentence on George Plant but Michael Walsh and Patrick Davern, instead of going to their deaths, were sentenced to penal servitude for life – so also was Thomas Hunt.

Yet the same Dev could in April '42, less than two months after displaying no pity for George Plant, oversee a Cabinet decision that allowed a Miss X to be readmitted to the Civil Service as a Post Office clerk Grade B in County Clare after she had decided to leave a convent.

It was on the personal recommendation of the Taoiseach that the Cabinet gave their unanimous approval to this course of action.

Dev's Government had in July, 1940 made plans for the evacuation of Dublin should the country be invaded and agreed on how the functions of government should be pursued outside of the capital city. It was agreed also that if Athlone Broadcasting Station should be of military advantage to an invader it would be destroyed "in order to prevent it falling into enemy hands". Powers were invoked also to restrict the entry of belligerent warships into Irish ports and anchorages.

When Jack Lynch with great courage began in Fianna Fáil the definition or re-definition of "Republicanism" and the taking of the "gun" once and for all out of the mythology that seemed to be inherent in the thinking of many of the "traditionalists", he was loath to pay homage to Rory O'Connor and the diehards with him like Liam Mellows who had taken over the Four Courts and created the situation initially where the Provisional Government was forced to act to show its authority – and Civil War inevitably followed. None of Jack Lynch's Ministers were sent to the commemorations at the graves of O'Connor and Mellows (at best some back-bench Deputy might go of his own volition).

Eamon de Valera in the maturity of years would always regret that he did not denounce Rory O'Connor there and then and ensure that the "political wing" held sway over those diehard elements who were prepared to plunge the nation into civil strife for the dream of the Republic (a lost dream as de Valera himself admitted when he brought Fianna Fáil into Dáil Éireann and accepted the hated Oath as an empty formula).

I am convinced that his ruthlessness against the "new" IRA in the years of the Emergency would have caused trouble in the streets if there had not been such stringent censorship of the newspapers and if the spotlight of television had been in vogue then as it was when Bobby Sands died on hunger strike in the North in 1981.

It was clear that de Valera would never again allow a challenge to the legitimate authority of the elected Government of the day.

Back in 1922 de Valera was weak and slow of decision at a crucial moment in Irish history. He failed to come to an "accommodation" with Collins and Griffith against the advocates of military dictatorship in the persons of Rory O'Connor, Liam Mellows and other Republican Army leaders, who seized the Four Courts as their headquarters on the night of April 15, '22. If de Valera at that point had thrown the full weight of his authority and undoubted statesmanship the right way to ensure that civil government held sway over the gunmen, the Civil War might have been prevented.

Even M. J. McManus in his sympathetic biography *Eamon de Valera* did not avoid the issue when he wrote that the question was asked at the time and has often been repeated since: "Why did not de Valera openly repudiate Rory O'Connor and his followers – who formed a G.H.Q. of their own, and occupied the Four Courts in Dublin and many other buildings?"

He may no longer have been leader (over the Republican military men) but he had not lost his influence in the nation and among the people as a whole and he could not overlook the fact that the Dáil had accepted the Treaty – even though that Treaty had not given full Irish freedom or his dream of a Republic.

That was the greatest tragedy of de Valera's career and it cannot be overlooked in any cold assessment of his life. It must be balanced against all that he achieved subsequently in the international sphere both at the League of Nations and in setting the State on a course of neutrality and maintaining it in face of all the odds during World War Two.

Jack Lynch, as Taoiseach, sent the Army to Béal na Bláth for the annual Michael Collins commemoration ceremony and the late Jerry Cronin, Cork North-East Deputy and later Euro parliamentarian for Munster, who was to become Minister for Defence in 1970 after Jim Gibbons, would always cherish a photo taken as he became the first Fianna Fáil Minister to lay a wreath on the grave of Collins.

Thus in a generous "ecumenical" gesture, Jack Lynch took Michael Collins out of the "Civil War sphere" and made him a hero to be admired as much by Fianna Fáil as by those who gave their allegiance to other Parties.

A hero to all the people and the nation.

*   *   *

After returning from Cork, where I had been the district staff man for almost a year for Independent Newspapers, I fitted back into the life of the Newsroom – Room 65 – and made the time to write my book on Father O'Flynn, titled *Father O'Flynn – The Well of Love*. And then on my return from my second trip to the Congo in 1961, I produced *The Fighting Irish in the Congo*, later to be re-issued in revised and up-dated form as *Under The Blue Flag*, covering not alone the involvement of the Irish Army with the United Nations peacekeeping units in the Congo but in Cyprus and the Lebanon.

In 1964 I left Independent House temporarily to research and write my histories of gaelic football and hurling, appearing in their initial editions as *Decades of Glory* and *The Football Immortals*. There would be a number of subsequent editions, the hurling book coming out as *The Clash of The Ash, The Hurling Immortals* and *The Greatest Hurlers of Our Time* while the football book was re-issued three times in up-dated form in 1971, '73 and 1983 and a further new edition was due to appear late in 1995.

Each history entailed a year's research – travelling the length and breadth of the country – and a year's writing. Four years in all. A back-breaking task, yes, but a labour of love.

Player-Wills, who were seeking to win a national image as Carrolls were setting out through their sponsorship of golf to build an international image, sponsored both books and later a film by Louis Marcus on Christy Ring.

Over a three-month period one summer I finished the final draft of *Decades of Glory* in Lahinch, which I came to love in a very special way. And much of the work on the final draft of *The Football Immortals* was done in winter on the Costa del Sol, which again holds its own corner in my heart and I have gone back there again and again to write or holiday in Marbella. I discovered Tenerife and the Canary Islands before they were overwhelmed by the hordes of package holiday-makers and the high-rise buildings and honky-tonk bars destroyed the uniqueness that once made them so appealing.

Hector Legge, Editor of the *Sunday Independent*, was always good to writers (he befriended Frank O'Connor for one) and he serialised extracts from both my hurling and football histories as they were being written and, again when they were completed, he bought the exclusive rights to both books. I was freelancing during all this time for the *Sunday Independent* and for the other Group papers, the *Irish Independent* and the *Evening Herald*. Thus, I was able to live the life of a full-time writer from 1964 to 1967 – not, let me stress, in any lavish fashion but I managed to survive. It is hard to believe it now but the serialisation of extracts from a book plus income from freelance work and sponsorship could nearly maintain you in Lahinch through a summer, or in Spain for much of the winter.

The Sixties and early Seventies represented an era in Dublin journalism when the scene was peopled by outstanding characters, whose like, I believe, will never surface again. Because they belonged to a period when everything was more carefree and less competitive, when, before the arrival of the computer age and the need to put your story over "on the tandy" or input it in the office, a colleague on a rival paper, who might be on "a bit of binge", could be slipped a black – or have the story with a different intro quietly sent to his office in his name. No one asked any questions as long as the copy duly arrived in time for publication and the co-operation and camaraderie was at a level that was unmatched.

I recall an outstanding journalist of the old school and a great NUJ man losing a tank at Fairyhouse races. The last he remembered before getting lost for a week was standing under the clock opposite Wynn's Hotel waiting for one of his favourite haunts to open. He was supposed to be part of the court team for that particular week (each paper provided its representative). His colleagues, knowing the score, did not let him down. I met him when he finally appeared out of the blue, unshaven and unkempt and he asked me if he was in trouble. I told him that his "copy" had arrived each day like clock-work and that he would be advised to stay away from the office until the Monday and stroll in nonchalantly carrying a rolled umbrella.

He took my advice and all was well that ended well.

12

"We'll Overwhelm Them With Our Indifference"

Kevin Collins was irrevocably linked with the *Irish Times,* though when it suited him he would move on – but always he would return to 'home' base.

The round of luncheons, cocktail parties and evening receptions appeared to be his natural habitat. He carried himself with such a sense of refined dignity that he made eager, bustling young Public Relations executives feel honoured with his presence. He had developed an approach and accommodation for these occasions, summed up in an ability to say nothing that was meaningful yet look the very personification of intelligence and erudition so that those leaning forward to catch the nuances of what he was propounding could only wonder where they had missed out in their education.

One afternoon he returned from a long, liquid, sumptuous lunch with a junior reporter in train who felt he had at last arrived in the big-time when given the opportunity to sit at the same table as Kevin.

The young man was surprised to notice that Kevin seemed to be in no haste to write anything. Indeed, after some time had elapsed, it began to dawn on him that the luncheon was going to be totally ignored. "But we have to show some kind of appreciation", he appealed.

"We'll overwhelm them with our indifference", came Kevin's immortal response.

Such was the affection felt for him by his colleagues right across the divide in the Dublin media and the respect for his wife, Pan (chief researcher on the *Late, Late Show*) that there was a tremendous turnout for the funeral service in St. Patrick's Cathedral. As Michael O'Toole recorded in his book, *More Kicks Than Pence,* Kevin had discussed with the Dean the final arrangements. As the coffin was borne down the long nave, many an eye among the hardened media folk present became moist as the organ played, and the choir took up, *Abide With Me.*

There was style in his going as there had been style always in the way he presented himself. And we were happy to think that day in St. Patrick's that Kevin had never, as in Kavanagh's line, heard, "the hysterical

Then Taoiseach (Irish Prime Minister), Jack Lynch chatting with the author on the day in Brussels in 1972 when he signed the EEC Treaty of Accession for Ireland with Foreign Minister, Dr.P.J. Hillery and (inset) Jack Lynch on the occasion he launched Smith's history of gaelic football, *The Football Immortals*. Also pictured Alan Buttenshaw, then Managing Director of Player-Wills, the sponsors of the book.

Dr.P.J. Hillery with Val Dorgan of the *Cork Examiner* (left) and the author in Tromso during a visit to Norway and (below) he gives a news conference on his arrival at Oslo Airport.

The Berlaymont Building (European Commission Headquarters) in Brussels with (on left) Dr.P.J. Hillery taking time off to relax on the golf course. Below (left) former Commissioner, Richard Burke with the author and (right) Peter Sutherland with the Pope.

Jacques Chirac (today President of France), speaking in Cork in 1979 as Fianna Fail launched their campaign for the first direct elections to the European Parliament, and made the famous *faux pax* that created headlines at the time and (below) Brian Lenihan who sought bravely to pour oil on troubled waters pictured at an Association of European Journalists function in the Killiney Court Hotel with on left Andrew Sheppard (President at European level) and the group of Elm Park Golf Club members, who provided a memorable evening's entertainment: John Dunne, Terry Nicholl (with bodhran), Maurice Rafter, Ciaran Kenny and Harry Cummins (with guitars).

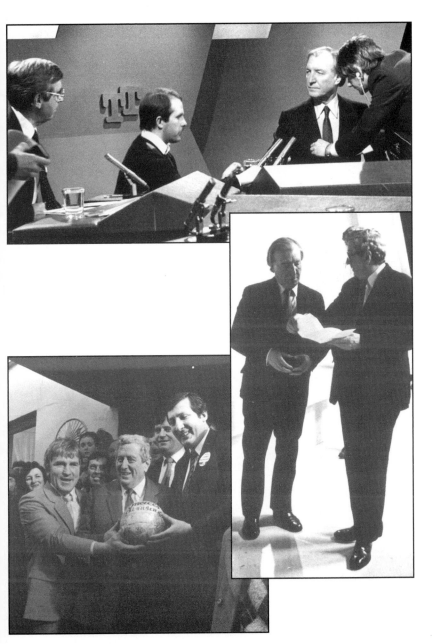

Charles J, Haughey prepares to face Dr Garret FitzGerald in a television head-to-head, with Brian Farrell on left and (right) Haughey has a word with FitzGerald before they both face the cameras and (below), after being well schooled in the traditions of the Green and Gold, Garret is presented by Jimmy Deenihan, Captain of Kerry's 1981 four-in-a-row team, with the ball used in the final. Deenihan is today a Dail Deputy for Kerry North.

CAUGHT IN THE ACT... media representatives line up (without knowing the cameras are on them!) for Dr. Fitzgerald's autograph on the evening of the launching in Buswell's Hotel of Raymond Smith's book, *Garret-The Enigma* and (below) Hugh O'Flaherty, now a Supreme Court Judge and his wife, Kay and Brendan Walsh, the well-known Dublin solicitor share a joke with Garret and the author at the launching reception.

David Andrews T.D., Ben Briscoe T.D., Senator Mick Lanigan and Jim Tunney T.D. with the author at the launching in Buswell's Hotel of *Charles J. Haughey-The Survivor* and (below) one of the keenest racing enthusiasts in the Fianna Fail Party, Charlie McCreevy T.D. recalls some coups he was involved in himself at the reception to launch *The High Rollers of The Turf* in the Burlington Hotel while former Taoiseach, Albert Reynolds, another great lover of the racing scene, has a word for one of the fruit vendors on Budweiser Irish Derby Day at the Curragh.

Members of the first Irish trade mission to China with media representatives, who covered the trip, after walking the Great Wall on a mist shrouded morning. Maeve Kennedy, *Irish Times* (centre picture), Raymond Smith, *Irish Independent* - Donal Musgrave, *Cork Examiner* (fourth in) are pictured left while the late John Wallace, *Irish Press* and Dermot Mullane (dark glasses) of RTE are just behind Des O'Malley towards right of picture. Inset (top left) the author in Peking beside one of the limousines laid on for the visitors and (top right) Des O'Malley, who led the trade mission, being greeted on arrival at Peking Airport, while (bottom) he talks business with one of China's top leaders over interminable cups of green tea.

laughter of the defeated".

Another notable and beloved character was Sean Lynch, who bore the affectionate middle-name "The Lip" because of the extraordinary stories he told in the gatherings of journalists. It always seemed to me that journalism in general or his role as Defence Correspondent in particular – simply could not contain the limitless horizons of his imagination.

Michael O'Toole remembered him in *More Kicks Than Pence* "flashing his cuffs in the Silver Swan as he told us about sorties he had flown in the Vietnam he had never seen". I remember him recounting how he was in a jumbo coming into San Francisco when the pilot got a heart attack and, responding to a desperate appeal over the intercom, he took over the controls and landed the plane safely.

Then there was the day I happened to take the Aer Lingus plane home to Dublin from Brussels. One of the last passengers aboard was Fergie O'Callaghan of the *Cork Examiner*, who as he sat down beside me kept mopping his brow, repeating aloud to himself: "That man, Lynch ... my God".

"Something the matter?", I enquired.

"Something the matter", he responded. "I count myself lucky to be here".

He went on to recount how they were on this American nuclear ship in the Mediterranean and at some point Sean Lynch suggested to one of the top U.S. Army experts that he point the nuclear warhead in the direction of Moscow. The guy duly obliged, so insistent was Sean. "I had this awful feeling for an instant that Sean was going to press the button to set off the Third World War and that a Soviet missile would blow the lot of us on that ship into eternity", said Fergie.

As he mopped his brow again, I pressed the button above my head and when the hostess appeared, I told her to bring us a couple of brandies – large and straight.

Again such was the great sense of loss and sadness permeating the world of Dublin journalism when Sean Lynch died from cancer at a tragically-young age that the funeral tribute showed the deep bonds binding the true professionals of the game, even though in the day-to-day round they might scoop each other on stories as part of the intense battle to boost circulations.

I must admit I didn't get home at all the night of the removal of the remains but exchanged stories with fellow-colleagues into the early hours. We saw the dawn come up over Dublin Bay – a dawn tinged with nostalgia – and it continued on after we had bade our last farewells at the graveside. We thought of him up there asking St. Peter to overlook the time he came in Robert Duval-style, complete with cowboy hat at a hawkish angle in a gunship with guns blazing and wiped out a Vietcong unit and an entire village with them plus the running, squealing, terrified pigs. No doubt Peter waved him through the Pearly Gates and Heaven is a better place now for Sean's arrival – and his stream of stories.

*   *   *

When I hit the Independent Newsroom first in 1960 it was peopled by reporters like Ned Murphy (Courts), Jim Brennan (Labour) and Maurice Hickey (Dáil) who had the total respect of the younger school like myself. For they had seen it all and more.

Later Jimmy Cantwell would make his mark as a crime reporter with great contacts. His opposite number in Burgh Quay was Sean Cryan, (brother of Tom), an outstanding character in his own right. "I'm off" Sean would tell the Newsdesk as he donned his hat – and every aspiring junior envied him for his knowledge of his particular beat and the scoops he landed.

Jimmy Cantwell would head off to lunch with Bill Shine, who in time would occupy the position of Group News Editor. If they did not wish to be delayed by the swish of traffic, Jimmy would shout at the Garda doing point duty at O'Connell Bridge, a fixture in himself: "Peter ... Peter".

And Peter, knowing Jimmy's distinctive voice, would stop the traffic with one wave of his hand.

Bill Shine, on returning to the Newsroom, basking in the after-glow of a mixture of shorts to begin with, then wine, followed by Irish coffees and ultimately pints, would get a call to the effect that there was a woman hanging out a window in Ballyfermot in danger of lunging to her death, having tried to rescue a cat and its kittens from a ledge. Spotting me at the Foreign Desk, he would ask me to take a taxi and get out there as quickly as possible. I would indicate in pained fashion that to cover a story about a woman hanging out a window in Ballyfermot was beneath any self-respecting EEC and Diplomatic Correspondent and that he might get a junior to do so.

Then Shine would throw his arms to the heavens and exclaim for everyone to hear: "He'll go to the Congo, to Brussels or China but he won't go to Ballyfermot ..."

And the entire Newsroom would split its collective side laughing.

On another occasion one of the reporters was in Derry at the height of the violence and some early-morning story broke across the Border that Shine wanted covered at short notice for the *Evening Herald*. This reporter had had little or no sleep and didn't think the story in question merited him pulling up camp. He tried to argue and reason with Bill, who finally in his exasperation, shot back: "When I'm sending a man to the moon, you won't be asked".

It was the era when Liam McGabhann and Liam Robinson, Seamus Brady, Jack Kenneally and Jim King were blazing a trail as the Irish Representatives for Fleet Street papers. With their cryptic, straight-from-the-shoulder style of reporting, they soon began to wipe away the cobwebs that for so long had hindered progress towards the adoption of modern-day norms in the Dublin dailies. For example, instead of saying that the Government was bringing in a Bill – listing its formal title in full – these men would go straight to the heart of the matter and announce to their readers that the Government was planning a free education programme or free travel for pensioners. The heavy baggage and civil-service-type language was eliminated in the cause of total simplicity.

Liam Robinson wrote beautifully when the occasion demanded in the *Sunday Express* while of all the journalists I have known, none had a greater social conscience than Liam McGabhann. Another fine writer was Tommy Kilfeather on the *Sunday Independent*.

*   *   *

The *Irish Times* in the Sixties at last began to emerge from the straight-jacket that had bound it in the Fifties and had hindered its progress to becoming a paper that could be bought by people who identified with things 'national' – in the broadest sense of the word. The old Protestant tag that had bedevilled it for so long was also eliminated, though it would continue to watch over the interests of this 'constituency'.

The era of Bertie Smyllie or 'The Editor' as he was known in Dublin (so well chronicled by Tony Gray in his book, *Mr Smyllie, Sir*) was over. So also that of his successor, Alec Newman of the brilliant mind and beautifully-modulated tones which we became so accustomed to on RTE Radio. Alan Montgomery – "Monty" to all his newspaper colleagues in Dublin – had established his reputation as News Editor and now as we entered the Sixties he began as Editor what might be described as the Great Leap Forward with an innovative approach.

However, the real tide of dramatic change swept over the *Irish Times,* when Douglas Gageby, founder Editor of the *Irish Press*, took over at the helm towards the end of 1963. Waterford-born Donal Foley, who had returned to Ireland from the London office, was appointed News Editor and, as Hugh Oram pointed out in his work *Paper Tigers*, "the two unleashed a creative volcano rarely seen before in the history of Irish newspapers".

Wesley Boyd, then the diplomatic Correspondent for the paper and later Head of News at RTE, summed up Donal Foley's impact when he told Hugh Oram: "He made people on the paper feel that journalism was a worthy thing to be in, that it should be associated with the everyday life of the country, that it should hold the life of the country up to the public and investigate it, examine it, tease it out and in his own column *Man Bites Dog*, make fun of it. It became a much more lively paper, but it is only fair to say that newspapers generally were evolving in that direction".

Donal Foley, as a lover of hurling and one for whom Munster Hurling Final Day had a place in Irish life that Flann O'Brien (Myles na Gopaleen) could never have understood, as he held court in the Pearl Bar, was the ideal General working hand-in-hand with former Army man, Field Marshal Gageby. It wasn't hurling alone that stirred Donal. It was Gaelic culture in the finest sense.

Donal was principally responsible for the policy of recruiting women journalists at a time when many 'markings' were seen to be the domain of male journalists. Yes, women writers could write about, fashion shows, babies' nappies and such matters but leave the big stories to the men.

Donal Foley wanted women journalists who had the ability and the drive to work side-by-side with their male counterparts – with no

155

apologies to anyone. Thus Mary Maher joined the paper and also Maeve Binchy, Mary Cummins, Nell McCafferty, Elgy Gillespie and later Ella Shanahan and Geraldine Kennedy.

Over on the *Irish Press* Mary Kenny as Features Editor, was breaking all the barriers. She was right in the van of the Women's Lib movement, "outrageous, completely and utterly outrageous", as Cathal O'Shannon put it so aptly to Hugh Oram.

She wore short mini-skirts at a time when any adventurous male reporter on the *Irish Independent* could be told politely not to wear a red shirt but a white one. And she posed for the photographer's camera with a plunging neck-line beneath the distinctive hat and the perennial pipe.

Later when she was European Correspondent of the *Evening Standard,* I remember her arriving at a reception in Brussels one evening sporting an "I Am For Free Love" button obviously to shock the staid diplomats. I smile today when I reflect back on that evening and note the sea-change that has occurred in her case as she raises the standard high in her articles to Right morals and Right thinking. Yes, Cathal O'Shannon is right – "She is completely turned around, almost like a Reverend Mother herself".

Gageby's editorship of the *Irish Times* will always be linked with other renowned names like those of columnist Seamus Kelly ("An Irishman's Diary"), who created his own special niche by getting a part in *Moby Dick,* and poet and critic, Bruce Williamson. Also, of course, Cathal O'Shannon, who was with me in the Congo and who had journalism in every vein and delighted in the get-togethers of those who were so hooked on it that they couldn't change for anything else (even though after moving on, first to RTE, he later became Public Relations Officer with Alcan but I always saw him essentially as a born newsman).

It was an inspired move by Gageby when he gave his head to John Healy, who will always be associated with the first of the really-informed political "insider columns". But then at the outset Healy had the contacts that enabled him to break a lot of good stories. And he had a penchant for coming up with the catchy phrase like dubbing the spin doctors of Dr Garret FitzGerald's first Coalition Government, "the National Handlers".

Later on his admiration for Charles J. Haughey may have coloured his writing in the political sphere but he never lost his passion for the West or the deprived areas. I came to know him as a good friend and fellow Committee-member of the Irish Section of the Association of European Journalists. He was the driving force behind a highly-successful gathering, involving all the sections on the European plane, in Ashford Castle. Naturally the theme hinged around the subject that was nearest to his heart, the peripheral regions of the Community.

When Gageby eventually retired in December, 1986 and Conor Brady assumed the editorship, the ship was well on course with its own established sale which has increased further under Conor's stewardship and with no financial worries clouding the sky. In time Conor O'Clery would move from Moscow on the establishment of a bureau in Washington.

There was more colour and more supplements. If there had been a period when the *Irish Times* was satisfied with P. D. Mehigan's report of the main hurling or football match of the day, it now sought to match its rivals in reports from the training camps in the count-down to All-Ireland finals and in dressing-room comments and with extensive use of colour.

But I have always felt that it lagged behind the *Irish Independent* in the sphere of hard news. It was almost a case of "if it's not in the *Times*, it's not worth reporting" or was it a case of the faithful core of readers being happy to 'take the Times' and not worry if they were missing out on a lot of good stories. A certain elitism perhaps!

In my days in the Independent Newsroom, we turned in scoop after scoop but no one seemed to bother that much about it over in Westmoreland Street – D'Olier Street. Life went on its merry way. Good journalists became columnists or were promoted to the Desk or to Features and that further diminished the news-gathering strength of the paper. They almost treated the "Indo" with a certain disdain.

Which explains maybe why I 'take the Times' for its arts pages, its features, its foreign coverage and good writing on sport but, frankly, I couldn't be without my *Irish Independent* each day – or I would miss out on much that is happening, outside the Pale in particular. And friends of mine could die and I would never get to their funerals (come to think of it, I heard a lady in the summer of '95 explaining to someone in the foyer of a Dublin hotel that she never got to the burial of a person she had been well acquainted with because the death notice wasn't in *the Irish Times*!).

On a funnier note, *the Irish Times* always seemed to cover seminars in a most exhaustive and detailed fashion. You might get some top professional type from the States addressing a group of medics in Dublin and I would be instructed to "pick up a few lines about it" on my way to another marking. I would collar the learned Professor in the corridor during the coffee break and come out in the *Evening Herald* with a story under the heading "Brown Bread and Long Walks The Secret of Longevity". The Professor, on seeing the headline, might ring up the News Desk in exasperation explaining that he didn't mean it as definite as all that – that I had included no qualifying sentences, that I mustn't have gone through every line of his script (naturally filled with the most involved and didactic medical terminology).

On being pressed, he would admit that the basic line of my story was okay... yes okay ... but no one survived to 90 or 100 on brown bread and long walks alone. The busy Desk would let it ride. And readers of the *Irish Times* probably got the full core of the Professor's thesis the next morning ... if they managed to understand him!

*   *   *

Initially when I hit Dublin, I had to take my turn on the roster in the Independent Newsroom in doing a monthly stint on Night Town. Paddy Clare ("Clare speaking") manned the fort for the *Irish Press* – was fifty years in all in the post – but the *Irish Times* and the *Irish Independent* alternated as the roster demanded (generally speaking the long-serving senior men were exempt). The approach was that each man in turn, be it either Paddy Clare, or Michael Foy for the *Times* when he was on, or myself rang the Fire Brigade at regular intervals to enquire if there was anything happening. Naturally in the case of a big fire, we always went out and I built up a close friendship with Michael Foy that was cemented further when he joined the Sugar Company as Press Officer and I became Press Officer of the National Farmers Association (later the IFA).

The stint each night on the *Irish Independent* extended from 8 o'clock until 4 o'clock the following morning. It suited me admirably in summer because, if things were quiet from 1.30 a.m. or 2 a.m. onwards, I could get down to work on a book and laze the next afternoon on the beach.

The young reporters making their way up the ladder naturally envied greatly the star names who wrote the gossip columns, taking in the social round in the evening time.

The Sixties then not alone gave us the phenomenon of the Showband Stars but the first of the big-name columnists – two of the most famous of all being Terry O'Sullivan, who had his own chauffeur-driven car and Tom Hennigan.

I remember Frank Hall wrote the *Evening Herald* around-town column for a time before moving to RTE to make his name on *Hall's Pictorial Weekly*. On a few occasions I stood in for Frank when he was on holidays and initially I felt that it was going to be my ticket to pastures new in the journalistic sense. I remember going along one evening to a 21st birthday party, the photographer and myself driving up a tree-lined avenue to a mansion in an exclusive suburb. When we duly presented ourselves to the father of the girl, he told us in no uncertain terms that he wanted no media presence and warned us that if we didn't get off his property in double quick time he would set the rottweilers on us.

Someone back in Middle Abbey Street had heard about this "society party" – but there was no formal written invitation as such (generally there was no shortage of invitations).

Another evening I was at the launch of a new lipstick that the P.R. executive claimed – as he pressed me to take a double whiskey – was the answer to any married man's prayers who was on the town as it didn't leave any tell-tale marks!

You started around 5 or 6 o'clock and finished around one o'clock in the morning, ensuring that your copy was left on the appropriate desk so that it could be subbed first thing next day.

It soon palled, of course, and in time we all wondered how Terry O'Sullivan had the enthusiasm and the stamina to keep going as long as he did. But then he was unique, almost an institution on his own, with one of the sharpest minds and sharpest pens in any journalist I have met, brilliant in the manner in which he could cut phoneys down to size.

Tom Hennigan was a lovable character, captured for posterity in *Paper Tigers* riding a penny farthing bicycle down Middle Abbey Street, outside the *Evening Herald* offices, for some promotion. They always had to have the apple-tart ready for Tom when he dropped into a reception. How many women workers I wonder now, broke their proverbial backs on a voluntary basis to ensure that the apple-tart was just right for Tom, fearing that if it wasn't then the charitable cause or some other venture they wanted highlighted in the social diary might never see the light of day.

Cathal O'Shannon's wife, Patsy Dyke wrote the social diary for the *Sunday Review* and then for the *Sunday Press*.

In time new editors wanted columns that broke new ground and eschewed the evening round of receptions that were often just organs used by clever P.R. people to plug their products or company ventures.

I like to think that John Feeney, tragically killed in the 1984 Beaujolais Nouveau wine-race plane crash at Eastbourne in southern England along with Kevin Marron of the *Sunday World*, Tony Hennigan of the *Irish Independent* (Tom's son) and Niall Hanley, Editor of the *Evening Herald,* was an innovator who smashed through all the accustomed norms for these social columns. Given a free hand by Niall Hanley, he became compulsive reading and certainly at his peak must have added thousands of copies to the overall sale of the *Evening Herald.*

John Feeney made the point to me over a drink one evening before he hit off on his round that people wanted to be entertained by his column – "they want a good laugh and more especially so if it is at the expense of some politician or captain of industry who has an inflated opinion of his own importance. And they want also to be brought on the inside track".

John, so brilliant in some ways and yet so reckless in others, was true to his own philosophy. If at times truth was sacrificed on the altar of ensuring that a column of his clicked in a fashion that was the talk of the town, he never lost any sleepless nights over it. He was such a hot property in boosting the paper commercially that Niall Hanley was loath to carpet him – even when his excesses made him a legend in his own lifetime.

During the funeral of Princess Grace of Monaco, he reported that Frank Sinatra and his wife were involved in a blazing row with Grimaldi officials in the Hotel de Paris about seating arrangements. As it turned out, the Sinatras were in California and never made it to the funeral.

He upset Cabinet Ministers. He upset Front Bench spokesmen for the Opposition. He upset heads of semi-State bodies and top executives of private concerns.

He was like the proverbial bull let loose in a china shop, such was the consternation and upset he caused on the widest possible plane.

But his fellow-journalists couldn't help but like him, for at heart he was extremely kind with a great sense of social justice and he was always only too willing to help a worthy cause.

When my book, *Under The Blue Flag* was being launched in 1980 in an Army barracks down by the quays, a pea-soup fog had descended on Dublin. It was so bad in fact, that many who had intended being there just couldn't make it as it was almost impossible to find one's way.

John Feeney did – rather late. And he painted a picture of the attendance being so large that the noise was akin to what you would find in a labour ward after a dozen or more babies had been born at one and the same time.

It was one occasion that I didn't mind him going over the top ...

One could not help but sympathise with Michael O'Toole who as *Evening Press* diary writer (Dubliner's Diary) had the unenviable task of 'marking' John Feeney. As he confessed in *More Kicks Than Pence*, Feeney's 'scoops' (whether true or not) naturally created pressure on him, yet "in fairness to Sean Ward (*Evening Press* Editor) and to the management of the paper, I have to say that it was never hinted to me that I should go down the same road".

Myles McWeeney (*Irish Independent*), Barbara McKeon (*Irish Press*) and Kathryn Rogers (*Sunday Press*) all made their special impact as social columnists. Angela Phelan produced each week for the *Irish Independent* weekender supplement a most informed and lively column that followed the trail of news-worthy events across the Atlantic to New York and Hollywood. She had the inside track to come up with those spicy items that are the life-blood of the game.

In the summer of '95 the *Sunday Business Post* had Trevor Danker of the *Sunday Independent* coming out No. 1 in a "vote among his peers" and, of course, that wasn't surprising considering his contacts both in this country and in Britain.

But of all the columns the one that had become essential reading with the "Dublin 4 Set" and all those who wanted to get an insider's view of things was the Terry Keane column on the back page of the Living Section of the *Sunday Independent*. Even if people confessed openly to hating the column, it didn't matter one iota – it was read. And read widely throughout the land. It touched on stories about marital problems among the socialites or lovers' quarrels among "The Set" that did not make the normal news pages. And it met the important criterion that it entertained.

The success of the column was based on the style of writing as much as anything else and Terry's penchant for the cutting edge. How she could plunge the dagger home when she felt the occasion warranted it.

Aengus Fanning had a very able Deputy Editor (Features) in Anne Harris who knew exactly what she wanted in her particular sphere and who realised only too well, as Aengus himself did, the role that the Terry Keane column played in providing constant talking points for the chattering classes.

*   *   *

In the *Sunday Tribune* on Sunday, September 10, 1995, Nell McCafferty under the heading "Death Of an Institution: Press Funeral 'An Appalling Sight' " wrote about the liquidation of Irish Press Newspapers the previous Friday at the R.D.S. in Ballsbridge. Adding to the irony was the fact that she reported that IPN owed her £800 and that the day before the papers were shut down, she had, as a freelance journalist working from home, bought a car.

One reflected back to the mid-Sixties when the *Evening Press* – still only twelve years old – was outselling the *Evening Herald*, the *Sunday Press*, with a massive six-figure sale, was ahead of the *Sunday*

Independent and the *Irish Press* was still solid with a sale of over 100,000 a day.

Major Vivian de Valera would have been appalled if he had been told in 1965 that thirty years on his son, Eamon would preside with Vincent Jennings over the last rites of Irish Press Newspapers, which had been founded as a national institution with high dreams and high principles.

No need to dwell here on the tragedy. For it was nothing less than a tragedy on a scale that only those who had given their lives to the Group papers could fully appreciate, many of them good friends of mine.

The late Conor O'Brien was Editor of the *Evening Press* in its glory days – the days when Con Houlihan, taking over the mantle of Joe (In The Soup) Sherwood, wrote a sports column that became an institution in itself and was valued by everyone who admired a distinctive style. During the death-throes of the Press Group, Con was seen on television news bulletins collecting on a bridge over the Liffey for his out-of-work colleagues. He himself would be snapped up by the *Sunday World* to write a weekly column for them.

Conor O'Brien in time became Editor of the *Sunday Independent*. Some journalists, like wines, don't travel well and Conor was seen and admired by his peers as basically an evening paper man. Frankly, I think he made a mistake in crossing the Bridge, as it never worked out for him at the helm of a Sunday paper as had been the case with the *Evening Press*. Hector Legge, who was still playing golf into his 90th year, had been Editor of the *Sunday Independent* when it had no competition and Hector in a way was unique, producing a paper to his own vision, satisfying the times that were in it and he didn't have to contend with pressure from the Board. Even after the *Sunday Press* made its appearance, the *Sunday Independent* had a sufficiently-strong core readership not to be unduly worried and Hector remained at the helm right to retirement age.

But it was a different era for Conor O'Brien and those who came after him.

The sure touch that he had displayed as Editor of the *Evening Press* somehow deserted him and the tragedy was compounded by the fact that he decided – against the best possible advice – to remain on in Independent House in a different capacity but with no input into the big decisions after he was replaced at the helm (it is one of the salutary facts of newspaper life that if you accept the editorial chair, you must be resigned to the fact from the outset that if matters don't work out for you, then you are likely to suffer the same fate as the manager of a soccer club in England).

Conor O'Brien was followed as Editor of the *Sunday Independent* by Michael Hand, one of the outstanding characters of Irish journalism in my time. Michael has so often had to contend with the problem of being mistaken for his twin brother, Jim and Jim in turn has been mistaken for Michael. When Michael was starting out on a local paper, he was covering the courts one day when the proprietor of the newspaper walked into a bar and spotted Jim having a drink. He caught him by the collar and demanded to know why he was drinking when he should be "down in the courts".

Around Christmas Eve on one occasion Jim dropped into Independent House to leave in a few bottles of the "right stuff". He opened one of them in the Editor's office while awaiting Michael's return and was happily sharing a drink with a few of the "boys" – his feet up on the desk – when one of the directors happened to look in. He went back up to the Fourth Floor rubbing his eyes in wonderment …

Michael was in his office one Saturday night glancing through proofs, with printing time for the country edition approaching, when his right-hand man, Michael Denieffe, later to become Editor of the *Evening Herald*, rang from "the stone" to tell him there was a crisis. The paper was about to go off with the picture of a male nude (frontal) in one of the pages.

"A what?", Michael shouted down the internal line as he nearly fell out of his chair.

"Yes, a nude … some artist or other", Michael Denieffe told him.

"Get it out … get it out right away".

"But what will I replace it with?"

"What have we got?"

Michael Denieffe said there was Curly Wee and some other items at hand that normally would have no place whatsoever in that particular page.

"I don't care if you fill the page with Curly Wee – but no nudes and that's final", came the Editor's command.

The picture of the artist in all his nude glory was duly consigned to the waste-paper basket, never to surface again.

And by the time the city edition was printed Curly Wee had vanished from the page also, to be replaced by an up-to-the-minute picture from the theatrical world that same evening.

Michael Hand had made his mark, as he liked to say himself, "at the barricades" when the Troubles flared first in the North and he did some outstanding on-the-spot reporting for the *Sunday Press*, which he left to join the *Sunday Independent*. At heart he was always a reporter in the field. How fitting then that he should be honoured by his peers and win one of the top awards for his coverage of the Rwandan crisis for the *Sunday Tribune*, which he had joined after being succeeded as Editor of the *Sunday Independent* by Aengus Fanning.

When Aengus took over at the helm in 1984, he could hardly have imagined that he would bring the paper to a position where it attained in 1995 a sale of 330,000 – a gain of 100,000 or so from 1984. The reality was that the *Sunday Independent* gained most of all of the Sunday papers from the death of the *Sunday Press*.

Aengus had soldiered with me, as I have recounted already, on the "European beat" and asked me to join him on the staff of the *Sunday Independent* (I duly moved up from the Newsroom to the Third Floor in '84).

We combined together in some ventures that proved very successful in boosting sales. There was the national poll of readers in the Centenary Year of the GAA in 1984 to pick the Sunday Independent/Irish Nationwide/GAA Teams of the Century in hurling and football. Later we came up with the idea of a cool £1 million prize to the person who would forecast the outcome of the General Election (i.e. the candidates who would win selected seats and the overall final total of seats won by each party).

The syndicates moved in to buy hundreds of papers. One syndicate took over a number of rooms in the Killiney Court Hotel and adopted a military-style approach to the filling out of the entry forms. it was a great moment when they arrived in Middle Abbey Street with their sacks of entries. No one succeeded in getting an all-correct entry but some went very close indeed, which was an indication in itself of the knowledge of politics in this country.

*   *   *

Vincent Browne, who had worked first in the Newsroom of the *Irish Independent* and subsequently on the *Sunday Independent* as one of the principal feature writers, had always been a courageous and crusading journalist (*Magill* in its heyday proved that most of all). The *Sunday Tribune* had its own distinctiveness when he was Editor and could be provocative and incisive on the big issues. While it failed to make a spectacular leap beyond the 100,000 barrier, it was doing all right financially when Vincent made the fatal decision to start a free-sheet weekly paper, hoping that the advertising revenue from this new venture would in time add strength and muscle to the *Tribune* itself.

But the venture back-fired sadly and brought about a downward plunge to near-disaster. The Independent Group stepped in to take an interest. The sale dropped as low as 60,000 but pulled back again after the *Sunday Press* ceased publication. Still, it failed to gain as spectacularly as did the *Sunday Independent*.

Former *Irish Times* security correspondent, Peter Murtagh was now at the helm, battling with an unenviable task – trying to reduce costs on the one hand and build up the sale, on the other to the point where the paper could be put on a footing where its financial problems could be put behind it once and for all.

At the same time the *Sunday Tribune* had to contend with the *Sunday Business Post* which was in there battling with it for many of the same potential readers. *The Post* had signed up Emily O'Reilly to write on politics and unquestionably she had the contacts to come up with exclusives and stories that made the right impact.

Aengus Fanning had the least worries of all the Irish Sunday paper editors – but the English Sunday quality papers, the *Sunday Times* in particular, were adding to the problems facing the *Sunday Tribune*. It was now a real rat-race to build on a low-base circulation in face of opposition on every side.

The *Irish Independent* had picked up much of the sale that was there to be garnered when the *Irish Press* ceased publication.

Under the Editorship of Vinnie Doyle, it was in a powerful position. I remember the time when Vinnie and Niall Hanley, under Aidan Pender's firm editorship of the paper, represented the finest lay-out duo that it was my pleasure to collaborate under. To see the two of them at work together at the height of a big story – like the climax of the counting of votes in a General Election, the formation of a new government or some dramatic happening on the international front – was to watch two men who gloried in the game and every facet of it. They were born newsmen who knew no other life and wanted no other life. The newspaper life was all. Aengus Fanning had the same outlook, the same compulsion.

Vinnie Doyle brought his penchant for brightness to the *Irish Independent* when he took over as Editor. And Niall Hanley did the same when he assumed the editorship of the *Evening Herald* and oversaw the change to a tabloid evening paper – a move that was to greatly benefit the *Herald* where it proved disastrous for the *Irish Press*.

Tim Pat Coogan, I always felt, had been a very courageous Editor of the *Irish Press* in that he moved it away from being under the wing of the Fianna Fáil Party and tried to give it a more independent voice. Mick Mills, when Political Correspondent, was deeply respected by Dáil Deputies in every party for his impartiality and the level of his independence. He was very good on radio and television too.

The demise of the *Irish Press* and what it meant to the options available to the Irish people, especially at election times, had to be set against the amazing success of the Irish edition of *The Star*. Michael Brophy, who had succeeded Niall Hanley as Editor of the *Evening Herald* and made his own mark in that position, was the inspiring force initially behind the onward advance of the *The Star*. It was carried on by Paul Drury and when Paul became Editor of the *Evening Herald*, Gerry O'Regan, who had cut his teeth in the battle lines with Vinne Doyle, assumed the editorial chair. At the time of writing in September, '95 Gerry had the satisfaction of seeing the sale jump beyond 90,000 a day. He had an outstanding team under him including John Donlon on the News Desk and Connie Clinton on the Sports Desk. They knew exactly what they wanted – and what caught the imagination of readers of the paper.

*   *   *

In 1967, having finished *The Football Immortals*, I decided it was time to take a full-time job again. As fortune would have it, the post of Press Officer of the National Farmers' Association (N.F.A.) fell vacant because the man in the job at the time had resigned suddenly. The Association was left without any proper Press Spokesperson for a period of some vital months. It was during this period that Rickard Deasy got a terrible press because of the action being taken by farmers in pursuit of their rights. It was even suggested – and believed by many – that he was a former British Army officer when, in actual fact, he had served his country in the Irish Army.

I joined the N.F.A. in the final months of Deasy's Presidency and did the best I could to correct the false image that had sprung up around his name. I came to admire him as one of the straightest men I had dealt with, as a person of total integrity, who didn't know what it was to tell a lie and a man with a very fine mind.

One evening, he flew in from Paris where he must have seen some of the action being taken by the students at the height of tense times in the French capital. He came straight to a meeting of the inner Cabinet of the I.F.A. and proposed that it might be a good idea to drop a few bales of hay outside Government buildings next day and set light to them as farmers carrying placards pressed home their case for certain concessions.

Sean Healy, the Secretary-General, Brendan Power, his Deputy and Dick Hourigan, the Chief Organiser remained silent. "That's the most cock-eyed proposal I ever heard", I remarked, knowing that it would be laughed out of court by the media when I issued a press release trying to explain the purpose.

Deasy rose from his chair and walked over to the window. "It's foggy outside, gentlemen, but its foggier in this room" – and with that he walked out.

I got knowing nods all round. In effect, it was being hinted to me silently that I might as well clear out my desk and prepare to move on.

Next morning, however, when Rickard arrived in his office, he called me down and told me he had been tired after the flight when he made his proposal the previous evening. "Forget all about it – I must have been back in my student days", he laughed and we both shook hands and it was on then to real business.

The eighteen months that Charles Haughey spent as Minister for Agriculture (1964-'66) saw him build up a very good relationship initially with the general body of farmers and with the National Farmers' Association.

I have little doubt that but for the historic Farmers Rights March from Bantry to Dublin (beginning on October 7, 1966), culminating in 30,000 farmers marching through the centre-city streets of Dublin (October 19, 1961) and the 20-day sit-down by the nine outside Government Buildings, Charles Haughey could have been judged by historians as one of the most dynamic and forward-looking Ministers for Agriculture in the history of the State and one of the most popular.

Indeed, as a veritable Cold War developed between the N.F.A. and Neil T. Blaney (only ended, incidentally, before the commencement of negotiations on Ireland's entry into the EEC through a historic handshake between Jack Lynch and T.J. Maher on the steps of Government Buildings), there were many farmers who privately regretted that Haughey had to go on carrying the can for the Government, as he had the vision to bring agriculture to the new frontiers in an enlarged European family of nations context.

When he refused to greet the farmers' representatives, it all turned sour between Haughey and the N.F.A., though it is significant that in retrospect he saw it stemming not from any personal differences between himself and N.F.A. President, Rickard Deasy but as a result of an economic clash between the farmers and the budgetary situation. "I had failed to get what they wanted and I had to carry the can for the Government," he admitted to Seán O'Rourke in an *Irish Press* interview.

My own information on that historic episode in farmer-Government relationship is that there had been a definite promise earlier that year, of a "penny (old) on the basic" to Rickard Deasy but Haughey apparently could not get the Cabinet to deliver (some contend that the seeds of tension had already been sown between Jack Lynch and himself). Later after their protest before the Presidential Election, the I.C.M.S.A. were seen by farmers to be more militant and their militancy paid off with a mild-price increase, which they claimed to have won.

Deasy decided to pull out his "troops" to regain lost ground for the N.F.A. and it culminated eventually in the various types of action of the Farmers Rights Campaign – but Haughey had gone from Agriculture before the crisis in the farming world was eventually solved.

At the height of the crisis the Army was called out in Kilkenny to support Gardaí in seizures of property from prominent N.F.A. men.

I recall John Healy writing in the *Irish Times* there was one Government for the country but there seemed to be a second over in Ely Place – a clear inference that Deasy could not be controlled. A message was conveyed to the effect that the N.F.A. would be proscribed – making it an illegal organisation – unless a document was signed giving full recognition to the Government.

I remember as if it was only yesterday – though it's now nearly thirty years ago – Sean Healy and Brendan Power and other senior figures arguing that if the Association did not bend to the Government's demands it would be dead as the voice of the farmers, because it would have been pushed underground in one stroke.

Sean Duignan was waiting downstairs with an RTE camera team to catch the 9 o'clock news. First Rickard Deasy produced a formula that did not quite meet the wishes of the Government. The emissaries were speeding to and fro. Finally, the required form of words was produced. Deasy's pen hovered over the page. For what seemed an eternity we waited. Finally, the pen came down and he signed.

I admired his bearing and his statesmanship at that moment more than at any stage in our short relationship. He rose from his chair and went down to be interviewed by Sean Duignan – his dignity intact. I realised that when it came down to the wire, he put the interests of the farmers he served and the Association that meant so much to him above every other consideration.

A much-maligned man but born to lead, whether people agreed with his style of leadership or not.

When T.J. Maher took over at the helm in '67 the Rights Campaign had still a distance to run before a new relationship was forged between Government and farmers that would blossom to the benefit of the country on Ireland entering the EEC.

*   *   *

I had no difficulty in "selling" T.J. Maher – the dairy farmer from Boherlahan in County Tipperary, who was a brother of the esteemed and eminent surgeon, Jamesie Maher.

I knew hectic times when there were literally two phones hopping off the desks in my room – one on my own desk and the other on that of my very able secretary, Donegal-born Kathleen Shovlin. Donal Foley telling me – indeed, commanding me – to send down a Press Release right away to the *Irish Times* and I telling him in the intense pressure of the moment that he would have to send up a reporter to collect it like every other paper – "or get lost." Next day I joked that I would send him a sack of potatoes for my attitude. He laughed.

There were farmers in jail and 2,000 of the womenfolk staged a mass rally outside Portlaoise jail. The total of farmers in prison had risen to 100 by May 13, 1967.

Yes, they were stirring times. I was proud to work for the farmers; through the N.F.A. and later the I.F.A. I forged friendships that were deep and lasting. I was proud to have as my colleagues during fiercely-pressurised days that seemed to have no end Sean Healy, Brendan Power, Dick Hourigan, Alan Dukes and also John Murphy, Tom Llewellyn, Seamus McCann, Jim Quinn, John Howley, and Denis Knox and, of course, I met one of the most outstanding characters of all in Tony Sherry.

I was prouder still to serve with T.J. Maher, who was unquestionably THE most outstanding President in the history of the Association with an uncanny knack of knowing exactly what his "troops" wanted.

My relationship with T.J. Maher worked easily and smoothly from the outset. He knew that I had no connection with any political party but was a journalist bringing my experience and know-how into the realms of the job of Press Spokesman. I would draft the big speeches and at Budget time, Alan Dukes, the Chief Economist would give the economic analysis. T.J. would then outline his thinking and we would work and re-work the speech. The final draft would mirror his thoughts exactly.

When he was making an appearance on television – for example, for a face-to-face grilling by Ted Nealon on the *Seven Days* programme – we would closet ourselves with him for hours and go over all the questions that we felt would be fired at him. On one occasion he did so well that I heard farmers in a pub on the road south actually cheering him as if he had scored the winning goal in an All-Ireland Hurling Final.

Talking of journeys south reminds me that once when I was travelling in the company of T.J. and Dick Hourigan, I happened to glance out the window to my right and remarked: "Fine field of oats".

"Corn", T.J. corrected me.

Further on, I noticed what I thought in the distance was barley and T.J. again interjected quietly to put me on the right track.

Eventually, I confined myself to saying: "Some fine grain over

167

beyond" and "they're excellent stock now, aren't they".

Every time I remind T.J. of that trip south, he cannot contain himself laughing.

By the time I left the I.F.A. – the exciting times were past and it was beginning to become a mundane round – to return to Independent House, it was as if I had gone through university and taken a degree. All the knowledge I acquired stood me in good stead when I began covering the negotiations on Ireland's entry into the European family of nations for the three papers in the Independent Group. This was especially so when the negotiations revolved around the nitty-gritty of deals on the milk price and the beet quota

*   *   *

At the time of the historic Rights Campaign, Irish farmers wanted to focus national attention on their dissatisfaction with their conditions at juncture (autumn '66) when livestock prices had slumped to rock-bottom and there was a general sense of disillusionment and little confidence in the future of farming.

Out of the Campaign a new spirit, a new sense of solidarity was born. Irish farmers discovered their identity. Before, there had been a feeling that their individualism would never permit them to march under a common non-party political, non-sectarian banner to assert their rights. Now all was changed, changed utterly.

They saw the new dawn. They discovered what they could do for themselves. They could respond to leadership and discipline as a body. They saw clearly too that without a strong, overall national organisation to crystallise their claims, they would get nowhere.

When a man is prepared to go to jail for a cause, he gains a new sense of fellowship with those who share a cell with him in the same cause. Small, medium and large farmers had walked side by side in the Long March from Bantry to Dublin (beginning October 7, 1966), culminating in the silent parade of 30,000 through the centre-city streets of the capital (October 19, 1966) and the 20-day sit-down protest by the nine outside Government Buildings.

When the farmers were released from jail on June 12, 1967, I was present at one of the big welcome-home functions – in Navan when 3,000 farmers crowded the Market Square and the new spirit of solidarity was never more evident.

I saw that spirit being channelled into constructive ends – into the formation of F.B.D. and into other ventures that made it all worthwhile.

On rejoining the Independent Group I was offered the News Editor's job on the *Sunday Independent* or the News Features job on the *Irish Independent*. After careful deliberation, I opted for the latter.

What gave me the greatest pleasure of all was the fact that my first marking was to accompany T.J. Maher and an I.F.A. delegation to Brussels. I was going now as a journalist and not as I.F.A. Press Officer. It was important in the eyes of farmers, I was convinced – and T.J. knew it also – that I should be seen as still totally at one with the leader they

168

admired so much.

The wheel had come full circle but those days in the I.F.A. were among the best and happiest – though the toughest – times in my professional career.

13

The Lord's Last Words
at The Last Supper

It was the time of one of the greatest sporting extravaganzas that Dublin had ever seen, the meeting of Muhammad Ali and Al 'Blue' Lewis in Croke Park on a summer's night in 1972.

In the count-down to the Big Fight they had invited Ali to Leinster House to be greeted by the Taoiseach, Jack Lynch in his office and to see the Dáil (Irish Parliament) in session. Later he sat down to a meal with his trainer, Angelo Dundee and the rest of us in the Leinster House restaurant. Ali, of course, was the guest of honour.

He had been out doing road-work in County Wicklow at around 5 o'clock that morning. His breakfast consisted of a cup of coffee. He ate no luncheon either. "When I'm training I take only one meal a day. I eat plenty of meat and vegetables but I don't eat no pork", he told me. Don't you feel hungry during the long day before that evening meal at 7 o'clock?, I ventured. "No", he replied. "When you're training, you miss meals, yes, but your stomach shrinks and you don't miss food".

Now he amazed us by eating not just one steak but two, washed down with coke and ice. Positively no chips and he did not take a sweet or coffee either. He never touched alcohol in his life.

I had been with him for all of that wonderful, stimulating and laughter-laden week. He had reminded me more than once in the breaks during the sweat and grind of training why he was "The Greatest" and where he stood in the popularity stakes world-wide. "Fly a plane over all the countries of the world and think of all the people assembled together in each of them and that is the kind of compressed interest you get around the globe when Muhammad Ali fights for the world crown. Everybody is interested, from China to the Arctic Circle and from the jungles of Africa to the Russian steppes and the cities of the United States".

In cold retrospect, could one dispute Ali's assessment of the spotlight he commanded when he boxed for the heavyweight championship of the world? He was 30 when he fought Al 'Blue' Lewis in that non-title fight in Dublin. Eight years on in the fading twilight of a brilliant career, he faced Larry Holmes in Caesar's Palace in Las Vegas – on October 2, 1980 to be exact – and the live gate of 25,000 paid 5,766,125 dollars, the largest in the history of boxing.

But that was not the sum total of it. The telecast was carried in China – the first time a boxing event had ever been shown on the television screens in that country. Ali had a total television audience for the night's fight of two billion – the greatest ever. And other statistics that made the mind boggle revealed that the title fight drew 1,200 media representatives to Las Vegas (with another 500 writers and photographers failing to get accreditation) while for the Nevada city itself, it grossed an estimated 100 million when account was taken of what was wagered at the tables.

"What were the last words the Lord uttered at the Last Supper?", Ali is asking from his seat at the head of the table in the Dáil restaurant, looking around at the twelve of us – like his Twelve Apostles – a mischievous gleam in his eye?

"Can't say, Ali", I remark.

"Let every man pick up his own check!"

In flashes of spontaneous wit in the classic mould like that, Ali proved that he was a born entertainer as well as being perhaps the greatest heavyweight in boxing history, though when I asked if he had ever considered going into the entertainment business as a full-time professional, he responded – clowning somewhat – that they couldn't pay him any more than he was earning out of boxing and then he added with a wink: "And they couldn't make me any more famous or more popular with the people than I already am".

Again there was the moment on the eve of the fight when I said to Ali that my Editor wanted to have some idea of when the 12-round bout might end, as it was important in planning the different editions.

"You go and tell your boss that I will knock the bum out in the fifth", he said. "cause he can only bring in enough money in advertising on television for that many rounds. I won't carry him for any longer than that".

And then after giving the Ali shuffle, he demonstrated for me the kind of killer punch that would take Al 'Blue' out.

Ali's prediction would have been right on target had not there been a dispute over the count when Lewis was floored in the fifth round and took a count of nine. The Ali camp claimed that the Long Count went on for over twenty seconds when it should have lasted less than ten seconds. American referee, Lew Eskin contended that there was nothing wrong with the count. What happened, in actual fact, was that he did not begin the count until Ali had moved away to a neutral corner and that naturally took up time – the time that allowed Al 'Blue' to be back on his feet before being waved OUT.

Be that as it may, the fight went to the eleventh round when it should have been over in the fifth. But the end result was the same, the referee stopping the contest one minute and 15 seconds into the round as Lewis could no longer defend himself.

*   *   *

Ali was on song from the moment he arrived at Dublin Airport. Sporting a shillelagh, he created the mood that turned his first news conference into a *tour-de-force*.

"It's hard to be humble when you are as good as I am", was just one of the quotable quotes he offered us for our evening paper stories and naturally the *Evening Herald* went front page with the heading "Muhammad Ali Comes To Town" over my three-column report and a picture of Ali waving his shillelagh in a mock threatening gesture.

"I have never been to the country before – where do the coloured hang out?" he asked with a smile towards the end of the press conference.

He talked about his fight the previous year with Joe Frazier, the great bruising contest in 'The Garden' in New York which saw him lose his title as a left hook from Frazier had him staggering around the ring at what Hugh McIlvanney so graphically described in *The Observer* as "a crazily reclining angle, like a surf-rider before he loses his board".

Now Ali is saying that some people were claiming that he would never meet Frazier again, that he would keep on raking in the cash against lesser fighters but that he would scrupulously avoid another confrontation with Smokin' Joe. "Money rules the world", Ali responded. "The whole world wants this repeat and it will be the greatest ever in the history of the planet Earth".

Then he added with an amused twinkle in his eye: "Frazier has need of it. He has seven children and one on the way".

Asked if it was true that he had Irish blood in his veins, he said: "You never can tell" and then he brought the house down when he added: "There was an awful lot of sneaking around then".

Somebody had written that he had an ancestor named O'Grady. Ali explained that in those times the slaves were named after their masters. If an O'Grady had ten slaves, they were all named O'Grady. That was why when he read history, he changed his name from Cassius Clay to Muhammad Ali.

Was he confident of beating Joe Frazier in a return match? "I am better now than I ever was in my whole career. I draw the people. Frazier does not want to meet me because he knows it will be his last big date".

Of the great fighters of history, which man would he have liked to have met? "Rocky Marciano".

Would he have beaten him? No comment

But then the old confidence surfaced again. "I could have whipped any of them".

*   *   *

The idea of staging the fight in Dublin was the brain-child of a great character, 48-year-old London-based Butty Sugrue who had as his adviser one of the outstanding names in American boxing, one Howard Conrad, who sported a moustache like Groucho Marx and who could rattle off the wise-cracks in machine-gun fashion like Groucho himself.

Butty Sugrue let it be known that any profits accruing from the fight would go to help the mentally handicapped children of Ireland.

His dignity was affronted though when doubts were raised about his ability to meet the estimated 300,000 dollars that it would cost to stage this extravaganza, with Ali taking a reported 215,000 dollars and TV contracts initially only bringing in around 75,000 dollars.

I wrote a report for the *Irish Independent* pinpointing these doubts and hinting that the Big Fight might even be in jeopardy. But all was well in the end. Like all the other media representatives, I was only too happy to spell out the exact position and hail Butty Sugrue for his courage in surmounting all the obstacles in his path towards the realisation of the ambition of a lifetime.

But Howard Conrad did not forget that initially I had been a Doubting Thomas. On the morning of the fight, as he swept into the Gresham Hotel, he spotted me in the circle around Billy Conn and shouted for everyone to hear: "Hey, you Smith, you'll get your Press ticket for the fight all right. We never lock out the media – but the crows will have a goddam better view than you'll have".

It was Tom Cryan, boxing correspondent of the Independent Group and one of the most experienced and knowledgeable writers in the business, who acquainted me of the heavyweight I had offended when I crossed swords with Howard Conrad. I was thinking then that I would be lucky after all to be up there with the crows. However, Conrad relented and I got a ring-side seat to write the Page One report for the *Irish Independent* on what I said was "a night that created the kind of atmosphere in the Croke Park stadium that I know will never be repeated".

Each day the very presence of Muhammad Ali in Dublin made a story for the evening paper and the morning paper. He was, in fact, THE story.

Ali had a suite in what was then Opperman's Country Club in Kilternan. A Garda squad car kept a watchful eye on the hotel and on Ali during his comings and goings.

He travelled everywhere in a chauffeur-driven Mercedes. Each time he left the hotel, it was like the exit of royalty. Admirers crowded the lobby and waited outside the entrance. The autograph hunters who mobbed him were not just wide-eyed youngsters but middle-aged people as well.

"He loves people", said Angelo Dundee when I asked him if Ali ever got tired from the pressure of the crowds pressing in around him. Dundee (whose wife of Irish decent on both sides of her family and daughter arrived from Miami for the fight) added that if they agreed to allow Muhammad to take in a lot of engagements, they just could not work out schedules "because every visit becomes a two-hour one in Ali's case. He just doesn't know how to pull himself away from people".

If Ali loved people, Dublin and the Irish people took him to their hearts also.

He was photographed at the hotel being shown how to handle a hurley by Eddie Keher, the famous Kilkenny star of that era and Ali tossed the ball on the stick in a manner that showed that he could have been an outstanding wielder of the caman had he been born in a stronghold of Ireland's national game.

He was photographed also trick-acting with John Huston after a training session in the Croke Park handball alley on the eve of the fight. That day, as Dublin basked in brilliant July sunshine, I accompanied Ali as he walked like a king the short distance from the Gresham Hotel to the Regent Cinema to see a private showing of John Huston's *Fat City*. Angelo Dundee came along also.

"That's me, that's me talkin', man," interjected Ali from his seat in the back row as a young black boxer talked in the film about his dream of being champion.

Ali had told me earlier why he would never allow his son, Muhammad Jnr. to take up a boxing career. "His brain might get shook up". That was his fear and towards the end of the film we saw a boxer whose brain had got "shook up". No wonder Angelo Dundee remarked coming out of the cinema: "It was good. It was reality".

Ali knew the game, its pitfalls and the ultimate quagmire into which the punch-drunks could sink. "You can buy guys on the way up but you cannot buy the champ – unless he wants to be bought", he said to me perceptively as he drew back the veil momentarily on the shadowy side of the game. And I knew then that Ali could NEVER be bought.

"I don't believe in war and now the American Government acknowledges I was right not to go to Vietnam", he said to Marie Corr in the course of an *Irish Press* interview four days before the Dublin fight.

But you make your money in a profession of aggression?, was the question she posed to him then. "Yes", he flashed back quickly. "But I don't ever hurt anybody deliberately. I never seek to knock out my opponent. Remember the Quarry fight? I asked the referee to stop the fight when I saw Quarry was in trouble".

In Ali's case we didn't concentrate on the colour of money but basically on the colour of his personality which naturally completely overshadowed that of Al 'Blue' Lewis.

Al 'Blue' Lewis emerged from a rough coloured quarter of Detroit, where he was a gang member and eventually ended up in prison on a second degree murder charge that was reduced to manslaughter. As in the case of Sonny Liston, it was in prison that he learned how to box. When he gained his freedom it became his life and his livelihood.

He had enjoyed significant victories over Eduardo Corletti and Cleveland Williams but, amazingly, in six years as a pro he had only thirty fights to his credit. He has won 26 of these. There was a lot of waiting between fights and this ate up the purse money from his successes. Not surprisingly he had reason to become disillusioned, even embittered, at times.

In the tradition of Charlie Burley and Holman Williams ("great Negro fighters who were never able to cash in on their ability because the champions gave them a wide berth"), Al 'Blue' Lewis found difficulty, according to Jim McNeill in an *Evening Press* piece in getting fights with Floyd Patterson and George Foreman – the word was spreading that he was a fighter to be avoided. If you beat him, so what? But if he hit you, he was liable to break you in half.

Don Elbaum, who was in Dublin as his adviser, told how Lewis sometimes didn't train as hard as he should "simply because he wasn't getting regular fights".

He was the victim of a vicious circle. Against Laotis Martin, a real good heavy, 'Blue' was slaughtering him but then ran out of gas. He just wasn't fit enough.

He was also at the wrong end of a few strange decisions. In the count-down to facing Ali in Dublin, he fought Oscar Bonavena in Argentina. Lewis was all over him, had him cut and half-way over the ropes when the referee stopped it. "We thought we had won", said Don Elbaum bitterly. "But the referee disqualified 'Blue' ".

"Chuck" Nary had become his manager when he hit Dublin and "Chuck" exuded confidence when I talked to him twenty-four hours before his boy went into the ring. "I have a funny feeling that Al 'Blue' will do it and the closer it gets to fight-time, the stronger this feeling becomes".

"Chuck", who was one of those outsize characters who seem to spring up like mushrooms in the American fight game, was holding a docket for a bet, laid with an English bookmaker, of £200 at 25/1 – Lewis to win by a knock-out. That was the measure of his confidence.

But even though, Al 'Blue' Lewis, standing 6' 4" and turning the scales at 219lbs, was acknowledged as "a formidable fighting machine", he still entered the ring on Wednesday, July 19 as the complete underdog, with odds of 7/1 to 12/1 being available on him. "I came here to beat Al 'Blue' and that is exactly what I will do", were Muhammad Ali's final words.

*   *   *

Even though he did not hold the world's heavyweight title at that point, Ali was still unquestionably "the people's champion", idolised by the fans around the globe.

Already he was thinking beyond Croke Park to a return bout with Frazier. "I dearly want to whip Frazier and prove to the world that I am the greatest", was how he put it.

Revealing to me his philosophy of what makes a real champion, he said: "The champ never runs. He never hides. Because he knows that in the end there is no place to hide. They will keep comin', wantin' to beat you, wantin' to prove that they have it in them to put you away. You take them as they come. Some just don't have it as they think they have it and it can be easy enough. Others have the punch but not the skills to do it over the length of a title bout or they may lack the courage or the killer instinct. Then you come up against someone who has the ability, the punch and the hunger. You know you are in a fight. You may be hurt more than in the body but you fight as the champion fights, with everything you've got and all the spirit you can summon up from the depths of your soul. You may get beat but even Joe Louis got beat but did it make him a lesser fighter in the end".

That rhetorical question seemed to hang in the air for a long time as I nodded my head in understanding. And I reflected on the fact that Ali had summoned up some of the finest writing from the finest writers of his time in victory – but, strangely, even more so in defeat.

Hugh McIlvanney, unsurpassed as a boxing writer, wrote in *The Observer* of hearing white American reporters screaming in The Garden the night Frazier beat Ali in March '71, "Kill the sonofabitch, take his head off, his time's here now" and next day he heard a hotel maid remark, "So the big mouth got shut good".

"They wanted a crucifixion … but the big man came out bigger than he went in", wrote McIlvanney.

Then he went on: "What is common to most of his detractors is a failure to let themselves become attuned to his spirit, to his dream. To those of us who believe in him, such a failure in astonishing. The beauty of his physical performances, his whole impact as a performer, are inseparable from his bizarre but ultimately heroic vision of himself. Arthur Miller's salesman is not the only man who has a dream. Whoever you are, it comes with the territory. The world would be uninhabitable if all of us dreamt on the epic scale of Ali, but it would be a considerably drabber place if one among us had not done so".

He summed up that in defeat Ali refused to let his dream be tarnished. He took the consequences with magnificent courage and admirable dignity. "I ain't the champ", he said quietly. "Joe's the champ. I call him champ now. Not before, but I do now. I ain't protestin' ".

"The Garden defeat far from diminishing Ali in the eyes of his admirers has deepened their feelings far beyond the normal limits of public respect and affection", added McIlvanney.

That respect and that affection was evident in overflowing abundance among the 20,000 attendance in Croke Park and, after his hand was raised aloft in victory, excited spectators invaded the ring to literally mob Ali. Gardaí battled with the fans the whole way from the ring to the tunnel under the Cusack Stand to clear a passage as the crowd tried to get near him. "It was just one more indication of the way he had captured the imagination of the Irish public since his arrival in Dublin", I wrote next morning in the *Irish Independent*.

A night of colour and excitement and the show the promoters staged before the fight bill itself got under way made the evening quite memorable in many ways, creating something of a carnival atmosphere that enthralled the casual spectator not acquainted with the finer points of boxing. Pat Quinn of Quinnsworth (later to emigrate to Canada) got a cheer worthy of Ali himself when he went £1,000 to buy the autographed painting of Arkle in the auction, the proceeds of which were earmarked to aid the mentally handicapped.

Famous names in the world of boxing like Terry Downes, the former world middleweight champion, Billy Conn (who once brought Joe Lewis to 13 rounds), Jose Torres of Puerto Rico (a former world light-heavyweight champion who wrote the bestselling book on Ali title *Sting Like A Bee*) and Freddie Gilroy were introduced to the crowd by Michael O'Hehir, M.C. for the night. Eamon Andrews was also there. He agreed that the setting for the contest was ideal and the evening just perfect for an open-air fight but he regretted the fact that the stadium was not packed to its 75,000 capacity.

The entry of the two boxers brought excitement to a peak in the stadium. The crowd rose to Al 'Blue' Lewis for coming back so strongly after being down for that count of nine in the fifth and he actually drew slight blood from Ali's nose in the sixth.

But in the final analysis he had no answer to the speed and punching power of the former world champion, who showed the full range of his talents through the contest.

From my ringside seat I marvelled at his speed, his ability to sway away from punches on the ropes, how he would open up with a succession of punches to the body or head, coming rat-tat-tat like machine gun fire. And then the manner in which he went for the kill in the fifth, like a matador going in over the horns in the Madrid or Seville bull ring, coldly and so professionally that Al 'Blue' would have been taken out then but for Ali's error in not going to a neutral corner right away when his opponent was sent sprawling to the canvas.

Bravely, Al 'Blue' lasted until the eleventh and then, just over a minute into the round, Ali cut loose again and a flurry of punches left Lewis helpless. Ali stepped away and looked at the referee, indicating that he did not want to punish his opponent further. Lew Eskin stopped it. And it was the signal for fantastic scenes as 20,000 spectators rose to acclaim their idol.

It remains a lifetimes's regret that I did not get to Kinshasa for the 'rumble in the jungle', when Ali beat the then seemingly unbeatable George Foreman. And I regret very much also that I did not get to Manila for the epic repeat encounter between Ali and Joe Frazier which Ali won.

And I missed out on the chance too of writing the Angelo Dundee Story. I struck up a very good friendship with him while he was in Dublin. He actually invited me to the States to do the research for the book and I had already thought of a title – *In The Corner With Ali*.

But it was not our time. At that point I was EEC and Diplomatic Correspondent for Independent Newspapers and deeply involved in covering the Brussels scene. To get six months to a year's leave of absence to research and finish the book was just not on.

Suffice it to say that Muhammad Ali was the greatest sporting figure I have met in a lifetime in journalism. Unparalleled in his lightning speed and footwork as a heavyweight who stood on a pedestal apart in his prime and who would have left an even more indelible imprint had he not lost four years because of his Vietnam protest. But, most of all, there was the charisma of his personality that shone out like a beacon for the media representatives who got close to him. I do not wish to dwell on the problems that came later. I can only think of the way he lit up the scene for a week in Dublin and the sparkling quotables quotes that sprang from his lips, whether it was in off-moments in his hotel, or in breaks in training or sitting down to that dinner in the Dáil restaurant.

177

You only wished that time could have stood still in his case and never ravaged the body beautiful.

The epilogue remains with Al 'Blue' Lewis. I accompanied him to the airport as he was catching a flight back to the States. I asked him where he had lodged his purse and he indicated a concealed pocket at his waist, that I noticed now was distinctly bulging from the wads of greenbacks (as far as I can recall he had asked to be paid in readies).

"You might get mugged?", I suggested diffidently.

He looked at me as if I was talking about someone stealing candy off a kid. He held up that big fist of his and remarked: "No one is goin' to take da money off Al 'Blue' ... just no one".

And patting that concealed pocket, he added: "It stays here ... until I get home ... right back inside my own front door".

Come to think of it, whatever happened to Al 'Blue' Lewis?

14

"Better One Day as a Lion"

From the chain around his neck hung the paw of a lion which he had killed on safari in Mozambique before the revolution. On it was inscribed the motto: "Better one day as a lion than one hundred years as a lamb".

It was the motto by which Jack "Treetop" Straus from San Antonio, Texas had always lived – and he was true to it right to the end. He was playing in a high stakes poker game into the early hours of the morning at the Bicycle Club Casino in Bell Garden, California in August, 1988 when he started feeling chest pains. He was escorted from the table and rushed to hospital in nearby Downey where, following treatment, he appeared to have pulled through. But then his heart just stopped beating and he was pronounced dead at 10.30 a.m. the following morning. He was only 58.

All his life he had operated as a free spirit outside the system. It galled him that his father – they were very close – had worked extremely hard as manager of a packing plant, and had looked forward to enjoying a happy and carefree time in retirement when he got to 65. But he died at 58, having never done any of the things he would so much have liked to have done.

Jack Straus vowed at his father's graveside that he would not make the same mistake. He would experience life to the full and not be bound by the constricts of time or money. "I have only a limited amount of time on earth, and I want to live every second of it" was how he put it. And to help him abide by his chosen dictum, he never wore a watch.

Ironically, Big Jack passed away at exactly the same age as his father. But there was a world of difference between the way father and son lived.

"The wonderful thing about the world of professional poker", he said to me during a break in the 1981 World Championship, "is that when you're broke, somebody will always stake you. Benny Binion laid it out for me a long time ago. I said, 'Benny, I'm really playin' with bad luck'. He replied, 'The only bad luck for a gambler is bad health. The rest is temporary aggravation' ".

Jack Straus was a master of the absolute, all-or-nothing way of life and could have starred in the lead in the film *Let it Ride*. In 1970, a terrible run at poker in Las Vegas reduced him to his last forty dollars. Instead of quitting, he took the forty dollars to the blackjack table and bet it all on a single hand. He won and continued to bet all the money in front of him until he had turned the $40 into $500. He took the $500 to the poker game and ran it up to $4,000, returned to the blackjack table and transformed the $4,000 into $10,000. He finally bet the whole sum on the Kansas City Chiefs in the Super Bowl and won $20,000. In less than twenty-four hours, he went from near-bankruptcy to relative affluence. The story is famous enough to have gone into gaming folklore in the States, but the real point of it was the refusal of Jack Straus to compromise.

He got the middle name "Treetop" from his fellow poker professionals because he stood 6ft 6ins tall. He was not alone THE most outstanding character I met on the American circuit but a student of life with a great feeling for people.

He told me a story that gave the greatest insight of all into his sensitivity and the principles by which he lived.

The Taxman had decided to make an investigation and, remember, Uncle Sam, apart from expecting the professional poker player to pay his share in taxes on his earnings, can bill his subjects for a cut from the winnings when someone hits the Jackpot at one of the Las Vegas slot machines.

The bill Jack Straus received was a mammoth one of $1,000,000 or more – emerging no doubt from some computer in Washington that made absolutely no allowance for losses incurred. Even a poker player as great as Jack Straus had to lose sometime!

Jack decided to appeal. While he was waiting his turn to be called, he could not help listening to the case of a man who was endeavouring to save his house because he had failed to meet liabilities of about 50,000 dollars.

His wife and kids, he complained, had walked out on him because of the mounting pressures after the tax bill arrived. The little Willie Loman-like character broke down and sobbed: "If you take my house from me, my wife is less likely to come back and bring the kids with her. Please leave me my home" he begged.

Jack Straus, from the back of the room, piped up at that moment – "Stick the 50,000 dollars on my bill. It won't make that much difference!"

*   *   *

He was one of the intrepid band of travelling "road pros" who played the Texas circuit and a book could be written on the adventures he had with men like Doyle (Texas Dolly) Brunson, Johnny Moss, Amarillo Slim Preston, "Sailor" Roberts, Puggy Pearson and other less-famous names. "Theirs was an era of excitement, danger and uncertainty. And always movement – somewhere down the river, or upstate some place", was how Tex Sheahan put it in a fine contribution in *Gambling Times* magazine.

A throw-back to an earlier era when "the gambling man was constantly on the move, following the action from rural hamlets to river towns and sometimes into the cities. At certain times, in particular places, the games came down almost like clockwork. Others were almost spontaneous".

"In some mysterious way, however, the gambling grapevine put the word out", Tex recalled, "and it was passed along; 'There's a big stud game comin' up at Louie's place in St. Joe!' There wouldn't be any specific day, just 'A lotta the boys will be there, sometime next week'. And a few days later, some of the 'road pros' would start drifting that way from various places".

They were a special breed – the rambling, gambling men that Jack Straus played with on the Texan circuit. Hold 'Em no-limit poker was normally their game and the knowledge they acquired of it was unmatched anywhere else.

The day in May, 1981 that I sat chatting with him in the Sombrero Room in Binion's, he told me that he was "well ahead" so far that year. "I have got a real good run of cards in private sessions outside the Tournament itself", he said. "I am getting plenty of action and I'm happy the way things are going for me".

After making his exit from the 1981 World Hold 'Em Championship, he did not depart the scene. One suspected that he was more at home in the private sessions where he was not constrained by trying to nurture a pile of $10,000 in chips and endeavouring to stay alive over four days to the concluding stages of the Tournament. Indeed, the real pros in the top league collect the bulk of their income from side games and private head-to-head sessions, maybe with oil-rich Texans who want to prove something to themselves and to the world. The stakes are always higher in these contests, the action at its fiercest and most intense. And the results are shielded from the prying eyes of the Internal Revenue Service. "If you win a tournament it can be emblazoned across the national media. The world knows what you did. Nobody knows what you win in a side game", was how one of the top pros put it.

I saw Straus go into a big private game that same evening that went on through the night and involved a confident young player being spoken of as a possible future world champion. Jack was at his most aggressive. I got the impression that he was playing for his peers – a small coterie of poker professionals who sympathised with the way he had been knocked out of the '81 Championship.

That was funny in itself – ludicrous, in fact, when you compared Jack's record with that of one Riviera Richmond, a millionairess from Beverly Hills, her fingers adorned with acorn-sized diamond rings. Somewhere along the line on the first day she got lucky, caught the card that eliminated Jack Straus and actually ended up leading the field. But the Texan breed, Amarillo Slim Preston, Doyle Brunson, Puggy Pearson and Johnny Moss were not impressed. For them she was like a swimmer who had gone out too far in shark-infested waters. There was the anticipation of blood being spilt, the very smell of it in the air.

As writer Steve Magagnini expressed it – "she glowered at her chuckling male opponents as if she were Lewis Carroll's Red Queen about to shriek, 'Off with their heads!'"

But the "sharks" got her – showing no pity for her in the end and when she was asked how she felt at the moment of exit, she replied: "Upset? With these garbage men? They didn't think I'd last this long".

Riviera Richmond had been coldly dismissed from his mind by Jack Straus as he became involved in some very big pots in the early hours of the morning, breaking the player who had gone into that game with such a high reputation. "It had to be done", he mused aloud. "It had to be done".

Now that it was all over, you kind of guessed that he was rather sorry for breaking the young player so ruthlessly – but during play with so much riding on each hand, there could be no pity, no pity at all. The school he had been brought up in with Doyle Brunson and the others down Texas way did not number the word "pity" in a professional's vocabulary – when you had a stack of chips in front of you. Pity was something you reserved for a fellow professional when he was broke or down on his luck and needed a hand until he rebuilt his bankroll.

Or when one of their own got hooked on drugs and looked like going down the river of no return. Then they would team together to put up the money to send him to the best possible rehabilitation centre and rejoice if he made it back and be saddened if their efforts failed to save him from the demon grip of cocaine or heroin.

*   *   *

I found a close similarity in the manner in which Jack Straus and Doyle Brunson, world champion in 1976 and '77 both became professional poker players and it proved to me that both from the very beginning had that essential freedom of spirit that is the hallmark of the true pros.

Jack Straus took a degree in business administration – just as Doyle did. He was a basket player in his youth – though he never attained the same high standard as Doyle. And he was in a regular job for just one year – the same as Doyle – before he quit in favour of making his livelihood as a gambler.

And like Doyle Brunson, Jack Straus showed a great fondness always for sports betting – all forms of betting, basketball, football, golf and horse racing.

While they were involved in big poker games, they constantly inquired about the progress and results of matches or races. Jack Straus could be in the big money one day after hitting a successful streak at poker and then proceed to blow all the winnings on bets that had nothing to do with the skill and nerve that earned him an honoured place in poker's Hall of Fame.

"Jack was a gambler's gambler", was how old Benny Binion aptly put it. "He would bet on anything. If there were 16 basketball games going on, he'd bet on every one of them".

He was a born athlete and, because of his height, he gravitated like a natural to the college basketball team at Texas A & M, where he took a degree in Physical Education. He liked to recall the moment when he decided to become a professional gambler. "I had just signed a high school teaching contract – I was going to be a coach – and I made this one bet for

$7,000. And I lost it. Then I looked at that contract that said it would pay me $6,500 for one year and I realized it was just going to take me too long to make up for that $7,000 bet. I came out to Las Vegas instead and stayed for three or four years playing poker".

From the time he began playing poker in high school and won a car in a game at the tender age of sixteen – before he could even drive – he loved every aspect of it and it wasn't surprising that later in life he would say, "Watching isn't fun. Playing is everything".

He easily made the transition to the professional ranks. He was likened in his time to Paul Newman's character in *The Sting* and it had to be said of him that he was one of the most colourful – and popular – of all the professionals who participated in his era in the World Series of Poker. The beard and glasses added a certain professorial touch to a born raconteur.

During our first meeting in 1981 I could not refrain from putting to him the direct question: Would you like to win the World Hold 'Em Championship some day?

His reply to that was to ask me a question that was really rhetorical: Would you like to win the Pulitzer Prize?

As Jack viewed it, the winning of the Pulitzer Prize might not make one a better writer but it would be seen as the final accolade. Likewise the winning of the World Poker Championship would make no difference to a top professional's standing with his peers but it would certainly have significance wherever poker is played in the world.

The Old Man and the Sea won a Pulitzer Prize for Ernest Hemingway in 1952 and was of critical importance in bringing him the Nobel Prize in 1954. In his acceptance speech to the Nobel Committee, he said ... "It is because we have had such great writers in the past that a writer is driven far out past where he can go, out to where no one can help him".

I saw Stu Ungar against Doyle Brunson in the 1980 World Poker Championship driven far out past where I thought he could go ... where he could only depend on his own courage and genius. Perhaps it explains why the World Poker Championship has produced such unforgettable moments and why it has gained in prestige with each passing year.

Jack Straus viewed the World Series of Poker as the annual get-together for the top professionals and top amateurs, and the setting for the meeting of old friends who might not see each other for the rest of the year. This aspect was even more important than the outcome of the various tournament contests.

He accepted the "risk factor" in a Tournament like this – "if fortune fails to smile on you, you just shrug your shoulders and wait until the next year". That's exactly what happened Straus in 1981.

*   *   *

His turn came, however, the following year when for the first time the field topped the 100 mark (104 players actually participated) and the total prize-money broke the million-dollar barrier for the first time. It was fitting that he should triumph in that epoch-making tournament in Binion's.

"Winning the title fulfilled a life-long dream", he said. "For years I thought I had been dreaming the impossible dream. Then all of a sudden I did it".

The final pot was another record – an astounding $950,000 dollars. The Horseshoe Casino room was crammed for the spectacular finish and the rail-birds – the guys and dolls who lean over the barriers separating the players from the spectators and watch every move as if their very lives depended on it – were left with the memory of moments that would stay with them always.

Straus, who had been quoted at 18/1 at the outset, had been down to his last $500 in chips on the first day but, bluffing his way back from the dead, was 3/2 favourite entering the last day's play.

It came down to a head-to-head between himself and Dewey Tomko, an outstanding professional and fine sportsman from Winter Haven, Florida. When both players exposed their down cards, Tomko was seen to have an ace and a 4 of diamonds. Straus had an ace of hearts and a 10 of spades. It remained for the dealer to deal the five remaining cards – the exposed cards common to both contestants. The flop came 4 and 5 of spades and 7 of diamonds. Now Tomko was ahead with a pair of 4s.

So it had all come down to what card would be turned "on the river" or fifth street (the final community card) – if Straus were to take the title.

You could hear the silence as Horseshoe dealer Brian McCandles of Las Vegas dealt the last card after what seemed an age. His slow flip of the card added to the adrenalin-pumping tension.

A 10 of clubs!

Pandemonium broke loose. Straus had won with a pair of 10s to Tomko's pair of 4s.

*   *   *

Jack Straus captured a record purse of $520,000 and, true to his reputation for being extremely generous in his hours of triumph, he retained the $500,000 and gave the odd $20,000 to the dealers and the cardroom staff.

It didn't end there. He announced that he was going to enjoy his winnings and relax for a while.

The Green Hills of Africa had always called him when he was not playing poker. He had gone on big game hunting trips to Kenya, Tanzania and Zimbabwe. Now he was off again and on this particular trip he would shoot one of the biggest lions ever entered in the trophy books.

He promised before his departure to buy a friend of his, Ray Miranda of Las Vegas an elephant. "He's worked with elephants before in circuses and I want to make him happy again", said Jack, those dark blue eyes of his mirroring the laughter that had lit up his countenance.

He talked about arranging a game of golf with me the next time I hit Las Vegas. But deep down I knew it was not on, for when he participated in fourballs involving Doyle Brunson and others the stakes could run to "ten, ten and ten", meaning $10,000 on the first nine, $10,000 on the second and $10,000 overall. My bank manager would have had a seizure on the spot if he heard I had got involved in that kind of game!

We talked about Jack coming to Ireland for a projected tournament for charity in the Killiney Castle Hotel. "I'll be coming now as the champion and not as a Texan bum", he remarked, again breaking into spontaneous laughter. He never did make it.

After he had been crowned champion, he was much sought after by the media for interviews spelling out his philosophy on the game and for advice to those aspiring to reach the top of the ladder.

He was a journalist's and writers' dream when it came to the quotable quote. "If there is no risk in losing, there is no high in winning" was a favourite maxim of his and again "chips don't have a home; if money is your god, you can forget no-limit poker because it's going to hurt you too much to turn loose of it. The way I feel about those pieces of green paper is, you can't take them with you ... if they wanted you to hold on to money, they'd have made it with handles on".

It came down for him to inner fortitude – to having ice water in the veins instead of blood when you went all in, maybe on a bluff or on a hand that you knew could be outdrawn. You can call it "heart" or you can call it "bottle" but, according to Straus, you had no place being at the table in a really high-stakes game unless you had that steely edge.

"Courage is an all-important ingredient in the make-up of any poker player", was how he put it to me. "You cannot hope to get anywhere without it".

And he added: "Before you go into any game, you must ask yourself the question – can I afford to play in it? You cannot play to your highest level of ability if you are concerned about your bankroll".

Al Alvarez, author of the classic book *The Biggest Game in Town*, thought it was fitting that Jack Straus should die in the middle of a marathon high-stakes game. "Personally, I hope he was losing when he had his heart attack. He was never a percentage player, the kind who always quits when he is ahead", said Al and he added: "If ever a man lived up to his motto – 'Better One Day as a Lion Than One Hundred Years as a Lamb' – it was Jack Straus".

*   *   *

I first became acquainted with the unique world of the big-time poker professionals when I flew to Las Vegas in May, 1980 to cover for the Independent Newspapers the attempt by Colette Doherty to win the title for Ireland. She had won the inaugural Irish Championship earlier that year and used her winnings to put down the $10,000 to compete in the World Hold 'Em Championship. In fact, she was the first competitor from Ireland ever to participate in the event. She made her exit the first day, being outdrawn on what might have well been a winning hand by Texas-born Bob Hooks and as Johnny Moss said to her: "You had to go on the hand – I would have bet on it too".

The fact that she had the courage to enter brought more world-wide attention than ever before to the World Series of Poker and 1981 saw competitors from Norway, Australia and Britain arrive in Las Vegas to participate in some of the tournament events, if not in all cases in the "Big One" itself. Therefore, she was the trail-blazer and Ireland sent more than one representative in 1981 and again in 1982.

Donnacha O'Dea, son of Siobhan McKenna, one of Ireland's most famous stage actresses and of film star, Denis O'Dea, who taught him the rudiments of the game, came in time to be accepted by Doyle Brunson, Bobby Baldwin, Stu Ungar, Bob Stupak, Chip Reese and others as well capable of holding his place in the "premier league". O'Dea proved his class in the Preliminary World Hold 'Em Tournament by reaching the last table and, more than once, he was in the firing line when the battle for the world crown itself reached its climactic stages. Like Jack Straus, he was turned on by the intensity of the action in private sessions, especially when it came down to head-to-head contests. The better the opposition, the more he was capable of producing in order to capture the big pots. His late father, who had played in the biggest game in town – Dublin that is – with Ireland's Prime Minister (Taoiseach), Sean Lemass must have smiled up there in the Great Beyond as he looked down on his son taking on *la crème-de-la-crème* of the High Rollers in Las Vegas.

From the day I first hit Binion's Horseshoe Casino and began rubbing shoulders with them in the Sombrero Room, I was fascinated by the characters I met and I knew then I wanted to give permanency to their stories in the pages of a book. Out of it all grew *The Poker Kings Of Las Vegas*, which was launched during the 1982 World Series of Poker.

I opened the book with a chapter on a legendary figure among the "Texan breed". The very first paragraph read: "His name is Thomas Austin Preston, Jr. but in the world of cards and wherever the game of poker has real significance, he is known simply as 'Amarillo Slim' ".

We were riding out in a chauffeur-driven limousine to the Helldorado Rodeo, organised by the Professional Rodeo Cowboys Association in the Las Vegas Convention Centre. It was a few days before the 1980 Hold 'Em Championship got under way in Binion's. Amarillo had invited Colette Doherty along to savour the excitement of the rodeo – a sport that they will tell you is the heritage of a unique breed, athletes tracing their expertise back to the cattlemen and cowboys who tamed a land with their professional skills.

"I will slit my throat if a lady takes the crown," said Amarillo with total frankness. Colette Doherty knew she was included in that sweeping comment. But while Amarillo could have dismissed her as a minnow thrown to the "sharks" of Las Vegas, he proved that Texan hospitality is a living reality just the same as Irish hospitality.

Amarillo Slim now began to reveal spontaneous wit as he conjured up the scene as the Roman soldiers at the foot of the cross on Mount Calvary, played dice as they waited for Christ to die – and gambled for his robe.

I remarked to Amarillo that if Christ were walking the earth in this present decade, he would probably be in there in the poker rooms mixing with the players – and no doubt would have chosen at least one of them as a disciple.

And Amarillo, not being irreverent for one moment, but just simply admitting that poker was his life as fishing had been Peter's, remarked that if he had been at the foot of the Cross on that Good Friday afternoon, he would have felt deep sympathy for "The Man up there" – "but knowing myself and how the action attracts me, I'm afraid you would have found me in there among the soldiers shooting the dice".

Amarillo Slim once faced this very good woman player, who was already being tipped as having an extraordinary future in the game. Amarillo looking out with those sharp eyes of his from under his Texan Stetson had noticed that under her flimsy, silk-thin blouse, her breasts swelled appreciably every time she got a good hand – while her face remained an inscrutable mask.

After a while he could almost read from the swelling of her breasts whether she had Jacks, Kings, Queens or Aces.

Amarillo realised that he had discovered the road to a "killing" next time round. But as he talked to two of the "old guard", someone happened to get an earful of what he was saying – and the word was passed along.

Next time he faced up to playing the dame, she was wearing a cardigan that revealed nothing – and was zipped right up to the neck. The odd third or fourth button from the top, carelessly but studiously open, was now for him but a mirage in the desert beyond Las Vegas!

*   *   *

He was born in Arkansas, an only son, but the family moved to Texas when he was nine months old. "I am a Texan," he would tell you simply and every bit of the 6' 2" tall and 165 pounds frame of his was Texan from his white Stetson to the soles of his white leather boots and, of course, that highly-distinctive, Texan drawl.

Everything about him was colourful. And no wonder when he became World Poker Champion in 1972, he was dubbed "Poker's Ambassador of Goodwill".

The belt around his waist had a horse's head on it, surrounded by a horseshoe. One of the rings he wore was a diamond insured for 90,000 dollars. On it was a map of Texas, inscribed with just one word – "Slim".

He had very limited schooling and never knew what it was to go to university – like some of the younger breed of professionals who would arrive later on the scene.

He was fifteen years old when he started playing poker – no limit. He got his initiation into the game in the back room of the pool hall in Forth Worth, near Dallas Texas. He discovered that it was easier to play with businessmen because the pickings were good. He learned to leave the hustlers alone.

Johnny Moss had emerged as the finest card player on the circuit. "We tried to duck Johnny but always wound up meeting him," he recalled.

Indeed, Amarillo and Johnny and "Sailor" Roberts were to be found on the southern circuit together. It was a tribute to the knowledge of cards they acquired in those days – and the ability also to endure the heat in the hottest kitchen – that all three would know the supreme honour of taking the world crown, Johnny Moss more often than any other player, three times in all.

Amarillo Slim first started coming to Las Vegas in the late Fifties and early Sixties. He recalled tremendous no limit games in The Dunes for high stakes. But he did not settle in Las Vegas – and never would. "If you gave me the whole goddam town, I wouldn't live here," he said.

His home was in Amarillo, Texas where he raised cattle (carrying the brand name "AS") and quarter horses on a 3,170-acre ranch.

But he was the first to admit that poker gave him his big break in life and his name became known far beyond the United States when he won the world title.

Amarillo became a true ambassador for the sport when he travelled outside the States to meet the best and, as the spotlight of the television cameras on the World Series of Poker increased his fame, there were many who wanted to test their skill at the game against him – including immensely-wealthy Arab Sheikhs, prepared to back their confidence in themselves with limitless money from their oil wells.

Once, in England on a trip with Johnny Moss, they were asked by a few Japanese to play "hari-kari poker". Johnny was rather sceptical, wondering if the two of them were being "set up" but Amarillo said challengingly: "We'll take them on".

It turned out to be the Japanese version of Texas Hold 'Em Poker but the Japs were kamikaze pilots against the two Texan professionals …

*   *   *

I saw Puggy Pearson bring colour to the scene at Binion's and make the television cameras whirr by dressing up on the opening morning of the World Hold 'Em Championship in the full regalia of an Indian Chief. "Me Great Big Chief", he would exclaim as he raised his right hand to the manner born. They loved it.

He came out of the blue grass country of Kentucky but he likes to think of himself as from Nashville, Tennessee – Johnny Cash country. He recalls a time when the family (nine children altogether) was so poor that he lived in nineteen different places. The reason? His parents had to move every time the rent fell due, as they could not pay. His father was "a handyman" with no formal education.

"In those depression days, you never saw a loaf of bread until you were perhaps ten years old," he recalled. All his mother could ask for when she went to buy the staff of life was "a piece off the end". Later when he hit the road, working his way up to be world poker champion, he knew what it was like to live on sardines and cheese and crackers and sleep rough in a car until there came a day when guys who recognised his ability took "a piece of the action" (for the uninitiated that means they took shares in him) and he ran over all opposition in 1973, standing on the top-most rung of the ladder as World Champion at Hold 'Em Poker.

He was christened Walter Clyde but among poker aficionados the world over, he is recognised by his huge cigars and by the first-name "Puggy" (he got the nickname "Puggy" when he flattened his nose in a fall when he was twelve).

A gambler has got to be different from ordinary people," he went on. "He has got to have the constitution to take it when he goes broke. You might get broke quite a number of times – completely broke. Gamblers know that this is going to happen. They learn how to be down and out. An accident may bring changes in the way you project yourself, even in your speech. It's the same when the gambler hits rock-bottom and loses all. He may find himself acting differently and talking differently."

"Like King Kong for ten or fifteen years, that was me. I ruled the world."

For four or five years he just travelled around from poker game to poker game.

He would hit Las Vegas two or three times a year. He remembers coming up in 1946 and getting broke, after his first trip overseas. "I was just like all the other suckers. Playing the tables. Playing craps. Playing the games in which the odds are with the House and you cannot win eventually. The House must always win."

So he came to realise that money didn't lie in the games of chance but in the game he knew better than others and could play better – poker.

These were the years of preparation, the years of acquiring knowledge. Later, after he had become world champion, he never had to worry about going hungry anymore. You see the champions are "comped" when they play in the big tournaments. The Casinos pick up the tab for their accommodation and for everything they eat and drink. The big names are part of the "circus". They draw the crowds who play poker for smaller stakes at other tables or who come to watch and gamble on the slots and all the other inducements a Casino offers for those seeking action and thrills. Without the colourful characters, the "circus" would have no pulling power.

*   *   *

I asked him why the best of the American poker champions do not travel more outside the States, like the top American golfers?

"The champions from every country wind up in Las Vegas eventually," he replied. "They all want to test their skill against the professionals who reside in Las Vegas or come here for the World Series from other parts of the States."

"Yes, believe me, if you wait around long enough, you will find that they all come to Las Vegas, be they home-town champions or the national champion of their own country. And they find out what they want to know – maybe at a cost in money or pride, but they have to know it, otherwise they would not come."

*   *   *

I saw a great similarity in the childhood days of Johnny Moss and Puggy Pearson. Like Puggy, young Johnny sold papers to live – did it, in fact, for seven years in Dallas, Texas and it was in that time that he also learned the rudiments of what a gambling career would entail.

In Las Vegas in May, 1973 in Binion's Horseshoe Casino the two men, like two gunfighters who had gone separate roads, faced each other – Johnny the fastest gun in his day, ageing now, Puggy the up-and-coming gunfighter, supremely confident and wanting to prove something to himself and the world. There was 30,000 dollars riding on the crucial hand – and what could not Johnny's parents or Puggy's have done with all that money back in the bitter times of the struggling childhood that both men had known.

Puggy had kings and sixes and Johnny tried to draw out on him but his rival didn't fold – and won the hand and went on to take the title.

Johnny had already known the glory of being champion more than once; for Puggy it was the realisation of a dream that would have seemed impossible back in his Nashville youth – and he wouldn't have to worry anymore about going hungry.

During our initial interview Johnny Moss unfolded for me a picture of Texas in the early decades of this century, a Texas that still retained much that people associate with the romantic Old West – but Western films did not always depict the deprivation that could exist hand in hand with what was romantically appealing.

I could almost smell the dust in the streets of Marshall where he was born in 1907 – in the heart of prairie country – the second son of the Deputy sheriff, John Hardie Moss. I could picture the sense of shock and disbelief that must have fallen on the Moss home when Da came home and told Ma that the Sheriff had lost his job because he failed to win re-election and that meant that the Deputy Sheriff had to go also.

So John Moss Sr. piled all the family belongings into a covered wagon and with his wife, Lena and the four children headed out of town – moving on from town to town in search of work. A long day's journey into night and another day dawning and night falling again and the cycle renewed. Johnny told me of the pain on his father's face in later years as he recalled that journey – and the tragedy that struck when they were about four weeks on the road. Lena died of a burst appendix. It was too late to do anything when they got her to Fort Worth Hospital. She was buried in that town. Johnny was too young to have really known his mother.

Later, after his father had got work as a lineman with the telephone company in Dallas, tragedy struck the family again. John Moss Sr. had his right leg amputated when a telephone pole fell on it. And, now handicapped with a wooden leg, he could no longer work. He had to give up his job with the telephone company, and with the insurance money he bought a small grocery store which kept them going until Johnny was about eight years old.

Eventually Johnny's father was forced to sell the store and Johnny had to give up school to sell papers in the streets of Dallas to help buy food.

He started playing poker when he was 15. In time he hit the road like Puggy Pearson, learning what it was like to be completely broke and to build up your bankroll again and then get broke a second time and a third. He agreed with the philosophy of other great players of his generation who maintained that you had to be completely broke before you acquired the art of managing money – and your own emotions.

He eventually arrived in the big time and the big action. He was capable of winning $100,000 and double that sum and more. Initially, the fortunes he won at poker, he lost on the horses and other forms of gambling. But then he had so much money by the values of the late Thirties and Forties that he saw it as an instrument in the life he had chosen – the life of a gambler.

There came a day, however, when he began to invest and acquire interests in oil wells and property. At last he was on his way to becoming a millionaire.

But his epitaph, I always liked to think, would comprise just seven words in bold capitals: **THE MAN WHO BROKE NICK THE GREEK**.

Johnny Moss had reached the point in his career when Benny Binion called him in Texas and asked him to come to Las Vegas to face The Man – the legendary Nick the Greek (Dandalos).

That marathon meeting of Nick The Greek and Johnny Moss was for those who had the good fortune to be present in Binion's Horseshoe Casino on a Sunday afternoon in January, 1949, like the World Heavyweight Championship bout between Muhammad Ali and the "unbeatable" George Foreman in Kinshasa in October, 1974.

Johnny Moss himself described it to me as "the biggest game of poker that ever was".

"The match lasted over a period of four or five months solid. I remember one $100,000 buy-in game. I would say two or three million dollars changed hands. We played all kinds of poker and when finally I got the better of The Man, who up to that point many had considered unbeatable, he made his memorable parting remark to me: 'I guess I got to let you go, Mr Moss'.

*   *   *

Tex Sheahan rated Doyle "Texas Dolly" Brunson "the best poker player of my era".

A graduate of the toughest school of all – the Texas circuit – he was the first after Johnny Moss to win two successive World titles (1976 and '77) – a feat emulated by Stu Ungar in 1980 and '81 and by Johnny Chan in 1987 and '88.

He told me that the biggest amount he ever won was $770,000 dollars – at a poker session that went on over two days and nights.

"I could walk away from big losses in my younger days", he confessed. "I learned what it was like to be broke one day and be in the money the next. I learned too that money is just a tool – it has no value!"

He had lived like a millionaire since he started playing poker as a full-time professional at the age of twenty-two. "We poker players live like millionaires whether we are or not", he said simply.

"I can't imagine anybody having a better life than we've had. When I say 'We' I'm speaking of all the poker players", he went on.

191

You answered to no boss, he explained. You travelled and went places and you were always meeting different people. No, he couldn't imagine a more exciting life – so different from a nine-to-five existence.

Doyle Brunson created a special niche for himself in poker history by compiling the classic 600-page work, originally title *How I Made Over One Million dollars Playing Poker*. It is considered by the pros one of the best books on poker ever and mandatory reading for anyone planning to enter a tournament.

His philosophy of life – like that of fellow-Texan Jack Straus was to live every minute of it to the full – was coloured by the fact that he fought back from a bout of cancer but he came back to put two world titles back-to-back and then in 1980 faced Stu Ungar in on of the greatest head-to-head of modern times.

In this classic of classics we had "The Kid" facing "The King". And when Ungar emerged the winner in the dramatic shoot-out after High Noon, Doyle Brunson paid this tribute to him: "He can become the best poker player ever. You do not find kids like him in poker parlours. This kid is a genius. He picks up things faster than I have ever seen in anybody of his age".

"I wanted to make it a shoot-out", said Stu Ungar to me. "I knew he would outplay me the longer it lasted, for , make no mistake about it, Doyle Brunson is the No. 1. Hold 'Em player in the world today. As far as I was concerned someone was going to go broke quickly by forcing him and carrying the play to him, I hoped it would not be me".

Picture the scene – The Kid pale and ascetic, almost gaunt-looking around the cheek-bones, yet, something of the suppressed fire of a James Dean about him. Not a spare ounce of flesh on that slight frame. Tension in all his movements, in every twitch of his face, in the very shrug of his shoulders beneath the casual dress.

Physically Doyle Brunson, with his heavy frame, commanded the table.

It's now the fourth and final day. Doyle Brunson had caught four aces to eliminate the ageless Johnny Moss, who had gone all in with $200,000 on a house of queens and who went out to spontaneous applause right around the cardroom. Then Brunson knocked out New Yorker Jay Heimowitz.

The showdown was the "dream ticket" between Brunson and Ungar, with the Texan, because of his vast experience, the odds-on favourite. He looked certain to justify the odds when he held a powerful hand of aces and sevens after the flop. But Stu filled a straight on Fourth Street and Doyle Brunson did not catch the ace or seven he needed on Fifth Street and that was it.

Stu Ungar was only 26 – the second youngest ever – when he won the title on May 19, 1980. He retained his crown the following year when beating Perry Green, "The Man from Alaska," in the final hand, taking new record prize money of $375,000.

*   *   *

The Kid came out of New York – though he had been resident in las

Vegas for almost a year and was already a fully-fledged professional when he first took the title. He knew no other life, as he put it to me, but "gamblin', sleepin' and eatin' ".

Stuart Ungar was his full name but they called him either "The Kid" or "Stuey" or just "Stu" and, looking at his boyish face in 1980, you would have been forgiven for asking: What is this baby doing among all these seasoned poker pros?

A baby he may have looked – but he was no child in his knowledge of cards. He was already recognised as one of the finest gin rummy players alive, a game mastered in his early teens by playing any – and all – comers in the up-market mountain resorts of upper New York State. His reputation at "gin" was so formidable, in fact, that he was beginning to find it extremely difficult to get anyone to play him.

"It was a case of being forced to take up poker", he told me. "The only way I could get a session of gin was to play an opponent an equal session of poker ... but I learned fast".

Stu Ungar grew up on Manhattan's Lower East side, where his father ran a corner bar and grill. He learned to play cards by his mother's side when the family went on holidays to resorts in the Catskill Mountains of New York State. "My mother was a good poker player", he said. "I started playing with the waiters and I got good. My father died when I was thirteen. I did not go to College. I went hustling. I was only fourteen when I started playing cards and I was already taking them seriously at 15."

"I started dealing and playing in private clubs in New York. I played the best players – and beat them. I suppose I had what you call 'card sense' from the cradle. The more I played, the better I got – and I picked up fast".

The 5 foot 6 inches tall "Kid", who turned the scales at around 8 stone, began to slip into suburban New York country clubs in his teens and the wealthy professional men among the membership must have considered it quite a novelty to play against such a frail-looking pale-face pint-sized youngster. They certainly paid for the pleasure – and Stu was soon reputed to be earning up to $50,000 some weeks and he began to build such a reputation that all opposition melted away when it came to gin rummy.

But he would never have become World Poker Champion so young if he had not come to Las Vegas where he quickly became involved in the superhot action in the Silverbird, learning what it was like to take on the "heavies" like Bobby Baldwin, Johnny Moss, Doyle Brunson and Puggy Pearson.

Stu was the first to acknowledge that the games he played in Las Vegas against champions like Bobby Baldwin and Doyle Brunson in the months leading up to the 1980 World Championship prepared him for the "Big One".

"I learned from them", he said. "But you've got to be lucky. You've got to have God on your side to win the title itself".

"I was a year learning professionally", he went on. "I was only a novice when I was in New York. Yes, I used to play in the subways of

Manhattan. Some would tell me, I know, that it was a misspent youth. What was misspent about it? If I had gone to school like a normal kid, I would not have ended up poker champion of the world".

*   *   *

I returned to Las Vegas in 1993 after an absence of some years to find that much had changed not alone on the poker front but along the glittering, neon-lit "Strip" with luxurious new hotels already making their impact, others in course of construction or at the planning stage – one of the new hotels boasting a full-scale sea battle that only the high-tech age and American inventiveness on the grand scale could contrive.

Bobby Baldwin, who blazed the trail for the "College Boys" when he won the World Hold 'Em Poker Championship in 1978, was now President of the imposing Mirage Hotel with its constantly erupting volcano, white albino tigers and tropical-forest ambience. He was still a very formidable opponent when he sat into high-stakes games with players of the calibre of "Chip" Reese, Doyle Brunson and Johnny Chan. The Golden Nugget and Binion's Horseshoe Casino in the downtown intersection of Fremont Street, where you also find Sam Boyd's Fremont Hotel and Four Queens squaring off in a blazing quadrangle of lights, had both been extensively refurbished and by 1995 Binion's would be building a new Tower. Yes, there seemed to be no end to expansion in Las Vegas.

Two Iranian expatriates, Mansour Matloubi, now living in Cardiff and Hamid Dasmalchi of Solana Beach, California had won the World Hold 'Em title in 1990 and '92 respectively. And Chinese-born John Chan (his family moved from Canton to Hong Kong when he was three and then when he was nine to Houston, Texas where his father set up a restaurant) had taken the crown in 1978 and '88. He had been thwarted of a fabulous three-timer in 1989 when beaten into second place by the brash, cocky Phil Hellmuth, Jr. who had dropped out of the University of Wisconsin in his senior year to become a professional poker player. At 24 Phil Hellmuth was the youngest ever to win the title (Stu Ungar, as we have already seen, was 26 when he won it for the first time in 1980 and Johnny Chan 29 when he became champion initially in 1987).

The break-through by Matloubi and Dasmalchi did not mean, of course, that American pros who were well-known names on the circuit were being eclipsed altogether. Far from it. Tom McEvoy from Grand Rapids was champion in 1983 and in 1985 Bill Smith, a hard-drinking Texan professional, outgunned fellow Dallas resident, T.J. Cloutier, one of the most colourful and successful players gracing the scene. The following year Las Vegas resident, Berry Johnston, the professionals' professional, who invariably adopts a quiet style with no histrionics, gained the reward for his consistency by at last landing the title. His overall tournament winnings were close to $900,000 at the time he became champion in 1992.

Another very likeable pro, Hans "Tuna" Lund, who was in his forties, listing his hobby as gold prospecting, had brought his total earnings from the World Series alone to $834,145 but he was very unlucky not to realise his great ambition of becoming world champion in 1990 when he had to

194

be content with runner-up position.

Lund was within one card of snatching the title. He held a strong two-pair (two aces and two nines) as it came down to Fifth Street. Mansour Matloubi looked to be in trouble with a pair of 10s. However, on the final card, the dealer turned over a 10 and Matloubi's hand of 3s beat out Lund's two-pair. "It hurts to watch your career-long dream slip away on the turn of one card", was all "Tuna" could say.

The romance of the World Hold 'Em Championship was shown once again in 1993 when Jim Bechtel, a 40-year-old cotton farmer from Arizona and a top-ranked amateur, who had been a regular player at the Horseshoe since he was 21, took the World crown.

*   *   *

The World Series of Poker had become such a world event and so good were some of the new breed who had hit the circuit that we had come a long way from the days when the World Hold 'Em title was contested by fields of 8, then 22 and 34. Tom McEvoy argued that with fields of 200 and more today for the "Big One", it was going to become almost impossible to make it two world titles back-to-back and a three-in-a-row looked completely out now.

And that made it all the more regrettable that Johnny Chan, the "Orient Express" did not complete the three-timer in '89. "You could play a million years and it would never happen again. Not only did Johnny win it twice-in-a-row and come in second the following year, he won two other tournaments in between. Therefore, he won four big tournaments in a row and came in second in the next one. It was extraordinary", was how Doyle Brunson but it to American write Steve Hirana of *Transpacific* magazine.

Chan had become the all-time high money-winner with tournament earnings of over $2,000,000.00. He had come a long way from the time he first hit Las Vegas with $120 and started playing at the three-dollar tables ("You don't have to have a lot of money to become a poker player, but you gotta have faith in yourself") and because of his lack of discipline and inability to manage money, not knowing when to quit, he went broke again and again. He was forced to get a job and worked in turn as a chef, a dealer and floor manager. "I finally learned when to quit. And I learned too that there's always another game tomorrow".

His tomorrows became good, so good, in fact, that he boasts a million-dollar home in Las Vegas, four cars and his suits never cost less than $5,000. He loves good food and admits that he is such a big spender that to leave a poker table with winnings of $75,000 wouldn't even cover his monthly expenses. He's a family man and stresses that "women and poker don't mix. They break your concentration".

This then is Johnny Chan, voted by his peers one of the greatest poker players in the world today. There are those who want to be able to say that they had the privilege of taking on THE MAN. Like the French billionaire, who was dying of cancer and wanted one last blow-out at the tables. He invited Chan and Doyle Brunson and other top American pros over to Paris for a two-week session. Chan returned home richer by $1 million.

The billionaire – "a very nice man, plus being an action guy", was Johnny's tribute to him – died a month later.

*   *   *

Seymour Liebowitz, one of the most colourful personalities on the circuit with his paunchy demeanour and his penchant for outsize cigars which he smoked continuously during play, never enjoyed anything like the success of Johnny Chan. Seymour came to Dublin some years ago with Stu Ungar, Mickey Appleman, Tom McEvoy, Amarillo Slim Preston, Bob Stupak, Bobby Baldwin and "Suitcase Jim" Ray, and others for a big charity tournament in the Killiney Castle Hotel.

When his close friend, Jack Straus got his fatal heart attack while playing in a tournament, Seymour said that it was the way he would like to go.

Ed Koch reported in the *Las Vegas Sun* that Seymour Liebowitz suffered a heart attack in the Mirage Hotel in mid-July 1995. "He died as he wanted to die – at the card table", added Ed.

One could only reflect on the words of Johnny Chan. "The government takes a bit of you, the mortgage takes a bit. Life is too short, you have to enjoy it".

15

"You Did Not Come Under Starter's Orders"

The fire alarm had gone off after midnight in the hotel in Cheltenham during Festival week and this guy, who had a race against time to get his trousers on, was making it as fast as he could down the stairs, a black prostitute ahead of him.

"Pay up, pay up", she shouted back at him, her boobs swelling beneath a flimsy white blouse over the tightest and shortest of minis.

"You must be kiddin' ", he shouted back. "You did not come under starter's orders".

It was during the era in the Seventies when Cheltenham was literally invaded by prostitutes and pimps, who were under the impression that there were rich pickings to be had out of the Irish, in particular. Nowadays, the hotels impose much stricter security at the doors. But the ladies of the night, who really want to do business, can get around it by booking into a hotel and the English police will tell you that unless one of them has a previous conviction and is actually caught in the act of soliciting, there is very little they can do to curb the blight.

Two prostitutes were overheard exchanging views and one of them remarked: "These bloody Irish are useless – all they think of is cards and horses".

The Kerryman's response to that, as he contemplated the vision of four beautiful Queens coming up before his eyes, was: "There's a time and a mood for everything".

There are wives I know who wouldn't be that perturbed about their husbands heading for Cheltenham with "a bunch of the lads" – certainly the great March Festival meeting has never been seen to hold out the same temptations as Paris and the Pigalle area during a rugby international week-end.

Jimmy (The Buck) Ryan summed up the lot of many a man returning from Cheltenham bleary-eyed and with every bone in the body aching with tiredness from the drinking and the singing, the card-playing and the "crack" generally, when he told us of the time he was in such bad odour when he got back to Fethard in County Tipperary that the only one to bid him the time of day and give him a knowing wink was "the ould gander" who had his own domestic problems and understood perfectly what one had to face in such situations.

Jimmy in the bar of the Queen's Hotel on the Friday morning of the '94 Festival meeting telling a group of us over the bucks fizz of the ingenuity of a character who did the rounds announcing to all and sundry: "Roll up, roll up and see the dancin' duck".

"He had an old bit of galvanised sheeting with an oil-burner under it," said Jimmy, "and you can bet that the goddam duck danced and danced like Fred Astaire or Gene Kelly as he felt his feet burning."

When one duck had had enough of the dancing, he was replaced by another. "Roll up, roll up and see the dancin' duck ..."

Meanwhile, the guy's wife was on the other side of the makeshift tent exclaiming: "Roll up, roll up and see the Holy Fryer."

The Holy Fryer happened to be a frying pan with a hole in it.

And then the three Irish nuns who went to London to attend the International Convention of the good sisters. At the luncheon break they go into Hyde Park to partake of their sandwiches and the flask of tea. They happen to take a seat right next to one occupied by three ladies of easy virtue.

Anyway, one of the ladies of the night had been out with a Greek shipping tycoon who had given her an island and an oil tanker; the second had been out with a German who presented her with a factory and a diamond as big as the Ritz while the third had met a Japanese tycoon who left the other two completely in the shade as the yen showered on her like confetti in addition to a plethora of gifts.

One of the nuns was heard to remark quietly, as she finished her ham sandwich: "To hell with the parish priest and his Mars bar!"

*   *   *

The golden era of the Queen's Hotel was unquestionably the decade from the mid-Seventies when J.P. McManus and other leading personalities in the invading 'army' from Ireland made it their headquarters. Standing at the top of the Promenade in the centre of Cheltenham, it presents a magnificent spectacle always when the facade is floodlit at night. It was the centre of the great victory dinners thrown by Dr Michael Mangan from Dunmore, County Galway in the seasons when Monksfield – 'Monkey' as he was affectionately known by those in the inner circle – won the Champion Hurdle in 1978 and '79.

And here too flamboyant John Mulhern from Celbridge, County Kildare added to the legends of how the Irish can celebrate in victory after his horse, Friendly Alliance had won the Grand Annual Challenge Handicap Chase in 1981.

You would see them at late breakfast in the morning when they had come in from watching the early work-outs on the course, browsing through the racing pages over their bacon and eggs, tea or coffee and toast – Mick O'Toole and Dessie Hughes, Jack Doyle, the legendary bloodstock agent and J.P. McManus, Ted Walsh and John Mulhern. Edward O'Grady

198

also stayed at the Queen's in that era.

The atmosphere was redolent with knowledge – and talk of how this one had gone that morning at exercise in the shadow of Cleeve Hill and the word was out that perhaps something else wasn't sparking. There was a depth of erudition in everything they had to say and all the time the patter was interspersed with banter and repartee.

There were those special occasions when you sensed it in the air that the ring would be rocked in the afternoon. J.P. McManus, deep in conversation with his close friend and confidant, Jimmy Hayes, brilliant student of the form book, as they prepared to "go to war" on what appeared to be a proverbial "good thing" in the National Hunt Chase – as often as not a graveyard for the punters and yet, ironically enough, the one event that provided the opportunity to pull off an awesome gamble – if you had the right animal for the job.

*   *   *

Yes, when I reflect back to the Seventies and early Eighties I know now that it was the golden age of the Queen's Hotel – a glittering era that leaves the writer with a sense of nostalgia for times past.

It was the era when the big poker games, played through the night could be seen in the lounge area of the Hotel. Big money changed hands in these 'schools' involving Irish and English players who played the circuit. It was a case of on to Liverpool from Cheltenham for the Aintree Grand National meeting and then to the Festival meetings in Ireland, right down to the Listowel meeting. Some missed out on the races completely, sleeping through the day to be refreshed for more all-night action at the card tables.

Card sharks and even cheaters were liable at times to get into a school. You might see a trio seat themselves so that they could give the right signals to one another. Once the late Tony O'Malley of Galway, a born sportsman and most likeable character (he is commemorated through the Tony O'Malley Memorial Handicap Chase during Galway Festival week) realised that he had gotten himself into the wrong school. He extricated himself without any fuss by having Reception announce that he was needed urgently on the phone and when he came back he excused himself by saying that a close relation was dying back in Ireland. He counted himself fortunate to get out when already deprived of £800 by the cheaters.

A friend of mine was in another school where again the cheaters were setting the situation up for a real killing. There was a very big crowd of eager onlookers around the table as they began to play it for a very sizeable pot. Everything rested on my friend filling a straight. The odds seemed stacked against him but he caught the one card that turned the tide on the cheaters and, rising from his seat, he exclaimed to the heavens as he stretched his arms out wide: "Lord, give me hands", and at the same time swept the mountain of notes to himself.

He ordered a bottle of the best champagne. As the cork popped, he put it to his lips and began to drink as if he was quaffing a bottle of

199

Budweiser.

The cheaters were looking very menacing. We knew they wouldn't accept the loss of this pot – and their own money in it. We got our friend away from the table and up to a back room – not his own. Someone agreed to sleep guard with him in the next twin bed. His winnings were quietly deposited by a friendly member of the Hotel staff where no one could lay hands on them. The sum was close to £1,000.

Not surprisingly, the cheaters came looking for my friend, seeking him out in his own room. They burst down the door but, to their consternation, the bird had flown.

Next morning my friend woke refreshed and ready for action. He was such an expansive character that when he hit a champagne mood the sky was literally the limit. He would have taken the first flight to Paris with a few of his pals but discovered to his grief that they were operating on restricted tickets. Instead they took a taxi to London later in the day, arriving too late to find any bar open. "Where can we get a drink?", they asked the taxi-man. "There should be a mini-bar in the room of your hotel", he replied.

They drank it dry. The bill for bed and breakfast left a mighty hole in the £1,000. But they weren't crying over it. They were content to celebrate in the knowledge that the cheaters had been totally outwitted for once.

Forgetting the cheaters, the card sessions provided absorbing entertainment for many people as did the backgammon.

J.P. McManus could be seen in backgammon games for stakes the size of which we could never learn. Always, one was drawn to the circle of onlookers around him as he switched the pieces with the smooth, easy, lightning touch of an assured master. Later I would learn that he had played in major tournaments in Monte Carlo, Florida, the Bahamas and other centres around the globe.

On one occasion he won the World Championship Consolation Tournament. Apart from the actual tournaments, one invariably found terrific action in side games and very serious gambling. "I have seen more heavy wagering on those occasions than I have seen on the racecourse. However, I always seemed to get my expenses when I took part in major tournaments", he revealed to me.

The fascination of the English media with all that surrounded the "Irish Connection" with the Festival meeting eventually killed the public card sessions and the backgammon sessions in the lounge area of the Queen's Hotel. Once the television cameras moved in, it was put onto an entirely different plane. The local police chiefs feared that London might get alarmed at the fact that heavy wagering on cards in public places was taking place without any curbs. Notices were put up to the effect that such wagering was debarred under a law that went back a long time. So the curtain came down on a facet of Cheltenham Festival week that we had come to take very much for granted.

*   *   *

The very same fascination of the English media resulted in J.P.

McManus and Jimmy Hayes suddenly being catapulted on to the international stage and nothing would ever be the same for them subsequently. The stories circulating in racing circles about J.P.'s tilts at the ring, especially when he hit Cheltenham and Royal Ascot, had already made him a legend in his twenties. His boyish features earned him the nomenclature "The Kid" from his fellow bookmakers when he first took out a licence and when he got down from his pitch to punt on a fancy of his, they would exclaim: "The Kid's having a go".

Hugh McIlvanney, the brilliant sports writer of *The Observer* then, wrote a feature article about him in which he named him "The Sundance Kid" – and from that moment he was on a pedestal apart as Ireland's most famous High Roller.

He could now no longer be taken for granted. The survivor in him meant that he never went under, despite shattering setbacks that would have broken the spirit of many a punter double his age. He had the happy knack of putting the setbacks of yesterday to the back of his mind and was invariably thinking forward to tomorrow.

He lived by the dictum that once you had the ammunition, your guns could keep firing. What had to be avoided at all costs was wasting that ammunition and ending up in hock to the bookies.

I remember my very first meeting with him during the week of the 1976 Rose of Tralee Festival, a six-man mobile Jazz Band playing *When The Saints Go Marching In* outside the Mount Brandon Hotel while at a table in the lounge area "The Sundance Kid" was playing backgammon. The racing, not the Festival merry-go-round, had drawn him to the Kerry capital and at his right elbow, holding as it were a watching brief, sat Jimmy Hayes of Fethard, son of one of the most respected members of the bookmaking fraternity, Dick Hayes, a gentleman to his finger-tips.

Jimmy Hayes was "Butch" to J.P.'s "Sundance" – an inseparable pair this duo who liked nothing better than to go gunning after the bookies but they did not want to go down in a blaze of glory, in the betting sense, as Newman and Redford did in the classic Western.

"I am not in the game for medals or glory", said J.P. to me on that occasion. "There is no future in picking losers. I don't want to be remembered as 'The King of the Ring'. I want to stay in existence as a punter ahead of the field. You ask me am I making it pay? Let's say I am still alive".

Sixteen years on from that day when I was researching my book, *The High Rollers of The Turf* I sat down for lunch with him in the Martinstown Stud near Kilmallock, County Limerick. It was a grey day in January, the Galtees in the distance were shrouded in mist and there was only the sound of the jackdaws in the trees to break the silence. Now, with his 41st birthday coming up during the '92 Cheltenham Festival meeting, he talked to me about his attainment of maturity as a professional gambler.

Outlining the principles by which the true professionals operate, he emphasised that the two basic ground rules were: (1) Never chase your losses and (2) There is never a last race.

Chasing losses, he said, was the bane of many a punter's life. "There is always tomorrow. You must scrupulously avoid seeing the last race as the 'getting out stakes' ".

He went on: "The professional operates differently from the amateur. His approach is to get the very best out of a good run and when in a bad run, to ensure that he lives to fight another day".

Discipline, he went on to assert, as he poured the white wine, was crucial, one of the most important ingredients of all, in fact. "I consider myself a professional gambler whether I am punting or making a book but I am not an addictive gambler. If I didn't have a bet at a particular race meeting, it wouldn't bother me."

The most successful punters, he contended, were those who believed in the form book and were able to interpret form. They were not swayed by tips from owners, jockeys, trainers or connections.

*   *   *

As with the High Rollers of the poker scene I had met in Las Vegas, J.P. McManus was not known to waver in his steely courage in face of initial setbacks, when these occurred, for example, on the first day of the Cheltenham meeting. While he retained ammunition for his guns, he could still "go to war" – but at the same time, if he did not get the price he wanted on a horse, he could immediately shut up shop, even if it was a horse carrying his own colours and was well fancied to win a particular race.

Nothing illustrated this better than what happened during the 1994 Festival meeting when "The Sundance Kid" rocked the ring over two days and then amazed all who knew him with his discipline.

Racecourse rumour had it that he backed his own Deep Run gelding, Gimme Five to win a cool £1 million in the last race on the Tuesday afternoon. There was pandemonium in the ring as the word got out that "The Kid" was on the warpath. It took some money, believe me, to bring Gimme Five crashing from 10/1 to 4/1 favourite in a field of 23 for a 3m 2f handicap hurdle. "It started when Stephen Little, in a single bet, laid him £250,000 to £30,000 – and there were other spectacular onslaughts", reported Hugh McIlvanney.

Gimme Five could only finish 20th.

Many a punter would have folded tent after suffering a hammer-blow like that and slipped quietly into the night. But resilience is J.P.s middle name. And always has been from the time he first started backing horses as a schoolboy in Limerick.

Next day came "the emerald revenge, with McManus riding shotgun," as Mick Cleary described it so colourfully and Mickey "Asparagus Kid" Fletcher bemoaned to *The Observer* writer "I've done my cobblers" after "The Sundance Kid" had hit town with a vengeance.

He had told me before he left Ireland for Cheltenham that Danoli was the Irish banker of the meeting. All he wanted was a price commensurate with his estimation of what was a certainty on the book.

His bombardment of the rails bookies included bets of £155,000 to

£80,000 and £60,000 to £30,000.

His winnings on Danoli were enough to restore the balance. "That put the wheel back on the bike," he told Hugh McIlvanney.

It could have been a day when "The Kid" could have written a special chapter in the history of Cheltenham gambling that would have emulated the flurry caused by Noel Furlong when he stood to win £4m in double bets had The Illiad won the 1991 Champion Hurdle.

Back ahead in his battle with the books, he was ready to go for the jugular on his own horse, Time For A Run in the Coral Cup Handicap Hurdle. He sent his trusted lieutenants to look for 10/1 or better. If Danoli had failed, the men J.P. did business with would have been only too willing to oblige him at 10/1 and maybe even slightly better odds. But now the shutters were up against any display of generosity and they knew from experience the scale of the bets he would have if he got the price he sought.

He told me himself that the best price on offer to him on the rails was 7/1 Time For A Run. You might ask why didn't he take the 10/1 that was going elsewhere to cash but J.P. is not the kind of man who carries around bundles of notes when he "goes to war" at Cheltenham. It's on credit and strictly on credit.

How must he have felt when Time For A Run, in the hands of Charlie Swan, won going away in a field of 30 at returned odds of 11/1.

And then Mucklemeg, also carrying his colours, won the Festival Bumper in very comfortable fashion at 7/2.

I have no doubt that if J.P. had got the 10/1 he sought on Time For A Run he could have taken £1 million out of the ring on that horse alone and then had another awesome cut on Mucklemeg. I leave it to the imagination of the reader to calculate what his total winnings for the day would have come to on Time For A Run and Mucklemeg on top of Danoli.

The big rails' bookies would have remembered it as "Black Cheltenham '94".

*   *   *

Come the '96 Festival meeting and I will have been a regular at Cheltenham for twenty years. How time flies!

The concept of the rendezvous, which is so much part and parcel of the World Series of Poker in Binion's Horseshoe Casino in Las Vegas each May, will be fully understood by all those aficionados of National Hunt racing who will never, while their health holds, miss the three days of the Cheltenham Festival meeting in March. Why is Cheltenham so special?

"Because it is about class in every sense of the word", is how J.P. McManus expressed it to me." It is about quality. Nothing can take the place of quality. The champions come out for the Cheltenham meeting. You get the best horses from Ireland locked in contention with the best from Britain and nowadays also the best that France can send over, like The Fellow, beaten in a photo finish in the 1991 Gold Cup and again in'92 and then gaining his reward in 1994".

And from the punter's viewpoint, you get a very strong ring at

Cheltenham, perhaps the strongest you get anywhere in national Hunt racing and, therefore, you can have a serious wager without it causing all that great of a flurry.

Nowadays, I invariably travel over on the Sunday and don't return home until the Friday evening, so that I can savour the week to the full. As you journey from Birmingham Airport, you begin to feel the adrenalin flowing in your veins at the prospect of what lies ahead. And then as Cleeve Hill comes into view and you see the glorious sweep of the racecourse itself, you know deep down that if you were diagnosed as having the "Big C" in the count-down to a Festival meeting and hadn't long to live, you would be content if you could get there for a last rendezvous with friends and to hear the "Irish roar" echo from the stands and enclosures, as it rose when Danoli scored his never-to-be-forgotten triumph in the 1994 Sun Alliance Novices' Hurdle.

There's immense joy and pleasure from simply walking down The Promenade in the morning, dropping into W.H. Smith's for the papers or browsing through the books in Waterstone's right beside it and then maybe to Ladbroke's or Hills to see what board prices are on offer on the different races and indulge in some doubles and trebles that will bring in a handy sum, should they come off. Cheltenham has been welcoming the Irish for a long time now and the people respond to Irish faces – and Irish wit and humour. It's a happy week all round.

Even if you don't stay in the Queen's Hotel, you will– if you are a real jumping enthusiast – make it there for the breakfast gatherings or for drinks before you leave for the racecourse. It may be early as yet and there's a long, long day ahead but the "crack" will still be good and over innumerable cups of tea or coffee, you will find the time ebbing away so quickly that soon it will be coming up to 11 o'clock, maybe even 11.30.

If the head is not too good and the stomach somewhat raw, you can slip into the bar and have a brandy and port. And if some of the real characters are about, you'll listen to yarns that will convince you that you may have thought you had heard them all before but Cheltenham invariably throws up new gems with each Festival meeting.

The same gang does not assemble in the Queen's Hotel as in the Seventies. J.P. McManus has long since moved out to a village in the Cotswolds where you will find him with his close friend, the financier Dermot Desmond, a great lover of racing over the jumps. Edward O'Grady has also moved on to pastures new and likewise John Mulhern. There are those who have discovered the privacy that comes with taking a cottage in the Cotswolds. To each man his own.

*   *   *

The memories will never die from the days in the Seventies when we saw Dessie Hughes establishing himself as one of the outstanding Cheltenham riders, scoring on Parkhill and Bit of a Jig for Mick O'Toole in 1976 and winning the Gold Cup on 14/1 chance, Davy Lad for O'Toole in 1977 when he also won on Mac's Chariot.

Monksfield, trained by Des McDonogh in County Meath and carrying the colours of Dr Michael Mangan, had won the Champion Hurdle for the first time in 1978 in the hands of Tommy Kinane, father of Michael. Now in 1979 he was ridden by Dessie Hughes in what Mick O'Toole described as "one of the greatest races I have seen over the Cheltenham course".

Jonjo O'Neill on Sea Pigeon threw down the gauntlet to 'Monkey' and Dessie Hughes. Television could never capture the sheer majesty of the climactic moments of that epic as Hughes and O'Neill got locked in battle from the last flight. There was something beautiful and timeless for me in the rhythmic movement of horse and rider towards the finishing post, the perfect balance maintained by two of the greatest jump jockeys of that era and yet the power they produced as they drove for victory was truly electrifying. Dessie Hughes prevailed by three-quarters-of-a-length to a surging "Irish roar" and his wife, Eileen has told me that they have the *Sean Graham Award* – the actual picture of the finish – in a spot over the fire-place at home. "If ever I happen to be down I look at it and it has the effect of making me feel good again", she said.

The champagne flowed freely in the Queen's Hotel at the celebratory dinner as it had in 1978. We didn't know it then but it was the "Last Hurrah" gathering honouring Monksfield before he surrendered his crown the following year.

Monksfield had £1 million riding on his back in bets in 1979. The Irish backed him at all odds down to 6/5 favourite on the day of the race itself – with Sea Pigeon going off at the very generous odds of 13/2. This time Monksfield finished seven lengths runner-up to Sea Pigeon.

Monksfield, however, could not be kept out of the headlines, even in defeat. Without any prior announcement, a 200-yard uphill stretch, taking in the area in front of the stands and behind the old Tote Prices display board, had been cut out of the course over which the Champion Hurdle was contested.

"The changing of the track made all the difference", Des McDonogh asserted and even Jonjo O'Neill admitted that the shorter trip helped in his case, though Dessie Hughes noted that "if anything was against Monksfield, it was probably the dead ground."

It would have been a fitting end to Monksfield's career if he could have joined the elite band of hat-trick winners, Hatton's Grace, Sir Ken and Persian War. But what a record he had over the Cheltenham course – he was never out of the first two in five appearances.

Dr Michael Mangan is a big man. Big in physique, in keeping with his days as a rugby player when his compatriots knew him as "Hopper". Big in heart and outlook and overwhelming in his generosity to his friends. A man who loves the flow of good conversation, especially when it hinges on National Hunt racing, who sparkles when good yarns are being spun.

A supreme sportsman who has shown that he can take defeat in the same spirit as victory and this was never typified better than the graciousness he displayed, especially in congratulating Jonjo O'Neill and the connections of Sea Pigeon, when Monksfield was thwarted of the three-timer.

You don't do to the reigning champion what Cheltenham did to Monksfield when they cut that 200-yard uphill stretch from the course. Certainly, you don't do it without telling the connections of the champion in advance because, in effect, it becomes a different race, calling for different tactics – over an altered course.

This would have summarised the sentiments we all felt, who were at the dinner party in the Queen's. But Cheltenham made no apology, even though more than once since then I have heard English racing writers I respect saying that it was wrong, very wrong.

Incidentally, I had one of my most embarrassing and at the same time funniest experiences as a journalist in the aftermath of Monksfield's triumph in 1978. Frankly, I had won enough money in ante-post bets and on the course itself on the day of the Champion Hurdle to cause the celebratory mood to last well beyond the victory dinner. Monksfield was going home and, as I adjourned to my room on the eve of Gold Cup Day, I knew that all the alka Seltzer in the world would not save me from waking with some "head" in the morning. I made the time though to jot down the intro for my *Evening Herald* story … "The bonfires will blaze in Moynalty this evening as Monksfield comes home to a hero's welcome". I then put in a time call for 8.30 a.m.

I awoke with a splitting headache. I called the *Herald*, got the copy-taker and was beginning to ad lib the rest of my story after the colourful intro when Padraig Byrne, then News Editor interjected to say: "Cut the crap, Smith … forget about the bonfires and all that …do you realise the racing is off because of the snow".

My God, snow … what the hell is happening … such were the thoughts running through my head in a mad whirl that everything I had conjured up about bands and cheering crowds and bonfires lighting the hills around Moynalty went out the window in a flash.

Or rather I came back to earth with a bang when I pulled back the blinds and looked outside and saw the carpet of white. I was being told from Dublin what I would have known if I had been up at cock-crow!

There was a new urgency in Padraig Byrne's voice when he conveyed to me that the *Evening Herald* was being inundated with calls from punters who had coupled Champion Hurdle winner, Monksfield with Brown Lad to win the Gold Cup and they wanted to know what was going to happen their ante-post wagers. "Give us a story fast", he said.

I must have broken the Irish hop, step and jump record as I skipped it down the stairs and, as luck would have it, collared the Ladbrokes man in the foyer. I was able to put over a new story, quoting authoritative sources in the bookmaking world, that would satisfy every punter from Ballyfermot to Ballybofey and beyond that their money wasn't automatically lost but that, assuming the Gold Cup was opened again, the doubles would become singles, as it would in effect, be a new race. I was back in the good books of the News Desk, who, I must admit, were rather surprised how quickly I managed to get in contact with those authoritative sources!

For the record, the Irish punters who had been singing "Brown Lad in the rain …" in anticipation of a famous triumph for the Jim Dreaper-trained gelding (winner of the Sun Alliance Novices Hurdle in 1974 and the Bonusprint Stayers Hurdle in 1975) were cruelly denied a clean-out of the bookies when the Cheltenham Stewards instead of putting racing back on the scheduled third day for twenty-four hours refixed the Gold Cup for April 12. On good ground that did not favour him, Brown Lad finished runner-up to Midnight Court, the mount of John Francome.

*   *   *

The West was truly awake again when For Auction won the Champion Hurdle at 40/1 for the Heaslip brothers, Danno and Mick in 1982. They put on a special bet for the champagne money, netting £2,000 in the process.

I travelled back with them and with trainer Michael Cunningham from the track to the Golden Valley Hotel. "You can open 100 bottles of champagne to begin with", Danno told a rather bewildered manager, who had rarely been hit on the spot with a celebratory order like that.

"And get a piano", he added.

"We don't have a piano in this area".

"Then buy one", said Danno.

Fortunately, they discovered that they had one in a function room upstairs – "and it was like seeing a coffin being brought downstairs", recalled Danno with a laugh.

Galway bookmaker, John Mulholland, a character in his own right and Mayor of his native city in his time, accompanied for the best sing-song I recall at any Festival meeting. Sometime after midnight he switched to Stephen Foster numbers of the deep South and we all joined in the chorus of *"Swanee"*. And then it was back to *Galway Bay* and *The Galway Shawl* to *The Fields of Athenry* and, yes, yet another rendering of *The West's Awake*.

The dawn was coming up over Cheltenham when it began to taper off. What a night!

Yes, memories are made of this.

The memory too of Golden Cygnet, owned by outstanding sportsman, Ray Rooney of Galway pulverising the opposition in the Supreme Novices Hurdle in 1978. And when later that same season he was fatally injured in a fall at Ayr it resulted in an amazing sense of loss among National Hunt enthusiasts throughout Ireland and in Britain also. "My phone never stopped ringing and there were cards and telegrams every day", said Ray Rooney. "It was as if a member of the family had died and I suppose in a way that is what happened. It may be pointless wondering now about what he would have achieved but he might have been another Arkle".

"He was really something special … but, well, that's racing", he added.

And the memory of the "Boys from Bohola", the Durkan brothers, Bill and Tony and the way they took Cheltenham by storm when the great mare Anaglog's Daughter won the Arkle Chase in 1980 with consummate ease. What an "Irish roar" greeted that triumph and never were there as

207

popular winning connections in the enclosure when Anaglog's Daughter came in to renewed acclaim.

She was ridden to victory by Tommy Carberry, one of the finest jump riders of his era. He had ridden L'Escargot to successive wins for Dan Moore (father of his wife, Pamela) in 1970 and '71 and, of course, won the Aintree Grand National on the same horse in 1975. He was successful again in the Gold Cup on Ten Up for Jim Dreaper in 1975.

Tied Cottage looked all over a winner coming to the last in the 1980 Gold Cup but although he got over the fence, he slipped up on landing and Alverton and Jonjo O'Neill had the easiest of victories. However, we got back our losses with interest the following year when Tommy Carberry rode a brilliant race to score at 13/2. Though the horse was disqualified subsequently on purely technical grounds, it didn't matter to the punters who had backed him – they had already got their money.

*   *   *

The romance of Cheltenham will always lie for me in the way the dreams of small trainers and unknown owners can be fulfilled and in how some young jockey by grabbing his opportunity can be catapulted onto an entirely new plane and make the big break-through.

The prophets of doom had been lifting their hands to the heavens in despair on the Tuesday of the 1990 Festival meeting when Kribensis, in the colours of Sheikh Mohammed, won the Champion Hurdle. They argued that it would only be a matter of time before the oil-rich Arab princes dominated the jumping scene and there would be no place anymore for the Willie Lomans of the racing world.

Sirrell Griffiths was to prove them all so wrong.

He milked 70 Friesian cows at 5.30 a.m. on the morning of Gold Cup Day before driving his cattle-truck (he did not have a horse-box) to Cheltenham to take on the reigning champion, Desert Coin.

It's history now how 100/1 outsider, Norton's Coin scored a famous victory for Wales. And that same evening in the village of Nangaredig, not far from the town of Carmarthen, which had given the legendary stand-off half Barry John and flying winger Gerald Davis to Welsh rugby, they put up a banner which read: "WELCOME HOME NORTON'S COIN".

The bonfires were blazing not for rugby heroes in an area where hero worship is legendary but for a steeplechaser who had upheld the honour of Wales against the most popular chaser since the incomparable Arkle.

Dylan Thomas could have written a poem about 50-year-old Sirrell Griffith's return to Wales with the Gold Cup trophy – transporting it back in the same vehicle in which he had headed for Cheltenham that same morning. And Norton' Coin ran with the cows in summer months.

Griffiths had blazed a trail out of the Welsh valleys. A year later the O'Sullivans of Lombardstown, Mallow, County Cork, enjoyed their finest hour as Lovely Citizen was led in after winning the Christies Foxhunters Chase. We heard the Cork anthem, *The Banks of My Own Lovely Lee* echo out from the unsaddling enclosure to Cleeve Hill and the Cotswolds.

The bonfires blazed in Lombardstown that night – and, yes, they had a party, quite a party, in the Becher's Brook pub in Mallow the night of the homecoming celebration with the Cup.

From the sheep country in Herefordshire emerged a success story in 1994 fit to stand beside the most romantic associated with the Festival meeting. Richard Price delivered 20 lambs on his 400-acre farm before travelling to Cheltenham with Flakey Dove and saw her succeed where her grand-dam had failed in the Champion Hurdle thirty-one years previously. And adding to the romance was the fact that Flakey Dove – the first mare to win this race since Dawn Run in 1984 – shared a Herefordshire field with a flock of sheep when not being asked to do the business on a racecourse.

*   *   *

But, of course, dwarfing all else was Danoli's triumph in the Sun Alliance Novices Hurdle that same year – leading to the most tumultuous and emotional scenes that I have witnessed since Dawn Run won the Gold Cup in 1986 and Jonjo O'Neill gave his arm-aloft salute to the skies as he passed the winning post.

Tom Foley would say to me with a twinkle in his eye that compared to Sirrell Griffiths with his herd of 70 Friesians he was "the smallest of the small men". And who was to argue with genial Tom when he said that.

Tom Foley had known days when he almost despaired of making a living out of the 62-acre farm at Aughabeg in County Carlow. Then he bought Danoli for £7,000 for his Myshall neighbour and friend, the bonesetter Dan O'Neill and his life was changed irrevocably.

The English loved all the elements of his story – the man who didn't wear a tie, who had never been in a plane before until he accompanied Danoli on the flight to Bristol, who had always to take a seat in the front of a car because he was a notorious bad traveller, "otherwise it's a certainty I will get sick". And, true to form, he never left the sick bag out of his hands from the moment of a rough take-off from Dublin in very strong winds to the stomach-churning descent itself. Green-faced from the buffeting, he was sick three times on the motorway between Bristol and Cheltenham.

Now he had arrived at the Mecca of the National Hunt game. As he caught his first glimpse of the course, as he looked over towards Cleeve Hill as dawn came over the countryside on Monday morning, the nightmare journey from Ireland behind him, burdened with the knowledge that all of Ireland was willing him and Danoli on, he said to himself: "This horse is my only chance. I will probably never have another good enough to run at the festival."

His wife Goretti (a local girl from Aughabeg despite the Italian-sounding Christian name) stayed at home with the children, three girls, Sharon (18), Adrienne (16) and Goretti ("we call her 'little Goretti' ") who is eleven and one boy, Pat who is nine.

They would watch the race on the television set in the sittingroom. They would all get very excited, yes, and Goretti Foley confessed to me: "Before the start the tension was unbearable because I knew how much was at stake for Tom and I thought too what it was going to mean to him and the rest of us if the horse won."

"I am what I am. I tell the truth and I know I cannot go wrong that way", Tom Foley had said to me in his home.

He came across to millions of viewers on television in Britain as someone totally different – a refreshing difference from what they had become accustomed to on the "talk shows" and the "phone-in" programmes

A non-drinking Irishman, a non-smoker, a non-gambler, who had never been out of his country before. A man who wasn't burdened by tradition or what the status quo demanded. Who said things simply and directly and with feeling.

They loved him for it. Later he would show me in his home the hundreds of letters he received from people in all corners of Britain, people telling him how he came across to them, that they were thrilled when Danoli won because they wanted to see the horse triumph – because of the man who trained him.

A small man, so different from the big men. The champion of all the underdogs in the mean back streets and out-of-the-way corners in Old England, aspiring to nothing more than a big win on the pools maybe and retirement to the sunshine of the Costa del Sol – all dreaming dreams that might never be realised.

"One of our own", they could say over their pints of bitter when they read in some tabloid of the Irish trainer who didn't wear a tie and thought nothing of it.

Danoli won to an "Irish roar" that was shattering, that echoed out beyond the course to the Cotswolds and back, you almost felt, to Aughabeg itself. Back then into the winner's enclosure. Again the Irish, crowding every conceivable vantage point to welcome their hero, opened their throats in a sustained wave of cheering, the like of which had not split the Cheltenham air since Dawn Run's Gold Cup triumph eight years earlier.

Later there was the renewed excitement of the homecoming celebrations for Tom Foley in Myshall ... mounting a trailer as the cheers of the people of the locality echoed in the night air out over the rural heartlands for him and Dan O'Neill. And, as Goretti would tell me, "the bands playing and the dancing into the early hours and all the local talent contributed to make it a night we will remember always."

"I am what I am" ... and Tom Foley was still himself in the homecoming, wearing no tie now.

And no one cared one iota.

Danoli had delivered for Aughabeg and Myshall and for Ireland.

The second act of Danoli's Cheltenham odyssey saw him fail to win the Smurfit Champion Hurdle at the '95 Festival meeting, beaten into third place behind Alderbrook and Norman Williamson. But he was back in the winner's enclosure when taking the Martell Aintree Hurdle at the Liverpool Grand National meeting and we marvelled at his courage on learning that he had suffered a serious injury in the course of that victory.

The racing world waited with bated breath the outcome of the operation of his injured leg and sighed with relief at the news that the insertion of two pins offered the hope that he might be able to race again. Tom Foley told me in the autumn of '95 that he was inundated with messages from racing enthusiasts in all parts of Ireland and Britain and there was a constant stream of callers to his stable, among them English people on holiday in Ireland.

Danoli may not have been crowned the champion hurdler but he was truly "the people's champion".

Charlie Swan, one of the most likeable of the present-day crop of jump jockeys and yet one of the most professional, was associated with Danoli's unforgettable Sun Alliance Novices' Hurdle triumph. At the '94 Festival meeting Charlie won the Ritz Club trophy for the second successive year as the leading jockey at Cheltenham. And, while Cork-born Norman Williamson would take this award in '95, Swan, deputising for Adrian Maguire, who stood down from taking part at the meeting because of the sudden death of his mother on the Sunday, left an indelible imprint through the magnificence of his horsemanship in winning the Queen Mother Champion Chase on Viking Flagship for David 'The Duke' Nicholson.

*   *   *

The wheel has come full circle.

In the count-down to Cheltenham '95 I flew to Geneva to meet J.P. McManus in an Alpine setting – so different from the Carribean where you will find him every January playing in the big Pro-Am organised by Robert Sangster at the Sandy Lane golf course.

J.P. had been resident in Switzerland for a year – operating strictly to the rule that governs all tax exiles from Ireland, that he can only spend 90 nights in any given year in his native country.

But the most feared High Roller of them all when it comes to "going to war" with the rails' bookies at Cheltenham scorned the very suggestion that he had chosen Geneva as his new base solely for tax reasons.

It was when he brought me down from his "pad" in the exclusive Cologny suburb overlooking Lake Geneva to the High building in the Rue du Rhone where his magnificent new suite of offices are sited, that I got a clear insight into the "Grand Design" that will see him from this out become a major player in the financial markets, far more than in the ring.

But Cheltenham, he confessed, still turns him on as no other race meeting does and nothing gives him greater pleasure than to hit the bookies for six.

Before breakfast he had been on the phone checking the present position of sterling against the dollar and the mark – getting the very latest on its fluctuating position. He brings the same professionalism to this facet of his business life, as he does when studying the form book in is preparations for Cheltenham.

"The difference that I see between Royal Ascot and Cheltenham is this – whereas everyone can have an opinion about something at Ascot,

211

whether it be the fashions of the strawberries or the champagne, the concentration at Cheltenham is on the horses and the opinions you hear expressed are about the comparative merits of the leading contenders for the big prizes", he said.

I sit with him as he selects from the many videos he has brought with him or which have been sent out to him – playing and replaying key moments in the races that matter in the assessment of form and the making of considered judgements on whether a leading contender will stay or jump or be able to contend with the hustle and bustle of big fields.

"I have not had a play this year in the ante-post market", he tells me. "I like to leave the decisions on what I intend to back as late as possible when it comes to Cheltenham. You see, three weeks ahead you can have made up your mind that a particular horse will win a particular race, then the going changes on the day and it can alter the whole situation. There are so many different factors that have to be taken into account before you decide to play. When you are playing big in the ring, it's crucial that you get it right, absolutely right".

He has come a long way from the time when to protect himself from his own impetuosity as a gambler, he wrote to all the bookies with whom he had accounts telling them that they must NOT giver him credit under any circumstance – in a word, that if he didn't have the cash, then he could not have a bet.

"Today, I know I have enough discipline in my forties, sufficient control of my emotions to be able to have credit accounts with the major layers in the ring", he said . "There is no question that I will bet on every race at Cheltenham. It's difficult enough to analyse four or five races properly but I don't see how you can have an opinion on twenty races and hope to come out on the right side at the end of the three days".

Where J.P. McManus differs from the majority of Irish punters heading for Cheltenham is that value means everything to him in betting and, having been a bookie himself and a leading rails' bookie at that, he can look at a board and immediately assess how a layer is betting "in the round" (that is to the 100 base by which they operate).

As we dined in the Restaurant Roberto on my first evening in Geneva, just around the corner from the "street of fashion", the Rue du Rhone ("never let your wife loose here with a credit card", said J.P. with a smile, "because rich men have been known to come out poor from it"), I brought him back to the '94 Festival meeting and his refusal to bet on Time For A Run when he did not get the 10/1 he sought. He wept no tears at the fact that he could have cleaned out the rails' bookies entirely on that Wednesday. "I was happy to see both Time For A Run and Mucklemeg winning for me and happier still that I bred both Time For A Run and So Proud, the runner-up in that race. That very, very rarely happens at Cheltenham, if indeed it ever happens".

His children did a painting for J.P. with the inscription under it … "It's Time For A Run Said Mucklemeg". It occupies a place of honour today in his penthouse suite in Geneva.

Dermot Desmond had hit town and was host in the Lion d'Or to J.P. and myself on the Tuesday night of my three-day stay in Geneva. It was impossible to keep him out of the headlines such was the high level of his successful operations in the financial sphere and yet, like the keen sportsman he is, he also found the time to take a stake in the Scottish club, Celtic.

Later Dermot would say to me – out of earshot of J.P. – that "The Sundance Kid" had one of the sharpest minds he had ever met – "and I have met a lot of razor-sharp minds and brilliant intellects in my time".

J.P. is in sparkling form on this evening, witty too. I get to understand and appreciate why he likes the life in Switzerland and why he has settled in so well in Geneva. The city is not too big and neither is it too small. You couldn't look for better communications anywhere in the world. "When you are operating in the world of high finance, communications mean everything", said Dermot Desmond. "You are only a phone call or a fax away from contacting those you want to contact but if time is the essence, bad communications can be very costly, especially to a man who can make £5,000 an hour".

J.P. is now recalling that in his early days in Cheltenham, he remembered waking up in the morning, maybe on the second or third day and thinking to himself how bad things were. "Come evening and I would find myself saying: 'If only it was morning again' ".

Gambling has been his life since he was nine. When attending the Christian Brothers School in Limerick he had a few bob on Merryman II to win the Aintree Grand National and the horse obliged at 13/2. Already he had been bitten by the betting bug and it would never leave him.

He laughed, as the Chateau Rotschild was poured, and reminded us of the philosophy propounded by an old Christian Brother: "You guys who think you are clever, be nice to the guys you see as no-hopers. Because they could be employing you one day!"

"The Sundance Kid" has never forgotten his roots.

He will continue from Switzerland to do a lot for good causes in Ireland. In '95 he organised a big Pro-Am Golfing Tournament over Limerick's Ballyclough course during the Whit week-end. It raised a substantial amount of money for the named charities he had chosen.

I bade farewell to him in Geneva as he entered the world of high finance, as he prepared for a new era and a new challenge in his life with his 44th birthday coming up during the Cheltenham Festival.Timeless Mont Blanc, I reckoned, would not oversee the fall of a man who had shown that he was a Survivor Supreme.

*   *   *

In Fethard, gateway to the Coolmore Stud complex and to the stables of "Mouse" Morris and Edward O'Grady, Jimmy (The Buck) Ryan is not concerned about how his shares are moving. He has none. Neither is he worried about how the pound sterling is faring against the mark or the dollar against the yen.

His concern is that he will have the continuing good health to get to

Cheltenham and the "tank" to enjoy the "crack" with Dr Michael Mangan, Dr Tony Healy, Ger Lynch, John Mannion and all the others he has got to know in close on twenty years' attendance at the Festival meeting (he once got a lift from "a fella hauling a load of Tipp cheese to Spain via London, coming back with oranges") and to have a few wagers.

His mythical suite of offices can be said to centre around McCarthy's pub, where Annette Murphy maintains the traditions set by four generations of her family. It is the most unique hostelry of its kind that you will find anywhere in the world and was aptly described by Clive Gammon in an American magazine as "the horsiest pub in Ireland".

I am sure that if Eugene O'Neill were alive today and looking for a place like Jimmy The Priest's around which to write a play on sporting characters and racing types, he would write a masterpiece as great as *The Iceman Cometh* with McCarthy's as the setting. Make it your business to drop in if you are ever down South Tipperary way.

Annette Murphy had some of the boys engaged in helping to restore the historic walls. It kept them off the booze in the count-down to Cheltenham and the fact that it was Lent helped also. "Half drunk and half sober", was how Jimmy Ryan described a few of the intrepid characters peopling his world.

His own house, down near the river, is called The White House. Cromwell was allowed through Fethard (after the Governor of the town averted a massacre by surrendering to him on very favourable terms) on his way to Clonmel which surrendered after a siege lasting for a period of days. It's anathema in Jimmy's eyes that when he dies his coffin should be taken along the same route as Cromwell.

"They'll shove it out the window into the waiting boat and my mortal remains will go down the river of no return like those of a Holy Man in India", was how he graphically described his departure from this life to me. "They won't place me on a pyre and make a bonfire. They'll find a spot for me in the graveyard beside Fr Phil Noonan, who asked that he be buried with the poorest of the poor. I accompanied Fr Phil on his last journey home from Dublin, where he had died in hospital, and we stopped the hearse opposite the Curragh racecourse where he had so much fun and enjoyment so that he could say farewell. I know he'll like the idea of me being buried beside him".

Such a man is Jimmy (The Buck) Ryan.

16

"You're Only a Face in the Crowd"

There will never again be a time in Irish politics to compare with the drama-laden period when three General Elections took place in a comparatively short space of time in the early 1980s and the Fianna Fáil Party was split wide open over the leadership of Charles J. Haughey. It led to the formation of what we came to know as the 'Club of 22' and eventually to the establishment of a new party, the Progressive Democrats.

Young entrants to journalism, especially those aspiring to be political correspondents or writers, are unlikely to be able to comprehend the emotions engendered when Haughey took the media on head-on at bruising press conferences that were invariably crowded affairs. It was obvious that the most hardened of the bunch were baying for his blood in the political sense. And always he gave as good as he got.

There was only one Charlie Haughey and there will never be another like him. This is not meant to convey that he was a leader and a Taoiseach who was head and shoulders above all others. No, I mean it in the sense that when it came to creating an atmosphere at a news conference that was akin to a no-holds-barred, bare-knuckle contest, Charlie was the one to do so. He was the last of the street fighters.

Instance the occasion when I fired a question at him aimed at eliciting an answer that he wasn't going to oblige me with – if he could help it.

"Who are you"?, came the response couched in biting cynicism.

"You can call me Raymond, Ray, Mr or even Miss – but you know me".

"You're only a face in the crowd".

At that the "groupies" burst into spontaneous laughter and applause.

A very good friend of mine from the annual Cheltenham Festival meeting and the racing round in general, Dr Tony Healy had just had a minor operation in St. Vincent's Hospital. He was listening to the radio. The press conference was being carried live. He recognised my voice immediately when I directed my Exocet missile at Haughey.

And when the Fianna Fáil leader hit back with his own heat-guided missile, Tony found himself laughing so much that he could only appeal to

215

one of the nurses: "Unplug that radio fast or my stitches will burst!"

During the Donegal by-election campaign of November, 1980, I recall accosting the then Taoiseach in a hotel lounge and asking him if he would go to the country should Clem Coughlan win the seat for Fianna Fáil. It was time for a snatched lunch on the road. Haughey glanced at the open smoked salmon sandwich he held in his hand and then, looking me straight in the eye, remarked: "Would you not agree that these are the best smoked salmon sandwiches we ever ate?".

That Donegal by-election campaign, incidentally, will always be remembered for the furore caused by Sile de Valera's speech from a platform in Letterkenny on Saturday night, November 1st 1980. John Wallace and myself were covering that particular Fianna Fáil rally for the Sunday *Press* and *Sunday Independent* respectively. The rain was already pouring down that evening as the band, which led the torchlight parade to the Fianna Fáil platform, played "Seán South of Garryowen", a fitting forerunner for Sile de Valera's address.

We stood, John and I, huddled each under a different doorway, trying to protect our notebooks, already sodden from being washed away altogether! Our brief was very much a watching one until Sile De Valera began to speak. John, a political reporter of wide experience and excellent judgment, nodded knowingly across at me and I at him. We began to take notes as fast as our shorthand permitted as Sile launched into a bitter attack on Mrs. Thatcher's handling of the H-Block issue, accusing her of lack of compassion and recalling that "not once but twice in the commons, the British Prime Minister issued callous unfeeling and self-righteous statements" on the British government stance.

She concluded by saying that if the situation was allowed to deteriorate further, then the British Government "must shoulder the responsibility for further deaths, whether it be in H-Block, on the streets or elsewhere throughout the Six Counties".

The bombshell effect of those climactic words delivered under a damp Donegal sky, can never be garnered from cold print. I can only reflect on the shocks waves reaching as far as No. 10 Downing Street that night as Sile de Valera, the 25-year-old Dáil backbencher and Euro M.P. and Grand-daughter of the late Eamon de Valera, finished her speech, a stunned and embarrassed silence falling over the platform party, which included eight Government Ministers. And, no doubt, Gerry Collins, Michael O'Kennedy and Charles Haughey himself were already only too well aware of the repercussions the speech would have on the plane of Anglo-Irish relations as the B.B.C. carried the gist of the blistering attack on Mrs. Thatcher in their later bulletins.

Haughey rushed past me and refused even a "no comment" when I approached him to ask if he approved of the sentiments expressed by Miss de Valera, who it was to emerge later did not submit her speech to the Taoiseach for clearance, though she issued the prepared script in advance to newspapers.

From the platform in the square thirty top Fianna Fáil people –

Raymond Smith (top right) interviewing ace Italian sharpshooter, Paolo Rossi, who scored three goals against Brazil in the 1982 World Cup and (top left) with American-born jockey cash Asmussen at Leopardstown and (centre right) J.P. (The Sundance Kid) McManus and his close friend, Dermot Desmond are pictured with John Berry after he had ridden Front Line to victory at the 1995 Cheltenham Festival meeting. Bottom left, Lester Piggott, who launched the biography of Vincent O'Brien, *The Master of Ballydoyle*. Vincent is seen receiving an autographed copy of the revised paperback edition from the author.

Dunmore County Galway-born Dr Michael Mangan leads in Monksfield (Dessie Hughes) after he had won the Champion Hurdle for the second successive year in 1979 and (below) the joy of victory in the winner's enclosure after Tommy Kinane, father of Michael Kinane had triumphed in 1978. Des McDonogh (trainer) and Paddy McGrath and his wife join in the congratulations.

Michael Kinane and fellow Tipperary-born jockey, Christy Kinane joined club members Raymond Smith (left) and Bobby Price (right) on the *Sunday Independent* team in the big Elm Park Golf Classic in 1994, coming into the winner's enclosure when taking fourth place. Seamus Greene, the Elm Park Professional, who welcomed Kinane and Roche on their first time playing the course, is pictured third from left, and (inset above) the Captains, the late Daniel McCoubrey of the Washington Press Corps (second from left) and Raymond Smith on the first tee at Killarney before the start of a mini "Media Ryder Cup".

Des Mullan of the *Evening Herald* drives in as Captain of the Dublin Journalists Golfing Society, of which the author was a founder-member.

Peter Doyle, Raymond Smith, Julian de Kassel and Joe Carroll (top) enjoy the "crack" on the famous train journey south during the 1977 Annual Congress of the Association of European Journalists. Centre: the late John Feeney (left) who covered the negotiations on Ireland's entry to the EEC for RTE and (right) Padraig Flynn, Ireland's current European Commissioner. (Below from left) Tom Earlie, Denis Corboy and Ed Fitzgibbon.

Andrew Sheppard, President at European level, addressing the Annual Congress of the Association of European Journalists in Athens and (inset left) Jim Downey, a prominent member of the Committee and (inset right) Dennis Kennedy, first chairman of the Irish Section. Below Eddie Keher, famous Kilkenny hurler, the late Niall Hanley, former Editor of the *Evening Herald*, Kitty Mackey, widow of Mick Mackey, the Babe Ruth of hurling in his prime, Vinnie Doyle, Editor of the *Irish Independent*, John Doyle, the legendary Tipperary hurler and Aengus Fanning, Editor of the *Sunday Independent* at the "Teams of the Century" awards dinner in Dublin in 1984.

THE FOUR MUSKETEERS...Paddy McCarthy, Raymond Smith, Steve Coughlan and Larry Lyons in happy mood together on the author's wedding day at Rockwell College, County Tipperary in 1970, and (inset left and right) Fr O'Flynn, the "Priest of the Stammerers" and Charles Lynch, the famous concert pianist. Below the author with Donal Byrne, Val Dorgan and Mike Burns at an AEJ dinner in Dublin.

Raymond Smith with his wife Sheila on Valentia Island in the early Seventies and (inset top) with daughter Bairbre in Connemara and (centre) son Stephen is quite a handful as a child and (bottom) the traditional family gathering with a rousing sing-song on All-Ireland Hurling Final morning. Rev Con O'Mahony is pictured second from left back row with the author.

Raymond Smith pictured with Rickard Deasy (left) and T.J. Maher (right) at an IFA remembrance function in Dublin to honour those who led the famous Long March and(below left) farmers carrying the banner proudly on the way to Dublin and (bottom right) T.J. Maher, second from right, with John Barry, Tom Blake and Sean Healy (Secretary-General) head a deputation for pre-budget talks in Government Buildings in 1969. Behind at left is Alan Dukes, then Economic Adviser to the IFA.

including Cabinet Ministers, Dáil Deputies and Senators – went at the instructions of the Taoiseach to the Golden Grill Restaurant in Letterkenny for a hastily-convened meeting, where a statement was prepared that was issued one hour later in the name of Director of Elections, Ray MacSharry. It was made clear in this statement, which Haughey himself went through line by line before approving it and handing it to the Press Secretary, Frank Dunlop, that Sile de Valera's speech did not reflect the views of the Government.

Meanwhile, Sile de Valera was driven from the town and the other newspapermen and myself were following extraordinary "leads" to the effect that Fianna Fáil campaign managers had put a watch on the Portnoo Hotel, where the republican firebrand Deputy was staying overnight to ensure that newshounds would not contact her; also that Minister for State, Pádraig Flynn, campaigning in another area of the constituency had received a message to find the "rebel" T.D. and order her not to address two after – Mass meetings she was scheduled to address next morning.

Later that evening after the "Kitchen Cabinet" meeting had concluded in the Golden Grill, Charles Haughey and Cabinet colleagues and by-election campaign field officers adjourned to the Ballyraine Hotel at the outskirts of the town. An unmistakable sense of high drama in the air. The Taoiseach refused point-blank to add anything to the statement already issued.

"Sile F.F. Fears Polls Blow"; "Miss Dev Flees In Black Mercedes"; "Sile Is Blamed From Donegal"; "De Valera Told To Tow The Line Or Be Expelled"; "Sile Ready To Sacrifice Her £30,000 Euro Job"; "Haughey Knew Of Sile's North Speech Contents – FG Claim"; "A Palace Revolution Puts Haughey In Hot Seat".

These made up just some of the banner headlines over two days – Monday and Tuesday – and there was still more to come.

The niceties of whether it was a black Mercedes or a white one that whisked her out of Donegal or whether Pádraig Flynn saw her in a personal or an official capacity (bringing a rebuke from the Party leader) didn't matter all that much. What mattered was that during the climax of the Donegal by-election campaign, Sile had made story, indeed had been the story day after day. If anyone thought those stories had been angled to make the headlines they were naive in thinking so, for those very headlines over the Page one stories were inevitable from the moment that Sile delivered her cold, blistering and remember scripted – attack on Margaret Thatcher from the platform in Letterkenny.

As Michael Finlan wrote in *The Irish Times*. "In the excitement of the night in Letterkenny, the utterance of one man at the end of the rally almost went unnoticed. But Bernard McGlinchey's words, harking back to other times, were grimly apposite on the night: 'When I was growing up in a Fianna Fáil home, de Valera's name was more revered than the Almighty himself'."

We were in the lounge of the Central Hotel in Donegal town on the Monday afternoon, Michael Finlan, John Wallace and myself wondering what the angle on the story would be for the next day when in walked one of the most senior of the Fianna Fáil campaign "generals". When we quizzed him for the latest Party reaction to Sile de Valera's controversial speech his firm response was that "if she continues on this course, she has certainly gone down the river of no return". In a word, she would be put out of the Party and he added that she had been "severely reprimanded" on behalf of the Taoiseach.

I was able to order a bottle of St. Emilion with my steak that evening with the certainty that the Gods had handed us another lead story without our even having to seek it. If Sile had walked into the dining room at that moment I would have bought a bottle of vintage champagne for her!

Next morning over the bacon and eggs the Page One single-word headline screamed out at me over five columns: "MUZZLED" and it was backed up by a secondary strip headline "Sile Warned on Eve of Poll".

*   *   *

It receded into something of a nine-days wonder when Fianna Fáil won a sweeping victory.

"Fianna Fáil Homage To King Charlie" was the Page One headline carried by the *Irish Independent* on Saturday, November 8, 1980 – the day after 37-years-old school-teacher, Clem Coughlan from Inver headed the poll with a first-preference vote that represented a swing of two per cent to the Government.

As the votes were counted in Ballybofey on the previous day, Charles Haughey knew that he was heading for a great personal triumph. Indeed long before the tallymen had finished the task of checking the papers and doing their tots – many hours before the first count was completed – the champagne corks were already popping.

In the euphoria of victory, the tension of the "Sile de Valera Affair" now dispelled, one of the Fianna Fáil campaign generals shouted at me: "Go back to your Blue Shirt friends: but more sober members of the campaign team apologised for his verbal onslaught and asked me to share a glass of champagne (the reporter in the front lines had to be prepared for such gunfire, especially when you hit the Hills of Donegal).

Even though the *Evening Herald* would not be on sale in the county itself until around six o'clock that same evening, I was able to file a lead story for the country edition of the paper with total certainty – just one hour after the checking of ballot papers had commenced and the first count had not yet begun – that it was a landslide and that "Charles Haughey was on his way to clinching his first victory as Fianna Fáil leader".

You might ask how that was possible – how I could put my head on the block with the country edition rolling off the presses at 11 a.m.

It stemmed from my total faith in the expertise of the tallymen who were masters of their art.

Albert Cummins, a solicitor from Tuam, was known to all the parties at the time as the "Computer King".

He had been forecasting by-election and General Election results since 1946. In fact in the Mayo by-election of November, 1975 which saw Enda

218

Kenny retain the seat for Fine Gael that had been held by his late father, the highly-popular Henry Kenny, he was able to tell Liam Cosgrave, then Fine Gael Party leader twenty-five minutes after the count began that Enda had won the seat.

I have always marvelled at such moments at the total professionalism of the tallymen, especially the O/C of the tallymen.

Invariably they lord it for the day – the day of a by-election of a General Election count.

The Party chiefs at local and national level don't have to wait until an actual count begins before they know – in a General Election situation – if there is a swing in a key marginal. And, in fact, as the ballot papers are actually being checked, the flow of information coming back from the tallymen in the various centres to the Party Headquarters will soon tell them the salutary truth of who is likely to form the next government.

The way they work is that they start counting as the ballot papers are being checked into bundles of 100 votes. By noting how many votes a particular candidate gets, they can calculate the average. There is no rivalry between the tallymen from the various Parties. They co-operate fully with each other on the day and will even check and cross-check figures and percentages with each other.

In the case of a five-seater, for example, the calculation of the average that a particular candidate is getting will soon indicate whether a Party will get two seats and what the indications are on how the vital fifth seat will fall. It is even possible for an experienced tallyman to predict that a sitting T.D. may be struggling to hold the fifth seat in the final counts.

As one tallyman put it to me: "It's not the total of votes from 100 checked that counts in the end, it's the average figure that emerges for the candidates whose progress you are following."

Each tallyman in the front line will bring his figures to the O/C of the tallymen, who will sit at a table like Rommel or Monty in his tent. The O/C of the tallymen is the Supreme Commander during the count. No one among the ordinary "troops" questions his authority. He will be a master at reading the averages. He will have to hand all the figures from previous elections, right down to how it went in each district, each village and even each street.

And his final reading and assessment of the trends – and the swings – can provide an invaluable bank of data for sitting TDs and prospective challengers for Dáil seats in the next election.

I could hardly have foreseen on the November day that the count concluded in the Isaac Butt Memorial Hall in Ballybofey that fifteen months on we would be mourning the death of Clem Coughlan, tragically killed in a road accident on his way to Dublin on Tuesday, February 1, 1983, the day before a crucial meeting of the Fianna Fáil Parliamentary Party leader.

The sweeping victory in Donegal led directly to Charles Haughey going to the country the following summer.

A caucus in the Parliamentary Party had propelled him a year earlier to the leadership of Fianna Fáil and to the realisation of his ambition to be Taoiseach – but he was still not satisfied.

He wanted to be able to stand on the pedestal that a clear-cut General Election victory would give him, satisfied in the knowledge that his mandate to serve a full term in office had come from the people and not just from winning a bitter and divisive internal "Succession Stakes" battle.

But, ironically, in going for the national mandate from the people that had almost become an obsession with him, Charles Haughey let Dr Garret FitzGerald in and, worse still, in failing to win an overall majority in the February, 1982 General Election, with everything in his favour, he created the platform for FitzGerald to come back the following November with 70 seats – only five behind Fianna Fáil.

Donegal was then the siren that flattered Haughey into the belief that what he was able to achieve in his first real electoral test as Fianna Fáil leader – admittedly on a localised plane – could be translated into national success.

Originally it was planned to make the Ard Fheis in the Spring the launching pad for an April General Election success. However, the terrible tragedy of the Stardust holocaust in the Fianna Fáil leader's own constituency caused a postponement to June – and the mood had changed dramatically by then.

Most significant of all was the H-Block hunger strike protest accelerated with first the death of Bobby Sands and then of Francis Hughes, one of the Provisional I.R.A.'s top men, what Frank Cluskey called "a slow dance of death" cast its shadow over Leinster House and, indeed, right across the political spectrum.

As he bade farewell to the Hills of Donegal, Charles Haughey could never for a moment have contemplated that H-Block candidates Patrick Agnew (Louth) and Kieran Doherty (Cavan-Monaghan) would take two "safe" seats from Fianna Fáil in the General Election that was to follow in '81.

I am convinced that the death of Bobby Sands more than any other single factor cost Haughey a national mandate and put him out of office when, before the turn of the year, the signs had looked so favourable for him.

It was a combination of circumstances beyond his control, rather than any gross electoral blunder on his part, that denied him victory first in 1981 and again in November 1982. And he could point to the fact that if the dissident elements had really pulled their weight properly in the February, '82 General Election campaign, the result could have been an overall majority rather than having to look to Tony Gregory and others to put Fianna Fáil back in power.

His critics, of course, would view things differently and argue that "the Haughey factor" played such an important role in the General Elections of June, '81 and February and November, '82 that it was only proper to assume that with any other leader at the helm – Des O'Malley for example – Fianna Fáil could hardly have fared as badly in those three Elections.

Charles Haughey had a fatal penchant for shooting himself in the foot when it came to making key appointments and was closely associated with people whose own failures landed him in trouble politically. I have little doubt that, as he celebrated his 70th birthday in September '95, one of his biggest regrets was that he ever decided to appoint Seán Doherty Minister for Justice at the age of 38, for this led on to "Liffeygate", the phone-tapping and bugging scandals that rocked the Irish nation and to Doherty eventually causing Haughey's own resignation as Leader of the Fianna Fáil Party.

But then one might conclude that Haughey was in debt politically to Doherty from the moment he achieved his long-term ambition in December, 1979 of becoming Leader of the Party and Taoiseach in succession to Jack Lynch. Doherty was one of the "Gang of Five" who had the famous caucus meeting in Room 460 in Leinster House on June 26, 1979 that set in motion the moves to propel Haughey to the leadership. And the initiative from Room 460 led in turn to the romantic version of late-night sessions in the Coffee Dock of Jury's Hotel helping to advance the plot – step by step by step to the achievement of the designated target.

The sands of time were running out for Haughey's short-lived Government that had come into power in March, 1982 when a deep-throat conveyed to me the information that a substantial five-figure sum of taxpayers' money had gone on a security wall around the Roscommon home of Minister for Justice, Seán Doherty.

"Take it from there," said the deep-throat – and then he was gone.

I took it from there. My enquiries continued after the fall of the Fianna Fáil Government by 82-80 in the Dáil confidence motion on November 4, 1982 and for weeks, indeed months after the Coalition had come back into power in December 1982.

The allocation for the wall became known to the new Minister for Justice, the eminently capable Limerick Fine Gael Deputy, Michael Noonan.

At that point my enquiries had reached the stage where I was almost ready to break the story in the *Evening Herald*. Of course, all the information at my disposal had to be closely and thoroughly scrutinised by the legal advisers to the paper. Naturally in any story of such consequence it is inevitable that deletions by made.

Michael Noonan at first, amazing as it may seem, was loath to respond. It was obvious that after the nation-wide reaction to the sensational data contained in the 13-page document he had made public at his news conference in Dublin on January 20, 1983 that he did not want to appear to be engaged in a witch-hunt for Seán Doherty. He would probably have preferred to have allowed the hare to sit – for some time at any rate.

By February 23, the legal advisers to the *Evening Herald* had cleared the draft version of my story for publication – granted the necessary reply to the queries I had put to Michael Noonan could be incorporated into the final version. I informed the Department of Justice that same afternoon that if they did not come up with an official response, then I would indicate that the Coalition government was not prepared to confirm or deny the facts unearthed – facts, I might again stress, that had come from unimpeachable sources and which were of deep public concern.

This brought confirmation the next day that "some works in the context of security under the direction of the Department of Justice had been carried out at Seán Doherty's home".

The statement continued: "As regards this particular work, whatever arrangements were made about walls, e.g. type, size, location etc. were made after joint inspection of the site by gardaí and the Office of Public Works representatives and, presumably, on the spot".

Meanwhile, dynamic *Evening Herald* Editor, Niall Hanley had detailed that a reporter and photographer be sent to County Roscommon to get extra background data to back up my story. Katherine Donnelly was the reporter who made the trip and Brian Farrell the photographer.

But Katherine Donnelly ran into a veritable wall of silence, Seán Doherty being viewed as "God" in his own constituency, irrespective of what the Coalition may have revealed about his involvement in the bugging and phone-tapping scandals.

What is more, she was to learn later that Seán Doherty, whose antennae extended into every corner of the constituency knew everyone she had talked to, where exactly she had gone in the course of her enquiries, what questions she had asked and what she had spent on meals. In a word, he could deduce what would be the claim in "expenses" for the day in the constituency.

Other reporters who went down to Roscommon following various "leads" or simply to write colour pieces had similar experiences and Olivia O'Leary would write in her *Magill* magazine feature on Seán Doherty in April, 1984: "He has a remarkable memory as I discovered over lunch when he was able to tell me in detail of one investigation I had initiated into his affairs over two years ago. He knew who had given me the information, who I'd asked to check out the information, who that person in turn spoke to. He spoke of various forays down to Roscommon by the newspapers and by RTE on Doherty stories. He knew within minutes that they were in town. He knew who they had spoken to, what questions they had asked; in one instance he was rung to be asked: 'Will I spin him a line?' He said no. He even knew what one journalist had charged his paper for a trip to Roscommon. He has eyes everywhere."

The adrenalin always flowed in Niall Hanley's veins when he got the whiff of a good story.

I remember during the 1977 General Election campaign Niall's reaction when I rang from his native town of Longford with a "colour" piece on how Frank Carter had been ditched at the Fianna Fáil Selection Convention that saw the arrival as the new kingpin of Albert Reynolds, self-made businessman. "Lets go with it, baby," said Niall as I told him my intro: "High noon in this bustling Midland town and in out of the sun yesterday, as men quenched their thirst in the Gold Rush Saloon, I heard them talk with an edge of bitterness of the sad rejection of 67-years-old Frank Carter ... But gunfighters get slow on the draw and ride on or fall victim in the heat of a saloon shoot-out when their speed has gone or the odds against them are too great. And so too politicians with whom time has caught up and who must accept the inevitable when the new breed of men decide that the sun has set for the old-timers."

Now from Niall Hanley came the same feeling of shared excitement.

On Friday, February 25, 1983, as men downed their pints or drank their G & Ts in Dublin pubs and lounges, they read the bold headline across the front page of the *Evening Herald* of "The Wall" around Séan Doherty's bungalow home at Cootehall, Boyle and Brian Farrell's photograph was enough to convince any doubting Thomas's of the reality of the protection the taxpayers had been asked to ensure that the former Minister for Justice would have at his Roscommon abode.

The story itself revealed that questions were to be asked in the Dáil about the security wall and that a detailed breakdown would be sought during Question Time on the bill for the wall with the emphasis on what work had actually been completed under the heading of "security".

Part of the overall sum had been allocated for the building of the wall and a further portion for the erection of gates.

The wall was no more than four feet high and when Olivia O'Leary went upriver with Séan Doherty in an Emerald Star cruiser from Carrick-on-Shannon to Cootehall while researching her *Magill* article on the Roscommon T.D., he suddenly cried: "And there's the wall." Then he mused: "Do you think Seamus Brennan would be able to climb over that?"

The Doc when in irrepressible mood like that could joke outrageously at himself – even to the extent that when the phone rang in the chemist's in Carrick-on-Shannon, he remarked" "It's all right, I haven't bugged it yet."

*   *   *

But behind the hail-fellow-well-met approach, the black humour, which in these days his constituents gloried in – because as far as they were concerned he could do no wrong – there were aspects of the man that frightened me. I became convinced that he was a man obsessed with the theory of "conspiracy" – when I interviewed him in a corner of the downstairs bar, the Molesworth Bar, in Buswells Hotel on an afternoon in November, 1983 for my book, *The Survivor*. It was an extraordinary interview.

Here was a man who was prepared to put a tap on the phones of two highly-respected journalists, Bruce Arnold and Geraldine Kennedy in the pursuit of his conviction that he had to ascertain who were the "politicians, power interests and financial interests" who were plotting to bring down Charles J. Haughey – the leader to whom he then professed total loyalty. And not alone was he prepared to tap journalists' phones but he thought nothing of asking the Deputy Garda Commissioner of the day to give a tape-recorder to the then Tánaiste, Ray MacSharry to bug a private conversation with a Party colleague, Dr. Martin O'Donoghue.

The arrogance of the man and his total misconception of what he had been guilty of when he authorised the phone-taps on Geraldine Kennedy and Bruce Arnold emerged clearly when he had the audacity to explain it away by stating publicly that it was because "national security was endangered through leaks of highly-confidential Government papers and memoranda".

"My actions were motivated solely by my concern for the security of my country", he added. Very few believed him.

During the amazing Buswell's Hotel meeting with him, I found no sense of regret in the man for any of his actions. He saw ministerial rank as meaning power, giving power and being all about the exercise of power. His interpretation of the role of a Dáil Deputy vis-a-vis a Minister for Justice and the overlapping of both into the area of serving one's constituents made me squirm when he indicated that he would never "fail to make representations on behalf of my constituents to the gardaí or, indeed, to any public service body".

When it was suggested to him that there had to be a differentiation between one's job as Minister for Justice and the role of the ordinary T.D. making representations on behalf of constituents, Seán Doherty replied: "The fact that I became Minister for Justice doesn't necessarily mean that I have to be silent when it comes to my constituents. If that were the situation they would have themselves a Minister for Justice and lose themselves a T.D. I am primarily a T.D. where my constituents are concerned – at a greater level I am Minister for Justice in the context of the national interest."

When pressed to agree that he had made phone calls to individual gardaí at garda stations, he said: "I have communicated to the gardaí as I have too many other public service bodies on many occasions insofar as the views of my constituents need to be expressed to them. I make no apology for having done that and I will do it again."

He added: "When I represent my constituents it's at the bottom and that's in my constituency and I represent them as Seán Doherty, Dáil Deputy."

Thus if you heard that he had pressed the claims of a constituent who wanted to enter the Garda Training College in Templemore but wasn't tall enough under the regulations for the job, you wouldn't be surprised. Sean would probably respond that the guy was a growing lad and liberal helpings of bacon and cabbage would do the rest!

It was obvious during the interview that Séan Doherty was only too consciously aware of being outside – outside in the sense that he had come from the position of holding one of the most powerful Cabinet portfolios in Government, that of Justice, to being no longer a member of the Fianna Fáil Parliamentary Party, as they occupied the Opposition benches in the Dáil after defeat in the November '82 General Election. It hurt him, hurt him deep down.

He intimated to me that he could only remain silent for so long. I formed the clear impression that if he was not eventually re-admitted to the Parliamentary Party, then he would speak out and one could only surmise who would be damaged politically, maybe irretrievably, if he were thwarted in this aim.

It was inevitable, considering the political debts that were owed to him, that Seán Doherty could not remain out in the cold forever.

It was on Monday, February 7, 1983 that he was forced to resign the Party whip. By December, 1984 he was back inside the fold of the Parliamentary Party.

In the course of an R.T.É. radio interview, he ruled out any involvement by Charles Haughey in his re-admission to the Party.

When asked if his re-admission was a mark of Mr. Haughey's loyalty to his friends, the Roscommon Deputy replied: "Mr. Haughey had nothing to do with it."

He emphasised also that prior to the Parliamentary Party meeting, he had not been talking with Brian Lenihan about the proposal for his re-admission and again he flatly rejected suggestions that Mr. Haughey had made arrangements about his re-admission.

When Seán Doherty's letter of application was read to the meeting, his re-entry was immediately proposed by Deputy Leader, Brian Lenihan and seconded by Denis Gallagher.

No one in his Roscommon constituency demurred at the restoration of the Party whip. Indeed, he was given a rapturous reception by 700 faithful followers who squeezed into the Royal Hotel in Boyle for a party to celebrate the return of the prodigal son from the political wilderness.

Seán Doherty was certainly "King" that evening and no less than 100 people had to be turned away because of the strain on space and facilities.

A year on from that famous night in the 'Royal', Seán Feehan of the Mercier Press, in an inspired stroke, decided to launch his book, *Operation Brogue*, in the same hotel and playwright John B. Keane and Seán Doherty were among the celebrities invited to attend.

Party dignitaries and members of the Party "faithful" in the area received invitation cards to the function. Naturally it was difficult to refuse, especially as it was announced as a wine reception – and Seán would be there.

The near-ecstasy and overflowing emotion at the moment Seán Doherty arrived ... then the bomb scare ... Seán Feehan on stage telling the crowd that he was willing to die with Seán Doherty and John B. Keane ... and the crowd's response indicating that they would gladly follow Seán Doherty to the Great Beyond, bomb scare or no bomb scare ... the book itself going like a bomb, as the faithful sought Seán Doherty's autograph on it ... and no one bothering with the Liebfraumilch, only creamy pints in the main and the man's right arm tired from pulling them ... and even the tea and sandwiches and cakes ignored ... and Seán Feehan telling the Doc that the book he wanted from him was "I Was A Victim Of The M.15" and intimating to Seán's wife, Maura at the same time that he would like to publish her memoirs – "My Life And Times With Seán (only that she seemed to have in mind a novel).

It was that kind of evening in Boyle when they launched *Operation Brogue*, the book that was so kind to Charles J. Haughey.

Come to think of it, when the issue of Seán Doherty's return was first about to be considered by the Fianna Fáil Parliamentary Party I wrote a very blunt feature article for the *Irish Independent* that not alone should he not be re-admitted to the Parliamentary Party but he should be forced to relinquish his Dáil seat.

Doherty, in the course of an interview with a local paper – picked up immediately by the national dailies – said that I would be advised not to leave my house and to keep in close touch with my doctor.

Friends of his claimed that it was only Seán's sense of black humour at work. I was never to know – though I did keep my doctor's number on me every time I ventured out in the following weeks and was inclined to look behind me, especially when I was in the precincts of the Dáil and dusk was falling.

Doherty wasn't joking when he pulled the plug on Haughey in January, '92 coming out with the allegation that he had shown the then Taoiseach transcripts of telephone conversations by the two journalists whose phones were tapped in 1982.

Haughey in a statement described Doherty's allegation as "absolutely false" and said it was ridiculous to be raking over events of ten years earlier.

He went further in the course of a press conference on Wednesday, January 22nd, '92 and hinted Doherty's supposed "revelations" were tied to the leadership struggle in the Fianna Fáil Party. He claimed that Senator Doherty's allegation about him was part of a campaign to oust him as leader of Fianna Fáil and Taoiseach.

Paul O'Neill reported in the *Irish Times* Haughey stating unequivocally that those behind the campaign were, broadly speaking a number of the people who were involved in putting down and voting for the parliamentary party motion against him.

He also referred to what he termed a significant little straw in the wind in the form of Mr Padraig Flynn, who either in his article in the *Sunday Tribune* the previous weekend or in a subsequent interview, had said that Senator Doherty would probably be clarifying his position with regard to the telephone-tapping incident. "That's a connection I think you should take into account," he added.

Asked if he believed Mr Albert Reynolds was involved, Mr Haughey said that he was not making any particular allegation of that kind.

Seán Doherty had plunged the dagger in and Haughey, like Caesar, could only say: "Et tu Seán".

*　　　　*　　　　*

I have always felt that in Haughey's case, there was the need to have around him people he could trust completely – men once they were welcomed into the close inner circle became totally loyal subjects and were expected to be so. The blunt truth was eschewed. Ben Briscoe put it well when he said that Haughey was "blessed with his enemies and cursed with his friends".

When I was researching my book *Charles J. Haughey – The Survivor* I discussed with Dr Ivor Browne, Chief Psychiatrist of the Eastern Health Board and a recognised authority on such matters what could be the effect on a man of a sustained period in the witness box in a long drawn-out court case with much hinging on the outcome. I was, of course, asking about the lasting effect of the Arms Trial on Haughey.

Dr. Browne made the very interesting point that it would depend ultimately on how far that person faced up to the crisis in his life and worked through it – rather than trying to deny to himself deep down that it ever happened. It was similar to a person suffering the death of a near or dear one, perhaps a loved parent or an only son or daughter, and endeavouring to avoid the hurt and the pain and the grief. If one experienced it frankly and went through the pain, then time would heal the wounds and there would not be the lasting legacy deep down that would certainly remain if there was an attempt to live a pretence as if nothing happened.

In 1968 he had been seriously injured in a road accident at Woodenbridge, Co. Wicklow and close friends, who saw the car afterwards, admitted that he was lucky to escape with his life. Twice he nearly died while in hospital. Two years later he was again badly hurt in a riding accident on the morning of Budget Day.

There are those who contend that he was never the same after the road accident, that it affected him far more than the events of the Arms Crisis, that his confidence was not quite the same. But, as I have already indicated, the Arms Crisis, which saw him dragged through the courts in the glare of a fierce, unrelenting public spotlight, had a far more traumatic effect on him psychologically than the physical injuries wrought by the road accident and the subsequent accident on the morning of Budget Day.

Just imagine a Minister for Finance, who had already forged an outstanding reputation for himself in this most testing of Cabinet posts, suddenly plunged from the heights to the back benches of the Dáil, his career as a politician in tatters and all ambitions to win the leadership of Fianna Fáil and attain the position of Taoiseach, set aside for a long time – if not eliminated entirely. And yet in that moment when he plumbed the depths, Haughey said to a fellow-Deputy in the Dáil: "I shall be back – no matter how long it takes".

The long haul as he went on "the chicken-and-chips" circuit with his faithful lieutenant, P.J. Mara, building up the support that would eventually pay off. He displayed a resilience that few politicians could have displayed in the circumstances. But yet the image he had so carefully built and nurtured in the Sixties was never the same again – as the mystique surrounding Ted Kennedy was never the same after the tragedy at Chappaquiddick.

Survival became the name of the game for Haughey – survival in order to keep the main chance always to the forefront and that meant winning the opportunity to get the ultimate mandate of the people in the form of an overall Dáil majority. He became cold and calculating, where in Cabinet in 1970 under the emotional strain of the happenings in the North, he became increasingly identified with the "hardliners", who did not want the Taoiseach "to stand by" while the Nationalist community in the Six Counties was crying out for protection.

Never again would he act in a headstrong manner as he did on Friday, October 23, 1970 when issuing a challenge cross the Atlantic to Jack Lynch (attending the United Nations session in New York), calling upon the then Taoiseach to resign. Sixteen years on in the adjournment debate in the Dáil on Friday, July 4, 1986, he gave a clear hint of how he regarded the "courage" of the Taoiseach, Dr. Garret FitzGerald in opting for a constitutional referendum on divorce. He likened it to "the courage of Lord Cardigan in leading the Light Brigade to destruction in the jaws of death at Balaclava".

Loyalty was everything to Haughey. He saw conspiracy among those who did not give him the loyalty he expected as leader. The politicians of his Party who violated in this area – and he was the final arbiter – were immediately consigned to the freeze-box while those who passed the loyalty test were rewarded, even when they weren't fit for it, with Cabinet or junior ministerial rank or honoured as Front Bench Spokespersons when the Party was out of power. No need for me here to list them. "You know them well", as Michael O'Muirheartaigh might put it.

This test of loyalty led Charles Haughey on one famous occasion to formally open a new milking parlour in Bruff (not far from Dev's own village of Bruree!) for one of his most loyal Deputies, Michael Noonan (not to be mistaken with Fine Gaels' Michael Noonan, a Limerick City deputy and Minister for Health at the time of writing in '95).

There was actually a plaque on the wall commemorating that historic act by a Taoiseach of the state. Gerry Collins was well and truly out in the cold on that occasion, which made Oliver J. Flanagan wonder for the sanity of the nation when its incumbent Taoiseach could take time off from the pressures of trying to right the economy to unveil a plaque outside a milking parlour belonging to a Fianna Fáil T.D.!.

If there was any machiavellian thought in Haughey's mind that it might all result in taking Gerry Collins down a rung or two in the electoral returns, he hadn't reckoned with the power of the Collins "machine", which never failed to deliver less than 12,000 first preferences (the Collins figure, which was 12,702 in the February '82 General Election jumped back to 12,719 in the November '82 Election whereas Michael Noonan fell from 7,535 first preferences to 7,061).

As Gerry Collins said solemnly to someone shaking his hand and commiserating with him on the loss of the State car after that second General Election in '82: "God's will be done", which would probably be interpreted another way to mean that God will look after his own (down to the return of the State car!), irrespective of a plaque on a milking parlour or the vagaries of the polls at a given moment in time …

Gerry Collins, the consummate politician, didn't allow the grass to grow under his feet when he lost the State car. He went for Europe and not alone became an M.E.P. but leader of the Fianna Fáil Group in the European Parliament.

When a storm of criticism broke over a group of the Fianna Fáil M.E.Ps for flying to a fact-finding gathering of members of the Parliament in an island in the sun, Gerry Collins when asked how he got sun-burnt, explained that it happened when he was going to Mass on the island.

But then Gerry was so experienced in the game of politics that no journalist was ever going to trap him into something he didn't want to say – even with the most cleverly-phrased question.

I remember when he was Foreign Minister he was guest speaker at a luncheon in Dublin of the Irish Section of the Association of European Journalists. As on all such occasions the question-and-answer session began at the coffee stage.

I put the question that if the Army of a totalitarian state had over-run Europe and was then invading Britain, would he back the sending of Irish troops to help defend the last bastion of democracy, as we were committed members of the European family of free nations?

Gerry's response was to put his hand on my wrist and exclaim aloud: "Your mother was a lovely woman like my own mother and I admired her every time I met her in Limerick".

The perfect "show me the coin" answer ... and not a single word about the saving of the last bastion of democracy ...

Again in the days when he was Foreign Minister, Gerry returned from China in November '82 at the height of the General Election campaign that saw Dr Garret FitzGerald return to power at the head of a Coalition Government.

Under the heading "Collins Puts Aside The Problems of China", Limerick-based staff writer, Noel Smith in a Limerick West Constituency Profile reported in the *Evening Herald* that "when Gerry Collins bade farewell to China and laid the trials and burdens of Foreign Minister behind him, he had to put out of his mind the problems of three very important Chinamen – Messrs. Zhao Ziyang, Huang Hua and Zheng Tuobin".

He went on: "The 1,000 million souls of the great Chinese Republic, enough to give any Irish politician a stutter and a population complex, the hordes of babies facing a life-time of bicycle riding and rice were a long way, a very long way from Abbeyfeale in the constituency of Limerick West.

"How to tackle the problems of Foreign Minister while conducting a winter's canvass on the doorsteps in the remote corners of the Kerry border with a north wind howling in your face might normally be a headache for any politician.

"But Gerry Collins, with a virtual lifetime of experience on the hustings takes it all in his stride – China is relegated firmly to the back seat. Zho Ziyang, Huang Hua and Zheng Tuobin it was nice meeting you, but will you continue now with your bicycle rides to the next commune while I try to grab another few number ones in Shanagolden, and a toasted ham sandwich in between?"

Scrap Saturday, the RTE Radio programme that used to give us so much pleasure on Saturday mornings, was always so amusing on Gerry Collins and Charles Haughey, especially when Ireland had the Presidency of the European Communities.

The two of them on a plane together and Haughey admonishing Gerry not to be eating "all the nice biscuits".

Or Gerry listing out all his favourite restaurants around Europe and pinpointing the Prado in Madrid as perhaps the one he liked best of all.

From his student days he created legendary stories that still survive to this day and are retold to us in social gatherings at Christmas by those who were in college with him.

Like the time he was hell bent on becoming President of the Student Body and he knew he could seal it if he did his bit for the U.C.D. boxing team in the inter-College annual joust.

The tactics were to put Gerry in against the best of the opposing university team from across the Irish Sea – a guy who was reckoned to be unbeatable because of the knock-out punch he packed. There would be a certain amount of points for just getting into the ring.

Gerry was instructed that when he was knocked down the first time he must stay down – to avoid the risk of being badly hurt.

But Gerry would have none of it. He survived the first round and well into the second before his rival finally realised that he wasn't up against one of the pick of the Irish and duly landed the killer punch.

Gerry was a hero among his fellow team-members for his courage and with onlookers who knew the score.

*   *   *

Politics are less fun now and so I have no regrets at no longer being in the maelstrom covering the scene.

I repeat that we will never see times like those between December, 1979 when Charles Haughey assumed the leadership of Fianna Fáil and February, 1983 when Ben Briscoe's motion calling for Haughey's resignation as Party leader was beaten by 40 votes to 33 in the parliamentary party.

The night of the famous rally outside Fianna Fáil Headquarters in Mount Street and the placards carried by diehard supporters proclaiming their loyalty to the man they adored ... the gatherings of the faithful in Buswell's Hotel awaiting the outcome of each wrench to dislodge Charlie ... the night when they screamed at the locked gates of Leinster House against anyone they thought was opposed to him and journalists who hadn't written too kindly about him had to run the gauntlet of a Bastille-like situation ... I thought better than to brave the mob and begged Michael O'Kennedy to allow me to sit into the back of his car ... and, as they opened the gate momentarily and we passed out into Kildare Street under a star-filled sky and full moon I kept my head well down and said to myself that the Congo and the Lebanon had nothing on this ... Mark

230

Killilea on the night when Haughey looked doomed and quite a number of his fellow Fianna Fáil T.Ds had already deserted ship telling me in the Dáil restaurant that even if everyone else left the deck he would stay there and go down with the Captain and I knew he meant it … what days … what drama …

In cold retrospect, history will be kinder, I feel to Charles J. Haughey than the media were to him during his tenure as Fianna Fáil party leader and in his days as Taoiseach. When cast against others, his statesmanship on the big occasions stands out. In the Dáil itself he was a true parliamentarian who knew the workings of the House, what went and what did not go. He would never abuse it for he knew that here was the beating pulse of our democracy. I have watched him in moments, for example, when a government has fallen. He would understand fully the magnitude of that moment. He was so different then from the man at a triumphalist rally or involved in the fierce cut-and-thrust of a bruising news conference during election times with the media like blood-hounds in full cry. So different from the man who could appoint Seán Doherty as Justice Minister.

The man who did so much for the arts and artists and for pensioners had his good points as well as his flaws. It was not all black and white in his case. The pedigree was not entirely flawed …

I meet him today at the races, as I met him at Fairyhouse on Monday, April 18th, '95 when his horse Flashing Steel won the Jameson Irish Grand National in the hands of Jamie Osborne in a thrilling finish with Rust Never Sleeps (Flashing Steel was trained by Charlie's son-in-law John Mulhern). The Taoiseach, John Bruton warmly congratulated him on his success, proving once again that in Irish racing there are no barriers, political, sectarian, class or otherwise.

All the clashes of the past are forgotten now. All passion is spent. We chat as if there was no past.

To his credit, I believe that the day C.J. Haughey bade farewell to the round of day-to-day politics, to the infighting and the jousts with the media, he put it all behind him, that he was prepared to see it as part of an era, as being on the political plane and not the personal. As he celebrated his 70th birthday in September '95 he received the kind of media coverage befitting an elder statesman.

Today, whether it is at Fairyhouse, as he leads in a winner or in Dingle as he mingles with the crowds on Regatta Day, he is allowed to be himself – and to enjoy unpressurised days. He seems to like it that way.

We have the knack in Ireland of allowing retired Taoisigh to bask in a warmth that crosses all political divides. Liam Cosgrave, Jack Lynch and Dr Garret FitzGerald know it as Albert Reynolds knows it and Charles J. Haughey too.

And as Sean Lemass and John A. Costello knew it also.

17

When Donegan Stormed
The Aran Islands

It was during the Galway West By-election campaign in 1975 that Paddy Donegan, then Minister for Defence, in the Coalition Government headed by Liam Cosgrave, decided to storm the Aran Islands and "take" them for Fine Gael. The "invasion" was to be launched on Inisheer, the smallest of the three islands.

The story was too good to miss, so I decided to accompany him on the trip. The Fine Gael Party worker, who was to have met Donegan on his arrival, found – conveniently – that he had business on the mainland that day. It didn't help the humour of the Minister for Defence, who also found himself on a cold night in February sleeping in a house that didn't have central heating and even extra blankets were no compensation!

He was drinking rum-and-blackcurrant. When Donegan was indulging, the sky was the limit. Suddenly, he decided that it was time that canvassing should commence. I knew then that we were going to have some fun.

Darkness had descended over the island. Donegan had picked up an "interpreter" – let's call him Tomasheen Beag – who wore an old battered raincoat with the buttons long gone and a sugán in place of a belt. We set off – Donegan, the interpreter, the Special Branch man (keeping a watchful eye on the Minister) and myself representing the media and someone with a flash-lamp to light our path. Dogs howled in the sharp coldness of the night and somewhere out there I could see the twinkling lights from the homes that were the target of Donegan's "sweep".

We were walking along a ledge with the strand down below us to our left and I can still hear the sound of the sea lapping on the shore-line. Suddenly there is a yelp and the interpreter trips over something and is gone – down onto the strand below with a thump. "My God," I say to myself as it all races through my mind in an instant. I can visualise the screaming headlines: "Man Dies in Mysterious Island Death Plunge: Minister and Journalist Held".

But Tomasheen Beag picks himself up and we can hear him shaking himself like a dog and soon he is back up beside us. "You okay?", asks

Donegan. "Yes, Sir," he says with due reverence to the Minister and, as the posse heads on towards the first beckoning light, I wonder how many broken ribs he might be suffering.

Two dogs bark at us continuously as we arrive at the first cottage. Donegan, with a few thumps on the door, puts his hand to the latch and swings it open and there before us sitting by the open-hearth fire is the man-of-the-house and his wife. The Minister goes straight to the point without even waiting for the interpreter to carry out his duties: "Votáil Fine Gael – Fianna Fáil Ins On Fharraige."

With that the man-of-the-house, who has got the message, even though Donegan is bereft of any blas, jumps to his feet, tall and strong and sinewy and takes off his crois in a threatening manner, his eyes blazing fire. Tomasheen Beag is spouting something in Connemara Irish to try and smooth the ruffled waters but I sound the retreat without any need for a bugle and the Minister and Special Branch man follow suit.

The canvassing is over for the night even before it has begun!

Next day Gerry Collins, like Montgomery on the mainland, read the headline at breakfast over the *Irish Independent* story that I had filed earlier that day: "Donegan in Bid to Storm Aran Islands".

He sends his wife, Hilary, over with a trusted company, knowing that Bobby Molloy will follow later with the main "task force" to retake the island for Fianna Fáil.

Paddy Donegan is standing on a cliff with his field glasses trained towards the sea, as the boat carrying Hilary Collins and the shock troops heads in towards the shore. He could have been Rommel overlooking the beach at Normandy on D-Day! He is chuckling to himself, enjoying every minute of it.

I go down to interview Hilary Collins – like a war correspondent – and, as her feet hit the strand, I cannot resist telling her that I have just heard Field-Marshal Donegan remark: "We will fight them on the beaches, we will fight them in the hills".

She wasn't at all amused.

Donegan told me he would send me some coloured prints he had taken during the "invasion" – a little memento of a unique occasion. I never expected for one moment that he would remember from those rum-and-blackcurrant waking hours. But, sure enough, they arrived six weeks later with a complimentary slip attached from an Aire.

That was the Paddy Donegan I got to know on Inisheer – and nothing was impossible afterwards …

*　　　　　*　　　　　*

Paddy Donegan coined his famous "a boot up the transom" phrase, which also passed into Irish Political history, during the "Claudia Affair" in late March, 1973.

After the Claudia, which was endeavouring to run a cargo of guns from Tripoli for the I.R.A., was intercepted off the coast of Waterford by the Irish Naval Service and taken to Cork, the Minister for Defence, who had maintained an all-night vigil at Army Headquarters in Dublin during the operation, travelled to Haulbowline by Air Corps helicopter to congratulate all the personnel that took part in the successful operation.

At a news conference on the afternoon of 29 March in Army Headquarters in Dublin, the Minister, pointing out that none of the crew of the Claudia would be charged, said: "The Claudia will get a boot up the transom and be put out of our waters fast … if they put their nose in again we will chop it off."

These colourful phrases tended to dwarf one of the most successful moments in Paddy Donegan's chequered period as Minister for Defence. Indeed, the high peak of his days as Minister might well be said to have come during this operation and it pleased him very much to strike so effectively at the Provisional I.R.A. And I must add that few Ministers were as popular with Army men as Donegan. They knew he had their interests at heart and would back them to the hilt.

Donegan revealed to me something that was never published during the time of "Operation Claudia". Two options faced the Army Command and Naval Services on the night the German-owned vessel steamed towards the Irish coast, carrying among its cargo of arms and explosives 250 Russian-made rifles and 20,000 rounds of ammunition. Should they just capture the Claudia or in one sweep "try and get the lot", as Donegan put it – that is the I.R.A. units waiting on the shore, along with the ship.

"There were enough bombs and guns in that cargo to keep the I.R.A. going for ten years," recalled Paddy Donegan. "But the most frightening aspect of the extent and potency of the cargo was that it included 100 anti-tank mines, each the size of a rugby ball in shape. Any one of these mines released in a supermarket would have blown the whole place to bits with appalling loss of life."

The Russian-made high-velocity rifles would have been ideal, according to the Minister, for Provisional I.R.A. snipers operating in Belfast. "The I.R.A. must have been very angry, indeed, with the Coalition Government for foiling their plans," he added.

Naturally, there was the temptation to close the net at the same time on the I.R.A. on land – but Paddy Donegan maintained, in retrospect, that this might have been at the risk of fouling up the operation in capturing the Claudia and the small boats. "We got the Claudia and we got the guns and ammunition and that was the essential task," he said.

*　　　　*　　　　*

Early in April of the same year – that is '73 – I had one of the luckiest breaks of my entire journalistic career when I was the only Irish journalist to get an interview with 41-years-old Herr Hans Ludwig Fluegel, the Captain of the Claudia.

The gun-running vessel had returned at this stage from Cork to Munich after receiving the "boot up the transom" that Paddy Donegan had promised to deliver.

I had been in Luxembourg covering a meeting of EEC Finance Ministers – the very meeting, incidentally, at which Dr Garret FitzGerald left his fellow-ministers almost open-mouthed with amazement with his knowledge of figures. Indeed, when I got word from the Newsdesk to fly immediately to Munich, I sent a message up to Garret that I needed something quickly, so that I could file my report before heading for the airport. He sent back down a scribbled note that was double-Dutch to me. Through one of his aides, I got another message to him asking him if he could oblige me by seeing me for "just a few minutes" – that is if he could manage it during a break in proceedings.

Happily, one did occur quite quickly. He swept down the stairs and painstakingly took me through the maze of highly-technical data. The problem with Garret always was that he assumed that everyone understood the most involved matters the same as he did. He couldn't bring himself down to the plane of the ordinary Joe Soap.

I caught the first plane from Luxembourg to Munich and asked the taxi-man to bring me to a convenient hotel in the centre of the city. Having booked in, I decided to have something to eat in the dining room. I overheard three men at the next table talking about their plans for the next morning. They happened to be reporters from English dailies who were calculating how much they would have to pay Herr Hans Ludwig Fluegel for his story. In my excitement at this piece of good fortune I let my soup go cold and asked them if they could cut me in and make it a four-way split. Naturally, an Irish paper represented no opposition to the scheme of things and, generously enough, they reduced my "contribution" to one that I knew the *Irish Independent* would have no qualms in meeting.

The upshot was that the *Irish Independent* was able to scoop all its rivals with a Page One lead telling the amazing story from Captain Fluegel himself of how the "Claudia Saga" began with armed Libyan troops loading the arms with just truck lights to guide them and then ended with the arrest off Helvick Head. In between, the Captain had to deal with "a mad Italian," take orders from I.R.A. men and worry about a mystery submarine shadowing them.

He told me that this Italian crew member went mad aboard and "did all sorts of crazy things". Just to have peace and quiet, they gave the Italian a rubber dinghy with a 25-horse power engine about 18 miles off Naples in fine weather. The seaman's wife later reported the man missing at sea, and the Captain of the Claudia made an official statement to the West German police clearing up the matter. No one seemed to know if the "mad Italian" was ever found.

"I am only a seaman. I obey my orders and the ship was chartered by the I.R.A.," Captain Fluegel began his dramatic tale.

"Normally we traded in cigarettes, but this time it was weapons. Anyhow weapons are not as dangerous to carry as petrol," he said whimsically.

Captain Fluegel said the vessel left Tunis for Tripoli, where there were no official port controls, after Herr Leinhaueser had met two I.R.A. men in Tunis and arranged the charter contract.

He went on to describe the voyage to the head of Waterford bay and finally the denouement. "A mile and a half off the coast around 10.30 p.m.

I began to pick up three or four vessels on the radar screen. These boats were three to four miles away.

"They remained on the screen for about an hour. They slowly closed in from each side. Though I had restarted the engines, I was in no position to do anything. I knew then that they were vessels of the Irish Navy.

"They began to flash the message, "Halt, Halt" in the international morse signal. I halted. Ten or fifteen minutes later a launch pulled alongside and a party of 18 to 20 armed men boarded the Claudia."

It was all over.

*   *   *

Paddy Donegan goes down in Irish political history as the man who caused the resignation of a President with one off-the-cuff remark.

The "Donegan Affair" undoubtedly created the greatest Constitutional crisis in the history of the State; it resulted from the Minister for Defence departing from his prepared script to call President Ó'Dálaigh a "thundering disgrace" when opening a new dining complex and central heating unit at Columb Barracks, Mullingar on October 18, 1976. His reason for doing so was that the President had referred the Emergency Powers Bill, passed by the Oireachtas, to the Supreme Court to test its constitutionality.

Paddy Donegan made several attempts to get a meeting with President Ó'Dálaigh to apologise to him personally. The President refused point blank to grant an audience. And Donegan would tell me later that he felt "slighted" at the President's refusal to see him.

One senior member of Liam Cosgrave's Government expressed the view to me that the Minister's apology should have been accepted in a gracious manner – on a *personal* basis at the very least – when it was so profusely given twice. Ó'Dálaigh, instead of seeking his pound of flesh in the form of the sacking of the Minister, could have shown a greater touch of humanity.

*   *   *

Cearbhaill Ó Dálaigh was known as a patron of the arts and artists, a linguist, a lover of the Irish language and European culture but the detachment of the high legal positions he held before he became the country's fifth President meant that he missed the common touch that you find in born politicians. No wonder he failed twice in his attempts to win a Dáil seat.

He stood out for a principle, the defence of the Presidency and the people – and the members of the media like myself who backed him fully at the time – will remember him for defending that principle. Politicians on all sides of the House, however, weren't in any way enamoured by his cold, legalistic approach. And there were no genuine tears shed on his departure from Aras an Uachtaráin. Indeed, the politicians of every Party were quite happy to get "one of our own" in the shape of Dr Paddy Hillery as his successor. At least "the Doc" knew what it was to take a drink in his day and to sing a song in a casual Aran sweater with the golfers at social gatherings in Lahinch Golf Club.

On one plane – the plane of of humanity and human relations – Ó Dálaigh came very badly out of the Constitutional crisis of October, '76.

The epilogue – indeed, the final irony – to that crisis was that Paddy Donegan had to go after all from Defence. In January, 1977 Liam Cosgrave was forced to demote one of his closest political friends and allies when he shifted him to Lands.

That was the price that Cosgrave knew he had to pay when Dr Hillery vacated the EEC Commissionership and became the unopposed candidate for the Presidency – Fianna Fáil's choice yes, if there had been a Presidential Election but the Coalition partners had no option but to indicate that they would not put up candidates against him.

It was obvious that Hillery could hardly have served as President and, under the Constitution, Commander-in-Chief of the Army, while Donegan was still in Defence.

*   *   *

They had come into power on March 14, 1973, as "the team of all the talents", including some of the best and brightest in Ministers of the calibre of Dr Garret FitzGerald, Justin Keating, Michael O'Leary and Dr Conor Cruise O'Brien and with Declan Costello whose name will always be linked with the "Just Society", as Attorney General.

Richie Ryan … Mark Clinton … Dick Burke … Peter Barry … Paddy Cooney … these were others in the Cabinet who added to its strength and solidity when it was contrasted with a Fianna Fáil Front Bench denuded of some of its most powerful personalities during the crisis surrounding the "Arms issue" in May, 1970; Jack Lynch dismissing two of his most senior Ministers, Neil T. Blaney and Charles J. Haughey while Kevin Boland resigned.

The contrast between the conservative and liberal wings of Fine Gael and likewise between the different wings of the Labour Party could not have been as stark.

The term "spin doctor" had not entered the political lexicon when Liam Cosgrave became Taoiseach in the 1973-'77 Coalition Government. He carried on the tradition of service to the State set by his founding-father, William T. Guarding the institutions of democracy was the driving force behind his philosophy – and, frankly, he needed no spin doctors to earn him the respect of friend and foe alike, whatever their feelings about his conservatism when contrasted with the attitudes and stance taken by those of the "liberal wing".

He had total loyalty to his family. Once when Liam Junr. was fighting a General Election campaign in Dun Laoghaire-Rathdown, I suggested through an intermediary to Liam Senr. that he might stand on Dun Laoghaire pier holding the new "arrival" – the pride and joy of Liam Junr. and his wife.

"But he would NEVER stand holding a baby for a picture", came the response.

"That IS the picture for the *Irish Independent* – the one they will splash", I insisted.

Liam Senr. did stand holding the baby and, of course, the *Irish Independent* had a readymade scoop – the line continuing through four generations.

The legends persist to this day of what evolved when the Wealth Tax Bill was introduced by Richie Ryan. It found no favour with Paddy Donegan and Paddy Belton, the wealthy Dublin pub and property owner and also with Maurice Dockrell, another Dublin businessman.

I was in the company of Paddy Belton one night in "The Cobweb" bar in Castlebar during the 1975 Mayo-West by-election when he was prepared to lay a bet of £6,000 on Enda Kenny retaining his late father Henry's seat. He was at the extreme end of the pole to the socialist visionaries to the left of centre in the Coalition. You could never imagine yourself getting involved in a long debate with him on revamping Fine Gael so that its liberalism would shine even more brightly for the young, emerging generations!

Maurice Dockrell, the former St Andrew's College and Trinity College student, walking into Leinster House immaculately dressed and with that distinctive hard hat, a character right out of a P. G. Wodehouse-type novel, set to a background of cricket on the village green and tea and crumpets on the lawn – certainly did not look a candidate in a desperate hurry to speak out in those refined modulated tones of his in support of the Wealth Tax. In fact, he went on record "profoundly to object" to the very principle of a Wealth Tax.

"I was not elected to bring in this piece of socialist legislation," he said – and come to think of it, he was right. You can imagine the echo that statement, with the emphasis on the word "socialist", found in the hearts of true-blue conservative Fine Gael supporters back in 1975 and particularly, I imagine, in Dun Laoghaire, where Maurice's brother Percy was then a Dáil Deputy and where walking the dog along the Prom was one of the primary afternoon considerations of some of the little "old dears".

Percy commanded only 2,206 first preferences in the 1973 General Election but got enough from Liam Cosgrave's surplus to ensure that he would win one of the four seats; and little wonder, with that kind of back-up that the story is told about him that he went one day to collect a cheque in Leinster House and evinced surprise when informed: "Sorry Percy, but don't you realise you are no longer a T.D.!"

Media speculation that a "revolt" by certain Fine Gael Deputies would lead to them breaking ranks when the crucial final division came on the Bill did not materialise. The Coalition Government had a majority of three – 69 to 66 – and Maurice Dockrell simply abstained but did not vote against it.

Richie Ryan brought in the measures in the Capital Gains Tax and Capital Acquisitions Tax aimed specifically, as he pointed out, to "get at the speculators".

Twenty years on from the fierce emotions engendered in that 1975-'76 era Richie Ryan's political courage still stands out and "little Liam" comes very well too out of that episode for backing him unswervingly.

*   *   *

In the Labour Party there could not have been a greater contrast than that between Justin Keating, Dr Conor Cruise O'Brien and Dr David Thornley and Michael Pat Murphy, Steve Coughlan, Jim Tully and Dan Spring.

I was still in my bachelor days during the excitement engendered by the 1969 General Election campaign. Larry Murphy's in Baggot Street was our "local". Labour brought a new dimension to that campaign by going forth on their "New Republic" slogan and on the theme, "The Seventies will be Socialist".

How Michael Pat Murphy and Steve Coughlan must have squirmed at those slogans and at the posters with the Starry Plough. And no doubt they died a thousand deaths when Conor Cruise mentioned Cuba and gave Fianna Fáil the opening to paint a picture for the farming community of what the "New Republic" was likely to mean for them …

Steve Coughlan, the stormy petrel of the Limerick political scene – a constant thorn in the side of the Labour Party establishment – but a character in his own right had no time whatsoever for militant socialists and spurned outright those he regarded as ultra-Leftists. He clashed constantly with Jim Kemmy in the era when, as Kemmy recalled to me once, "there was hardly a socialist in Limerick and the very word 'socialist' seemed to be anathema in the city".

Steve Coughlan came out strongly against the opening of a bookshop in Limerick selling Leftist literature and, in particular, the little red book, "Quotations from Chairman Mao Tse-Tung" and he also made a speech to the Credit Union that led to his being dubbed what he admitted in a *Sunday Press* interview "a Jew hater and a Fascist but only by my enemies. The people of Limerick know what I stand for".

Michael Pat Murphy in his heyday could be described as the doyen of the rural-conservative Labour politicians, who could have fitted as easily into a Fianna Fáil or Fine Gael "coat" as into a Labour one. It just happened that they were winners among rural voters carrying the Labour "tag". Unlike Michael D. Higgins, whose brilliance of mind, grasp of socialist principles and political integrity I admired, they gave nothing intellectually whatsoever to the Party or to the nation. They were the worker ants and were happy to remain so. Let Michael D. have sleepless nights over Nicaragua and the Sandanistas and the Contras. He was welcome to it!

Who was the politician who said to me once that any T.D. worth his salt should not be pipped by a few hundred votes in a General Election. This same politician painted a picture for me of the early bird catching the worm – going in a car to the mental home and ensuring that he got the votes of those capable of being brought to the local polling station and reminding the road ganger on the way of "services rendered" and maybe even picking up a few votes from itinerants on the register – if you were really nervous of being caught in a photo finish.

239

Justin Keating was one of the "Class of '69" – the celebrated group of media personalities, including also Dr Conor Cruise O'Brien and Dr David Thornley, who entered the Dáil for the first time in the General Election of that year – joining men of the previous generation such as Dr Noel Browne and John O'Donovan with whom they would have had sympathy.

Keating was undoubtedly one of the deepest and most brilliant minds in the 1973-'77 Coalition Cabinet – the man who was cut out to be an Irish EEC Commissioner in the mould of a Dr Sicco Mansholt or a Claude Cheysson, as was also Garret FitzGerald. But Garret was not prepared to go to Brussels as EEC Commissioner, even if nominated by Liam Cosgrave, as long as the North remained an outstanding issue to which he felt he could contribute.

So Dick Burke was rewarded by Liam Cosgrave for his unswerving loyalty to him even when the ship looked like going down at one point on a "family issue". And Dick never had to worry afterwards about looking his bank manager straight in the eye.

Justin Keating made himself the *bête noir* of the Fianna Fáil Party, who saw him as the the one man they had to "take out" – even more so than Dr Conor Cruise O'Brien.

Incidentally, it was a fatal blunder for the Labour Party not to leave their options open on going into Coalition with Fine Gael in 1969; the transfers that would go the way of Fine Gael and Labour when they produced a joint programme for Government in '73, did not materialise. A salutary lesson was learned by Labour's pragmatists but the euphoria of '69 and the go-it-alone approach still lingers to this day.

Dr Hillery made the point to me more than once when he was Foreign Minister that Fianna Fáil should have lost the General Election of 1969 and won in 1973. They increased their vote in '73 but failed because of classic transfers between Fine Gael and Labour. The mood of change among the electorate was even greater, I believe, in 1969 that it was in 1973 but the people were not given a clear option of an alternative Government in '69 – as Liam Cosgrave and Brendan Corish gave them in '73.

*   *   *

Dr Conor Cruise O'Brien, dubbed by one Fianna Fáil T.D. as the "anti-Christ", was a hated figure to the diehard Republicans of the Party. He brought their wrath on his head by striking continually at the very heart of much that was dear to the Party traditionalist.

The pro-Haughey wing of the Party detested him most of all for his constant attacks on the man who carried their unstinted loyalty.

During an election campaign in Cork I walked into the Commodore Hotel in Cobh where I met Cruise O'Brien having lunch. I did an impromptu interview with him. He said that the *raison d'etre* of his political life was to try and get rid of Haughey from the scene. He didn't go so far in that particular interview as to paint a picture of Haughey at a cross-roads with a stake through his heart! But he certainly pulled no punches.

One of Conor Cruise's aides told me afterwards that as I was walking out of the room he turned and said: "That will be the lead story in the *Irish Independent* tomorrow".

And it was.

Conor Cruise O'Brien with his intellectual brilliance – some critics might even say his arrogance of mind – was so out of touch with what moves the ordinary Irishman at the grass-roots that he was a blessing in disguise ultimately to Fianna Fáil at election times. I know men, like my close friend, the late Martin Fogarty (reciting with fire and passion Pearse's "The Fool" in my sitting-room, his elbow resting on the mantel-piece) who while totally relaxed in the company of Fine Gael and great GAA friends of his like Jim Egan and Des Kennedy, would hit the counter in Hartigan's of Leeson Street and proclaim to the world at large: "I hate Conor Cruise". There was nothing personal in that statement, I hasten to add – just in case Conor Cruise might think that there was a contract out on him at the time.

Martin Fogarty had friends reaching right across the political spectrum (a classic among those close to him was the one of how he came to have breakfast after a long night with Paddy Belton in the Mansion House when Paddy, as true-blue a Fine Gaeler as they come, was Lord Mayor of Dublin. It has gained in the telling to the extent that some vouch that the Lord Mayor was wearing his chain of office over the bacon and eggs while Martin, on his own admission, was like the King in the fable!).

*   *   *

Dr David Thornley never became the "hate" figure for Fianna Fáil that Conor Cruise and Justin Keating both managed to become. He succeeded Conor Cruise as the intellectual voice of the Labour Party in the European Parliament. I recall David on a plane back from Strasbourg one evening making the point to me that after a speech attacking the regime of the Colonels in Greece that might earn him a standing ovation, he would return to find a man on his doorstep wanting to know why the house-repair grant from "The Corpo" was so slow in arriving.

David, wayward but brilliant – so wonderful to converse with about the philosophies that move men to reject totalitarianism in favour of democracy with all its faults – became a victim in the end of forces which he could not handle, taking the road down to the depths of despair and nihilism that had claimed Dylan Thomas at an age when for many in the artistic world life is only beginning.

But you wondered if David Thornley with his unique mind was really cut out for politics with all its petty frustrations, the confessional boredom of clinics and the interminable boredom of the Dáil itself, outside of the great moments, and the pettiness too that you found in many small-minded Deputies, concerned only with the perks of the job and the number of letters they could have posted each week on headed paper from Leinster House in the effort to hold on to their seats at any cost.

I remember the twilight days – when we knew he had sadly slipped down the final slope – dropping in one morning to The Duke for a coffee and seeing him there at the back with a large brandy before him. In the lost world of the no-hopers now. In his eyes a strange twinge of embarrassment and appeal almost but I was even more embarrassed. I slipped out quickly.

We, as journalists, had afforded him in the European Parliament the total protection that the Irish media invariably gives to those who have "a problem". Protected too by his own colleagues – Brian Lenihan helping to ensure one evening that he would make it to the plane when he seemed to be unconcerned and unaware of the final announcement.

Even in the last sad days of decline we respected David Thornley's mind for the vistas it had opened when he was in full flight intellectually, a brilliance shining like a beacon over seas of much mediocrity. We thought of all the politicians who had nothing to offer us but who survived. We could only conclude that politics is death for some, as it is the very elixir of life for others.

When news reached us one morning of his death, there should have been no sense of shock. Yet we were shocked and deeply saddened. In our tribute for Page One of the *Evening Herald* that day we wrote simply of his "problem" and of the cruel loss of one who had so much to offer and somehow the promise had not been realised. The poetry of Dylan Thomas was in our mind all that long day.

And as I was green and carefree, famous among the barns
About the happy yard and singing as the farm was home,
in the sun that is young once only,
Time let me play and be
Golden in the mercy of his means,
And green and golden I was huntsman and herdsman, the calves
Sang to my horn, the foxes on the hills barked clear and cold,
And the sabbath rang slowly
in the pebbles of the holy streams.

*   *   *

Four years on from 1973, having brought the ship of the economy successfully through the worst of the oil crisis and having survived a major challenge to the security of the State from the Provisional I.R.A., Liam Cosgrave's national Coalition Government, was "rewarded" by being swept out of power in one of the worst defeats ever inflicted on any government since the founding of the State.

In 1973 Fianna Fáil actually increased its share of the vote from 45.7 per cent (in 1969) to 46.2 per cent but because of classical transfers between Fine Gael and Labour, the Coalition partners won enough seats to effect the first change of government in the history of the State in sixteen years.

Justin Keating put it well when he said that the Coalition was only in its first autumn in power when bits of the ceiling began to fall in on it. In fact, the Arab-Israeli conflict – the Yom Kippur War – setting off as it did a quadrupling of oil prices and bringing Europe to its knees in deep and sudden recession, meant that the ceiling had fallen in for Fine Gael and Labour (if they had only realised it then).

A study of the 1973-'77 Coalition shows a Government, under the firm leadership of Liam Cosgrave, battling most courageously with economic problems not of their own making.

And yet Richie Ryan, one of the best Ministers for Finance the country has had, managed to bring the ship of the economy to port in '77 with the books balanced and no crippling external debt. Those who put the tag "Red Richie" on to him at the height of the fierce battle over the Wealth Tax conveniently forgot all that, of course. He took on head-on a powerful lobby who did not want that Tax at any cost and his courage was admirable.

Brian Lenihan said to me one day that when historians look back on that period, they would acknowledge that it was a far better government than many gave it credit for after the fall in 1977.

A study of that 1973-'77 government shows clearly the unswerving determination of Liam Cosgrave as Taoiseach and his Cabinet colleagues not to bend the knee to the Provisional I.R.A. in a continuous silent battle, heightened by the drama of the kidnapping of Dutch industrialist, Dr Tiede Herrema, in October 1975 and the assassination of the British Ambassador, Ewart-Biggs in July, 1976.

In the final analysis Cosgrave's Coalition Government went out of power in 1977 simply because Fianna Fáil made it a "Dutch auction" with their famous manifesto, comprising a package of "goodies" that no voter could resist. In fact, the fulfiling of the promises made in that Election campaign would subsequently do untold damage to the economy. Fianna Fáil friends of mine have said privately that there was no need for the Party to have gone so far. It can be argued that Jack Lynch would have returned to power offering less than half the "goodies" he dispensed.

There are men in the Fianna Fáil Parliamentary Party who have made the point to me also that the very size of the 1977 victory contained seeds of a self-destructive nature; to begin with, it induced complacency where a hung Dáil would have kept the Deputies on their toes. Without having to look over their shoulders constantly at the prospect of being brought down in a snap Dáil division, they looked inwards – and there was ample time for plotting among the hawkish elements that could never accept Jack Lynch's leadership after 1970.

On the other side of the coin, it can be argued that had Fine Gael returned victorious in the 1977 General Election, it would not have made the dramatic internal changes in structures that came about once Garret FitzGerald took over at the helm. So the defeat and the shattering scale of it was in the long-term a blessing in disguise – causing such a revolution that the road was opened for victory in 1981 and, more important, for the "Leap Forward" to 70 seats in the November '82 election.

18

"How Did it Go, Minister?"

D r Garret FitzGerald during his time as Minister for Foreign Affairs was returning from a particularly tough session in Brussels at the climax of the negotiations on Lome One the Convention linking independent African, Caribbean and Pacific countries with the European Community in a unique system of co-operation.

Aengus Fanning, then Agricultural Correspondent of the *Irish Independent* (later to become News Analysis Editor of the paper and then Editor of the *Sunday Independent*) had gone to Dublin Airport to interview Agricultural Minister, Mark Clinton, also, as it happened, on his way home from Brussels. Gerry Connaughton, Press Spokesman in the Department of Agriculture, spotted Aengus and told him that for protocol reasons it would be helpful if he would first have a word with Garret as he came through the VIP lounge.

Aengus pointed out to Gerry that he wasn't briefed at all on what Garret had been involved in that day on Lome. What he was concerned about was sugar beet. There was a deadline to meet – but he was willing to oblige Gerry if it solved a protocol problem.

As Garret approached, all hustle and bustle, Aengus Fanning greeted him with the non-committal: "How did it go, Minister?".

Garret, his brain awhirl with percentage calculations, the bushy crop of hair not cut and stylised as it was later, with a sheaf of papers under his arm adding to the look of the born academic, launched into a long explanation about the problems of Botswana beef and Burundi tea and how when they seemed to have surmounted these, someone intervened on the question of a better quota for a banana-producing ACP State and then he remarked to Aengus who was writing furiously or appeared to be – "Do you understand?"

"Yes, Minister," came the reply.

Garret rambled on through the maze of Botswana beef, through rum quotas in hectolitres of pure alcohol, through ACP sugar, through fish, dried, salted and in brine and Stabex and finally ended by saying: "Have you got all that?"

"Yes, Minister." said Aengus, now reeling on the ropes under the sheer weight of Garret's enunciation of detail.

"And if there is any point you don't understand, you can ring me," said the ever-helpful Garret, as he rushed away to the waiting ministerial car.

"Yes, Minister, … thanks."

Meanwhile an impatient Mark Clinton was waiting to give the real story of the day that would inevitably grab the headlines next morning, for who among Ireland's farmers wanted to read about Botswana beef and Burundi tea or banana quotas when there was an emotive battle (with even bishops involved on the sidelines) being fought at that time on sugar beet. And who better than our Mark to lay it on the line to the Brits or anyone who seemed to be standing in the way of Ireland's "vital interests" in the agricultural sector?

No doubt, Garret glancing at the *Irish Independent* next day must have wondered how he got pushed off the front page – and every other page into the bargain and how sugar beet so transcended the culminating negotiations on Lome. Ah well …

The legends have grown with the passing years – and with every election.

Like the morning on the road during one election campaign, rather than disturb Joan when rising for an early-morning appointment, he did not put on the light when reaching for his shoes and ended up putting on two odd shoes. A lynx-eyed photographer later that same day caught the picture for posterity.

And the time campaigning by the Lee, Garret was handed a life-size teddy bear in the Red and White colours – after Cork had won an All-Ireland senior hurling title. He looked puzzled. Not to recognise the old "blood and bandages" in such a situation – impossible you might think but then Garret never moved in that world of the dust-flying-in-the-square, or meat-teas-and-plain-teas and the songsters singing *The Valley of Knockanure* or *The Banks of My Own Lovely Lee*.

It was all like the lost world of the Incas to him.

In the November '82 General Election campaign the Fine Gael campaign planners in North Kerry wanted to ensure that there would be no repetition when Garret visited the constituency, especially as Jimmy Deenihan, who had led the Kingdom to the fourth-in-a-row All-Ireland senior football crown the previous year, was a candidate. The story goes that Garret was given a thorough "grind" on the colours all the way down to Tralee and a final "refresher" in a hotel room in town. "What are the Kerry colours?" "Green and Gold." Repeat? "Green and Gold."

And when Garret came out for his walk-about and was handed the No.2 jersey that Jimmy Deenihan had worn against Offaly in the All-Ireland final, he was heard to remark with a knowing nod of the head: "Ah, the Green and Gold."

* * *

The stories that you found doing the political and social round showed that Garret was human. However whether true or apocryphal, they were never as colourful as those surrounding the late Lord George Brown, who as British Foreign Secretary in the Government of Harold Wilson left a memory of being one of the most flamboyant politicians ever to hold the office – a man, who acknowledging his own flaws and weaknesses, could remark: "Emotion in a politician has become a dirty word" or, after being banned for three years from driving: "If I were advising God on how to make me the second time, there are parts of my temperament which I would suggest he left out."

Like the story related about George by Geoffrey Levy in the *Daily Express* after his death on June 3, 1985. The occasion was a glittering reception in South America, where as the band struck up, the ever-ebullient George asked a purple-robed figure to dance, and was refused. When asked why, the figure hissed: "Firstly, because you are drunk, secondly because this is the National Anthem, and thirdly because I am the Papal Nuncio."

First as Foreign Minister and then as Fine Gael leader and Taoiseach, Garret was Garret. Everyone loved him all the more for the absent-minded professor-like qualities, unable to change a fuse or cook a meal when mother was away. Garret's faults stemmed not from a too-human weakness that had brought good men down but rather a Clouseau-like fumbling in the figurative sense that made him rather distinctive among the Irish politicians of his generation.

Another man might be damaged beyond repair if stories were constantly repeated about him. Because these things are separate as it were from Garret the brilliant intellect, the man with the total grasp of figures and economic factors and above all the man of integrity who shone like a beacon when the "Liffeygate Scandal" was rocking Fianna Fáil to its foundations.

Someone who had been close to him put it well when he said: "You never knew in the figurative sense when he was liable to put his eye-drops in his ears and his ear-drops in his eyes".

This same man went on:

"Garret would fill a travelling bag with all the essential documents and the books he felt he had to read on a journey but he might forget his razor or his toothbrush or his cuff-links. He was quite liable to put salt in his tea instead of sugar or maybe reach over and put the sour-cream or horse-radish sauce instead of ordinary cream in his coffee at dinner table. It didn't worry him when he was made aware of what he had done – or if he was pictured in the newspapers wearing two wrong shoes. His mind was so caught up with what you might call the Grand Design that he was always getting it wrong in smaller and less important matters."

The legends persist from his days as Foreign Minister and have gained in the telling – and retelling.

Was it in the King David Hotel in Jerusalem that an aide was seen scurrying down a corridor in a desperate search before a formal dinner for a pair of braces (or was it cuff-links) – and came up from the nether regions of the Hotel with the needful?

But it was in Moscow certainly that he amazed the Russians with his knowledge of trains and trams. These have always held a small-boy's fascination for him and few are aware that he has a collection of tram and train tickets from various parts of the globe, as others collect rare stamps. Garret, in fact, will take a ride on a train just for the sheer enjoyment of it and, the experience he gleaned in his days in Aer Lingus of timings and schedules gives him a computer-like accuracy in making comparisons between electric trains and steam-engined models.

He took a train from Moscow to Leningrad and was able to tell the Russians in a speech to the Leningrad Soviet an hour or two before his departure on that rail trip how it compared on his reckoning in timing with the one that left St. Petersburg for Moscow at precisely the same time – 23.55 – in 1914. They are still rubbing their eyes in wonderment.

Anyone who visits Moscow will want to see the Bolshoi Ballet. Garret had the privilege of being brought along as the personal guest of Foreign Minister, Andrei Gromyko, later President of the Supreme Soviet. And the ballet, interestingly enough, was based on Shakespeare's *Much Ado About Nothing*.

Garret is not exactly a lover of the ballet or an opera buff; his pleasures are of the mind rather than the artistic heart and, of course, he revels in good conversation at dinner table.

When Garret, on a visit to Vienna discovered that on the schedule was a Night at the Opera – the opera in question being Wagner's *Gotterdammerung*, which normally starts around 5.30p.m. and goes on until after 10.30p.m.

Garret, who would find it hard to sit quiet for that length of time – even if it was a question of a replaying of the unabridged Nixon tapes, expletives and all – put out discreet feelers in advance to get the programme altered. But the word came back from Vienna – "no go". The Austrian Foreign Minister was going along too – and would be in the VIP box beside Garret.

So Garret had to sit through it all and what surprised him was that the Austrian Foreign Minister arrived quite late, with appropriate apologies to him. Next day he called Garret aside and said in his ear: "Really, I am not an opera lover at all".

You should have seen Garret's face at that moment …

I happened to be covering that trip of Garret's and was fortunate at all to get a seat (courtesy of the Press Section of the Austrian Department of Foreign Affairs) in a packed Opera House. But I missed the strawberries and cream and champagne served to Garret and the other distinguished guests during one of the intervals.

I could have warned Garret that the heavy-bosomed women in Wagnerian operas take much longer to die than those in popular Verdi or Puccini operas. It was rated the greatest performance of that particular Wagnerian opera seen in Vienna since 1946. The climax was truly breath-taking.

I think Garret found it less exacting to listen to the piano recital that

John O'Connor gave at a private dinner hosted by the Irish Foreign Minister for his Austrian counterpart. And I for my part found an afternoon at the races next day drinking mulled wine to background music like *The Blue Danube* and other Strauss waltzes, less demanding than *Gotterdammerung*.

But then no one goes to Vienna without going to the Opera and no one goes to Moscow without trying to get to see the Bolshoi.

Garret got to both -with different effects ...

          *   *   *

In the early Seventies his wife, Joan and himself were not happy flying and it was supposed to have stemmed from Joan having a nightmarish dream in which she saw the plane go down that was conveying Garret on some Government business, though another theory was that she was deeply affected by the loss of the Aer Lingus plane that simply vanished off the east coast on a flight out of Dublin (the inside theory on that was that it was hit by a British missile during exercises in the Irish Sea).

Garret amazed his aides in Iveagh House in his initial days as Foreign Minister by presenting them with a perfectly worked-out schedule on how to get to Tokyo by boat and train (I am not certain whether it took in the Trans-Siberian Express!) He never did make that journey to Japan the way he had planned it.

Of course his schedules became so hectic that he had to overcome the fear of flying.

Even before he graduated into politics he created his own legend when promoted at the age of 25 to a position in Aer Lingus that saw him in charge of the planning of new routes, scheduling aircraft, selling charters, making provision for extra services in peak periods and recommending fare structures.

When he left, it was said it took four executives and a computer to replace him!

The public could forgive Garret his foibles and accept them, for they saw him at heart as the true academic, a man as it were in temporary exile for the good of the nation from his natural abode – a chair in some university. As night follows day, they reckoned that he would go back to things academic – and with an even greater devotion to matters literary and of the mind.

The lasting impression of Garret is of a man whose trousers always seemed a size too big. Perhaps if you gave Garret a walking-stick, he could have strayed in other times into a Charlie Chaplin film like *Gold Rush*.

When I was researching my book, *Garret – The Enigma* I was given thirty minutes with him in his office one morning in Government Buildings at the time he was Taoiseach.

Joan must have rung at least twice before Garret finally said to her kindly but firmly: "I'm with Raymond Smith and time is running out".

On another day he had agreed to meet me again in his office but this time had gone down with a touch of flu and I was told by one of his secretaries that he would see me instead at his home.

There was no fire in the sitting-room. Garret didn't seem to notice. And there was no suggestion that he might make a cup of tea or coffee. You didn't think any less kindly of him for it. You simply concluded that to prepare for himself a full Irish breakfast of bacon and eggs would never be on the Garret agenda. He lived and moved in a different world from the rest of us.

I recall once on the road with the Boys in the Bus. Garret met us after dinner for what might be styled an impromptu remains-of-the-day press briefing and it gave him the opportunity also to talk off-the-record afterwards over a drink. It provided those of us who had to file for the evening papers next morning with an angle on stories that might need a new top – or Garret, again being Garret, might even come up with something that might make a lead.

On this particular evening Joan was there – holding court, you might say. "Now who is this young man – should I like him?", she ventures as she is introduced to a reporter she does not immediately recognise. "Did he write something the other day that was critical of Garret?".

Said in half-jocose, banter-like style – but with a hint of ice.

Joan could never be described as a simple, home-loving housewife with no idea of what Garret's plans were or what was revolving around him. A graduate from U.C.D in economics and history, she had been a brilliant University student in her own right. In fact, Garret met her in College as Joan Farrell and they fell in love. After being appointed to a post in Aer Lingus in January, 1947, he was married nine months later at the age of 21.

It did seem at times to her critics that Joan's influence over her husband was too great. He, for his part, appears to have always deeply respected her judgement and again this goes back to their days in College and to the time when she was closely involved with him in establishing the Economic Intelligence Unit of Ireland, an economic consultancy organisation of which she was a director in the early sixties.

It was claimed on the political grapevine that she had an input into the final shape and composition of Garret's Cabinets when he was Taoiseach, though none of the political correspondents could ascertain this for certain. They could only surmise on the "favoured son" syndrome and ponder and analyse who was "in" and who was "out" at a given moment.

Contrast Garret on the road creating a family atmosphere over dinner with Joan and Mark with C.J. Haughey's approach. You inevitably expected to meet C.J. alone in the ring – with the gloves off, ready to fight bare-knuckle!

But I remember one revealing moment when Mrs Maureen Haughey had to be with her husband at an official function in the West of Ireland. There she was in the lobby of the hotel greeting local dignitaries as we came in. Earlier in the day we had been at another of those bruising press conferences in the Burlington Hotel.

When we of the media paid our respects to Mrs Haughey, she greeted each one of us warmly and without the slightest indication that she knew which of us had been in there giving the old rabbit punch to Charlie and catching him with a one-two for good measure in the kidneys if we could manage it. Did I mention to her that I was proud to shake the hand of Sean Lemass's daughter – the man I admired as possibly the best Taoiseach this country has had?

That's immaterial. What I am glad of is that through all those hectic, frenetic times in the Eighties we left Mrs Haughey and her family untouched in the white heat of an era that will never be repeated in Irish politics.

It would be ludicrous to suggest that the Haughey family members were not hurt or didn't have feelings when the headlines screamed that C.J.'s demise was at hand and the *Irish Press* even went into print with his political obituary. The journalist, however, can't begin to think at the height of the big battles what the side-effects will be on the family plane. All he can do is scrupulously leave wife and family out of it in any criticisms and concentrate on the issues at the heart of the matter.

*   *   *

Frankly, I have not met any politician with the same breadth of knowledge of foreign affairs on a global level as Garret FitzGerald. The only one who could be entered in the same league was Professor and later Senator James Dooge, who was Foreign Minister in the short-lived Coalition Government from June '81 to March '82.

Garret's knowledge was awe-inspiring. But it sometimes caused him to overlook certain happenings, vote-catching in their appeal, that an early-bird politician would immediately grasp and turn to his own advantage.

Instance the time that Garret did a whirlwind tour of the Middle East countries and I caught up with him in Luxembourg. I asked him if he would be taking action to try and free the young chap from Dublin who was being held by the Belgian authorities because he had strayed – unwittingly it appeared – into an out-of-bounds area near a military installation and was apprehended because he was taking photographs.

There had been an outcry in the media back home while Garret was flitting from capital to capital in the Middle East. He looked at me blankly now, not knowing who in earth I was talking about. No doubt he expected me to bombard him with questions about his initiatives to ensure that relations would not deteriorate further between Israel and the Arab world.

Meanwhile, a few other politicians from Dublin constituencies who happened to be on the Continent on European business headed with all possible speed for the prison where the young Dubliner was being held. And captured all the kudos they could for the trouble they had taken, building up in the process a bank of sympathy votes.

It was only when he got back to Dublin that Garret realised how he had been beaten to the punch but really he should have made it his business before he ever hit Luxembourg to see to it that he was fully briefed – even on matters that would not normally engage his mind or his full attention.

Garret as Foreign Minister always rode the High Sierras. He was right

251

in the thick of things when the Summit of Heads of Government and State was held in Dublin Castle during Ireland's Presidency of the European Communities in '75. He worked non-stop to find a balanced solution to the British renegotiation with the EEC, wanting to keep Britain in at all costs while striving at the same time to see to it that Irish interests were not sacrificed or damaged in any way.

And he played a key role in the successful conclusion of the first Lome Convention. He actually signed this agreement on behalf of the European Community and later Michael O'Kennedy was to sign Lome Two and Peter Barry Lome Three, linking then sixty-five ACP States with the member-States of the Community.

*   *   *

In cold retrospect, it has to be contended that Garret FitzGerald showed political naivety and a total failure to acknowledge geographical considerations when he came to select his first Coalition Cabinet in the summer of '81. He omitted Tom O'Donnell, who had been an excellent Minister for the Gaeltacht in the Liam Cosgrave Government of 1973-'77, also Dick Burke, Minister for Education in that same Government and Richie Ryan. Through pressure from the grass-roots, Tom O'Donnell and Richie Ryan had been brought back to the Front Bench after the failure of the Party to win the Donegal By-Election in November, 1980. There was naturally fury among Tom O'Donnell's supporters in Limerick and in the Shannon area at the manner in which he was snubbed in the allocation of Cabinet posts.

Dick Burke did not hide his shock at failing to get the portfolio of Foreign Affairs over Professor Jim Dooge. Making it even more galling for the former EEC Commissioner was the fact that he had answered a call to Harvard University to come back and fight the Election for Fine Gael and had been pitched into the Dublin West five-seater, embracing Ballyfermot – strange country, you might say, for a man living among the Diplomatic set in Ailesbury Road in Dublin's South-side. He helped in a singular triumph for Fine Gael, Jim Mitchell heading the poll with 9,326 first preferences, Dick Burke himself polling 5,301 and Brian Fleming 5,052. Brian Lenihan (7,169) and Eileen Lemass (4,953) took the other two seats for Fianna Fáil and sitting Deputy, Liam Lawlor (Fianna Fáil) lost his seat.

The story is told from that time that Dick Burke was absolutely shattered as he sat down beside Richie Ryan in the back benches. When Richie told him he had got nothing, Dick replied that he had got nothing either. Richie shrugged his shoulders and indicated that he wouldn't simply be languishing as a backbencher in the Dáil – but would be devoting a lot of attention to his role as leader of the Fine Gael Group in the European Parliament. Dick Burke, not trying to conceal his feelings, turned to him and said: "But I got nothing, nothing, NOTHING".

Dick Burke never forgave Garret FitzGerald for omitting him from the Cabinet. Tom O'Donnell took it very badly also. Richie Ryan, who always talked about "my Taoiseach" when Liam Cosgrave was at the helm kept his thoughts to himself.

I believe that Garret FitzGerald in passing over Tom O'Donnell and Dick Burke for Cabinet posts and also ignoring Richie Ryan simply accentuated the clash in basic understanding and outlook between the "Donnybrook Set" and the "Cosgrave-ite wing" of the Party. He left a legacy of bitterness that was to surface in a number of different guises later.

But nothing could ever excuse his political "innocence" in ignoring some of the biggest areas of population in the country. Not alone was Limerick left without a Cabinet Minister but even without a Minister of State. Galway got no Cabinet Minister and no Minister of State either. Waterford got a Minister of State in the person of Eddie Collins. No wonder John Donnellan was rightly angry when he saw Jim Dooge, who had not contested the General Election, being appointed to the Cabinet while prominent Deputies, who had been in the front "trenches" throughout the campaign, were ignored.

Not surprising then that in the Spring of 1982 when Dick Burke got the call from then Taoiseach, Charles Haughey to go to Brussels in place of Michael O'Kennedy as Ireland's EEC Commissioner, he accepted the offer. The "hard men" of the Fine Gael Parliamentary Party who saw Haughey's offer as simply a case of a Greek bearing gifts, had left him like a man who had been put through a clothes wringer when I interviewed him in his home for the *Irish Independent*. His wife, Mary, was helpless to assuage the wounds that had been opened. As Dick saw it, he was guilty of no crime in serving the national interest in Brussels as an EEC Commissioner for a second spell. He owed no apologies at any rate to Garret FitzGerald who had treated him abominably after he had come back from Harvard University – in response to Garret's own initiative – and won that famous victory in Dublin-West.

Let it be noted here that Alan Dukes at the age of 36 was appointed by Garret FitzGerald a Cabinet Minister on his very first day in the Dáil – emulating Dr Noel Browne, Kevin Boland and Dr Martin O'Donoghue.

Garret saw him as a favoured son. When Garret eventually resigned as Party leader, he was no doubt very happy that Alan took over at the helm. This was to prove disastrous for the Party. Alan Dukes had time on his side. From my days with him in the N.F.A. (later the I.F.A.), I have always admired his outstanding qualities and, in particular, his grasp of economic matters. But he should not at that point have become Party leader. It was unquestionably the heavyweight figure of a senior politician like Peter Barry, who came across so well on television, who should have assumed the leadership and the young contenders to the "throne" would have been given ample time to establish their credentials. Fine Gael paid a very heavy price for that moment of madness and the haul back to winning again the reins of power was to be a bitter and bruising one with, ironically enough, Alan Dukes suffering most of all.

*   *   *

When final assessments are made of Dr Garret FitzGerald's outstanding qualities as a Taoiseach and the flaws in his pedigree, one of the greatest flaws of all – indeed, his achilles heel – will be seen to be his inability to grasp what was of overriding importance to grass-roots people over and above the "national interest". For example, putting a tax on children's shoes could constitute to Jimmy Kemmy a matter of deep-seated emotion, hinging on every tenet of socialism and to appeal to him – as Garret did – to vote for it on the basis that he was serving the national interest in doing so was sheer nonsense.

Gilbert and Sullivan, if they were alive at the time, could have written a rollicking and sparkling operetta as good as *The Pirates of Penzanze* on the fall of the Coalition Government on the January '82 Budget. I chronicled the absurdity of that fall in my book, *Garret – The Enigma*, the impossibility of Garret's approach as the ship began to sink until ultimately he was like a captain on deck appealing to Jim Kemmy to throw him a life-belt and Jim dismissed him with the immortal words: "I am sorry, Garret, the die is cast. I cannot go back on my decision. It is too late now".

Too late, yes, far too late. Those words were uttered by Kemmy when Garret knelt on the bench in front of him in the Dáil chamber just before he entered the division lobbies for the fateful vote on John Bruton's budget.

Garret didn't understand – could never have understood until it was too late – what the 18% VAT on children's footwear (on clothing also) meant to the Limerick Deputy.

On Budget Day – Wednesday, January 27, 1982 – Jim Kemmy took a call to inform him that Sean Bourke had died. "My friend Sean Bourke was dead. It was a bad omen", he said simply.

Behind that statement it was obvious that Kemmy was deeply moved and upset at Bourke's passing. Both had had a lot in common in the remembrance of childhood days – in Kemmy's case his father dying of T.B., leading on to his taking the emigrant ship to England. And out of those images from the time he left his native city and homeland ("stark and searing and remaining with me with a terrible intensity of feeling") he wrote his poetic statement, *Exiled Memory '57* which has echoed down the years for those who know him and admire the principles that have always dominated his life ("Life-long dwindling to/That lone option:/The inescapable move/For survival and self-respect/Forced out to a "pagan" world/By hopeless unemployment.")

Sean Bourke died a comparatively young man alone in a caravan over 50 miles from his native Limerick and it was the "damn booze" that finally got him, as his doctor had warned him it would, if he didn't stop.

Noel Smith, who was a friend of his over a number of years, touched the heart of the matter when he wrote in a tribute in the *Irish Independent* to the Man who sprang British masterspy, George Blake about Bourke's childhood. He recalled Sean Bourke's own words.

"Love was so easily stifled in my youth – the poverty and the degradation of those days provided a soil far too barren for the survival of

anything more than a somewhat tenuous family loyalty. Who or what are you supposed to love as you walk to school barefoot, through the snow on a breakfast of tea and bread and margarine."

Sean Dublin Bay Loftus voted against the Budget along with Jim Kemmy – and it was just after 8 o'clock on that fateful Wednesday night that Garret knew he was out of power. John Bruton would admit to me later that the Cabinet did not realise how emotive the 18% VAT measure would prove to be and he added: "With the benefit of hindsight, of course, we would not have introduced it, if we were framing that Budget now".

Garret FitzGerald fully accepted later also that it was a major mistake to put VAT on children's clothing and footwear.

Garret became the laughing-stock of the country over one simple remark during the news conference at which he tried to defend what was impossible to defend. It is remembered as the "women with small feet" syndrome.

Garret has explained to me since that this remark was made jocosely but that it was reported in all seriousness by the daily papers next morning. "You should never make jokes in politics," he added wryly.

The *Irish Times* reported that fateful remark in the following manner on page one of its edition of January 28, 1982: "Pressed on the point of the 18% VAT imposition on clothing and footwear, if the Government ought not to have exempted children's wear, the Taoiseach said that this could have led to a situation where some women, with small feet, could have bought their shoes cheaper than their children, who had larger feet."

John Bruton became the sacrificial lamb for a decision taken by the Cabinet as a whole. When the Coalition won the November '82 General Election and took office again on December 14 of that year, he was replaced by Alan Dukes as Minister for Finance and switched to Industry, Commerce and Tourism.

But out of the humbling experience he endured, John Bruton, whose integrity as a politician remained unsullied, became a much tougher and wiser politician today, close on fourteen years on, he has known what it is to be in power and out of it. He has known the cruel ups and downs of the game in a way that gives him a distinct advantage as Taoiseach and Fine Gael leader over Bertie Ahern, Albert Reynold's successor at the helm as Fianna Fáil leader. Bruton's silence is his strength as it was in the case of Liam Cosgrave.

He is street-wise in the cut-and-thrust of Dáil debate and street-wise also when it comes to what is demanded in a television confrontation.

As I write this in September, '95 the intriguing questions being asked in political circles are: How will John Bruton fare against the 'Young Pretender' for the job of Taoiseach, Bertie Ahern when the two square up against each other in the ring in the next General Election?

Can Bruton ever hope to emulate Garret FitzGerald, who hit a total of 70 seats in the Dáil for Fine Gael in the November '82 General Election or can he at least show that he is a real winner as a leader at the polls?

Can Bertie Ahern show that he has the winning touch of a Jack Lynch, the most successful of all Fianna Fáil leaders at the polls, as proven by his achievement in 1977 in winning 84 seats?

As I see it, Bertie Ahern's task is to convince the Fianna Fáil faithful and the electorate as a whole that behind the "nice guy" image – behind his unquestionable popularity – he has the killer instinct to take out John Bruton and Dick Spring at the polls and, in addition to that, the statesmanship to become a dominating Taoiseach, should he be given the requisite mandate.

*   *   *

Back in the days when Liam Cosgrave was Taoiseach the term "spin doctor" was unknown. And it was the same when Jack Lynch was at the helm. Indeed, it was an import to this country in recent times from Britain.

I like to think that the first of the real spin doctors to grace the Irish political scene was Galway-born Peter Prendergast, who as General Secretary of Fine Gael played a notable role in masterminding the General Election victory of '81. Under him we had the institution of the high-powered back-up team, dubbed "The National Handlers" by John Healy in the *Irish Times*.

A graduate in commerce from U.C.D., Prendergast had made his mark as a business consultant. Cynics would contend that coldly and without any emotion whatsoever, he packaged Garret and presented him to the electorate in the summer of '81 as he would a product produced by Unilever while he was attached to that concern. It was with Unilever, in fact, that he learned the business of selling and he acquired it the hard way.

In a dairying country like Ireland, there is a natural built-in resistance to anything that is not made from pure fresh Irish milk, especially to margarine, even of the ten per cent butter variety, in many households (because there was a time when margarine at table was associated with poverty). But like a true professional, Peter Prendergast went about his job selling the Unilever brand in the face of the tide of consumer resistance.

He knew that even if there was resistance to Fine Gael among voters who were not traditional Party supporters, he had a highly-marketable "product" in Garret FitzGerald – much, much easier to market than margarine! Indeed, Peter admitted to me one day that, as he saw it, Garret was the hottest property Fine Gael had – "people liked Garret, they trusted him and they wanted him to succeed because he was somehow removed from the usual run of politicians".

Therefore, the Fine Gael emphasis going into the 1981 General Election was on "Garret". His face, frank and open, peered out from full-page advertisements – as Jack Lynch's face had looked out at the electorate in 1977 – and, as with the Fianna Fáil leader, there was a personal message above Garett's signature. In every provincial paper, the focus was firmly on "Garret's Team" and he appeared in full-page advertisements flanked by the Party candidates running in each constituency.

"The National Handlers" became the envy – and the target – of Fianna Fáil just as in a later era Fine Gael and Labour would accept that Fianna

256

Fáil came up with a real winner in P.J. Mara. The time makes the man.

Frank Dunlop would be succeeded as Fianna Fáil Press Officer and later Government spokesman when Jack Lynch was in power by P.J. Mara, P.J. took over after Lynch retired and Charles Haughey was elected Party leader and Taoiseach. Frank Dunlop was a thorough professional in his approach and had a very good working relationship with the media, who admired him for his competence and his respect for the truth.

But even Frank will be the first to admit that P.J. Mara was an unique personality – different from anyone who had previously performed the role of Government Press spokesman. It was not for nothing that he was affectionately dubbed "The National Fondler" and he gained immortality from the *Scrap Saturday* programme on RTE Radio and the humour it derived from his relationship with Haughey.

He had the full confidence of his leader and, even through the worst of times, nothing seemed to dampen his effervescent manner or kill his enthusiasm. *Uno Duce, Uno Voce* was not lightly said.

His greatest single achievement, I have always felt, was to keep the lines of communication open to correspondents and writers that the "Groupies" would have viewed as "baddies" because they were constantly clashing with C.J. P.J. Mara showed true professionalism and it was to the benefit in the long-term of the party he served, as much as the leader.

In a word, he did not alienate any group of journalists. He did not divide them into two camps. By taking an even-handed and cool approach he brought the media with him and created the impression that he was always on top of the situation.

The playboy, wise-cracking, fun-loving aspects of his character, which would reveal themselves when we gathered in the Berkeley Court Hotel or some hostelry after a soccer international involving the Republic of Ireland at Lansdowne Road, masked a man who was a professional to his finger-tips.

Then would come Sean Duignan, or simply "Diggy" to his friends. His time as Government Press Secretary when Albert Reynolds was Taoiseach was an era in itself … an era that created its own legendary stories, already immortalised in the haunts where the members of the Fourth Estate meet in Dublin.

"Diggy" was maintaining the modern tradition whereby it's to RTE that a new government will look for its Press Spokesman. One has only to reflect back to Ted Nealon and also to Liam Hourican, who after serving as Deputy Chef in the Cabinet of Peter Sutherland – the man I rate as definitely the best EEC Commissioner from this country – became Press Spokesman to Garret FitzGerald's second Coalition Government. And today Shane Kenny is Government Press Secretary to the Government headed by John Bruton.

Liam Hourican had established a lasting name for himself when he was RTE's man in the North and later he built on this when returning to Dublin to become Diplomatic Correspondent. Following his sojourn as Government Press Secretary, he would return again to Brussels to work in a key post in the EEC Commission. He died at a tragically-young age of a heart attack while on holidays with his wife and family in Cahirciveen in County Kerry. I still remember the very moving and inspiring tribute during the Requiem Mass from his close friend, Michael Lillis, recalling too their last dinner at a venue in South America. Of all the people I have known, Liam Hourican had one of the most brilliant minds and finest intellects. It was a privilege to have been numbered among his friends, to have savoured the hospitality of his home in Brussels and to have golfed with him.

Sean Duignan, a product of the *Connacht Tribune* and then the Independent Newsroom, made his mark first with his close friend, Mike Burns on Radio Eireann as the pioneers of the news programmes *This Week* and *The News at 1.30* with which Kevin O'Kelly was also very much involved. Duignan and Burns with their dynamic approach, their sheer elan when they caught the scent of a good story and the impact of their personalities, were mould-breakers in an arena that could so easily be hand-bound by conservatism and the need to conform. In 1968 they won a Jacobs award for their coverage of the Civil Rights agitation. They did brilliant reporting also from the United States and gloried in the opportunities provided for evocative on-the-spot coverage of all the razzmatazz surrounding the Democratic and Republican conventions.

Sean Duignan graduated to become Political Correspondent just before the 1977 General Election. The pundits were calling it an easy triumph for the Coalition Government headed by Liam Cosgrave and "Diggy" went with the tide. On radio he said that if Fianna Fáil won, it would represent "the greatest comeback since Lazarus".

He had to eat his words after Jack Lynch led Fianna Fáil to a landslide victory, ruefully conceding – on air – that not alone had Lazarus returned "but he had brought a lot of his friends with him".

He learned a salutary lesson from that particular episode and his motto for the future would be – "don't jump because everybody else jumps".

During the heaves against the leadership of Charles Haughey in the early 1980s, he admits now that he was very careful about making predictions. "There were times naturally when I felt he was gone and I am convinced that he himself thought it was curtains for him but something came out of the blue each time to keep him going for another 24 hours. So this image of the implacable survivor seeing clearly what he was going to do is part of legend".

At the same time, "Diggy" thought that Haughey's performance during that crisis period in Fianna Fáil was an "astonishing" one and he does not hide his admiration for the man's "sheer will to survive. There were dark moments when he gave up and was geed up by extraordinary events".

The transition to becoming the presenter of the *Six-One News* was another milestone in "Diggy's" life.

The litmus test of any news programme is, in his view: "Can you afford to miss it?".

Who will ever forget Brian Lenihan's appearance on the *Six-One News* on the night the Duffy tape was played and those rivetting moments, tragic for Lenihan, as his aspirations to make it to the Presidency were blown away?

Who will forget Albert Reynolds declaring that he would be voting against Charles Haughey at the Fianna Fáil Parliamentary party meeting and setting the platform for his own bid for the leadership?

Who will forget Gerry Collins making his famous plea into camera to Albert not to "burst the Party"?

"Diggy" was there, gently probing or simply giving the man his head – and if the man plunged over a precipice of his own making, there was no one afterwards who could blame it on the presenter. His style was the style of one who had mastered the art of making it all look so innocuous and it stemmed from the fact that he was a born actor who could leave so much hang in the air.

I remember how "Diggy" would gather his papers and make it seem inconclusive as he remarked: "The problem just won't go away".

His colleague David Davin Power, now doing so well as RTE's Man in Northern Ireland, recalls how after one such brilliant piece of stagecraft, "Diggy" was buttonholed in a pub the following day to be told by the lads drinking their pints – "ye could have heard a pin drop in here when you were on last night. We all agreed that you said nothing but you knew something".

One of his great gifts is to be able to spin yarns at his own expense and to turn his bloomers on radio or television to advantage in social gatherings. Like the time he covered Charles Haughey's trip to Australia. He began one of his 16-a-day live reports with the legendary intro: "This morning, the Taoiseach, Mr Haughey met the Australian Premier, Bob Hope ..."

To get him to "perform" is not easy. But there have been memorable evenings when I have listened to him singing one of my favourite numbers, *Sally* in a way that no one else can sing it and giving maybe *Sweet Sixteen* as an encore. And in such moments I have realised why back in the late Fifties when the actress Barbara Bel Geddes (later to be known as Miss Ellie of Southfork, Dallas, Texas) spotted "Diggy" on stage in Galway while she was holidaying in the area, she should have offered to introduce him to repertory in New York, leading on in time maybe to a career on Broadway.

But if "Diggy" had taken up that offer, he would never have realised his last great ambition and that was to see the workings of government from the inside. He got his big chance when Albert Reynolds sounded him out about taking over from P.J. Mara. "Diggy" had turned down a similar approach from Charles Haughey but now his very personable Kerry-born wife, Marie encouraged him to "give it a lash". Harking back to his theatrical days, he has described the decision as a scene from *Butch Cassidy and the Sundance Kid* – should he jump or should he stay put?

By the time he met the new Taoiseach privately, he was able to give him his answer, which, of course, was in the affirmative.

He could never have foreseen what he was really letting himself in for – the hectic hours, the hectic pace, the frenetic last days as the Government fell apart and Albert was left numb and shell-shocked by how cruelly and swiftly power had slipped from his grasp. It would inspire "Diggy" to capture it all in a brilliant vignette. It was like, he said, being the magician's parrot on board a liner like the *Titanic,* watching him do his magic tricks and then suddenly the ship hits an iceberg and sinks and the parrot thinks, 'Amazing, how the hell did he do that?'.

"Diggy" returned to Montrose and in the returning, they didn't have to kill the fatted calf for the prodigal son. They had only to recall what he said once to an interviewer when he was surrounded by all the hype of his appointment to the £47,000-a-year-plus Government Press Secretary job: "It wasn't just journalism I loved. It was journalists. The whole ambience. The whole fun thing of journalism. The weird people who inhabited it. I just thought it was fabulous".

At heart he was always the young reporter from the *Evening Herald* heading out to cover a fire, fascinated, as he admitted himself, by the way it was done, looking for an angle, the something that made it different.

"You didn't come back with a fire, you got a hero. If you were stuck, you got a dog that barked and woke everybody. Did the dog bark? The dog barked. So make a hero out of Fido".

This then is Sean Duignan, who was Government Press Secretary for a time …

19

Erskine and "The Wanderley Wagon"

It was somewhere out around Maam Cross in Connemara and the faithful had been waiting for hours in the rain for Erskine to appear. I mean Erskine Childers, Fianna Fáil candidate for the Presidency in 1973.

The original schedule had long since gone by the board, such was the welcome he was receiving. Erskine earlier suggested that Maam Cross should be dropped as it wasn't exactly a formal stop on the tour and, anyway, there was a bigger engagement that evening with RTE cameras moving in to cover it (and Seán Duignan doing the voice-over) that could not be missed. His advisers, aghast at this, told him that there was no way Maam Cross could be omitted, even if it only meant a few quick words and a wave to the waiting crowd. He concurred.

He stood there under the canopy looking out at them, as the rain still poured down the backs of their necks but they seemed oblivious to everything, only the words he was delivering. He could have been the Messiah come suddenly among them. He seemed to be staring at a point over beyond their heads, somewhere in the mist-shrouded mountains, the bleakness of Connemara in the rain forming the backdrop to his words. "Tis ye that have it. Ye are the lucky ones. Hold on to it like a jewel. It is precious. Lose it and it can never be regained ...".

And on he went for another five minutes in the same nebulous vein ...

As they shuffled from one foot to another in the continuous downpour, now drenched to the skin beyond caring, they wondered what it was they had and what they must not lose. But they caught something spiritual as it were going out from the man, the women listeners in particular. They did not rush to touch his garment but they voted for him – solidly to the last one of them in that crowd – on the day that mattered.

Seán Duignan, Political Correspondent of RTE at the time, was privy to that amazing moment in Erskine's grand tour in the "Wanderley Wagon" as the campaign coach came to be known by the media representatives who had the good fortune – or misfortune – to accompany the candidate in his swing through the country. I can never catch the nuances of the story the way Seán can with his Taibhdhearc na Gaillimh acting experience.

While Erskine was talking about the "jewel in the crown" out around Maam Cross, Dr Conor Cruise O'Brien was marching in the van of a parade down O'Connell Street calculated to get the electorate to vote for Tom O'Higgins as an endorsement of the National Coalition programme. And later Erskine would nod his head sadly, after his great triumph, and remark to me that he thought it was a mistake, a very big mistake, this effort to connect the Presidency with the National Coalition and what it had done since it won the General Election.

Could Conor Cruise every understand ...

I still wince when I reflect on my good friend Gerry Flanagan of the *Irish Press* who was trapped for the entire duration of the campaign on "The Wanderley Wagon".

On mornings when the *Irish Press* gave splash treatment to one of Erskine's speeches, Gerry would find himself invited up to the front of the bus for coffee – and maybe something even stronger and more stimulating!

But the next morning if the campaign speech or speeches had got little or no show – worse of all if they were subbed into a few measly paragraphs – Gerry found himself banished to the back of the bus for the day and left there to kick his heels. It took a lead story or at least top-of-the-page billing to restore him to Erskine's good favours ...

Erskine Childers was a world removed when compared to born politicians like Brian Lenihan or the late Sean Flanagan. To put it bluntly he was a rare species, totally foreign in a way to the Irish political scene but it was his very uniqueness that somehow or other captured the imagination of the Irish electorate during that Presidential campaign in '73 when his rival Tom O'Higgins started out looking odds-on to emerge victorious.

When Erskine Childers was inaugurated President of Ireland on June 25, 1973, it was the 103rd anniversary of his father's birth – the father, Erskine Childers, who had faced a firing squad in Beggar's Bush Barracks almost 52 years previously, on November 24, 1922, to be exact. Born in England, he had served with the British forces in the Boer War and was afterwards an intelligence officer in the British Army.

He it was who, imbued with the spirit of Irish nationalism, ran the guns for the Irish Volunteers to Howth in 1914, the episode which led to the massacre of civilians at Bachelor's Walk later that Sunday by the King's Own Scottish Borderers.

His rejection of Civil War politics and his unequivocal rejection of violence were facets of the character of Erskine Childers II that impressed all those who came to know him as a Fianna Fáil politician and later as President.

He told me once that being called in as a boy of 16 to speak to his father before he was executed left an indelible imprint in his mind and he promised then never to refer to the Civil War from any platform if he went into politics and to do all he could to speed reconciliation.

He remained faithful to his word.

Remembered too is the famous moment at a Fianna Fáil Ard Fheis when others shook hands with Charles Haughey as he was welcomed back into the "official" fold – but Erskine Childers kept reading his paper.

He always struck me as a man who stood aloof from the common herd, who hardly knew some of the backbenchers in his own Party. And there was that occasion when one of them made his famous "bags of guns" comment in the Dáil and I rang Erskine from the reception desk of a hotel in Sligo right in the middle of the Presidential campaign to ask him for his reaction. He was having breakfast in his room with Rita. I believe that he had to ring Dublin to ascertain who, in fact, was the T.D. who had made the comment, even though it was headline news in all the papers and to be filled in on his background.

He came downstairs shortly afterwards and with fire in his eyes remarked to me: "What are you trying to do to me?".

The Presidential campaign showed facets of the man that had made him the despair of the hard-nosed Fianna Fáil "machine" during general elections and by-elections but, strangely enough, did not damage him at all in this particular contest. For example, he was wont, right in the middle of a General Election or By-Election campaign, to visit the home of someone in a locality who might be the centre of agitation to have his land divided. Erskine would dismiss the objections of the officers of the local Cumann with the comment that the member of the landed gentry in question was a friend of his of long standing.

In Monaghan on one occasion the rent-a-crowd Fianna Fáil Party men had ensured that there would be a big turn-out for "the Minister" in his own constituency by telling "the lads" that there would be pints up for them on the counter – after they had done "the needful". Sure enough, as Erskine came through in the ministerial car, sitting in the back with Rita, he got a welcome fit for royalty. But the story goes that he was reading *The Times* (of London!) and that Rita saved the day in the nick of time by exhorting: "Wave to the left, Erskine, now wave to the right".

*   *   *

In his moment of triumph, after he had beaten Tom O'Higgins by 48,000-plus votes, I suggested to Erskine Childers that he had come across exceedingly well on television and that he had been a big hit with women voters, who appeared to have gone solidly for him. A satisfied smile spread across his countenance as he replied: "You said it, not I, Raymond".

He explained that the television gift was like playing the piano. "If you have not got the gift, it places you at a disadvantage in the modern world".

It was four months after Fianna Fáil went out of office that Erskine Childers was inaugurated President in June '73. When Jack Lynch took over as Taoiseach in November, 1966 in succession to Sean Lemass, Childers had become his right-hand man and second in command, being Tanaiste during explosive and highly-charged emotional times.

Childers backed Lynch to the hilt in his stance on the North and in setting his face courageously against the ultra-Republican elements in his own party.

When the North erupted in rioting and violence in 1969, with refugees pouring south and troops being sent to the Border to protect the interests of the State, the "hawks" in Fianna Fáil hardly felt in tune with Jack Lynch when he outlined his reasons for not sending the Irish Army across the Border on the night of August 14, 1969 when Derry's Bogside was in open conflagration and parts of Belfast in turmoil. Lynch had gone on radio and television to broadcast to the nation and made his now-famous "We shall not stand idly by" address, construed by the "ultras" as meaning that he was prepared to go all the way.

"Let history judge me as it will, but looking back now I believe I acted absolutely correctly in shunning any decision that would have led to the commitment of our soldiers across the Border", he said to me in the course of a wide-embracing interview for the *Irish Independent* when the dust had settled on the events of that extraordinary era.

"To have acted in any other way would have been contrary to my judgement and instincts and my abhorrence of the legacy of bitterness which the Civil War of 1922-'23 had left", he stressed.

He went on then to talk about leadership – when the buck stops at your desk. "It is at moments like that night in August '69 that you realise later what leadership is all about. The destiny of a people and the nation is in your hands. It is then one must keep ones head and not be swayed by emotionalism and one must examine coldly the consequences of any hasty action one might take".

He revealed to me why in the final analysis he was deterred from sending in the troops. "I thought of all the Catholic communities in out-of-the-way rural districts who would almost certainly have been annihilated immediately the word went out that troops from the South had crossed the Border.

"I know it has been argued since that Irish Army units could have been sent into the Bogside, simply and solely as a protective measure, and not have advanced further and then an appeal could have been made to the United Nations to move in.

"But that would have been overlooking entirely what would have been happening elsewhere in the Six Counties and forgetting how many Catholics might have died before assistance could be rushed to them. Once our troops had been sent in, one could not control the situation."

Jack Lynch faced another major crisis on Sunday, January 30, 1972 – the day that would pass into the history of the North as "Bloody Sunday".

The fierce tide of emotion and seething anger over the killings in Derry swelled over in Dublin the following night when the British Embassy, then sited in Merrion Square, went up in flames. The British Ambassador, Sir John Peck, emerged as a diplomat of the highest standing when next morning he sought to cool the situation, separating overall Anglo-Irish relations and the friendship between the Irish and British peoples from the terrible incident in Derry.

Perhaps the people of Dublin and the nation were appalled at the "ultimate act" of burning down an embassy; it was like the bursting of a boil, and members of the Cabinet privately realised that passions would subside in the cold reality of dawn. But at the same time no one could overlook the lasting link between North and South or that "Republican" feelings would well up when ever the minority of the North were victims of what the south saw as a cold-blooded act.

I heard grown men talk in the immediate aftermath of "Bloody Sunday" in terms of taking up guns and "marching on the North".

Against the swell-tide of passion Jack Lynch maintained his pipe-smoking coolness. To his lasting credit, he laid the groundwork for the "politics of reality and pragmatism" when it came to the bulk of Fianna Fáil members and the people of the South generally looking North. The emerging generations – the generations of the Eighties and Nineties – would come to accept that one million Protestants in the Six Counties could not be bombed into a United Ireland. The simplicity of Dev's time, when it was all left hanging in the air and, as Christian Brothers Schools' boys, we thought the Border was simply a line on the map that if it were taken away it would mean unity overnight, was dispelled forever.

We came to realise that there could be no true unity unless it was of the hearts and minds.

Dr Garret FitzGerald, with his dream of bringing Protestant, Catholic and Dissenter together on a common platform that were all part of the one small Ireland, worked through his Crusade while in Government to achieve a genuine pluralist society in the Republic that in time would help achieve unity by consent.

There was a special bond across the political divide between Jack Lynch and Garret FitzGerald. Their concept of the "Republican dream" may not at all times have been popular with those brought up with a different vision but they were unswerving in their determination that the gun must be taken out of Irish politics.

When Albert Reynolds took over as Fianna Fáil leader from Charles Haughey, I remember a two-page release being issued from the Party Press Office for the first press conference he gave in the Martello Room in Jury's Hotel on the evening of February 6, 1992.

There were two paragraphs in that release which may not have struck us at the time as meriting a lead the next day when there were so many other issues to raise with the man who would be confirmed as Taoiseach by the Dáil the following week. In retrospect now they explained how he was able to maintain the single-mindedness and commitment that would be vital to the achieving of the Peace Process. A similar single-mindedness was shown by John Hume right down to the wire. The SDLP leader with great courage rode the tide of criticism – even personal invective from certain quarters – as he was not deterred in continuing his contacts with Gerry Adams, the Sinn Fein President, leading to the cease-fire announced by the Provisional IRA in August '94 and responded to by the Loyalist para-militaries.

Albert Reynolds spoke that evening in Jury's Hotel of feeling diminished, as an Irishman, by the killings in the North. "So often have we condemned these murderous acts that we have impoverished the vocabulary of outrage. But we must prove that we have **not** bankrupted our determination to find a solution to this problem", he said.

Then he added significantly: "I look forward to working with the British Prime Minister (John Major) to try to end the cruelty of this continuing conflict. That cruelty comes from a dwarfed and twisted patriotism which sees inflicted deaths as instruments of change".

I wrote to Albert Reynolds after the fall of his Government that when all the details of the Fall had been forgotten, the monument to him that would remain was his role in the Peace Process. Nothing, I emphasised, could take that from him.

*   *   *

The irony of Albert Reynolds choosing Jury's Hotel for his first press conference as Fianna Fáil Party leader was not lost on veteran newsmen who had covered the dramatic shifts inside the Party in the period 1979-'83.

In fact, before I took the lift up to the Martello Room I made a point of going into the new Coffee Dock for a pot of tea for reasons of my own that conjured up memories that would never fade. I was remembering, of course, that it was in the old Coffee Dock that the "Gang of Five" – Albert Reynolds among them – had their late-night sessions plotting Haughey's advent to the leadership. I was remembering too how I wrote in the *Irish Independent* that the "hawks" soared proudly on a clear December night at Leinster House after Haughey had beaten George Colley in a bruising contest by 44 votes to 38.

Padraig Flynn and Sean Doherty would be on the floodlit platform when Albert Reynolds came home to a hero's welcome in Longford town on Saturday, February 16, 1992.

"We have no doubt that Albert Reynolds is the Messiah that we have looked for to lead us to the Promised Land", declared the late Sean Fallon, then the Cathaoirleach of the Seanad while Padraig Flynn led a succession of triumphant cheers as he exclaimed: "I do not think this kind of political gathering has been seen since de Valera came here in the Thirties".

Charles Haughey spoke in his going of the "Western Alliance" moving against him.

The wheel had come full circle ...

As we drank our tea in the Coffee Dock, we remembered the epic clip RTE had shown before Christmas '91 of Albert Reynolds in broad-rimmed cowboy hat and high-heeled shoes singing "Put Your Sweet Lips A Little Closer To The Phone" in some Ballroom of Romance. A throw-back to the days in the Sixties when he opened no less than fourteen ballrooms with his brothers, Jim and Joe and the nostalgia from classic names like "Cloudland" and "Dreamland" linger to this day for those of an older generation who danced in them to the Big Bands.

We remembered too how Albert, the self-made man, became wealthy by setting up a highly-successful pet food manufacturing concern with another Longford businessman. "If you drive over a dog or cat on your way through Longford, you are killing one of my constituents!", he said to me once.

Albert came to the leadership of Fianna Fáil with no "Republican baggage". It was the Lemass-like pragmatism, the very essence of the successful businessmen that allowed him to deliver on the North what Charles Haughey would have dearly loved to deliver – but it did not fall his way before he stepped down.

Such is the hinge of history ...

*   *   *

As I finish this book in a picturesque little village along the east coast in the Indian summer setting of a September week-end in '95, I find it hard to believe that 25 years have passed since I went to Luxembourg for the formal opening of the negotiations on Ireland's entry into the European family of nations and the Tricolour flew with the other flags from the building on the Kirchberg.

It was in 1972 that I missed a classic All-Ireland Hurling Final between Cork and Kilkenny as a result of getting a call from the office, while relaxing in the garden at home, and being instructed to proceed to Munich as fast as possible. The then Taoiseach, Jack Lynch and British Premier, Ted Heath had decided to meet during the Olympic Games.

Arriving in Munich late on Saturday evening, I managed in the special Accommodation Office that had been set up to book the last available room in the last hotel down by the railway station. No opportunity was presented to me to go and look at the room. You either paid the deposit there and then or refused. If you refused, you would have to go twenty-five miles or so out from the city to find a place to sleep for the night. Naturally, I wasn't being choosey and, as it turned out, I was the luckiest man alive to grab that last-chance room.

We went out to the airport on the Sunday evening to meet Jack Lynch on his arrival from Dublin. He had left Croke Park at the point in the second half when Cork hurlers looked to be coasting to victory and supporters, sporting the Red and White colours, had come on to the pitch dancing with joy in anticipation of what the final whistle would bring.

On the flight the pilot was able to convey to the Taoiseach that Kilkenny, inspired by Eddie Keher and the irrepressible Paddy Delaney, had staged an amazing fight-back to win by seven points.

My first question to Jack Lynch on the tarmac was not concerned with what he would be discussing with Ted Heath but came down to two words: "Who won?".

After the killing of the Israeli athletes, tension ran high in the German city and the security men were prepared to take no chances whatsoever. The Special Branch men with Jack Lynch knew me well from the domestic political scene at home but not so the "heavies" around Ted Heath. The gaberdine I had grabbed on my way out the door when rushing to Dublin Airport had, sadly, seen better days. I was carrying a bundle of papers under it as I approached the British Prime Minister to ask him a question. For all the world I could have been carrying a sub machine-gun. In a twinkling I was surrounded and would have ended up on the ground, my hands tied behind my back had not one of Jack Lynch's men intervened to tell the 'heavies' that I was an Irish newsman and not a terrorist bent on taking out Ted.

*   *   *

It was much easier for me to get close to Princess Grace of Monaco when she flew into Dublin Airport for the funeral of de Valera. I walked across the tarmac with other newsmen and she chatted in an informal, friendly manner about her previous meeting with the late former President. The epilogue to that came in Monaco itself when I journeyed to Nice for an Association of European Journalists' meeting.

There was an invitation to the officers from each national delegation of journalists to go down the coast to the Palace in Monaco to be received by Prince Ranier and Princess Grace. Dennis Kennedy of the *Irish Times* was just behind me in the line of journalists approaching Princess Grace.

As I shook her hand, her brow puckered and then she remarked: "Have I not met you somewhere before?".

I told her about her arrival at Dublin Airport for the funeral of de Valera and she smiled and nodded – and it was on to Dennis Kennedy, who said to me subsequently: "Now I have seen it all!"

In 1977 it will be twenty years since the Irish section of the AEJ agreed to take on board all the planning for the staging in Ireland of the Annual Congress of the Association of European Journalists.

When we said 'Yes' to the venture, we hardly realised the magnitude of the task. And yet such was the commitment and dedication of those who rallied to the call to give a helping hand – on a completely voluntary basis – that it exceeded all expectations and was voted unquestionably one of the most successful annual gatherings of its kind.

Overshadowing all else was the train journey from Dublin to Limerick – a journey into the "crack", the laughter and the bonhomie. Then on to Knappogue Castle and dancing after the medieval banquet. Oysters in Burkes of Clarenbridge. The smell of pints pulled in quaint pubs during impromptu stops on the road to Galway. The singing of *Galway Bay* and *The West's Awake* and other numbers that delighted the visitors from other European countries, accustomed to much more regimentation and rigidity in their lives.

The lack at the time of hotels that could take a few hundred delegates and give single rooms to those who needed single rooms meant that there had to be enforced doubling-up of male delegates and females. It was certainly a tall order to ask two men – even from the same national delegation – to share a room together when they had not done so before. Fortunately, it was in the pre-AIDS era and we got away with it. Only the Irish would!

We had drunk the train to Limerick dry and it was the same in the case of the rail journey back from Galway to Dublin – a journey full of

268

memories and friendships forged that lasted and were cemented further in following years.

Yes, even the best-stocked trains could not stand an assault by the Irish and Dutch together …

I remember Link Van Brugen, a famous Dutch radio journalist and foreign correspondent, telling me how he got word when covering a session of the United Nations in New York that his Auntie Alida had died in Arkansas. He headed off to pay his respects at her funeral, but wasn't prepared for what evolved.

On arrival he found that her husband had gone into a deep depression and had spent two days drinking gin. Her body was still in a back bedroom awaiting burial. He had to ring the undertakers to make all the necessary arrangements. It then emerged that her last request was that, after she had been cremated, her ashes should be spread in the Green Meadow at the very spot where she had lost her virginity at the age of 18 with her first love.

Link van Brugen duly headed off in a coach-and-four with the plumed horses immediately ahead of him holding the urn with the ashes on his lap, wondering how in the heavens he had gotten' himself into this – and the husband in the back seat behind him holding his head in his hands and moaning aloud as a result of all the gin he had consumed. They reach the Green Meadow. Link pulls back the black curtain and decides that he will get it all over with quickly and simply tosses the ashes into the meadow.

A gust of wind catches the ashes and much of Auntie Alida's mortal remains float back into his hair.

Link decides that he must have a quick shower when he gets back from the final "obsequies".

After he had thoroughly washed his hair, he looks down at the black dust around his feet and says aloud to himself: "Farewell my Auntie Alida".

There was the Luxembourg journalist who was gastronomic correspondent for his paper, giving him the kind of power in a small country that was almost impossible to contemplate. He could make or break a restaurant with one article.

He was dining this evening in a newly-established restaurant and wasn't particularly happy with the lobster bisque which the Chef considered one of the specialities of the house that would put it firmly on the map. He actually sent it back.

Out came the Chef and fell on his knees, tears of emotion welling up in his eyes as he pleaded: "You can take my wife and bring her for a week-end to my summer cottage in the Alps as long as you don't dismiss my lobster bisque. You can have her for a month and longer if you wish … but please, oh please, don't destroy me".

My gastronomic correspondent friend told him, despite his dog-eared pleading, he didn't want his wife but wouldn't write this time what he thought of the soup, entering a note of warning at the same time: "Remember, this is your one and only chance".

He was kissed on both feet and up the ankles and on both cheeks. He was still being showered with kisses as he walked out into the night.

*   *   *

Incidentally, Denis Corboy as Head of the EEC Commission Office in Dublin and Peter Doyle who was Press Spokesman both played a major role in contributing to the success of the Congress. Denis, who is today in Georgia (formerly part of the Soviet Union), heading the European Union Office there, had the most style of any Eurocrat I have known. At a time way back in my bachelor days when I used to have what I considered a casual evening meal in the Grill of the Shelbourne Hotel, Denis would invariably dine in the Saddle Room.

I remember when he left Dublin for Washington to take up a post of Director of the EEC Information Office on the Hill the farewell party was something else. As obituaries in the provincial papers in the old days listed every Vicar-General, Canon, Parish Priest and ordinary Curate, so you could have filled a column with the representatives of the various sectors of Dublin society that attended – from politicians to media men and women, to ardent supporters of the arts – and the gardaí had to lend a hand in easing the traffic outside Denis's house, there were so many C.D. cars on hand. Yes, a night to remember – into the dawn!

Peter Doyle, who was later in Washington before moving to Brussels, invariably showed style. But he was really good at the job of Press Spokesman and complemented Denis perfectly. When Denis Corboy was at the helm in Dublin he personalised the office in a way that the European Commission had an individual, high-profile presence. And Peter Doyle was able to cut through the bureaucratic language and jargon that inevitably has to be part of any big international organisation and simplified matters for the journalists in daily contact with him. It was a golden era. And the lustre remains undimmed for those of us fortunate enough to be part of it.

The Annual Congress of the Association of European Journalists was held again in Ireland in 1977 – this time in the magnificent setting of Ashford Castle in Cong, County Mayo. President Reagan, Jacques Chirac and the Grand Duke and Grand Duchess of Luxembourg can be counted among the notables who stayed in the hotel.

In this hotel too in 1979 Michael O'Kennedy chaired an informal week-end meeting of the EEC Foreign Ministers.

I recall a funny incident from that same week-end. The fish were actually jumping in the lake when Lord Carrington and Michael O'Kennedy were taking a stroll in the grounds. The British Foreign Secretary was so impressed that he asked had they been specially imported for the occasion of the gathering of the Ministers!

*   *   *

When I got the call from Aengus Fanning, after his appointment as Editor of the *Sunday Independent* in 1984, to join him on the paper, I bade farewell to the job of EEC and Diplomatic Correspondent. In one way it was a wrench but in another way I was rather glad as I had done an immense amount of global travelling in the fourteen years from 1970. You found yourself coming in over Dublin on a glorious Friday evening on a plane from Brussels and looking down at people playing golf over some course in the city or its environs and saying to yourself: "What the hell am I doing up here?"

There was more time for golf now and overall, life assumed a much more regular pattern. The EEC and Diplomatic Correspondent becomes accustomed to living out of a suitcase and to being ready always to answer the call from the Newsdesk to go anywhere at a moment's notice.

Aengus wanted me to bring my experience as a feature writer to help build up the sports pages. It was a challenge that inspired me as at this stage I had written quite a number of books on hurling and gaelic football and had been editing the *Irish Racing Annual* since 1976. To his credit, Aengus wanted it to be a team effort as we had been team players together on the European plane. The "beat" he gave me was a broad one which wouldn't confine me to the gaelic games and racing scene alone.

Thus, I found myself in Manchester doing a feature on Paolo Rossi, the Italian sharpshooter who had scored three memorable goals against Brazil in the 1982 World Cup. He came out of the dressing-room at Old Trafford wearing an old casual gaberdine instead of a blazer and my intro was that if he had been living in Ireland he might have been a poacher of salmon rather than a poacher of goals.

Later, when he came to Dublin I met him again and he told me that he had been sent the cutting of my piece and it had caught his fancy.

There was another trip to Manchester to see Maradona in action and I think it was then that I saw Paul McGrath, who, of course, was overshadowed that night by the Argentinian super-star – but there was a memory left that did not fade from my mind. One day I casually bumped into Paul in Davy Byrne's in the aftermath of the '94 World Cup in the States and I could not help but remind him of an evening in Old Trafford when he was finding his way up the ladder and his budding genius was unnoticed by all but a few.

When Eamon Dunphy broke with the *Sunday Tribune*, I suggested to Aengus Fanning that he sign him up immediately as he commanded a public of his own in the soccer arena and wrote in the controversial manner that would boost sales. Aengus moved quickly and another foundation stone was laid for the position the *Sunday Independent* occupies today as the leading Sunday paper in this country.

Later Mick Doyle was contracted to write on rugby. I now gave up writing on soccer and rugby and was able to devote my entire attentions to hurling, football and racing – the areas I was happiest covering.

However, I had enjoyed my stint on the rugby front during winter days. The morning I heard on an early RTE Radio news bulletin that Tony Ward had retired I rang him at home and suggested that I would "ghost" his story in a series of articles for the *Sunday Independent*. Aengus Fanning and myself met him later that same day in the Gresham Hotel and the deal was done.

I had the pleasure of meeting Jackie Kyle when he came into Dublin from Zambia and delivered a memorable homily at a function organised by the *Sunday Independent*. I recall the next morning presenting him with a copy of Patrick Kavanagh's Collected Poems in the Berkeley Court Hotel. We have been good friends since.

I was young when I saw Kyle playing at outhalf for Ireland. He was unquestionably the greatest Irish outhalf of his time and played to the strength of his pack. In modern times, Paul Dean had the finest tactical brain of anyone to play at stand-off half for Ireland. I remember calling to his flat to interview him one evening when he was single and getting his views on whether Ireland would beat Wales the following Saturday in Cardiff. "Ring me again when I have studied the videos and I will be more definite", he said. I did. He predicted victory – and so it came to pass.

Ken Goodall had the greatest charisma of any back row forward of his time and later Fergus Slattery was a dominating personality while Ciaran Fitzgerald proved himself one of Ireland's outstanding captains. No one could match the electrifying dynamism and body swerve of Mike Gibson when he was in his prime as a centre.

Aengus Fanning loved the scent of the chase when it came to beating the opposition to the stories of big-name sportsmen when they announced that they were stepping down.

The biggest name of all was Mick O'Connell, the man from Valentia. I struck up a very close friendship with Micko from the time I first met him and made many visits to the island and spent happy times fishing with him and his close friend, Ned Fitzgerald, a former Kerry captain and father of Maurice, off the coast around Valentia. Mick O'Connell was not alone the finest gaelic footballer I have ever seen, breath-taking in his fielding ability and in the pinpointed accuracy of his kicking, but a man of depth and feeling who with his wife Rosaleen has worked unselfishly in the cause of raising funds for Down's Syndrome children. I am proud to say that Mick is my friend.

In the racing arena, under the arrangement I had with Aengus Fanning, the *Sunday Independent* had first run on the serialisation of my biography of Vincent O'Brien, which I wrote with the co-operation of the Master of Ballydoyle and which was launched at a Bollinger champagne reception in the Berkeley Court Hotel by Lester Piggott, who flew in specially for the occasion.

When Lester spent a time in prison over tax problems I wrote to him that if I was sitting with some racing friends at Fouquet's on the Champs Elysees on the morning after the Prix de l'Arc de Triomphe and he passed by, we would say: 'There goes the greatest Flat racing jockey in the world'. All else would be irrelevant. And I concluded the letter by telling him that all his racing friends, including the members of the Racing Press, in Ireland sent their best regards.

His wife, Susan told me on the phone that the letter had given him a special lift at a bad time. The Maestro did not forget.

* * *

272

In the "university" that represented my days in the Irish Farmers Association, I became adept at drafting speeches and, frankly, I could come up with one at very quick notice. There was the occasion when a top executive in Independent Newspapers had to deputise for Dr Tony O'Reilly at a dinner in the Old Belvedere Club and my brief was to come up with at least one gem of a story that had never made the rounds in the Dublin rugby circuit before.

I took the train south to Cork and I knew that my expenses would not be questioned if I could deliver as I was expected to deliver.

I put up in Jury's Hotel. I contacted Noel Murphy, acquainting him of the pressure I was under and that he must not fail me at any cost.

"Don't worry", said Noel. "I have one that I bet you Tony O'Reilly himself hasn't heard and which he would love to tell in his own inimitable fashion if he were speaking at the function".

A chap from Kerry, a born footballer, had emigrated to England and in time joined the Harlequin's Club. He graduated up the line through his ingrained talent to the second team.

In the count-down to the Cup Final, the left-winger on the first team got injured and your man from the Kingdom was called up as the eleventh-hour replacement. His destiny lay in his own hands.

With time ticking away, it's level pegging. A loose maul and the ball is swept out to the Kerryman, who hares off, running almost the length of the field.

With the opposing line at his mercy, he hears the cry from the little group of avid fans from his own county who have come to watch him in action on this day: "Up the Kingdom".

He stops in his tracks and momentarily his mind seems to go blank. He is back in a different world as he steadies himself and kicks the ball – over the bar.

Yes, it brought the house down …

*   *   *

One day Dr Tony O'Reilly was coming through the *Sunday Independent* office accompanied by an entourage comprising a few top executives and experts in the new technology. The typewriters by now had almost all given way to the computers but I was still hammering away on my old machine. And, as it happened, I was alone in the Sports Department of the open-plan office on this day. I had seen it all from the hot-metal era and subbing "on the stone" as a page of the *Tipperary Star* was put to bed to watching subs now doing it on screen.

As Tony waved a greeting to me, I exclaimed: "We'll fight them on the beaches, we'll fight them in the hills".

He laughed spontaneously at that , though I must admit that one or two of his entourage weren't all that amused at my last-ditch stand from the trenches.

Of course, I succumbed to the "invasion" like all the rest. The cursed cursor now dictates our day.

EPILOGUE

$\boxed{\textbf{\textit{20}}}$

The Way I Would Like To Go

The way I would like to go is to die of a heart attack at the Killinan end in Semple Stadium, Thurles on a sun-drenched Munster Hurling Final Day.

Ideally, Tipperary and Cork, those ancient rivals, would be doing battle in a torrid match, with the scores level coming up to half-time as I collapsed in the fierce tension and excitement.

They would lift my body out over the wire and place it on the sideline in front of the crowded Open Stand, draped in the Blue and Gold of Tipperary.

At the interval would come the announcement that I had died. A hushed silence would fall over the attendance. Then 45,000 voices would rise in singing *Slievenamon* as I was wafted into the Great Beyond in a manner befitting one who had gloried in watching great matches and great men on this sod from schoolboy days.

In a salubrious Dublin suburb on the Monday morning, the Lady in Black is having breakfast down table from her company managing director husband, who is totally preoccupied with the crisis Board meeting that lies ahead for him that morning. She has already heard of my passing the previous evening and is now glancing through the obituary notices and the tributes in the *Irish Independent* and *Irish Times*.

She mentions to her husband that she will be heading out of town for a golfing engagement but will be back for dinner. He simply nods his head. He's accustomed to these excursions. But then her handicap is down to single figures and by now the sideboard has evidence of her prowess.

In the car she plays the tapes that bring up moments from her storehouse of memories that will never fade – the music from *Elvira Madigan* and the haunting climax to *Death In Venice* ... then *Giselle* and *Swan Lake*.

The miles pass quickly. Now and then she smiles her private smile, content in the thought that the ephemeral in life cannot touch the moments that reach out beyond the mundane Board meetings and the pressures that kill men in the city.

When she reaches Thurles, she is lucky to find a parking spot in The Mall down from the broad expanse of Liberty Square.

She slips into the back pew of the Cathedral unnoticed. Her head is bowed through most of the Mass, her face invisible behind the black veil. Her hand strays to her eye as the organ soars in *The Old Rugged Cross* and there is a hint of a sob as the choir gloriously sing *Nearer My God To Thee*. She turns away, the profile of her sad pale ascetic features rigid now, as the procession comes down the aisle and it doesn't seem to strike her that the Archbishop of Cashel and Emly, Patron of the GAA, has graced the occasion.

She doesn't mind the long walk to the cemetery where the grave bought way back for £2 when that was a week's salary for a young cub reporter on *The Tipperary Star* is open and ready. She is lost in the press of the moving tide of humanity. Just another mourner among the many dignitaries from every walk of life.

The prominent politicians are there crowding the graveside, wanting to be seen ... the famous names from hurling and football ... the big names from the racing world ... the professional punters who have rocked the Cheltenham ring in their time ... the doggy men ... the poker players ... men and women of the arts ... a plethora of members of the Fourth Estate ... old school pals.

She stands there tall and upright as the last rites are performed. Val and Andy and Mike are together. In another group Mick D. and Denis, Dick and Timmy and the boys who used to frequent Murphy's of Baggot Street in bachelor days.

When the first sod hits the coffin, she steps forward and tosses in a red rose.

It is too much for Val. He has to know who the Lady in Black is. He goes over and enquires: " Did you know him?"

She draws back the black veil with her little finger and, not caring to hide the tears now, she replies softly: "Know him? Why, I loved him".

Somewhere back in Dublin the Board meeting has gone well for her husband. He greets her on her return with the query: "How did the golf go?"

"The usual", she responds. He deduces that she has played another round that will soon warrant the purchase of a new sideboard.

James brings the duck a l'orange and pours the Chateau Margaux. She is at one end of the long table, her husband is at the other. Half way through, she pushes the plate away from her.

"I'm not feeling all that well", she remarks. Turning to James, she says, ever so quietly now: "You can serve me coffee in my room".

The strains of Mahler's music from *Death in Venice* echo later from her room.

275

content in the thought that the ephemeral in life cannot touch the moments that reach out beyond the mundane Board meetings and the pressures that kill men in the city.

When she reaches Thurles, she is lucky to find a parking spot in The Mall down from the broad expanse of Liberty Square.

She slips into the back pew of the Cathedral unnoticed. Her head is bowed through most of the Mass, her face invisible behind the black veil. Her hand strays to her eye as the organ soars in *The Old Rugged Cross* and there is a hint of a sob as the choir gloriously sing *Nearer My God To Thee*. She turns away, the profile of her sad pale ascetic features rigid now, as the procession comes down the aisle and it doesn't seem to strike her that the Archbishop of Cashel and Emly, Patron of the GAA, has graced the occasion.

She doesn't mind the long walk to the cemetery where the grave bought way back for £2 when that was a week's salary for a young cub reporter on *The Tipperary Star* is open and ready. She is lost in the press of the moving tide of humanity. Just another mourner among the many dignitaries from every walk of life.

The prominent politicians are there crowding the graveside, wanting to be seen ... the famous names from hurling and football ... the big names from the racing world ... the professional punters who have rocked the Cheltenham ring in their time ... the doggy men ... the poker players ... men and women of the arts ... a plethora of members of the Fourth Estate ... old school pals.

She stands there tall and upright as the last rites are performed. Val and Andy and Mike are together. In another group Mick D. and Denis, Dick and Timmy and the boys who used to frequent Murphy's of Baggot Street in bachelor days.

When the first sod hits the coffin, she steps forward and tosses in a red rose.

It is too much for Val. He has to know who the Lady in Black is. He goes over and enquires: " Did you know him?"

She draws back the black veil with her little finger and, not caring to hide the tears now, she replies softly: "Know him? Why, I loved him".

Somewhere back in Dublin the Board meeting has gone well for her husband. He greets her on her return with the query: "How did the golf go?"

"The usual", she responds. He deduces that she has played another round that will soon warrant the purchase of a new sideboard.

James brings the duck a l'orange and pours the Chateau Margaux. She is at one end of the long table, her husband is at the other. Half way through, she pushes the plate away from her.

"I'm not feeling all that well", she remarks. Turning to James, she says, ever so quietly now: "You can serve me coffee in my room".

The strains of Mahler's music from *Death in Venice* echo later from her room.